The Conservative Tradition
in European Thought

The
Conservative Tradition in European Thought

An Anthology Selected and Edited
by Robert Lindsay Schuettinger

G. P. PUTNAM'S SONS: NEW YORK

*To my colleagues
and students
in the
University of St. Andrews*

Second Impression

Copyright © 1970 by Educational Resources Corporation

Library of Congress Catalog Card Number: 69-18194

PRINTED IN THE UNITED STATES OF AMERICA

Preface

The selections from the writings of conservative thinkers which are represented in this anthology have been chosen to provide a broad cross section of conservative political theory as developed in Europe. I have attempted to include representatives from every major European country, but Britain, as might be expected, is the source of a high proportion of the authors. Although the main British tradition of Burkean empirical conservatism is for obvious reasons more relevant to American readers than the restorationist philosophy of De Maistre and Donoso-Cortés, I have tried not to neglect any major school of European conservative thought. The selections span the eighteenth, nineteenth, and twentieth centuries with some particular attention to the origins of many of our political ideas in the classical era. The book closes with a demonstration of how the principles of the conservative tradition are being applied in our time by contemporary thinkers.

Although I am inclined to think that complete objectivity in political matters is a chimera, there can be little doubt that students of politics have an obligation to be as fair as is humanly possible. Biases should be frankly stated. I should therefore warn the reader that my own sympathies lie with the empirical conservative and moderate classical liberal tradition of Burke, De Tocqueville, Acton, Hayek, Röpke, and Oakeshott; in compiling this anthology, however, my object has been to present each thinker as honestly and sympathetically as

7

possible so that the reader may decide for himself what value, if any, to place upon a particular set of ideas.

This book would have many more faults than it does if it were not for the help and advice of many friends. The dedication is a small gesture of appreciation for a debt which never can be repaid. The hospitality, kindness, and intellectual stimulation which I always found in St. Andrews University in my too brief stay of two years will never be forgotten. In particular, I want to thank the professor of political economy, J. W. Nisbet, and the professor of modern history and vice-principal, Norman Gash, both of whom read the introduction and made many valuable comments, as well as my good friends Douglas C. Mason, Duncan Madsen Pirie, J. Allan Stewart, and other members of the University Conservative Association.

I want to acknowledge with gratitude the way in which Miss Renate Fröhlich, of Educational Resources Corporation, persistently shepherded the manuscript for me. It is also a pleasure to acknowledge the assistance, given at various times, of the following persons: Isaiah Berlin, W. F. Buckley, Jr., Herbert Frankel, Milton Friedman, Philip Goodhart, Charles W. Hallberg, Ralph Harris, F. A. Hayek, Geoffrey Howe, John Jewkes, Russell Kirk, Anthony Lejeune, Russell Lewis, Frank S. Meyer, John O'Sullivan, Noel E. Parmentel, Jr., John Parsons, Michael Pinto-Duschinsky, W. H. Roberts, Arthur Seldon, Michael Uhlmann, T. E. Utley, Ernest van den Haag, and E. G. West.

As all of these gentlemen would be the first to point out, what faults remain must of necessity remain my own responsibility.

ROBERT LINDSAY SCHUETTINGER

St. Salvator's College
University of St. Andrews

Contents

Introduction

How do we define the word "conservative"? There is a great temptation to employ some purely personal description such as: "A conservative is someone like Winston Churchill or Charles de Gaulle or Konrad Adenauer or Barry Goldwater," or (even less helpfully): "A conservative is someone who says he is one. Period."

There are also epigrammatic definitions which are scarcely more revealing: "A conservative is someone who believes nothing should ever be done for the first time." Or: "A conservative does not want to set the clock back; he wants to set it right."

It does seem, however, that we should not give up so easily; there is a certain set of ideas and principles connected with the conservative tradition which originated in Europe and which has been carried to every corner of Western civilization. Although it is also true that conservative principles are notable for the frequency with which they are mislaid (which explains the perennial lament among conservatives: "Where are our principles?"), they still do exist, if only as goals toward which men strive.

In the first part of this introductory essay we will examine the broad basic principles of conservatism (which distinguish the great majority of conservatives from the great majority of liberals), the three underlying modes of thinking common to most conservatives, the three major political groupings into which most conservatives may be divided, and finally the essential differences between all constitutional democrats, whether liberal or conservative, and totalitarians of various hues. In the second part of this essay, we will briefly survey the origin and subsequent career of conservatism as a political movement in the countries of Western Europe since the outbreak of the French Revolution, paying special attention to the roles of those thinkers represented in this volume.

Conservatism is not an ideology or a firm set of doctrines on man and the universe. We will be nearer the truth if we view conservatism as a disposition and turn our attention to five principal beliefs toward which many conservatives are clearly disposed. Not all conservatives, of course, hold to these beliefs, while at the same time many liberals are by no means hostile toward all of them. But conservatives are more likely to stress their importance than do most liberals. In brief, modern conservatism can be understood as arising from five basic principles or "dispositions":

1. There is a divine intent in history and man has a duty to conform himself to God-given and immutable laws of morality.

2. Order and stability are the first requirements of good government; these goals can best be achieved by restraint and respect for tradition.

3. Variety, for many reasons, is more desirable than uniformity, and liberty more important than equality.

4. The good life, not just life itself, is the proper goal of a man. Honor and duty, therefore, take precedence over personal indulgence.

5. There are definite limits to the power of man's reason. Because of this, a healthy skepticism toward abstract principles, toward intellectualism, and toward grandiose plans for reform should be encouraged.

From these five principles follow most of the chief canons of the conservative tradition. The disposition toward religion leads conservatives to adopt a humble attitude toward the mysteries of the universe. "We know," wrote Edmund Burke, "and it is our pride to know, that man is by his constitution a religious animal. . . . We know, and what is better, we inwardly feel, that religion is the basis of civil society, and the source of all good, and of all comfort." Even those conservatives who do not believe that a divine plan rules history still accept the idea of original sin, in the sense that human nature is fatally flawed and capable of evil as well as good. There is more disagreement on the precise nature of those laws which govern our morality, but even those who are skeptical about natural law are reluctant to embrace ethical relativism. Almost all conservatives would maintain that a shared respect for a fundamental morality is an essential prerequisite to a stable and free society. As Burke urged, if there are not restraints from within, there must be surely restraints from without. Many conservatives would go further and hold that all political problems are, in essence, theological problems.

The personal religious commitments of any particular individuals aside, it remains true that liberalism as a political creed is less opposed to a secular society than is conservatism. Liberalism tends to a more optimistic estimate of man's nature, puts a greater reliance on education, and is readier, if need be, to face an unknown future without divine guidance. On the other hand, few if any liberals would deny the overriding value of a common moral tradition to the social order. It should also be said that conservatives too often have a tendency to equate their own deeply felt beliefs with the unquestioned laws of God Himself.

No matter what his views of the supranatural, no conservative would question the second principle of our list: the primary need for order in this world. Without stability nothing else (not justice, not equality, not liberty, not prosperity) can be accomplished. This first duty has seldom been so well expressed as it was by R. J. White in *The Conservative Tradition*:

> To discover the order which inheres in things rather than to impose an order upon them ; to strengthen and perpetuate that order rather than to dispose things anew according to some formula which may be nothing more than a fashion ; to legislate along the grain of human nature rather than against it ; to pursue limited objectives with a watchful eye ; to amend here, to prune there ; in short to preserve the method of nature in the conduct of the state . . . this is Conservatism.

Conservatives have always known that the political structure of a state, if it is to be stable, must reflect the traditions and customs of that society; "the method of nature," in short, must be preserved. Constitutions transplanted from societies which differ widely cannot be expected to flourish; still less can "paper" institutions be created out of abstract principles. Society, conservatives insist, is not a machine which can be tinkered with and altered without limit; rather, it must be understood as a living organism and therefore must develop gradually and naturally if it is to survive.

Some conservatives forget that order is not an end in itself but a necessary means to a great many other ends: justice, freedom, civilization, equality, happiness, and so on according to the values of each society. The intelligent conservative, therefore, will not be content simply to stand like a rock for order and tradition. He will work for the kind of society where everyone benefits by stability and has a stake in preserving it. He will want to bring all groups in the society into the political framework and will therefore favor constitutional democracy—not because democracy produces the best or wisest government but because it is the strongest safeguard of peace and order.

As Henry A. Kissinger astutely remarked in an essay on Metternich, it is the task of the conservative "not to defeat but to forestall revolutions . . . a society which cannot *prevent* a revolution, the disintegration of whose values has been demonstrated by the *fact* of revolution, will not be able to defeat it by conservative means . . . order once shattered can be restored only by the experience of chaos."

Liberals would have little difficulty in seconding Kissinger's warning; many, however, would have qualms about according stability pride of place among earthly goals. Order in itself, they would probably say, can all too easily be an excuse for oppression. We should therefore emphasize justice and freedom, and order will naturally follow as a by-product. Many liberals would agree that political arrangements must be rooted in the needs, desires, and customs of people; they would add, however, that respect for tradition should not be allowed to obstruct new ideas which will improve the lives of people. Liberals too can often be paternalistic; many are eager to play philosopher-king and erect a near-utopia based on reason and good sanitation facilities where before there was ignorance and backwardness.

Liberals would not deny that they have often brought progress to less-favored peoples at the expense of variety and liberty—the third principle we have imputed to conservatives. Liberals, in this century, have a tendency to look upon centralized planning, hopefully by an enlightened government, as the quickest and surest means to social progress. Planning from the top down necessarily involves an increase in uniformity and decrease in regional autonomy; variety and liberty are supplanted by sameness and (hopefully) equality. Conservatives sense instinctively that the liberal passion for furthering equality can only be brought about by greater and greater uniformity. In self-defense, they have taken up the cause of local autonomy, of "states' rights," in opposition to the growing leviathan state. "The love of the whole is not extinguished," wrote Burke, "by [a] subordinate partiality. . . . To be attached to the subdivision, to love the little platoon we belong to in society, is the first principle . . . of public affections. It is the first link in the series by which we proceed towards a love of our country, and of mankind."

Conservatives also know that the natural institutions of an organic society (churches, trade unions, universities, newspapers, bar associations, farmers' unions, businessmen's clubs) have a special role in standing between a citizen and his government. By strengthening the power of one, they ensure the stability of the other.

A leveling kind of equality finds little sympathy from conservatives, since they strongly suspect that only the rulers will prosper when all subjects are equal. Men who are outstanding in some way (rich, famous, heroic, learned, pious, amusing) serve, as do institutions and regional traditions, as further checks on the power of the central authority. The proper function of government, say conservatives, is not to concentrate power but to diffuse it.

With this goal in mind, some form of guaranteed independence for citizens becomes necessary; conservatives have therefore always been defenders of the rights of property, recognizing that "property" includes more than material things. For example, the academic freedom of university teachers, earned through years of hard work, is a property right.

The necessary relation of property and liberty is forcefully expressed by Quintin Hogg in his book *The Case for Conservatism*: "The possession of property by the individual is the essential condition of . . . liberty. No man is fully free unless possessing some rights of property in something, since property is the means whereby he develops his personality by impressing it upon his external surroundings without dependence of the will of others. . . ." Hogg points out that property imposes a duty upon the owner to develop it as a thing of beauty or utility and to make use of it in such a way that it does not intrude upon the rights of other persons.

Liberals would agree that a good deal of individualism and local responsibility is eminently desirable; they would probably want to add, however, that a certain amount of uniformity is necessary for fairness, just as some centralization is required for efficiency. Most liberals realize that complete equality is not only impossible but very likely undesirable as well. On the other hand, they would note that since nature seems to encourage inequality it should be the duty of government to redress the balance. Almost all supporters of constitutional democracy would, of course, unite on the importance of equality before the law and of equality of opportunity; those differences remaining would again be matters of emphasis and degree.

As we come to the fourth principle, however, we may at last be discovering a fundamental division between the liberal and the conservative. Many commentators have maintained that the parties can be determined by those who follow the classical philosophers in asserting that only the good life is worth living and those (like Thomas Hobbes and Adam Smith) who will settle for mere contentment and security. What is right, many conservatives insist, cannot be determined by some utilitarian standard purporting to measure various degrees of pleasure. For them, honor and duty are far more important than material well-being; they are more concerned with the quality of civilization than with its gross national product. Some conservatives would go so far as to urge that there have always been two distinct sets of human ideals: the "Athenian" goals of liberty, progress, open-mindedness, equality, and individual happiness and the "Spartan" virtues of loyalty, honor, courage, faith, fraternity, and self-sacrifice. Certainly in any given nation there are probably as many (perhaps more) liberals who are patriotic and self-sacrificing as there are conservatives who practice these virtues, and conversely, there are doubtless many not calling themselves liberals who are passionately interested in liberty and equality. And yet it must be said that liberals seem to prefer the *rhetoric* of progress and welfare while conservative speakers often appeal to the loyalty or patriotism of their listeners.

In any event, it is fair to say that the average conservative makes a sincere effort (even if his baser nature sometimes gets the better of him) to place moral above material values and ends. "He holds it more important," Clinton Rossiter tells us in his *Conservatism in America,* "to sharpen men's minds and lift up their spirits than to glut their bellies and relieve their toils, more necessary to advance intellectually and spiritually than materially and technologically. . . ." The conservative prefers a cherished value to a labor-saving gadget, tradition to comfort. He regards a high standard of living as only one, and by no means the most important, of the criteria by which the greatness of a nation is to be determined. To a conservative, the condition of "culture, learning, law, charity and morality" are of far more interest "than the annual output of steel or aluminum."

The idea that there is a "good life" which can be discovered by using the rules of human reason will be viewed with skepticism by most liberals and many conservatives. The majority of liberals and a minority of conservatives prefer to evaluate their policies by pragmatic and utilitarian norms, not absolutist standards. Few liberals will fail to admit, however, that honor, loyalty, duty, and patriotism are admirable qualities; but if they were to respond to criticism, they might very well tell conservatives to put their own houses in order before preaching moral virtues and high ideals.

Although conservatives disagree among themselves on many specific issues, although there are diverse interpretations of even the most general tendencies, almost all are united on one great question: the place and limits of human reason in the affairs of men. The fifth and last great "disposition" of conservatives is a tendency to view with the utmost skepticism extravagant claims for the powers of human reason.

This does not mean, of course, that conservatives are irrationalists. It does mean that, like David Hume, they prefer to use reason to "whittle down the claims of reason." Fundamentally, there are two approaches to the place of reason in political thought. The first, which might be called the ultrarationalist school, found great favor in the French tradition and is ably represented by Descartes and the Physiocrats. The second, the empirical or antiultrarationalist approach, is characteristic of the British tradition, of Locke, Hume, Smith, and Burke. De Tocqueville, among other French scholars, finds his place in this mode of thought.

Most modern liberals have tended to be closer to the "French" or ultrarationalist school than to the more empirical outlook of most conservatives. Characteristically, liberals are disposed to look for and to rely upon deliberate human design in the social order; empirical conservatives, on the other hand, maintain that most of the order in human society is the unforeseen result of the actions of many individuals. They hold, therefore, that most progress is made in spite of the imperfections and limitations of individual reason. Man's great social achievements are due to impersonal social processes by which individuals, acting separately, create social arrangements, such as the market economy or the common law, which no centralized mind or team of minds could have brought about. Because of this conviction, conservatives place reliance on tradition and long-standing customs as a means of accomplishing things which individual men of today, having only the wisdom of their own experience, could not hope to do successfully.

David Hume, in many ways one of the principal founders of modern conservatism, went to the heart of the matter with great precision. "To balance a large state," he wrote, ". . . on general laws, is a work of so great difficulty that no human genius, however comprehensive, is able, by the mere dint of reason and reflection, to effect it. The judgment of many must unite in this work: Experience must guide their labours, time must bring it to perfection: And the feeling of inconvenience must correct the mistakes which they inevitably fall into, in their first trials and experiments."

It was said of Hume that he trained the weapons of the Enlightenment on the Enlightenment; that is, he used reason to expose the false claims of reason. This is not opposition to rational investigation and scientific argument; it is opposition to pretensions which cannot be substantiated by facts. One may admire scholarship and learning without turning society over to the intellectuals.

Aware as they are of the distinct limitations of human reason in general, conservatives are not very sanguine about the possibilities of governmental action in particular. They know that no one man or group of men (whether they are aristocrats, plutocrats, Marxist guardians, or proletarians) has the capacity to foresee all the consequences of any single government policy. For this reason, caution, humility, and the broadest base of democratic support ought to be among the first requirements of sensible government.

In this "disposition," conservatives are at one with their contemporary allies in practical politics, the classical liberals. The followers of Adam Smith, Alexis de Tocqueville, Lord Acton, and John Stuart Mill have been less concerned with what man *as a politician* might achieve at his best; they have been more determined to ensure that political man should have, in the words of F. A. Hayek, "as little opportunity as possible to do harm when he was at his worst." Most conservatives and classical liberals would agree that a chief object of politics is to contrive a decentralized system of limited government where evil men can do the least harm. As F. A. Hayek said of the ideal polity of the British liberals of the eighteenth century,

It is a social system which does not depend for its functioning on our finding good men for running it, or on all men becoming better than they now are, but which makes use of men in all their given variety and complexity, sometimes good and sometimes bad, sometimes intelligent and more often stupid. Their aim was a system under which it should be possible to grant freedom to all, instead of restricting it, as their French contemporaries wished, to "the good and the wise."

This is not to suggest a lack of interest in cultivating superior talent and in encouraging greatness; unlike most modern liberals most conservatives simply believe that the gradual betterment of man is best done by society as a whole—by education, religion, the family, private associations of all sorts—rather than by the government. For this reason, politics is not as important to conservatives as it is to many modern liberals. "To the great majority of Conservatives," wrote Quintin Hogg, "religion, art, study, family, country, friends, music, fun, duty, all the joy and riches of existence of which the poor no less than the rich are the indefeasible free-holders, all these are higher in the scale than their hand-maiden, the political struggle. . . . The simplest among them prefer fox-hunting—the wisest religion."

Hogg reminds us that the power of politics to do good in this world is not unlimited. This is partly true because there are inherent limits to political action; the inherent difficulty, however, is in the nature of man himself. He is, after all, an imperfect creature with the capacity for evil as well as good. Certainly, the ultimate aim of politics, as of all else, is the good life. The good life, however, is not something which can be comprehended in some slogan or formula (such as "New Frontier" or "Great Society") about the social order, and even if it could, Hogg points out, it could not be achieved by government edict. The conservative approach is to try to make sure that at least some of the conditions in which the good life can flourish are present and, more important, to try to keep simpletons and charlatans from creating situations where the good life is all but impossible. "All the great evils of our time," Hogg maintained, "have come from men who mocked and exploited human misery by pretending that good government, that is, government according to their way of thinking, could offer utopia."

In contrast to the ingrained skepticism shared by most conservatives, most modern liberals, inclined as they are to be more optimistic about the perfectibility of man, are similarly more hopeful about the efficacy of governmental action. Progressive, humanistic education, liberals are convinced, is the means whereby men will eventually be able to ameliorate—if not solve—their pressing social and economic problems. While realizing that no one is omniscient, they would argue that we must at least attempt to rationally plan our complex social structures. Conservatives (or classical liberals) such as Dr. Ludwig Erhard of Germany would counter that we have only to examine the record of planned economies and of market economies to realize that central planning has for the most part been a failure and that the nations with the most consumer goods are the nations with the least governmental restrictions.

Modern liberals, on the other hand, charge conservatives with defeatism, negativism, and a lack of concern; they regard themselves as positive activists and are proud to be at least trying to improve the world. The conservative disdain for politics is a quality they frankly find irritating. To many liberals, in fact, politics is what makes life worthwhile—they find it exciting, ennobling, and, they would stress, *useful*.

The intelligent conservative, of course, is not at all disturbed when he is called "negative." He patiently reminds his liberal friend that the most important political goods are peace, liberty, and justice, all of which are in their essence negative. Governments do not *grant* peace, liberty, or justice; they strive to create the underlying framework within which these goals may be achieved; their duty is to prevent malefactors from denying the right of self-development to their citizens. Conservatives know that governments often attempt to do too many things, many of which are outside their proper province, with the result that the basic responsibility of government— enforcing the rule of law under which individuals are able to live their own lives and prosper—is often poorly done or not done at all. As Michael Oakeshott put it: "Briefly, the office [the conservative] attributes to government is to resolve some of the collisions which this variety of beliefs and activities generates; to preserve peace, not by placing an interdict upon choice and upon the diversity that springs from the exercise of preference, not by imposing substantive uniformity, but by enforcing general rules of procedure upon all subjects alike."

We have examined the five basic principles or "dispositions" which motivate and guide most modern conservatives, and we have noted the wide divergence of attitudes among persons united by a common political name. There are, in addition, three underlying modes of thought to be found among conservatives: (a) the empirical, (b) the rationalist, and (c) the intuitive. On the political level, the vast majority of modern conservatives may be roughly classified into three broad groupings: (a) liberal conservatives, (b) conservative liberals or classical liberals, and (c) antiliberal conservatives or restorationists.

Empirical conservatives have long been dominant in Britain, and their influence in all English-speaking countries is great. Their mentors have been men such as Aristotle, Hume, Montesquieu, Burke (in most of his moods), Melbourne, Stephen, Salisbury, Churchill, and Oakeshott; they have been evolutionists rather than revolutionaries, menders of the old rather than creators of the new. They preferred to stick closely to given facts and put greater store in precedents than in general principles. The English common law, based on *stare decisis* (let the previous decision stand), is a product of their method of thought, just as the Continental legal system, founded on general principles, proceeds naturally from rationalist premises. Empirical conservatives (like empirical liberals) resist the temptation to dogmatism and absolutism; they are more comfortable making gradual progress by trial and error, by testing and retesting in the light of experience, than they would be by trying sudden "great leaps forward." They tend to be wary of long chains of rationalist demonstration and are not terribly worried if they are not always rigorously consistent or even coherent; in short, they would rather be *reasonable* than rational. As Judge Learned Hand said of the spirit of liberty, the spirit of empiricism is not too sure that it is right.

As conservatives, empiricists are not by any means equally disposed toward all of the five basic canons that we have enumerated. They are most at home with the fifth principle, being deeply averse to ideologies and planning on a large scale, though they are reformers and welcome what Sir Karl Popper has called "piece-meal social engineering." They would, however, have no quarrel with principles two and three, since they are committed to such goals as stability, variety, and the widest liberty consistent with other values. They would likely hesitate to venture an opinion on the first and fourth canons, preferring to let everyone decide for himself what God and the good life might mean. Immutable laws of history or of morality they would find difficult to accept, though they would defend the need for moral principles and rational judgments in ethical matters. Like all conservatives, they treat ethical relativism with disdain.

Rationalist conservatives tend to be found more often on the Continent than in the English-speaking world. They look for their guidance to such thinkers as Plato, De Maistre (in most moods), Hegel, Cortés, Newman, Voegelin. When their own society reflects their principles they are the staunchest of men, but when, as often happens, their ideas are rejected they can quickly become partisans of radical change. Unlike empirical conservatives (with whom they are often uneasily allied) they are devoted to abstract, universal principles and much prefer deductive, *a priori*, reasoning to inductive, *a posteriori*, arguments. Instead of fearing dogmatism, many welcome it. Logic is highly prized; these conservatives strive to erect a case of rigid rational consistency even at the cost of being unreasonable. Rather than accept a reality which interferes with their deductive conclusions, many rationalists will attempt to remake it to fit their preconceived ideas. As Hegel phrased it in his supremely self-confident analysis: "The real is rational and the rational is real."

Most rationalists like to pursue an argument to its logical conclusions—something empiricists try to avoid. If private enterprise is superior to socialism, rationalist conservatives might say, then why do we not denationalize the Post Office and the schools? Empirical conservatives, on the other hand, are content to debate one issue at a time, face it on its own merits, and attack problems as they arise. The rationalist is also inclined to argue problems in terms of limiting cases, that is, in either-or propositions, so that we may be told to choose between socialist dictatorship and absolute *laissez-faire* on the grounds that if a man cannot dispose of *all* his earnings as he wishes, he is not free.

As may be expected, the rationalist no more than the empirical conservative is wholly happy about our five principles of conservatism. He is most enthusiastic about the first and fourth canons; he may not necessarily believe in God (although he usually does), but he almost always believes in universal laws of morality and often of history. As a latter-day Platonist, he will also generally believe that reason will tell us how to live the good life. He will not value stability and order quite as highly as will the empiricist, since he may decide that some overriding goal is more important than stability. The empirical conservative will sacrifice stability only with the greatest reluctance, but for the rationalist, rightness is all. Some rationalists are firmly devoted to the third principle (variety and liberty); others are just as firmly opposed to it. Almost all rationalist conservatives, however, agree with part of the fifth principle: a healthy skepticism toward grandiose plans for reform—by means of governmental action—should be encouraged. Although obviously not as skeptical of man's reason in general as is the empiricist, rationalist conservatives are almost all convinced that the attempt to govern most major aspects of society from the top down is a misuse of reason, a violation of the principle of subsidiarity.

Not all conservatives can be clearly identified as either empiricists or rationalists; some prefer to rely on intuition and can only be called romantics or even irrationalists. This group, it should be said, holds an honored place in the conservative tradition and may be the most influential of all. Their inspiration has come from such predominantly "cultural" conservatives as Coleridge, Wordsworth, Carlyle, Scott, Yeats, and (in some of their moods) Burke, Disraeli, Dostoyevsky, Melville, Nietzsche, and Henry Adams. They have usually held that their own times were out of joint and have often been intellectual revolutionaries or restorationists. They have defended the old values and fought what is called progress often without being able to say why. They have sensed instinctively that our modern industrial civilization contains the seeds of woes we cannot now imagine. Their mood is well expressed by Coleridge:

> It is this accursed practice of forever considering *only* what seems *expedient* for the occasion . . . of never listening to the true and unerring impulses of our better nature, which has led the colder-hearted men to the study of political economy . . . in a few years we shall either be governed by an aristocracy, or what is still more likely, by a contemptible democratical oligarchy of glib economists, compared to which the worst form of aristocracy would be a blessing.

"The true and unerring impulses of our better nature"! This, not reason, has been their battle cry. They have opposed capitalism as much as communism, an urban plutocracy as much as a socialist state. They have been proud of their past and honored it above the gadgets of what passes for progress. They speak from the heart rather than the mind, and so they have no qualms about embracing any or all or none of our five principles.

The romantics, as well as the empiricists and rationalists, all contribute to the variety of conservatism; it is perhaps this variety which is the chief explanation for the durability of conservatism. In addition, they serve as correctives, for they continually remind one another that there is more to life than facts alone, or logic alone, or feeling alone.

The various strands of practicing conservatives today may be divided into three paramount groups, all of which derive their substance from the ideas we have been discussing.

The first are liberal conservatives, the heirs of Burke and Montesquieu, of Hume and Disraeli. The largest segment of contemporary conservatism, they favor evolutionary tactics to accommodate themselves to gradual change; most of them tend to be empiricists and prefer to avoid dogmatic political positions. Their overriding goal is to reform in order to preserve. They are distinguished from conservative liberals principally by a streak of paternalism which sometimes urges them to use governmental powers in order to promote their personal social ideas. It often happens, therefore, that they are found making common cause with modern liberals or democratic socialists when they happen to agree on a particular social goal. Their commitment to such liberal ideals as the maximization of personal freedom and equality of opportunity separates them on their other flank from the antiliberal conservatives. Liberal conservatives generally accept our second, third, and fifth principles, but their bias toward empiricism forces them to view principles one and four with a certain coolness despite the personal devotion most of them have in their religious faith.

Conservative liberals or classical liberals might at first appear to be not really conservatives at all. It would seem no accident, however, that this tradition of liberalism has collaborated with liberal conservatives on most issues of practical politics since the turn of the century. Quite simply, they share a common skepticism toward the efficacy of government action and a common belief in gradual progress through the spontaneous natural forces of society as opposed to the large-scale planning favored by modern liberals and socialists. The majority of classical liberals today are probably empiricists in the tradition of Smith, De Tocqueville, Acton, Erhard, De Jouvenel, and Hayek; there has always been, however, an influential minority tradition of rationalists from Bentham to Ludwig von Mises. Probably Wilhelm Röpke in his *A Humane Society* has come closest to unifying the various strands of classical liberalism with liberal conservatism to form a coherent social philosophy. Although classical liberals and liberal conservatives have fallen into a harmonious working arrangement, differences still remain. Classical liberals are generally opposed to paternalism and fail to respond as enthusiastically as do most conservatives to appeals to nationalism. They probably have more in common with democratic socialists, however, than they do with our third group, the antiliberal conservatives. Like most liberal conservatives, they adjust easily to the second, third, and fifth principles, with the proviso that the minority tradition of rationalist classical liberals is less skeptical of the powers of human reason and is hospitable to the idea of universal law implied in the first principle. Almost all classical liberals would hold that the meaning of God and the good life are reserved for every individual's own conscience.

Creating a virtuous society, however, is more important to most antiliberal conservatives than is the sanctity of the individual conscience. De Maistre and Donoso-Cortés have been their chief teachers, together with Carlyle, Barrès, Maurras, Pius IX, and Pobiedonostsev. Their strength is on the Continent rather than in the English-speaking world, and most of their partisans would be called romantics or rationalists rather than empiricists. They are often called reactionaries, but perhaps restorationists—they wish to restore the virtuous principles of a previous golden age—would be a more appropriate term. Progress as the word is understood today is anathema to them, for they are opposed to the goals of the modern liberals and not merely to their methods or techniques. They are as firmly critical of the classical liberals as they are of the socialists; they are able to cooperate some of the time with some empirical conservatives, since the latter are at least not devoted to accelerating the deterioration (as they see it) of Western civilization. Representing as they do the outer edge of conservatism, it is not surprising that some of them have flirted with fascism. The great majority, however, are sharply distinguished from fascists by their respect for persons and for the law, including a higher law than man's. As conservatives, they could never worship the state or ascribe to a leader qualities belonging to God alone. The rejection of *will* as the sanction for law is, after all, an inseparable element of their tradition. All but a very few would subscribe with enthusiasm to our first principle, that a divine intent rules history and that God has issued universal moral laws which must be obeyed. Principles two and four are also congenial to restorationists, but number three would present some difficulties: antiliberals are able to endorse variety and liberty only so long as they contribute to the furthering of their own goals. Starting with the same premise as the classical liberals and liberal conservatives, that human reason is weak, restorationists arrive at the exactly opposite conclusion: a strong, paternalistic government is needed to help its citizens toward earthly happiness and eternal salvation.

Each of these three political groupings is in its own way a valuable part of the larger conservative movement. The classical liberals remind their allies of the importance of material progress, of the rights of individuals, of toleration of minorities, and of internationalism. The liberal conservatives, on the other hand, provide a necessary sense of moderation, of prudence and cautiousness. They are not likely to give wholehearted support to any new and untested proposal, no matter how much it may appeal to their personal prejudices. The sometimes dampening fact that significant (and lasting) political change can be brought about only *with* the grain of a particular region's cultural tradition is constantly (and usefully) emphasized by the antiliberal conservatives. Their paternalism (which sometimes borders on authoritarianism) probably supplies a needed corrective to the classical liberal's readiness to repeal most restrictions on freedom of expression and private morality. It should be stressed once again that this tripartite division is by no means hard and fast; there is considerable overlapping and exchange of ideas within these three general groups. It is not at all uncommon, in fact, for individual conservatives to espouse ideas from two or even all three of these broad traditions.

Conservatives, it will be readily observed, also differ among themselves on their attitudes to change. It is all but meaningless to say that a conservative is someone who believes in the status quo or who favors gradual change. If this were so, doctrinaire Marxist-Leninists in some countries would be "conservatives," as would democratic socialists in Sweden as well as supporters of the free enterprise system in the United States. Obviously, such widely divergent political factions cannot be said to share a common philosophy of government, no matter how broadly defined. The term "conservative," if it is to be of any use at all, must mean someone who wishes to conserve certain selected principles from a particular tradition, that is, most of the five basic canons of conservative thought discussed in this essay. Our thinking is confused rather than clarified if we use the word as a synonym for other more precise words. (Thus, the term "conservative socialist," depending on the context, could mean one of several things. The man so described could be a doctrinaire socialist, or an old-fashioned socialist, or a moderate, *i.e.*, not-very-socialist socialist, or even a socialist who happens to dress and act in an inconspicuous manner.)

We have seen that many conservatives wish to emphasize particular principles while still working within a broadly shared tradition. Classical liberals will tend to stress internationalism, whereas antiliberal conservatives are likely to be more nationalistic. Similarly, rationalists are more often doctrinaire and rigid in promoting their ideas than are empiricists, who usually favor adopting compromise proposals after careful thought and experimentation. There are also, of course, differences in temperament and in prudential judgment. Some will simply feel more deeply about their own ideas and will be more eager to see them widely adopted than will others. It seems evident, however, that it tells us little to say of a man that he is in favor of "going forward rapidly" or of "going backward slowly" unless we know *what it is* he wishes to move toward. Many liberals, after all, are likely to support the status quo if they happen to be in power or may even wish to return to the policies of a previous liberal government if their opponents happen to be in office.

We can assume that except for a very few contented souls all the members of Western civilization favor some changes in their social and political environment. Conservatives will want changes to be made (gradually or more urgently according to their disposition) in order to promote goals generally in accordance with the five principles we have been examining. Liberals, on the other hand, will want changes to accord with principles of their own—to be instituted, again, at a rate compatible with their own temperaments.

The essential issue is not the relative rates of speed at which one intends to bring about social changes but the *means* one uses to do so. Conservatives prefer to rely on the spontaneous forces of society operating within a framework of general rules provided by the government; liberals, having greater faith in the powers of human reason and the efficacy of state bureaucracies, are more inclined to look to government as the mainspring of social improvement. This, it must be stressed, is the essential identifying mark of the political conservative. It is, in the last analysis, irrelevant whether or not a political conservative is moderate in his personal views or habits, is devoted to his country's well-being, or believes in some system of natural law. The point at issue, surely, is his attitude to *government* and not to anything else. Anyone who believes in limited government and gradual progress through natural social forces is a political conservative, no matter what his views may be on any other question.

If we have had any doubts that the differences between liberals and conservatives are ones of emphasis and degree, we have only to compare both with totalitarians. It will then be clear that all constitutional democrats share a common belief that there are definite limits to the powers of the state and that there are some things which simply are not done. The totalitarian acknowledges no such self-imposed limitation; his actions are circumscribed only by the technology at his disposal. In this essential respect, of course, there is no difference between Communists, Fascists, Nazis. Lenin once declared to a group of Young Communists, ". . . morality is entirely subordinate to the interests of class war. Everything is moral which is necessary for the annihilation of the old exploiting social order." And in 1945 a Nazi prisoner of war told his captors: "The enemy we could not buy or break was the aristocratic individualism of the ordinary citizen of the West. If only we had hanged—as Himmler was always itching to do—all those outdated legalists, with their squawks about moral dignity, then our movement would have swept the world" (quoted by Peter Viereck in his *Conservatism Revisited*).

"As Himmler was always *itching* to do." Constitutional democrats of all persuasions are perhaps best differentiated from their opponents by the fact that the enemies of democracy are, in a fundamental sense, *impatient*. They are bored with discussions, rules of law, and elections; they *itch* to "get things done"—for what they call "direct action." Spanish philosopher José Ortega y Gasset, who had fought both Communism and Fascism, analyzed this phenomenon in 1930 in his *The Revolt of the Masses*:

> Under the species of Syndicalism and Fascism there appears for the first time in Europe a type of man who does not want to give reasons or to be right but simply shows himself resolved to impose his opinions. . . . Here I see the most palpable manifestation of the new mentality of the masses, due to their having decided to rule society without the capacity for doing so . . . Hence, the "new thing" in Europe is to "have done with discussions"; and detestation is expressed for all forms of intercommunion which imply acceptance of objective standards, ranging from conversation to Parliament, and taking in science. This means a renunciation of the common life based on culture, which is subject to standards, and a return to the common life of barbarism. All the normal processes are suppressed in order to arrive directly at the imposition of what is desired. . . .
>
> Civilization is nothing else than the attempt to reduce force to being the last resort . . . "direct action" consists in inverting the order and proclaiming violence as the first resort, or strictly as the sole resort. It is the norm which proposes the annulment of all norms. . . . It is the Magna Charta of barbarism.

Conservatives, even the best of them, are far from perfect, and like many liberals and democratic socialists, many will be found to be motivated by some selfish or narrow-minded interest a good part of the time. They all, in company with other constitutional democrats, acknowledge the civilized values and share a common disdain for the proponents of "direct action," whether or not they embellish it with the rhetoric of the "right" or the "left."

A REVIEW

Conservatism, as we understand the term today, owes its birth to the French Revolution. It was then that the barricades went up and sides were chosen; those who wished to radically alter human society stood on one side and those who wished to preserve it took their places on the other.

The great issue which divided men into two camps was not, it should be stressed, their attitude toward the respective claims of the rich and the poor, as it is so often suggested. The arch-antagonist of the Revolution, Edmund Burke, declared in the clearest terms: "When, indeed, the smallest rights of the poorest people in the kingdom are in question, I would set my face against any act of pride and power countenanced by the highest that are in it; and if it should come to the last extremity, and to a contest of blood,—God forbid! God forbid!—my part is taken: I would take my fate with the poor and low and feeble." The decisive issue was, in fact, the place and efficacy of human reason in the affairs of men.

To the conservative mind, the beheading of the king, the massacre of the nobility, even the destruction of the laws, were as trifles compared with the profound blasphemy of worshiping the Goddess of Reason in the Cathedral of Paris. By this act the revolutionaries denied the reality of original sin and asserted that evil could be swept away by good will and good arguments.

On the continent of Europe, Joseph de Maistre in Sardinia and Friedrich Gentz in Austria continued the intellectual counterattack against the new doctrines so ably begun by Burke. In the next generation, men like Donoso-Cortés, Cardinal Newman, and Pope Pius IX carried on the defense of the old values against the new. Only in a time when standards were being challenged, when the basic structure of society was no longer generally accepted, was there a need for a self-conscious conservatism. When the "cake of custom" was broken in 1789, all over Europe men wedded to the old ways stepped forward to defend them.

This newly articulated conservatism took the form, as we have seen, of five basic predispositions. To support these principles of reverence, order, liberty, honor, and moderation the leaders of the counterrevolution drew upon the experience and thoughts of the molders of the Western tradition, of such men as Plato, Aristotle, Cicero, Aquinas, Dante, and Hooker, among many others.

At about the same time another revolution appeared in Europe whose effects were even more drastic and far-reaching than the French. The Industrial Revolution's initial beneficiaries were the newly enriched plutocracy. The forces of the new conservatism were as insistent in pointing out the dangers in the one revolution as in the other. They saw what the rise of the factory system would do to the society they knew and loved. It was the literary conservatives—

Coleridge, Wordsworth, Carlyle, Burckhardt, Dostoyevsky, Ortega y Gasset—who saw that individual men would feel more and more helpless in the developing mass society. Throughout the nineteenth century these men, and many others, did their best to delay the destruction of humane values in the name of progress. Most of the legislation of this time protecting the interests of workers was, in fact, passed by conservatives. Although sometimes done for selfish reasons, the usual motive was a sincere desire to humanize the growing powers of machines.

The new era of steam and steel brought with it new struggles for power and precedence. The rising middle classes wanted the political franchise extended—to themselves. In Britain, the Reform Bill of 1832 was fiercely opposed by the Lord Chancellor, Lord Eldon, who prided himself on being against *every* new piece of legislation on the grounds that no one could ever foresee all the consequences of any change.   Most conservatives were not nearly as rigid as Eldon, of course. Many opposed the Reform Bill because they foresaw that a government claiming its power from the people (instead of from prescription) would grow in power until it became the omnicompetent state. Still other conservatives, led by Disraeli and Randolph Churchill, became Tory Democrats and took as their motto "Trust the People!" The second Reform Act, in 1867, extending the vote to the upper working class, was of course passed by Disraeli.

As the Age of Discussion gradually dawned, established ideas in every country on the nature of liberty, of authority, and of equality were questioned more and more often. De Tocqueville in France and Acton in Britain defended liberty as valuable in and of itself regardless of any utilitarian justification. This emphasis on the importance of freedom in a time of increasing governmental power was congenial to conservative thought, which had always taught the duty of rectifying the balance in the perennial debate between liberty and authority. Another Englishman, James Fitzjames Stephen, was to counter the optimism and rationalism of John Stuart Mill with commonsensical (and brilliant) arguments defining the proper limits of liberty in morals and society. De Tocqueville, Acton, and Stephen were all active members of the liberal parties of their respective countries, and they represent the point at which most of the classical liberals imperceptibly passed over the line into conservatism. Any one of the three could have stood for his parliament as a member of the conservative party (as Gladstone once did—at the same period when Disraeli was standing as a radical). Like Walter Bagehot, another paradigm of the conservative liberal (or liberal conservative), they were "between sizes in politics." For that reason, if for no other, they are important as surrogates of a great movement that has largely merged, while retaining an identity of its own, into the more inclusive tradition of empirical conservatism.

While De Tocqueville and Acton were arguing the case for liberty in France and England, Hegel in Prussia and Metternich in Austria had been solicitously upholding the claims of authority and nationalism on the one hand and of stability and order on the other. The cosmopolitan, empirical Metternich was closer in temperament to that steadfast critic of nationalism, Lord Acton, than he was to the rationalist, patriotic Hegel, who thought the Prussian state the highest creation of historical development. Metternich, like his spiritual descendant Archduke Otto von Habsburg, dreamed of a federal Europe without barriers to goods or ideas. As a conservative, however, he knew that he must deal with the problems of his own time and country first, and, for post-Napoleonic Austria, the first need was peace and order.

In 1848 the *Communist Manifesto* was published, and at about the same time in most countries of Europe forces were unleashed which were eventually to wreak havoc in the twentieth century—the forces of ideological nationalism, dictatorial socialism, racism, and incipient fascism. Henceforth, the struggle for peace and the traditional order, for the survival of their world, was to occupy the energies not only of conservatives but of liberals and democratic socialists as well.

It was, of course, the maverick Conservative, Winston Churchill, who did more than any other single man to keep liberal democracy from becoming a fading memory on our planet. Although the struggle against dictatorship in its many and recurring forms obviously takes precedence over all other issues, men such as Churchill, in peacetime at least, could turn their attention to less vital but still pressing problems.

Among these is the growing power of the nonelected bureaucracy over our daily lives; Churchill himself had a good deal to say on this subject, as did the Italian political sociologist Gaetano Mosca, well known for his analysis of the ruling elite in modern democracies. It is becoming increasingly clear that men elected to power who are necessarily an elite are losing touch with the real wants, needs, and ideas of the ordinary men and women who elected them.

Conservatives have always been concerned to work toward a humane and just society as well as a free and prosperous one; Wilhelm Röpke in Germany and Switzerland and Bertrand de Jouvenel in France have devoted much of their thought to this goal, as their many books attest. Ludwig Erhard, when directing the rebuilding of war-shattered Germany, taught the world a lesson in how to create the material well-being which is the basis for a happy and civilized nation. In Britain, Arthur Seldon and John Jewkes have contributed many valuable ideas on the best ways of reforming the welfare state in order to achieve efficient social services and a fair distribution of the necessities and amenities of life.

On a philosophic level, F. A. von Hayek, a conservative liberal born in Austria, and Michael Oakeshott, a thoroughly English traditional and empirical conservative, have both stressed in all their work the need for a healthy respect for the limits of human reason in political affairs and an appreciation of the vital role of tradition in a creative, free, and progressive society.

In this short review there has been only space to touch briefly on the relationships between the conservative scholars and statesmen represented here. The interested reader who wishs to broaden his knowledge of these men and their ideas may wish to consult some of the books listed in the Suggestions for Further Reading.

I
Man and Society

The conservative view of man and society was set out in the eighteenth and early nineteenth centuries by the giants of the tradition: Edmund Burke, Samuel Taylor Coleridge, and Georg Wilhelm Friedrich Hegel. These three drew from the democratic philosophy of Jean-Jacques Rousseau. The tradition has been carried on in our time by such contemporary scholars as Röpke, Hayek, and Oakeshott.

These thinkers have disagreed among themselves on many issues, but they have been united in their condemnation of the misplaced self-confidence of utilitarian liberals who believe that the end of the world may be realized, that heaven may be brought down to earth, that an ideal society can be created by man's reason.

Modern conservatism was born as a reaction to the follies of the French Revolution. Burke, Coleridge, and Hegel—all intellectual giants—devoted much of their time to exposing the fallacy that a committee of intellectuals could sit down and write a constitution for a given state without reference to the customs, traditions, and habits of that society.

The fathers of conservatism knew that society was necessary to the full development of man as an individual and that it was something more than just the sum of its parts, that any given society was something more than the government of the day or the inhabitants of the time. In the words of Burke, they all agreed that any society is indeed "a partnership in all science ; a partnership in all art ; a partnership in every virtue, and in all perfection. As the ends of such a partnership cannot be obtained in many generations, it becomes a partnership not only between those who are living, but between those who are dead, and those who are to be born."

Just as society is worthy of reverence, so, conservatives would always insist, is individual man himself. Men must, as Kant argued, always be treated as ends in themselves, never as mere objects or things. From its inception conservatism has opposed those theories of society (whether of the "right" or the "left") which relegated the individual to a secondary role and glorified the political state as all-important.

Wilhelm Röpke and F. A. von Hayek, two of the most eminent social philosophers and economists of this century, have devoted much of their thought to reconciling the conflicting claims of the individual and society.

Men must employ their reason (while recognizing the limitations of reason) to devise social arrangements which allow for the greatest possible free development of individuals, preserving at the same time the institutions and traditions of society which are themselves necessary for individual development. Hayek, in particular, has emphasized the dangers of a false individualism which prepares the way for its opposite: collectivism.

The moral weaknesses and subtle threats to freedom which are often encouraged by the restrictive regulations of a collectivist society have been discussed with considerable insight by John Jewkes, one of the most prominent British critics of the planned society. Another English scholar, Michael Oakeshott, has often stressed the need for humility in the face of the mysteries of social life and of the universe; he has given us a penetrating critique of the errors of extreme rationalism and an affirmation of that time-tested approach to politics which has placed the English-speaking nations among the most stable and democratic in history.

Conservatives maintained that politics has its limitations and that, in fact, there are many things in life more important than politics, among them "religion, art, study, family, country, friends, music, fun, duty." * The conservative distrust of politics stems basically from the view that man is an imperfect creature whose inmost nature is a mixture of good and evil. They are concerned, therefore, to so order society that bad men have the least opportunity to do harm. This is a more modest goal than the liberal's, but it is more realistic and, it may be added, it allows for the spontaneous and the unexpected.

* Enumerated by Quintin Hogg, *The Case for Conservatism* (London, 1947).

1 BURKE

The Nature of
Society and Government

Edmund Burke (1729–1797), the great Anglo-Irish statesman and orator, more than any other man was responsible for the founding of modern conservatism. He was a member of the Whig Party. In his youth he strongly defended the struggle for freedom of the American colonists and warmly condemned arbitrary rule in India. In 1791 he published what has been called "the best single essay on conservatism," his *Reflections on the Revolution in France*. Most of the following selections are taken from that book and Burke's "Speech on the Impeachment of Warren Hastings" and "Letter to a Noble Lord." Other speeches and essays are included.*

Society is, indeed, a contract. Subordinate contracts for objects of mere occasional interest may be dissolved at pleasure; but the state ought not to be considered as nothing better than a partnership agreement in a trade of pepper and coffee, calico or tobacco, or some other such low concern, to be taken up for a little temporary interest, and to be dissolved by the fancy of the parties. It is to be looked on with other reverence; because it is not a partnership in things subservient only to the gross animal existence of a temporary and perishable nature. It is a partnership in all science, a partnership in all art, a partnership in every virtue and in all perfection. As the ends of such a partnership cannot be obtained in many generations, it becomes a partnership not only between those who are living, but between those who are living, those who are dead, and those who are to be born. Each contract of each particular state is but a clause in the great primeval contract of eternal society, linking the lower with the higher

* See Edmund Burke, *Works* (Boston: Little, Brown & Co., 1865).

natures, connecting the visible and invisible world, according to a fixed compact sanctioned by the inviolable oath which holds all physical and all moral natures each in their appointed place. This law is not subject to the will of those who, by an obligation above them, and infinitely superior, are bound to submit their will to that law. The municipal corporations of that universal kingdom are not morally at liberty, at their pleasure, and on their speculations of a contingent improvement, wholly to separate and tear asunder the bands of their subordinate community, and to dissolve it into an unsocial, uncivil, unconnected chaos of elementary principles. It is the first and supreme necessity only, a necessity that is not chosen, but chooses, a necessity paramount to deliberation, that admits no discussion and demands no evidence, which alone can justify a resort to anarchy. This necessity is no exception to the rule; because this necessity itself is a part, too, of that moral and physical disposition of things to which man must be obedient by consent or force: but if that which is only submission to necessity should be made the object of choice, the law is broken, Nature is disobeyed, and the rebellious are outlawed, cast forth, and exiled, from this world of reason, and order, and peace, and virtue, and fruitful penitence, into the antagonist world of madness, discord, vice, confusion, and unavailing sorrow. . . .

It is no wonder, therefore, that, with these ideas of everything in their Constitution and government at home, either in Church or State, as illegitimate and usurped, or at best as a vain mockery, . . . [the revolutionists of France] look abroad with an eager and passionate enthusiasm. Whilst they are possessed by these notions, it is vain to talk to them of the practice of their ancestors, the fundamental laws of their country, the fixed form of a Constitution whose merits are confirmed by the solid test of long experience and an increasing public strength and national prosperity. They despise experience as the wisdom of unlettered men; and as for the rest, they have wrought under ground a mine that will blow up, at one grand explosion, all examples of antiquity, all precedents, charters, and acts of Parliament. They have "the rights of men." Against these there can be no prescription; against these no argument is binding: these admit no temperament and no compromise: anything withheld from their full demand is so much of fraud and injustice. Against these their rights of men let no government look for security in the length of its continuance, or in the justice and lenity of its administration. The objections of these speculatists, if its forms do not quadrate with their theories, are as valid against such an old and beneficient government as against the most violent tyranny or the greenest usurpation. They are always at issue with governments, not on a question of abuse, but a question of competency and a question of title. I have nothing to say to the clumsy subtilty of their political metaphysics. Let them be their amusement in the schools. . . .

But let them not break prison to burst like a Levanter, to sweep the earth with their hurricane, and to break up the fountains of the great deep to overwhelm us!

Far am I from denying in theory, full as far is my heart from withholding in practice, (if I were of power to give or to withhold,) the *real* rights of men. In denying their false claims of right, I do not mean to injure those which are real, and are such as their pretended rights would totally destroy. If civil society be made for the advantage of man, all the advantages for which it is made become his right. It is an institution of beneficence; and law itself is only beneficence acting by a rule. Men have a right to live by that rule; they have a right to justice, as between their fellows, whether their fellows are in politic function or in ordinary occupation. They have a right to the fruits of their industry, and to the means of making their industry fruitful. They have a right to the acquisitions of their parents, to the nourishment and improvement of their offspring, to instruction in life and to consolation in death. Whatever each man can separately do, without trespassing upon others, he has a right to do for himself; and he has a right to a fair portion of all which society, with all its combinations of skill and force, can do in his favour. In this partnership all men have equal rights; but not to equal things. He that has but five shillings in the partnership has as good a right to it as he that has five hundred pounds has to his larger proportion; but he has not a right to an equal dividend in the product of the joint stock. And as to the share of power, authority, and direction which each individual ought to have in the management of the state, that I must deny to be amongst the direct original rights of man in civil society; for I have in my contemplation the civil social man, and no other. It is a thing to be settled by convention.

If civil society be the offspring of convention, that convention must be its law. That convention must limit and modify all the descriptions of constitution which are formed under it. Every sort of legislative, judicial, or executory power are its creatures. They can have no being in any other state of things; and how can any man claim, under the conventions of civil society, rights which do not so much as suppose its existence,—rights which are absolutely repugnant to it? One of the first motives to civil society, and which becomes one of its fundamental rules is, *that no man should be judge in his own cause.* By this each person has at once divested himself of the first fundamental right of uncovenanted man, that is, to judge for himself, and to assert his own cause. He abdicates all right to be his own governor. He inclusively, in a great measure, abandons the right of self-defence, the first law of Nature. Men cannot enjoy the rights of an uncivil and of a civil state together. That he may obtain justice, he gives up his right of determining what it is in points the most essential to him. That he may secure some liberty, he makes a surrender in trust of the whole of it.

Government is not made in virtue of natural rights, which may and do exist in total independence of it,—and exist in much greater clearness, and in a much greater degree of abstract perfection: but their abstract perfection is their practical defect. By having a right to everything they want everything. Government is a contrivance of human wisdom to provide for human *wants*. Men have a right that these wants should be provided for by this wisdom. Among these wants is to be reckoned the want, out of civil society, of a sufficient restraint upon their passions. Society requires not only that the passions of individuals should be subjected, but that even in the mass and body, as well as in the individuals, the inclinations of men should frequently be thwarted, their will controlled, and their passions brought into subjection. This can only be done *by a power out of themselves,* and not, in the exercise of its function, subject to that will and to those passions which it is its office to bridle and subdue. In this sense the restraints on men, as well as their liberties, are to be reckoned among their rights. But as the liberties and the restrictions vary with times and circumstances, and admit of infinite modifications, they cannot be settled upon any abstract rule; and nothing is so foolish as to discuss them upon that principle.

The moment you abate anything from the full rights of men each to govern himself, and suffer any artificial, positive limitation upon those rights, from that moment the whole organization of government becomes a consideration of convenience. This it is which makes the constitution of a state, and the due distribution of its powers, a matter of the most delicate and complicated skill. It requires a deep knowledge of human nature and human necessities, and of the things which facilitate or obstruct the various ends which are to be pursued by the mechanism of civil institutions. The state is to have recruits to its strength and remedies to its distempers. What is the use of discussing a man's abstract right to food or medicine? The question is upon the method of procuring and administering them. In that deliberation I shall always advise to call in the aid of the farmer and the physician, rather than the professor of metaphysics.

The science of constructing a commonwealth, or renovating it, or reforming it, is, like every other experimental science, not to be taught *a priori*. Nor is it a short experience that can instruct us in that practical science; because the real effects of moral causes are not always immediate, but that which in the first instance is prejudicial may be excellent in its remoter operation, and its excellence may arise even from the ill effects it produces in the beginning. The reverse also happens; and very plausible schemes, with very pleasing commencements, have often shameful and lamentable conclusions. In states there are often some obscure and almost latent causes, things which appear at first view of little moment, on which a very great part of its prosperity or adversity may most essentially depend. The science of government being, therefore, so practical in itself, and intended for such practical purposes, a matter which requires experience, and even more experience than any person can gain in his whole life, however sagacious and observing he may be, it is with infinite caution that any man ought to venture upon pulling down an edifice which has answered in any tolerable degree for ages the common purposes of society, or on building it up again without having models and patterns of approved utility before his eyes.

These metaphysic rights entering into common life, like rays of light which pierce into a dense medium, are, by the laws of Nature, refracted from their straight line. Indeed, in the gross and complicated mass of human passions and concerns, the primitive rights of men undergo such a variety of refractions and reflections that it becomes absurd to talk of them as if they continued in the simplicity of their original direction. The nature of man is intricate; the objects of society are of the greatest possible complexity: and therefore no simple disposition or direction of power can be suitable either to man's nature or to the quality of his affairs. When I hear the simplicity of contrivance aimed at and boasted of in any new political constitutions, I am at no loss to decide that the artificers are grossly ignorant of their trade or totally negligent of their duty. The simple governments are fundamentally defective, to say no worse of them. If you were to contemplate society in but one point of view, all these simple modes of polity are infinitely captivating. In effect each would answer its single end much more perfectly than the more complex is able to attain all its complex purposes. But it is better that the whole should be imperfectly and anomalously answered than that while some parts are provided for with great exactness, others might be totally neglected, or perhaps materially injured, by the over-care of a favorite member.

The pretended rights of these theorists are all extremes; and in proportion as they are metaphysically true, they are morally and politically false. The rights of men are in a sort of *middle,* incapable of definition, but not impossible to be discerned. The rights of men in governments are their advantages; and these are often in balances between differences of good,—in compromises sometimes between good and evil, and sometimes between evil and evil. Political reason is a computing principle: adding, subtracting, multiplying, and dividing, morally, and not metaphysically or mathematically, true moral denominations.

By these theorists the right of the people is almost always sophistically confounded with their power. The body of the community, whenever it can come to act, can meet with no effectual resistance; but till power and right are the same, the whole body of them has no right inconsistent with virtue, and the first of all virtues, prudence. Men have no right to what is not reasonable, and to what is not for their benefit. . . .

*   *   *

The object of the state is (as far as may be) the happiness of the whole. Whatever makes multitudes of men utterly miserable can never answer that object; indeed, it contradicts it wholly and entirely; and the happiness or misery of mankind, estimated by their feelings and sentiments, and not by any theories of their rights, is, and ought to be, the standard for the conduct of legislators towards the people. This naturally and necessarily conducts us to the peculiar and characteristic situation of a people, and to a knowledge of their opinions, prejudices, habits, and all the circumstances that diversify and color life.

The first question a good statesman would ask himself, therefore, would be, How and in what circumstances do you find society? and to act upon them. . . .

*   *   *

It is one of the finest problems in legislation, and what has often engaged my thoughts whilst I followed that profession,—What the state ought to take upon itself to direct by the public wisdom, and what it ought to leave, with as little interference as possible, to individual discretion. Nothing, certainly, can be laid down on the subject that will not admit of exceptions,—many permanent, some occasional. But the clearest line of distinction which I could draw, whilst I had my chalk to draw any line, was this: that the state ought to confine itself to what regards the state or the creatures of the state: namely, the exterior establishment of its religion; its magistracy; its revenue; its military force by sea and land; the corporations that owe their existence to its fiat; in a word, to everything that is *truly and properly* public,—to the public peace, to the public safety, to the public prosperity. In its preventive police it ought to be sparing of its efforts, and to employ means, rather few, unfrequent, and strong, than many, and frequent, and, of course, as they multiply their puny politic race and dwindle, small and feeble. Statesmen who know themselves will, with the dignity which belongs to wisdom, proceed only in this the superior orb and first mover of their duty, steadily, vigilantly, severely, courageously: whatever remains will, in a manner, provide for itself. But as they descend from the state to a province, from a province to a parish, and from a parish to a private house, they go on accelerated in their fall. They *cannot* do the lower duty; and in proportion as they try it, they will certainly fail in the higher. They ought to know the different departments of things,—what belongs to laws, and what manners alone can regulate. To these great politicians may give a leaning, but they cannot give a law. . . .

*   *   *

In a plan of reformation, it would be one of my maxims, that, when I know of an establishment which may be subservient to useful purposes, and which at the same time, from its discretionary nature, is liable to a very great perversion from those purposes, *I would limit the quantity of the power that might be so abused.* For I am sure that in all such cases the rewards of merit will have very narrow bounds, and that partial or corrupt favor will be infinite.

2 BURKE

The Nature of Law *

Nothing in Mr. Hastings' proceedings is so curious as his several defences; and nothing in the defences is so singular as the principles upon which he proceeds. Your Lordships will have to decide not only upon a large, connected, systematic train of misdemeanors, but an equally connected system of principles and maxims of government, invented to justify those misdemeanors. He has brought them forward and avowed them in the face of day. . . .

He has told your Lordships, in his defence, that actions in Asia do not bear the same moral qualities which the same actions would bear in Europe. My Lords, we positively deny that principle. . . . These gentlemen have formed a plan of *geographical morality,* by which the duties of men, in public and in private situations, are not to be governed by their relation to the great Governor of the Universe, or by their relation to mankind, but by climates, degrees of longitude, parallels, not of life, but of latitudes: as if, when you have crossed the equinoctial, all the virtues die, as they say some insects die when they cross the line. . . . This geographical morality we do protest against; Mr. Hastings shall not screen himself under it. . . .We think it necessary, in justification of ourselves, to declare that the laws of morality are the same everywhere, and that there is no action which would pass for an act of extortion, of peculation, of bribery, and of oppression in England, that is not an act of extortion, of peculation, of bribery, and oppression in Europe, Asia, Africa, and all the world over. This I contend for not in the technical forms of it, but I contend for it in the substance.

* See introductory remarks to Selection 1.

Mr. Hastings comes before your Lordships not as a British governor answering to a British tribunal, but as a subahdar, as a bashaw of three tails. He says, "I had an arbitrary power to exercise: I exercised it. Slaves I found the people: slaves they are,—they are so by their constitution; and if they are, I did not make it for them. I was unfortunately bound to exercise this arbitrary power, and accordingly I did exercise it. It was disagreeable to me, but I did exercise it; and no other power can be exercised in that country." . . . Will your Lordships submit to hear the corrupt practices of mankind made the principles of government? No! it will be your pride and glory to teach men intrusted with power, that, in their use of it, they are to conform to principles, and not to draw their principles from the corrupt practice of any man whatever. Was there ever heard, or could it be conceived, that a governor would dare to heap up all the evil practices, all the cruelties, oppressions, extortions, corruptions, briberies, of all the ferocious usurpers, desperate robbers, thieves, cheats, and jugglers, that ever had office, from one end of Asia to another, and, consolidating all this mass of the crimes and absurdities of barbarous domination into one code, establish it as the whole duty of an English governor? I believe that till this time so audacious a thing was never attempted by man.

He have arbitrary power! My Lords, the East India Company have not arbitrary power to give him; the king has no arbitrary power to give him; your Lordships have not; nor the Commons, nor the whole legislature. We have no arbitrary power to give, because arbitrary power is a thing which neither any man can hold nor any man can give. No man can lawfully govern himself according to his own will; much less can one person be governed by the will of another. We are all born in subjection,—all born equally, high and low, governors and governed, in subjection to one great, immutable, pre-existent law, prior to all our devices and prior to all our contrivances, paramount to all our ideas and all our sensations, antecedent to our very existence, by which we are knit and connected in the eternal frame of the universe, out of which we cannot stir.

This great law does not arise from our conventions or compacts; on the contrary, it gives to our conventions and compacts all the force and sanction they can have. It does not arise from our vain institutions. Every good gift is of God; all power is of God; and He who has given the power, and from whom alone it originates, will never suffer the exercise of it to be practised upon any less solid foundation than the power itself. If, then, all dominion of man over man is the effect of the Divine disposition, it is bound by the eternal laws of Him that gave it, with which no human authority can dispense,—neither he that exercises it, nor even those who are subject to it; and if they were mad enough to make an express compact that should release their magistrate from his duty, and should declare their lives, liberties, and properties dependent upon, not rules and laws, but his mere capricious will, that covenant would be void. The acceptor of it has not his authority increased, but he has his crime doubled. Therefore can it be imagined, if this be true, that He will suffer this great gift of government, the greatest, the best, that was ever given by God to mankind, to be the plaything and the sport of the feeble will of a man, who, by a blasphemous, absurd, and petulant usurpation, would place his own feeble, contemptible, ridiculous will in the place of Divine wisdom and justice? . . .

Law and arbitrary power are in eternal enmity. Name me a magistrate, and I will name property; name me power, and I will name protection. It is a contradiction in terms, it is blasphemy in religion, it is wickedness in politics, to say that any man can have arbitrary power. In every patent of office the duty is included. For what else does a magistrate exist? To suppose for power is an absurdity in idea. Judges are guided and governed by the eternal laws of justice, to which we are all subject. We may bite our chains, if we will, but we shall be made to know ourselves, and be taught that man is born to be governed by law; and he that will substitute *will* in the place of it is an enemy to God.

Despotism does not in the smallest degree abrogate, alter, or lessen any one duty of any one relation of life, or weaken the force or obligation of any one engagement or contract whatsoever. Despotism, if it means anything at all defensible, means a mode of government bound by no written rules, and coerced by no controlling magistracies or well-settled orders in the state. But if it has no written law, it neither does nor can cancel the primeval, indefeasible, unalterable law of Nature and of nations; and if no magistracies control its exertions, those exertions must derive their limitation and direction either from the equity and moderation of the ruler, or from downright revolt on the part of the subject by rebellion, divested of all its criminal qualities. The moment a sovereign removes the idea of security and protection from his subjects, and declares that he is everything and they nothing, when he declares that no contract he makes with them can or ought to bind him, he then declares war upon them: he is no longer sovereign; they are no longer subjects.

*   *   *

What the law respects shall be sacred to me. If the barriers of law should be broken down, upon ideas of convenience, even of public convenience, we shall have no longer anything certain among us. If the discretion of power is once let loose upon property, we can be at no loss to determine whose power and what discretion it is that will prevail at last. It would be wise to attend upon the order of things, and not to attempt to outrun the slow, but smooth and even course of Nature. There are occasions, I admit, of public necessity, so vast, so clear, so evident, that they supersede all laws. Law, being only made for the benefit of the community, cannot in any one of its parts resist a demand which may comprehend the total of the public interest. To be sure, no law can set itself up against the cause and reason of all law; but such a case very rarely happens, and this most certainly is not such a case. The mere time of the reform is by no means worth the sacrifice of a principle of law. Individuals pass like shadows; but the commonwealth is fixed and stable. The difference, therefore, of to-day and to-morrow, which to private people is immense, to the state is nothing. At any rate, it is better, if possible, to reconcile our economy with our laws than to set them at variance,—a quarrel which in the end must be destructive to both. . . . [I]t is necessary from the demands of the people, whose desires, when they do not militate with the stable and eternal rules of justice and reason, (rules which are above us and above them,) ought to be as a law to a House of Commons.

3 BURKE

Tradition and Progress *

There is another advantage in taking up this business singly and by an arrangement for the single object. It is that you may proceed by *degrees*. We must all obey the great law of change. It is the most powerful law of Nature, and the means perhaps of its conservation. All we can do, and that human wisdom can do, is to provide that the change shall proceed by insensible degrees. This has all the benefits which may be in change, without any of the inconveniences of mutation. Everything is provided for as it arrives. This mode will, on the one hand, prevent the *unfixing old interests at once:* a thing which is apt to breed a black and sullen discontent in those who are at once dispossessed of all their influence and consideration. This gradual course, on the other side, will prevent men long under depression from being intoxicated with a large draught of new power, which they always abuse with a licentious insolence. But, wishing, as I do, the change to be gradual and cautious, I would, in my first steps, lean rather to the side of enlargement than restriction.

*　　*　　*

I knew that there is a manifest, marked distinction, which ill men with ill designs, or weak men incapable of any design, will constantly be confounding,—that is, a marked distinction between change and reformation. The former alters the substance of the objects themselves, and gets rid of all their essential good as well as of all the accidental evil annexed to them. Change is novelty; and whether it is to operate any one of the effects of reformation at all, or whether it may not contradict the very principle upon which reformation is

* See introductory remarks to Selection 1.

desired, cannot be certainly known beforehand. Reform is not a change in the substance or in the primary modification of the object, but a direct application of a remedy to the grievance complained of. So far as that is removed, all is sure. It stops there; and if it fails, the substance which underwent the operation, at the very worst, is but where it was.

All this, in effect, I think, but am not sure, I have said elsewhere. It cannot at this time be too often repeated, line upon line, precept upon precept, until it comes into the currency of a proverb,—*To innovate is not to reform*. The French revolutionists complained of everything; they refused to reform anything; and they left nothing, no, nothing at all, *unchanged*. The consequences are *before* us,— not in remote history, not in future prognostication: they are about us; they are upon us. They shake the public security; they menace private enjoyment. They dwarf the growth of the young; they break the quiet of the old. If we travel, they stop our way. They infest us in town; they pursue us to the country. Our business is interrupted, our repose is troubled, our pleasures are saddened, our very studies are poisoned and perverted, and knowledge is rendered worse than ignorance, by the enormous evils of this dreadful innovation. . . .

It was, then, not my love, but my hatred to innovation, that produced my plan of reform. Without troubling myself with the exactness of the logical diagram, I considered them as things substantially opposite. It was to prevent that evil, that I proposed the measures which his Grace is pleased, and I am not sorry he is pleased, to recall to my recollection. I had (what I hope that noble Duke will remember in all his operations) a state to preserve, as well as a state to reform. I had a people to gratify, but not to inflame or to mislead. I do not claim half the credit for what I did as for what I prevented from being done. In that situation of the public mind, I did not undertake, as was then proposed, to new-model the House of Commons or the House of Lords, or to change the authority under which any officer of the crown acted, who was suffered at all to exist. Crown, lords, commons, judicial system, system of administration, existed as they had existed before, and in the mode and manner in which they had always existed. My measures were, what I then truly stated them to the House to be, in their intent, healing and meditatorial. A complaint was made of too much influence in the House of Commons: I reduced it in both Houses; and I gave my reasons, article by article, for every

reduction, and showed why I thought it safe for the service of the
state. I heaved the lead every inch of way I made. A disposition to
expense was complained of: to that I opposed, not mere retrench-
ment, but a system of economy, which would make a random expense,
without plan or foresight, in future, not easily practicable. I proceeded
upon principles of research to put me in possession of my matter, on
principles of method to regulate it, and on principles in the human
mind and in civil affairs to secure and perpetuate the operation. I
conceived nothing arbitrarily, nor proposed anything to be done by
the will and pleasure of others or my own,—but by reason, and by
reason only. I have ever abhorred, since the first dawn of my understanding to this its obscure twilight, all the operations of opinion,
fancy, inclination, and will, in the affairs of government, where only
a sovereign reason, paramount to all forms of legislation and administration, should dictate. Government is made for the very purpose of
opposing that reason to will and to caprice, in the reformers or in
the reformed, in the governors or in the governed, in kings, in senates,
or in people.

*   *   *

We are afraid to put men to live and trade each on his own private
stock of reason; because we suspect that this stock in each man is
small, and that the individuals would do better to avail themselves of
the general bank and capital of nations and of ages. . . .

The people of England well know, that the idea of an inheritance
furnishes a sure principle of conservation and a sure principle of
transmission; without at all excluding a principle of improvement.
It leaves acquisition free; but it secures what it acquires. . . . By a
constitutional policy, working after the pattern of nature, we receive,
we hold, we transmit our government and our privileges, in the same
manner in which we enjoy and transmit our property and our lives.
The institutions of policy, the goods of fortune, the gifts of providence,
are handed down to us, and from us, in the same course and order.
Our political system is placed in a just correspondence and symmetry
with the order of the world, and with the mode of existence decreed
to a permanent body composed of transitory parts; wherein, by the
disposition of a stupendous wisdom, moulding together the great
mysterious incorporation of the human race, the whole, at one time,
is never old, or middle-aged, or young, but, in a condition of unchangeable constancy, moves on through the varied tenor of perpetual

decay, fall, renovation, and progression. Thus, by preserving the
method of nature in the conduct of the state, in what we improve, we
are never wholly new; in what we retain, we are never wholly ob-
solete. . . .

At once to preserve and to reform is quite another thing. When the
useful parts of an old establishment are kept, and what is superadded
is to be fitted to what is retained, a vigorous mind, steady, persever-
ing attention, various powers of comparison and combination, and the
resources of an understanding fruitful in expedients are to be exercised; they are to be exercised in a continued conflict with the combined force of opposite vices, with the obstinacy that rejects all improvement, and the levity that is fatigued and disgusted with everything
of which it is in possession. But you may object,—"A process of this
kind is slow. It is not fit for an Assembly which glories in performing
in a few months the work of ages. Such a mode of reforming, possibly,
might take up many years." Without question it might; and it ought.
It is one of the excellences of a method in which time is amongst the
assistants, that its operation is slow, and in some cases almost imperceptible. If circumspection and caution are a part of wisdom, when we
work only upon inanimate matter, surely they become a part of duty
too, when the subject of our demolition and construction is not brick
and timber, but sentient beings, by the sudden alteration of whose
state, condition, and habits, multitudes may be rendered miserable.
But it seems as if it were the prevalent opinion in Paris, that an un-
feeling heart and an undoubting confidence are the sole qualifications
for a perfect legislator. Far different are my ideas of that high office.
The true law-giver ought to have a heart full of sensibility. He ought
to love and respect his kind, and to fear himself. It may be allowed
to his temperament to catch his ultimate object with an intuitive
glance: but his movements towards it ought to be deliberate. Political
arrangement, as it is a work for social ends, is to be only wrought by
social means. There mind must conspire with mind. Time is required
to produce that union of minds which alone can produce all the good
we aim at. Our patience will achieve more than our force. If I might
venture to appeal to what is so much out of fashion in Paris,—I mean
to experience,—I should tell you, that in my course I have known,
and, according to my measure, have coöperated with great men; and
I have never yet seen any plan which has not been mended by the
observations of those who were much inferior in understanding to

the person who took the lead in the business. By a slow, but well-sustained progress, the effect of each step is watched; the good or ill success of the first gives light to us in the second; and so, from light to light, we are conducted with safety through the whole series. We see that the parts of the system do not clash. The evils latent in the most promising contrivances are provided for as they arise. One advantage is as little as possible sacrificed to another. We compensate, we reconcile, we balance. We are enabled to unite into a consistent whole the various anomalies and contending principles that are found in the minds and affairs of men. From hence arises, not an excellence in simplicity, but one far superior, an excellence in composition. Where the great interests of mankind are concerned through a long succession of generations, that succession ought to be admitted into some share in the councils which are so deeply to affect them. If justice requires this, the work itself requires the aid of more minds than one age can furnish. It is from this view of things that the best legislators have been often satisfied with the establishment of some sure, solid, and ruling principle in government,—a power like that which some of the philosophers have called a plastic Nature; and having fixed the principle, they have left it afterwards to its own operation.

To proceed in this manner, that is, to proceed with a presiding principle and a prolific energy, is with me the criterion of profound wisdom. What your politicians think the marks of a bold, hardy genius are only proofs of a deplorable want of ability. By their violent haste, and their defiance of the process of Nature, they are delivered over blindly to every projector and adventurer, to every alchemist and empiric. They despair of turning to account anything that is common. Diet is nothing in their system of remedy. The worst of it is, that this their despair of curing common distempers by regular methods arises not only from defect of comprehension, but, I fear, from some malignity of disposition. Your legislators seem to have taken their opinions of all professions, ranks, and offices from the declamations and buffooneries of satirists,—who would themselves be astonished, if they were held to the letter of their own descriptions. By listening only to these, your leaders regard all things only on the side of their vices and faults, and view those vices and faults under every color of exaggeration. It is undoubtedly true, though it may seem para-doxical,—but, in general, those who are habitually employed in finding and displaying faults are unqualified for the work of reformation; because their minds are not only unfurnished with patterns of the fair and good, but by habit they come to take no delight in the contemplation of those things. By hating vices too much, they come to love men too little. It is therefore not wonderful that they should be indisposed and unable to serve them. From hence arises the complexional disposition of some of your guides to pull everything in pieces. At this malicious game they display the whole of their *quadrimanous* activity. As to the rest, the paradoxes of eloquent writers, brought forth purely as a sport of fancy, to try their talents, to rouse attention, and excite surprise, are taken up by these gentlemen, not in the spirit of the original authors, as means of cultivating their taste and improving their style: these paradoxes become with them serious grounds of action, upon which they proceed in regulating the most important concerns of the state. . . . Mr. Hume told me that he had from Rousseau himself the secret of his principles of composition. That acute, though eccentric observer, had perceived, that, to strike and interest the public, the marvellous must be produced; that the marvellous of the heathen mythology had long since lost its effects; that giants, magicians, fairies, and heroes of romance, which succeeded, had exhausted the portion of credulity which belonged to their age; that now nothing was left to a writer but that species of the marvellous, which might still be produced, and with as great an effect as ever, though in another way,—that is, the marvellous in life, in manners, in characters, and in extraordinary situations, giving rise to new and unlooked-for strokes in politics and morals. I believe, that, were Rousseau alive, and in one of his lucid intervals, he would be shocked at the practical frenzy of his scholars, who in their paradoxes are servile imitators, and even in their incredulity discover an implicit faith.

Men who undertake considerable things, even in a regular way, ought to give us ground to presume ability. But the physician of the state, who, not satisfied with the cure of distempers, undertakes to regenerate constitutions, ought to show uncommon powers. Some very unusual appearances of wisdom ought to display themselves on the face of the designs of those who appeal to no practice and who copy after no model. Has any such been manifested? . . .

4 BURKE

Religion and the State *

We know, and, what is better, we feel inwardly, that religion is the basis of civil society, and the source of all good, and of all comfort. In England we are so convinced of this, that there is no rust of superstition, with which the accumulated absurdity of the human mind might have crusted it over in the course of ages, that ninety-nine in a hundred of the people of England would not prefer to impiety. We shall never be such fools as to call in an enemy to the substance of any system to remove its corruptions, to supply its defects, or to perfect its construction. If our religious tenets should ever want a further elucidation, we shall not call on Atheism to explain them. We shall not light up our temple from that unhallowed fire. It will be illuminated with other lights. It will be perfumed with other incense than the infectious stuff which is imported by the smugglers of adulterated metaphysics. If our ecclesiastical establishment should want a revision, it is not avarice or rapacity, public or private, that we shall employ for the audit or receipt or application of its consecrated revenue. Violently condemning neither the Greek nor the Armenian, nor, since heats are subsided, the Roman system of religion, we prefer the Protestant: not because we think it has less of the Christian religion in it, but because, in our judgment, it has more. We are Protestants, not from indifference, but from zeal.

We know, and it is our pride to know, that man is by his constitution a religious animal; that atheism is against, not only our reason, but our instincts; and that it cannot prevail long. But if, in the moment

* See introductory remarks to Selection 1.

of riot, and in a drunken delirium from the hot spirit drawn out of
the alembic of hell, which in France is now so furiously boiling, we
should uncover our nakedness, by throwing off that Christian religion
which has hitherto been our boast and comfort, and one great source
of civilization amongst us, and among many other nations, we are
apprehensive (being well aware that the mind will not endure a void)
that some uncouth, pernicious, and degrading superstition might take
place of it. . . .

The consecration of the state by a state religious establishment is
necessary also to operate with a wholesome awe upon free citizens;
because, in order to secure their freedom, they must enjoy some deter-
minate portion of power. To them, therefore, a religion connected with
the state, and with their duty towards it, becomes even more necessary than in such societies where the people, by the terms of their
subjection, are confined to private sentiments, and the management
of their own family concerns. All persons possessing any portion of
power ought to be strongly and awfully impressed with an idea that
they act in trust, and that they are to account for their conduct in
that trust to the one great Master, Author, and Founder of society.

This principle ought even to be more strongly impressed upon the
minds of those who compose the collective sovereignty than upon
those of single princes. Without instruments, these princes can do
nothing. Whoever uses instruments, in finding helps, finds also impedi-
ments. Their power is therefore by no means complete; nor are they
safe in extreme abuse. Such persons, however elevated by flattery,
arrogance, and self-opinion, must be sensible, that, whether covered
or not by positive law, in some way or other they are accountable
even here for the abuse of their trust. If they are not cut off by a
rebellion of their people, they may be strangled by the very janissaries
kept for their security against all other rebellion. Thus we have seen
the king of France sold by his soldiers for an increase of pay. But
where popular authority is absolute and unrestrained, the people have
an infinitely greater, because a far better founded, confidence in their
own power. They are themselves in a great measure their own instruments. They are nearer to their objects. Besides, they are less under
responsibility to one of the greatest controlling powers on earth, the
sense of fame and estimation. The share of infamy that is likely to
fall to the lot of each individual in public acts is small indeed: the
operation of opinion being in the inverse ratio to the numbers of those

who abuse power. Their own approbation of their own acts has to them the appearance of a public judgment in their favor. A perfect democracy is therefore the most shameless thing in the world. As it is the most shameless, it is also the most fearless. No man apprehends in his person that he can be made subject to punishment. Certainly the people at large never ought: for, as all punishments are for example towards the conservation of the people at large, the people at large can never become the subject of punishment by any human hand. It is therefore of infinite importance that they should not be suffered to imagine that their will, any more than that of kings, is the standard of right and wrong. They ought to be persuaded that they are full as little entitled, and far less qualified, with safety to themselves, to use any arbitrary power whatsoever; that therefore they are not, under a false show of liberty, but in truth to exercise an unnatural, inverted domination, tyrannically to exact from those who officiate in the state, not an entire devotion to their interest, which is their right, but an abject submission to their occasional will: extinguishing thereby, in all those who serve them, all moral principle, all sense of dignity, all use of judgment, and all consistency of character; whilst by the very same process they give themselves up a proper, a suitable, but a most contemptible prey to the servile ambition of popular sycophants or courtly flatterers. . . .

5 BURKE

The Aristocracy and the People *

I am accused, I am told abroad, of being a man of aristrocratic principles. If by aristocracy they mean the peers, I have no vulgar admiration, nor any vulgar antipathy towards them; I hold their order in cold and decent respect. I hold them to be of an absolute necessity in the Constitution; but I think they are only good when kept within their proper bounds. I trust, whenever there has been a dispute between these Houses, the part I have taken has not been equivocal. If by the aristocracy (which, indeed, comes nearer to the point) they mean an adherence to the rich and powerful against the poor and weak, this would, indeed, be a very extraordinary part. I have incurred the odium of gentlemen in this House for not paying sufficient regard to men of ample property. When, indeed, the smallest rights of the poorest people in the kingdom are in question, I would set my face against any act of pride and power countenanced by the highest that are in it; and if it should come to the last extremity, and to a contest of blood,—God forbid! God forbid!—my part is taken: I would take my fate with the poor and low and feeble. But if these people came to turn their liberty into a cloak for maliciousness, and to seek a privilege of exemption, not from power, but from the rules of morality and virtuous discipline, then I would join my hand to make them feel the force which a few united in a good cause have over a multitude of the profligate and ferocious.

*   *   *

A true natural aristocracy is not a separate interest in the state, or

* See introductory remarks to Selection 1.

separable from it. It is an essential integrant part of any large body rightly constituted. It is formed out of a class of legitimate presumptions, which, taken as generalities, must be admitted for actual truths. To be bred in a place of estimation; to see nothing low and sordid from one's infancy; to be taught to respect one's self; to be habituated to the censorial inspection of the public eye; to look early to public opinion; to stand upon such elevated ground as to be enabled to take a large view of the wide-spread and infinitely diversified combinations of men and affairs in a large society; to have leisure to read, to reflect, to converse; to be enabled to draw the court and attention of the wise and learned, wherever they are to be found; to be habituated in armies to command and to obey; to be taught to despise danger in the pursuit of honor and duty; to be formed to the greatest degree of vigilance, foresight, and circumspection, in a state of things in which no fault is committed with impunity and the slightest mistakes draw on the most ruinous consequences; to be led to a guarded and regulated conduct, from a sense that you are considered as an instructor of your fellow-citizens in their highest concerns, and that you act as a reconciler between God and man; to be employed as an administrator of law and justice, and to be thereby amongst the first benefactors to mankind; to be a professor of high science, or of liberal and ingenuous art; to be amongst rich traders, who from their success are presumed to have sharp and vigorous understandings, and to possess the virtues of diligence, order, constancy, and regularity, and to have cultivated an habitual regard to commutative justice: these are the circumstances of men that form what I should call a *natural* aristocracy, without which there is no nation. . . .

*   *   *

The Chancellor of France, at the opening of the States, said, in a tone of oratorial flourish, that all occupations were honorable. If he meant only that no honest employment was disgraceful, he would not have gone beyond the truth. But in asserting that anything is honorable, we imply some distinction in its favor. The occupation of a hair-dresser, or of a working tallow-chandler, cannot be a matter of honor to any person,—to say nothing of a number of other more servile employments. Such descriptions of men ought not to suffer oppression from the state; but the state suffers oppression, if such as they, either individually or collectively, are permitted to rule. In this you think you are combating prejudice, but you are at war with Nature.

I do not, my dear Sir, conceive you to be of that sophistical, captious spirit, or of that uncandid dullness, as to require, for every general observation or sentiment, an explicit detail of the correctives and exceptions which reason will presume to be included in all the general propositions which come from reasonable men. You do not imagine that I wish to confine power, authority, and distinction to blood and names and titles. No, Sir. There is no qualification for government but virtue and wisdom, actual or presumptive. Wherever they are actually found, they have, in whatever state, condition, profession, or trade, the passport of Heaven to human place and honor. Woe to the country which would madly and impiously reject the service of the talents and virtues, civil, military, or religious, that are given to grace and to serve it; and would condemn to obscurity everything formed to diffuse lustre and glory around a state! Woe to that country, too, that, passing into the opposite extreme, considers a low education, a mean, contracted view of things, a sordid, mercenary occupation, as a preferable title to command! Everything ought to be open,—but not indifferently to every man. No rotation, no appointment by lot, no mode of election operating in the spirit of sortition or rotation, can be generally good in a government conversant in extensive objects; because they have no tendency, direct or indirect, to select the man with a view to the duty, or to accommodate the one to the other. I do not hesitate to say that the road to eminence and power, from obscure condition, ought not to be made too easy, nor a thing too much of course. If rare merit be the rarest of all rare things, it ought to pass through some sort of probation. The temple of honor ought to be seated on an eminence. If it be opened through virtue, let it be remembered, too, that virtue is never tried but by some difficulty and some struggle.

Nothing is a due and adequate representation of a state, that does not represent its ability, as well as its property. But as ability is a vigorous and active principle, and as property is sluggish, inert, and timid, it never can be safe from the invasions of ability, unless it be, out of all proportion, predominant in the representation. It must be represented, too, in great masses of accumulation, or it is not rightly protected. The characteristic essence of property, formed out of the combined principles of its acquisition and conservation, is to be *un-*

equal. The great masses, therefore, which excite envy, and tempt rapacity, must be put out of the possibility of danger. Then they form a natural rampart about the lesser properties in all their gradations. The same quantity of property which is by the natural course of things divided among many has not the same operation. Its defensive power is weakened as it is diffused. In this diffusion each man's portion is less than what, in the eagerness of his desires, he may flatter himself to obtain by dissipating the accumulations of others. The plunder of the few would, indeed, give but a share inconceivably small in the distribution to the many. But the many are not capable of making this calculation; and those who lead them to rapine never intend this distribution.

The power of perpetuating our property in our families is one of the most valuable and interesting circumstances belonging to it, and that which tends the most to the perpetuation of society itself. It makes our weakness subservient to our virtue; it grafts benevolence even upon avarice. The possessors of family wealth, and of the distinction which attends hereditary possession, (as most concerned in it,) are the natural securities for this transmission. With us the House of Peers is formed upon this principle. It is wholly composed of hereditary property and hereditary distinction, and made, therefore, the third of the legislature, and in the last event, the sole judge of all property in all its subdivisions. The House of Commons, too, though not necessarily, yet in fact, is always so composed, in the far greater part. Let those large proprietors be what they will, (and they have their chance of being amongst the best,) they are, at the very worst, the ballast in the vessel of the commonwealth. For though hereditary wealth, and the rank which goes with it, are too much idolized by creeping sycophants, and the blind, abject admirers of power, they are too rashly slighted in shallow speculations of the petulant, assuming, shortsighted coxcombs of philosophy. Some decent, regulated preëminence, some preference (not exclusive appropriation) given to birth, is neither unnatural, nor unjust, nor impolitic.

It is said that twenty-four millions ought to prevail over two hundred thousand. True; if the constitution of a kingdom be a problem of arithmetic. This sort of discourse does well enough with the lamp-post for its second: to men who *may* reason calmly it is ridiculous. The will of the many, and their interest, must very often differ; and great will be the difference when they make an evil choice. A government of five hundred country attorneys and obscure curates is not good for twenty-four millions of men, though it were chosen by eight-and-forty millions; nor is it the better for being guided by a dozen of persons of quality who have betrayed their trust in order to obtain that power. At present, you seem in everything to have strayed out of the high road of Nature.

6 COLERIDGE

The Continuing Social Contract

British poet and essayist Samuel Taylor Coleridge (1772–1834), like most "cultural conservatives," was less concerned with party politics than with the life and mind of the individual. He has been called "the purest of all conservatives" because he never compromised with material self-interest. He defended the Church of England as a necessary civilizing body and espoused the sanctity of the person as the basis for all law and morality. He repudiated the mechanistic and atomistic model of society which English liberalism had derived from Hobbes and Locke. He regarded the organic theory of society, developed from Rousseau, Kant, and Hegel, as a more accurate and more profound description of social processes. As John Stuart Mill was to point out, Jeremy Bentham was the foremost proponent of the atomistic model in the first half of the nineteenth century, and Coleridge was the foremost proponent of organic theory. The following selection is taken from Coleridge's *On the Constitution of the Church and State* (1852 edition), primarily from Chapters I and X.

Every reader of Rousseau, or of Hume's Essays, will understand me when I refer to the original social contract assumed by Rousseau, and by other and wiser men before him, as the basis of all legitimate government. Now, if this be taken as the assertion of an historical fact, or as the application of a conception, generalised from ordinary compacts between man and man, or nation and nation, to an alleged actual occurrence in the first ages of the world; namely, the formation of a first contract, in which men should have covenanted with each other to associate, or in which a multitude should have entered into a compact with a few, the one to be governed and the other to govern under certain declared conditions; I shall run little hazard at this time of day in declaring the pretended fact a pure fiction, and the conception of such a fact an idle fancy. It is at once false and foolish.* For what if an original contract had actually been entered into and formally recorded? Still I cannot see what addition of moral force would be gained by the fact. The same sense of moral obligation which binds us to keep it, must have pre-existed in the same force and in relation to the same duties, impelling our ancestors to make it. For what could it do more than bind the contracting parties to act for the general good, according to their best lights and opportunities? It is evident that no specific scheme or constitution can derive any other claim to our reverence, than that which the presumption of its necessity or fitness for the general good shall give it; and which claim of course ceases, or rather is reversed, as soon as this general presumption of its utility has given place to as general a conviction of the contrary. It is true, indeed, that from duties anterior to the formation of the contract, because they arise out of the very constitution of our humanity, which supposes the social state—it is true, that in order to a rightful removal of the institution or law thus agreed on, it is required that the conviction of its inexpediency shall be as general as the presumption of its fitness was at the time of its establishment. This, the first of the two great paramount interests of the social state, that of permanence, demands; but to attribute more than this to any fundamental articles, passed into law by any assemblage of individuals, is an injustice to their successors, and a high offence against the other great interest of the social state, namely, its progressive improvement. The conception, therefore, of an original contract, is, I repeat, incapable of historic proof as a fact, and it is senseless as a theory.

But if instead of the conception or theory of an original social contract, we say the idea of an ever-originating social contract, this is so certain and so indispensable, that it constitutes the whole ground of the difference between subject and serf, between a commonwealth and a slave plantation. And this, again, is evolved out of the yet higher

---

* I am not indeed certain that some operational farce, under the name of a social contract or compact, may not have been acted by the Illuminati and constitution-manufacturers at the close of the eighteenth century; a period which how far it deserved the name, so complacently affixed to it by contemporaries, of "this enlightened age," may be doubted. That it was an age of enlighteners no man will deny.

idea of person in contra-distinction to thing; all social law and justice being grounded on the principle that a person can never, but by his own fault, become a thing, or, without grievous wrong, be treated as such; and the distinction consisting in this, that a thing may be used altogether and merely as the means to an end; but the person must always be included in the end; his interest must form a part of the object, a mean to which he by consent, that is, by his own act, makes himself. We plant a tree and we fell it; we breed the sheep and we shear or we kill it; in both cases wholly as means to our ends; for trees and animals are things. The wood-cutter and the hind are likewise employed as means, but on agreement, and that too an agreement of reciprocal advantage, which includes them as well as their employer in the end; for they are persons. And the government, under which the contrary takes place, is not worthy to be called a state, if, as in the kingdom of Dahomey, it be unprogressive; or only by anticipation, where, as in Russia, it is in advance to a better and more man-worthy order of things. Now, notwithstanding the late wonderful spread of learning through the community, and though the schoolmaster and the lecturer are abroad, the hind and the woodman may, very conceivably, pass from cradle to coffin without having once contemplated this idea, so as to be conscious of the same. And there would be even an improbability in the supposition that they possessed the power of presenting this idea to the minds of others, or even to their own thoughts, verbally as a distinct proposition. But no man, who has ever listened to labourers of this rank, in any alehouse, over the Saturday night's jug of beer, discussing the injustice of the present rate of wages, and the iniquity of their being paid in part out of the parish poor-rates, will doubt for a moment that they are fully possessed by the idea.

In close, though not perhaps obvious, connection with this is the idea of moral freedom, as the ground of our proper responsibility. Speak to a young Liberal, fresh from Edinburgh or Hackney or the hospitals, of free-will as implied in free-agency, he will perhaps confess with a smile that he is a necessitarian,—proceed to assure his hearer that the liberty of the will is an impossible conception, a contradiction in terms,* and finish by recommending a perusal of the

---

* In fact, this is one of the distinguishing characters of ideas, and marks at once the difference between an idea (a truth-power of the reason) and a conception of the understanding; namely, that the former, as expressed in words, is always, and necessarily, a contradiction in terms.

works of Jonathan Edwards or Dr. Crombie; or as it may happen he may declare the will itself a mere delusion, a nonentity, and advise the study of Mr. Lawrence's Lectures. Converse on the same subject with a plain, single-minded, yet reflecting, neighbour, and he may probably say, (as St. Augustine had said long before him, in reply to the question, What is time?) "I know it well enough when you do not ask me." But alike with both the supposed parties, the self-complacent student, just as certainly as with our less positive neighbour; if we attend to their actions, their feelings, and even to their words, we shall be in ill luck, if ten minutes pass without having full and satisfactory proof that the idea of man's moral freedom possesses and modifies their whole practical being, in all they say, in all they feel, in all they do and are done to; even as the spirit of life, which is contained in no vessel, because it permeates all.

Just so is it with the Constitution.* Ask any of our politicians what is meant by the Constitution, and it is ten to one that he will give a false explanation; as for example, that it is the body of our laws, or that it is the Bill of Rights; or perhaps, if he have read Thomas Payne, he may say that we do not yet possess one; and yet not an hour may have elapsed, since we heard the same individual denouncing, and possibly with good reason, this or that code of laws, the excise and revenue laws, or those for including pheasants, or those for excluding Roman Catholics, as altogether unconstitutional; and such and such acts of Parliament as gross outrages on the Constitution. Mr. Peel, who is rather remarkable for groundless and unlucky concessions, owned that the late Act broke in on the Constitution of 1688: whilst in 1689 a very imposing minority of the then House of Lords, with a decisive majority in the Lower House of Convocation, denounced this very Constitution of 1688, as breaking in on the English Constitution.

But a Constitution is an idea arising out of the idea of a State; and because our whole history from Alfred onwards demonstrates the continued influence of such an idea, or ultimate aim, on the minds of our forefathers, in their characters and functions as public men, alike

---

* I do not say, with the idea: for the Constitution itself is an idea. This will sound like a paradox or a sneer to those with whom an idea is but another word for a fancy, a something unreal; but not to those who in the ideas contemplate the most real of all realities, and of all operative powers the most actual.

in what they resisted and in what they claimed; in the institutions and forms of polity, which they established, and with regard to those against which they more or less successfully contended; and because the result has been a progressive, though not always a direct or equable, advance in the gradual realisation of the idea; and because it is actually, though even because it is an idea not adequately, represented in a correspondent scheme of means really existing; we speak, and have a right to speak, of the idea itself, as actually existing, that is, as a principle existing in the only way in which a principle can exist,—in the minds and consciences of the persons whose duties it prescribes, and whose rights it determines. In the same sense that the sciences of arithmetic and of geometry, that mind, that life itself, have reality; the Constitution has real existence, and does not the less exist in reality, because it both is, and exists as, an idea. . . .

Now, in every country of civilised men, acknowledging the rights of property, and by means of determined boundaries and common laws united into one people or nation, the two antagonist powers or opposite interests of the State, under which all other state interests are comprised, are those of permanence and of progression.*

It will not be necessary to enumerate the several causes that combine to connect the permanence of a state with the land and the landed property. To found a family, and to convert his wealth into land, are twin thoughts, births of the same moment, in the mind of the opulent merchant, when he thinks of reposing from his labours. From the class of the *novi homines* he redeems himself by becoming the staple ring of the chain, by which the present will become connected with the past, and the test and evidence of permanency be afforded. To the same principle appertain primogeniture and hereditary titles,

---

* Let me call attention to the essential difference between "opposite" and "contrary." Opposite powers are always of the same kind, and tend to union, either by equipoise or by a common product. Thus the + and − poles of the magnet, thus positive and negative electricity, are opposites. Sweet and sour are opposites; sweeter and bitter are contraries. The feminine character is opposed to the masculine; but the effeminate is its contrary. Even so in the present instance, the interest of permanence is opposed to that of progressiveness; but so far from being contrary interests, they, like the magnetic forces, suppose and require each other. Even the most mobile of creatures, the serpent, makes a rest of its own body, and, drawing up its voluminous train from behind, on this *fulcrum* propels itself onward. On the other hand, it is a proverb in all languages, that (relatively to man at least) what would stand still must in fact be retrograde.

and the influence which these exert in accumulating large masses of property, and in counteracting the antagonist and dispersive forces, which the follies, the vices, and misfortunes of individuals can scarcely fail to supply. To this, likewise, tends the proverbial obduracy of prejudices characteristic of the humbler tillers of the soil, and their aversion even to benefits that are offered in the form of innovations. But why need I attempt to explain a fact which no thinking man will deny, and where the admission of the fact is all that my argument requires?

On the other hand, with as little chance of contradiction, I may assert that the progression of a State in the arts and comforts of life, in the diffusion of the information and knowledge, useful or necessary for all; in short, all advances in civilisation, and the rights and privileges of citizens, are especially connected with, and derived from, the four classes, the mercantile, the manufacturing, the distributive, and the professional. . . .

The Role of the State

The chief object for which men, who from the beginning existed as a social band, first formed themselves into a state, and on the social super-induced the political relation, was not the protection of their lives but of their property. The natural man is too proud an animal to admit that he needs any other protection for his life than what his own courage and that of his clan can bestow. Where the nature of the soil and climate has precluded all property but personal, and admitted that only in its simplest forms, as in Greenland for instance, —there men remain in the domestic state and form neighbourhoods, not governments. And in North America the chiefs appear to exercise government in those tribes only which possess individual landed property. Among the rest the chief is the general, a leader in war; not a magistrate. To property and to its necessary inequalities must be referred all human laws, that would not be laws without and independent of any conventional enactment; that is, all State-legislation.

Next comes the King, as the head of the National Church or Clerisy, and the protector and supreme trustee of the Nationality: the power of the same in relation to its proper objects being exercised by the

King and the Houses of Convocation, of which, as before of the State, the King is the head and arm. . . .

And if superior talents, and the mere possession of knowledges, such as can be learned at Mechanics' Institutions, were regularly accompanied with a will in harmony with the reason, and a consequent subordination of the appetites and passions to the ultimate ends of our being;—if intellectual gifts and attainments were infallible signs of wisdom and goodness in the same proportion, and the knowing and clever were always rational;—if the mere facts of science conferred or superseded the softening humanising influences of the moral world, that habitual presence of the beautiful or the seemly, and that exemption from all familiarity with the gross, the mean, and the disorderly, whether in look or language, or in the surrounding objects, in which the main efficacy of a liberal education consists;—and if, lastly, these acquirements and powers of the understanding could be shared equally by the whole class, and did not, as by a necessity of nature they ever must do, fall to the lot of two or three in each several group, club, or neighbourhood;—then, indeed, by an enlargement of the Chinese system, political power might not unwisely be conferred as the *honorarium* or privilege on having passed through all the forms in the national schools, without the security of political ties, without those fastenings and radical fibres of a collective and registrable property, by which the citizen inheres in and belongs to the commonwealth, as a constituent part either of the Proprietage, or of the Nationality; either of the State or of the National Church. But as the contrary of all these suppositions may be more safely assumed, the practical conclusion will be—not that the requisite means of intellectual development and growth should be withholden from any native of the soil, which it was at all times wicked to wish, and which it would be now silly to attempt; but that the gifts of the understanding, whether the boon of a genial nature, or the reward of more persistent application, should be allowed fair play in the acquiring of that proprietorship, to which a certain portion of political power belongs as its proper function. For in this way there is at least a strong probability that intellectual power will be armed with political power, only where it has previously been combined with and guarded by the moral qualities of prudence, industry, and self-control. . . .

The Role of the Church

I respect the talents of many, and the motives and character of some, among you too sincerely to court the scorn which I anticipate. But neither shall the fear of it prevent me from declaring aloud, and as a truth which I hold it the disgrace and calamity of a professed statesman not to know and acknowledge, that a permanent, nationalised, learned order, a national clerisy or Church is an essential element of a rightly constituted nation, without which it wants the best security alike for its permanence and its progression; and for which neither tract societies nor conventicles, nor Lancasterian schools, nor mechanics' institutions, nor lecture bazaars under the absurd name of universities, nor all these collectively, can be a substitute. For they are all marked with the same asterisk of spuriousness, show the same distemper-spot on the front, that they are empirical specifics for morbid symptoms that help to feed and continue the disease.

But you wish for general illumination: you would spur-arm the toes of society: you would enlighten the higher ranks *per ascensum ab imis?* You begin, therefore, with the attempt to popularise science: but you will only effect its plebification. It is folly to think of making all, or the many, philosophers, or even men of science and systematic knowledge. But it is duty and wisdom to aim at making as many as possible soberly and steadily religious; inasmuch as the morality which the State requires in its citizens for its own well-being and ideal immortality, and without reference to their spiritual interest as individuals, can only exist for the people in the form of religion. But the existence of a true philosophy, or the power and habit of contemplating particulars in the unity and fontal mirror of the idea,—this in the rulers and teachers of a nation is indispensable to a sound state of religion in all classes. In fine, religion, true or false, is and ever has been the centre of gravity in a realm, to which all other things must and will accommodate themselves.

7 RÖPKE

A Humane Economy

Wilhelm Röpke (1899–1966) was not only a distinguished economist who was credited by Ludwig Erhard with preparing the theoretical groundwork for the postwar German "economic miracle"; he was also an insightful critic of modern mass society. For many years professor of economics at the Institute of Higher International Studies in Geneva, he was the author of many influential books, including *The Social Crisis of Our Time* (London, 1950) and *A Humane Economy.* The following selections are from the latter work, especially from the chapters "Centrism and Decentrism" and "The Conditions and Limits of the Market."*

Democracy is, in the long run, compatible with freedom only on condition that all, or at least most, voters are agreed that certain supreme norms and principles of public life and economic order must remain outside the sphere of democratic decisions. This *unitas in necessariis* encompasses more than the principle of the rule of law, which, though admittedly important, is ultimately only formal. It is this fundamental agreement which imbues the concept of inviolable law as such with an absolute content, and once it can no longer be taken for granted, we are in the presence of mass democracy of a pretotalitarian kind. We hardly need the lessons of the Jacobin government of the French Revolution to remind us forcibly of the inevitable socialist tendencies of such mass democracy. Conversely, socialism is fatefully ranged among the forces responsible for the transformation of liberal democracy into mass democracy. To divest such funda-

---

* *A Humane Economy: The Social Framework of the Free Market,* transl. by Elizabeth Henderson (Chicago: Regnery, 1960). By permission.

mental institutions as property and economic freedom of their inviolability and to make their fate dependent on the ballot box is tantamount to destroying the very foundations of liberal democracy, since the latter must rest on above-party agreement with respect to the unchallenged validity of the state's ethical, social, and political principles. Democracy is then no longer an instrument of internal peace, security, stability, and freedom but becomes a tool of revolution, and of permanent revolution at that.

This kind of radicalism, typical of a spirit which is not content to accept what is but must forever reopen every question, is precisely the mark of mass society and mass man. It is the spirit of men who, together with their social roots, have lost the sense of tradition, principles, and history and who have become the prey of the moment's whims and passions, as well as of the demagogy of leaders translating these whims and passions into ephemeral slogans and inflammatory speeches. Matters are yet made worse by the skepticism and positivism, sometimes bordering on nihilism, for which the intellectuals are to blame. Thus modern mass democracy becomes the breeding ground for the revolutionary social religions of our times and the rallying point for the crusades on which the inflamed masses set out to conquer some millennium, some New Jerusalem. What Michel Chevalier (*Lettres de l'Amérique du Nord* [1836]), at the same time as Tocqueville, rightly or wrongly said of the American people applies without reservation to mass democracy: it has "the morale of an army on the march." And it has all the attributes of such an army, too: the clockwork precision of the march, collective high spirits, noise, the "here today and gone tomorrow" outlook, the moment's enjoyment without thought of the future, the transience of life, the rousing banners, a nomad and rootless existence, practical action unburdened by disdained theory, pragmatism, grabbing and wasting, and good-fellowship.

We shall have more to say later about the significance for today's economic and social life of this mass democracy cut loose from the moorings of natural law and tradition. . . .

This is the moat across which the eternal dialogue goes on: on one side are those who think that the economy is best planned by the market, competition, and free prices and who regard the decentralisation of economic decisions among millions of separate producers and consumers as the indispensable condition of freedom, justice, and well-being; on the other side are those who prefer planning from above, with the state's compulsory powers. And so it goes on.

The centrist is none other than the social rationalist, whom we met before. Seen from his central point, the individual is small and eventually dwindles to a statistical figure, a building brick, a mathematical magnitude encased in equations, something that can be "refashioned," in short, something that may well be lost sight of. We know with what optimism our social rationalist views the success of his constructions and refashioning. By contrast, the decentrist, who thinks in terms of human beings and also knows and respects history, is skeptical or pessimistic and in any case bases his arguments realistically and unsentimentally upon human nature. The centrist is doctrinaire, the decentrist undoctrinaire and unideological. The latter prefers to hold on to established principles; he is swayed more by a hierarchy of norms and values, by reason and sober reflection, than by passions and feelings; he is firmly rooted in ultimate and absolute convictions for which he requires no proof because he would regard it as absurd not to believe in them. . . .

The "left" moralist all too often reaches the point where his big words of love and freedom and justice serve as a cover for the exact opposite. The moralist, with his lofty admonitions, becomes an intolerant hater and envier, the theoretical pacifist an imperialist when it comes to the practical test, and the advocate of abstract social justice an ambitious place-hunter. These moralists are a world apart from the decentrists' attitude, of which the hero's father in Adalbert Stifter's *Nachsommer* says that man does not primarily exist for the sake of human society but for his own sake, "and if each one of us exists in the best possible manner for his own sake, he does so for society as well." I used to know an old servant who had discovered this wisdom for herself; she always wondered why so many people kept racking their brains about how to do good to others, while, so she thought, it would surely be better if everyone simply and decently did his duty in his own station. The centrist's moral ideal frequently enough amounts to a desire to make the world into a place where, to quote Goethe again, everyone is nursing his neighbor—which presupposes a centralized compulsory organization.

The further we proceed with our analysis of the two modes of thought, the more we are led to assign each attitude to one or the other camp. The contrast between centrism and decentrism is, in fact, unusually comprehensive. In the economic sphere, the contrast is most clearly epitomized by monopoly and competition, and the collectivist economy corresponds to the centrist's ideal, just as the market economy corresponds to the decentrist's. Every economic intervention is a concession to centrism—made lightheartedly and in pursuit of his own ideal by the centrist and unwillingly by the decentrist. The latter demands strict justification for all concessions, and the burden of proof is on their advocates because it is his principle that there is always a presumption in favor of shifting the center of gravity of society and economy downwards, so that every act of centralization and every upward shift of the center of gravity requires convincing proof before the decentrist will condone such deviation from his ideal.

The position of equality and inequality cannot be in doubt. Equality and uniformity obviously belong to centrism; inequality, diversity, multiformity, and social articulation to decentrism. This requires no further explanation, but there is a special problem here . . . namely, the particular form of "equality of opportunity." This problem reminds us that life is not an equation which is soluble without a remainder; unless we are very careful, decentrism might involve itself in self-annihilating contradictions on this point. The ideal of decentrism, in common accord with one of the unchallenged aims of liberalism, certainly demands that individuals should try their strength against each other in free competition, and this implies that they start the race from the same starting line and on the same conditions. Is it, then, to be a continuous race of all for everything? Do we always have to be on the lookout for better opportunities, wherever they may appear? Do we always have to regret the opportunities we missed and always chase after those we think are better? This cannot be the true meaning of the ideal. If it were so, it would obviously be a dangerous ideal and one most uncongenial to the decentrist, and to pursue it would cause general unhappiness. Our star witness, Tocqueville, observed long ago that the Americans, in whose country equality of opportunity always held pride of place, are so dedicated to the restless hunt after better opportunities that they end up as nervous and ever dissatisfied nomads. . . .

Apart from many other insights which the centrist lacks, the decentrist also knows that it is always easier to centralize than to decentralize and to widen the powers of the state than to curtail them. There is

yet another thing which the decentrist knows better, and this is that
the centrist's path is bound to lead to regions where the air of freedom
and humanity becomes thinner and thinner, until we end up on the
icy peaks of totalitarianism, from which nations can hardly hope to
escape without a fall. The trouble is that once one takes this road, it
becomes increasingly difficult to turn back. Centrism is in danger of
encountering no check any more, least of all in itself. . . .

The temptation of centrism has been great at all times, as regards
both theory and political action. It is the temptation of mechanical
perfection and of uniformity at the expense of freedom. Perhaps
Montesquieu was right when he said (*Esprit des Lois,* XXIX, 18) that
it is the small minds, above all, which succumb to this temptation.
Once the mania of uniformity and centralization spreads and once the
centrists begin to lay down the law of the land, then we are in the
presence of one of the most serious danger signals warning us of the
impending loss of freedom, humanity, and the health of society. A
century ago, John Stuart Mill wrote: "If the roads, the railways, the
banks, the insurance offices, the great joint-stock companies, the universities, and the public charities, were all of them branches of the
government; if, in addition, the municipal corporations and local
boards, with all that now devolves on them, became departments of
the central administration; if the employés of all these different enterprises were appointed and paid by the government, and looked to the
government for every rise in life; not all the freedom of the press
and popular constitution of the legislature would make this or any
other country free otherwise than in name. And the evil would be
greater, the more efficiently and scientifically the administrative
machinery was constructed." . . .

Society as a whole cannot be ruled by the laws of supply and
demand, and the state is more than a sort of business company, as
has been the conviction of the best conservative opinion since the time
of Burke. Individuals who compete on the market and there pursue
their own advantage stand all the more in need of the social and
moral bonds of community, without which competition degenerates
most grievously. As we have said before, the market economy is not
everything. It must find its place in a higher order of things which is
not ruled by supply and demand, free prices, and competition. It must
be firmly contained within an all-embracing order of society in which
the imperfections and harshness of economic freedom are corrected

by law and in which man is not denied conditions of life appropriate to his nature. Man can wholly fulfill his nature only by freely becoming part of a community and having a sense of solidarity with it. Otherwise he leads a miserable existence and he knows it.

The truth is that a society may have a market economy and, at one and the same time, perilously unsound foundations and conditions, for which the market economy is not responsible but which its advocates have every reason to improve or wish to see improved so that the market economy will remain politically and socially feasible in the long run. There is no other way of fulfilling our wish to possess both a market economy and a sound society and a nation where people are, for the most part, happy.

Economists have their typical *déformation professionelle,* their own occupational disease of the mind. Each of us speaks from personal experience when he admits that he does not find it easy to look beyond the circumscribed field of his own discipline and to acknowledge humbly that the sphere of the market, which it is his profession to explore, neither exhausts nor determines society as a whole. The market is only one section of society. It is a very important section, it is true, but still one whose existence is justifiable and possible only because it is part of a larger whole which concerns not economics but philosophy, history, and theology. We may be forgiven for misquoting Lichtenberg and saying: To know economics only is to know not even that. Man, in the words of the Gospel, does not live by bread alone. Let us beware of that caricature of an economist who, watching people cheerfully disporting themselves in their suburban allotments, thinks he has said everything there is to say when he observes that this is not a rational way of producing vegetables—forgetting that it may be an eminently rational way of producing happiness, which alone matters in the last resort. Adam Smith, whose fame rests not only on his *Wealth of Nations* but also on his *Theory of Moral Sentiments,* would have known better. . . .

To the economist, the market economy, as seen from the restricting viewpoint of his own discipline, appears to be no more than one particular type of economic order, a kind of "economic technique" opposed to the socialist one. It is significant of this approach that the very name of the structural principle of this economic order has been borrowed from the language of technology: we speak of the "price mechanism." We move in a world of prices, markets, competition, wage rates, rates of interest, exchange rates, and other economic magnitudes. All of this is perfectly legitimate and fruitful as long as we keep in mind that we have narrowed our angle of vision and do not forget that the market economy is the economic order proper to a definite social structure and to a definite spiritual and moral setting. If we were to neglect the market economy's characteristic of being merely a part of a spiritual and sccial total order, we would become guilty of an aberration which may be described as social rationalism.

Social rationalism misleads us into imagining that the market economy is no more than an "economic technique" that is applicable in any kind of society and in any kind of spiritual and social climate. Thus the undeniable success of the revival of the market economy in many countries gave quite a few socialists the idea that the price mechanism was a device which an otherwise socialist economy could well use to its own benefit. In this concept of a "socialist market economy," which Tito seems to want to translate into practice, the market economy is thought of as part of a social system that is best described as an enormous apparatus of administration. In this sense, even the Communist economic system of Soviet Russia has always had a "market sector," although it is undoubtedly no more than a technical device and contrivance and not a living organism. How could a genuine market, an area of freedom, spontaneity, and unregimented order, thrive in a social system which is the exact opposite in all respects? . . .

To grasp the full significance of ownership to a free society, we must understand that ownership has a dual function. Ownership means, as in civil law, the delimitation of the individual sphere of decision and responsibility against that of other individuals. But ownership also means protection of the individual sphere from political power. It traces limits on the horizontal plane, and also vertically, and only this dual function can fully explain the significance of ownership as an indispensable condition of liberty. All earlier generations of social philosophers agreed on this point. . . .

The economic function of private ownership tends to be obstinately underestimated, and even more so is its moral and sociological significance for free society. The reason is, no doubt, that the ethical universe in which ownership has its place is hard for social rationalism even to understand, let alone to find congenial. And since social rationalism is in ascendancy everywhere, it is not surprising that the institution of ownership has been badly shaken. Even discussions on questions concerning the management of firms are often conducted in terms which suggest that the owner has followed the consumer and the taxpayer into the limbo of "forgotten men." The true role of ownership can be appreciated only if we look upon it as representative of something far beyond what is visible and measurable. Ownership illustrates the fact that the market economy is a form of economic order belonging to a particular philosophy of life and to a particular social and moral universe. This we now have to define, and in so doing the word "bourgeois"* imposes itself, however much mass public opinion (especially of the intellectual masses) may, after a century of deformation by Marxist propaganda, dislike this designation or find it ridiculous.

In all honesty, we have to admit that the market economy has a bourgeois foundation. This needs to be stressed all the more because the romantic and socialist reaction against everything bourgeois has, for generations past, been astonishingly successful in turning this concept into a parody of itself from which it is very difficult to get away. The market economy, and with it social and political freedom, can thrive only as a part and under the protection of a bourgeois system. This implies the existence of a society in which certain fundamentals are respected and color the whole network of social relationships: individual effort and responsibility, absolute norms and values, independence based on ownership, prudence and daring, calculating and saving, responsibility for planning one's own life, proper coherence with the community, family feeling, a sense of tradition and the succession of generations combined with an open-minded view of the present and the future, proper tension between individual and community, firm moral discipline, respect for the value of money, the courage to grapple on one's own with life and its uncertainties, a sense of the natural order of things, and a firm scale of values. Whoever turns up his nose at these things or suspects them of being "reactionary" may in all seriousness be asked what scale of values and what ideals he intends to defend against Communism without having to borrow from it.

---

* The word "bourgeois" is here used to correspond to the German word *bürgerlich,* in a completely non-prejorative and non-political sense. As will be seen from the context, the word is used to designate a particular way of life and set of values.

To say that the market economy belongs to a basically bourgeois total order implies that it presupposes a society which is the opposite of proletarianized society, in the wide and pregnant sense which it is my continual endeavour to explain, and also the opposite of mass society as discussed in the preceding chapter. Independence, ownership, individual reserves, saving, the sense of responsibility, rational planning of one's own life—all that is alien, if not repulsive, to proletarianized mass society. Yet precisely that is the condition of a society which cherishes its liberty. We have arrived at a point where we are simply forced to recognize that here is the true watershed between social philosophies and that every one of us must choose for himself, knowing that the choice is between irreconcilable alternatives and that the destiny of our society is at stake. . . .

8 JEWKES

Moral Values in a
Socialist Society

John Jewkes (1900–   ), professor emeritus of economic
organization, Merton College, Oxford, has been an unflagging critic of
the socialist society which two postwar Labour governments have
attempted to erect in Great Britain. The many organizational faults of
the National Health Service have been exposed in his two studies
(written jointly with his wife, Mrs. Sylvia Jewkes) *The Genesis of the
British National Health Service* and *Value for Money in Medicine*. His
comparison of the respective moral qualities of collectivist and private
activities in the economic and cultural life of a nation was published
in 1965 under the title *Public and Private Enterprise*. Democratic socialists
have often claimed that the kind of society they advocate is somehow
morally superior to the capitalistic way of life prevalent in the United
States. In his latest book, *The New Ordeal by Planning*,* Jewkes has
set out to refute his argument with a wealth of examples drawn from
more than twenty years of experience in Britain with economic planning
by both Tory and Labour governments. The selection is taken from
Chapter IX of that work, entitled "The Moral Sickness of a Planned
Society," and subsequent pages as indicated.

> The prime principle of the Socialism for which we stand
> lies not in the methods of organisation of our society that
> we adopt but in the high purpose at which we aim.
> SIR STAFFORD CRIPPS, *Democracy Alive.*

Socialists have always held that, apart from its other deficiencies,

*(London: Macmillan, 1968). Reprinted by permission.

the market economy is fundamentally immoral. The profit motive, it is argued, is unchristian since it breeds selfishness, acquisitiveness and the idolatry of wealth. Inequality of income divides communities into non-sympathetic classes and leads to exploitation. Competition puts a premium upon dishonesty and deception and forces producers to make shoddy and adulterated goods. The growth of big business debauches public life and corrupts the legislature. The ostentatious display of wealth by the rich destroys taste and judgment in the arts. The rich become a ruling class to whom the rest are subject through economic necessity.[1] The injustices which men create for themselves can only be removed by the State, "which is, in fact, accepted as the nearest we can get to an impartial judge in any matter." [2]

Now the centrally directed economy is the ultimate manifestation of State activity. Does the experience of planning in Great Britain suggest that this form of economic organisation stimulates the life of the spirit and fosters those simple, upright human associations which are universally regarded as the test of civilised living?

The answer can be given very briefly. Since 1945 the Supreme Planners have been increasingly engaged in searching for alibis, in hunting for scapegoats and in trailing red herrings. The public have increasingly devoted themselves to the evasion of the law and to operations upon the black markets. Contempt for authority has increased; class consciousness has become more acute; cynicism regarding corruption in public life more prevalent; personal and class irresponsibility more in evidence; gambling practices more widespread. Liberal society in all its aspects is being eaten away.

This, of course, is not the fault of any individual or group of individuals. It is the fault of an economic system which multiplies unenforceable laws and hence the opportunities of breaking them, and which places upon the materialistic conception of life so great an importance that the spiritual values are weakened or stamped out. Under it, men of integrity and good will may just as easily be dragged down to lower moral standards as are the crooks and the law-breakers. . . .

[1] Those who feel that this summary of the socialist attitude is overdrawn should read the Webbs' *The Decay of Capitalist Civilisation;* R. H. Tawney, *The Sickness of an Acquisitive Society;* Sir Stafford Cripps, *Towards Christian Democracy.*

[2] Sir Stafford Cripps, *Towards Christian Democracy,* p. 55.

LAW-BREAKING AND THE BLACK MARKETS

As the planned economy unfolds its consequences the ordinary member of the public is conscious of a group of Supreme Planners making large errors, and a host of minor planners who are enforcing regulations in which there seems to be neither rhyme nor reason. It is in this atmosphere that disregard for the law grows apace and the black markets flourish.

Great Britain is not naturally a fertile field for black marketing. The people are law-abiding by habit and tradition. There is no large agricultural population from which, as in many other countries, food can be acquired illegally or by barter. But there can be little doubt that, by the middle of 1947, a large part of the British population were breaking some of the laws of which they were aware, a greater part were breaking laws of which they were not aware, and a still greater part would have been prepared to break the laws if they had had the opportunity.

The anxiety of the Government regarding "spivs and drones" was, in itself, good evidence of this. Responsible and independent public men, not given to exaggeration, were warning us of the decay of morals. Thieving and petty pilfering abounded. Barter, for those who had scarce commodities to exchange, became common. The use of pound notes for the settlement of debts was employed as a method of tax evasion. The black markets were particularly prevalent in house repairing, food and clothing. A Minister lamented, "we cannot have a policeman behind every hedge."

THE DECLINE IN THE QUALITY OF PRODUCTION

By the middle of 1947 it was a matter of common observation that a high proportion of the goods in the shops were of bad design and poor quality.

The trend towards the production of rubbish was undeniable, the causes of it obscure and diverse. In part it was undoubtedly attributable to the existing inflationary condition, for when manufacturers are certain that whatever they produce can be sold, their anxiety to maintain the good will of the consumer evaporates. In part it was due to the shortages arising out of the bad distribution of raw materials under planning which compelled producers to do their best with the materials that came to them. In part it was a reflection of the emphasis, common among planners, placed on mass production and standardisation. The upshot was a declining sense of service by the producer to the consumer, contributing to the dreariness of existence and representing a real waste of economic satisfaction.

The Growth of Class Consciousness

All real progress in society consists of the growth of charity, freely and spontaneously expressed, through which the material distinctions between individuals are smoothed away in the consciousness of their common human heritage. This was the philosophy providing the foundation for the growing humanitarianism of the nineteenth century. At best, it implied a classless society. At worst, it presumed that if classes were created through differences in income, in occupation, in taste or in ability, the class distinctions should be secondary in the sense that movement between the classes should be unimpeded by privilege and that no class should have it in its power to dominate another. The socialist attacks on the social rigidities and privileges of Victorian England were sound and, being sound, were successful in paving the way for a greater measure of economic equality and the break-down of many vested interests.

But it is becoming clear that the centrally directed economy germinates a new crop of privileged groups and thus weakens social cohesion based upon consent.

There is, first, the clash between the planners and the planned, between those who wield the power and those who must submit to it. The planner is confronted with the baffling administrative problems raised by the diversity of individual needs and individual circumstances. He must simplify and standardise, frame his rules in relation to the average, aim at dealing with masses. By definition, therefore, the rules will not fit individual cases. The planned, recognising the arbitrariness of the general rule and perceiving how badly it fits his special case, strive to evade regulations apparently neither just nor rational. The more widespread the evasion the more stringent and repressive must be the laws. The vicious circle is then complete. For whilst the planner always sees the solution of his problems in just one more set of controls to block some new form of evasion, each member of the planned class sees his salvation in more skilful evasion or the sweeping away of controls altogether. The circle of mutual distrust can grow almost indefinitely. This is why the British Civil Service, probably the least corruptible and the most hard-working and able cadre that has ever operated, is so popularly derided that Ministers must come to its defence in public. This is why the civil servant must constantly add to his unpopularity by seeking for fresh powers of repression if he is to try to carry out the behests of his masters, and why planners in all countries have ultimately found it necessary to raise cries against the recalcitrant classes — be they capitalists, Jews, kulaks, the middle classes or merely spivs and drones.

Secondly, there are the jealousies and envies created between the greater part of the public and those groups which, for the moment, enjoy economic privileges. When planning blunders are made, compulsion can be used to patch up the broken system. But economic incentives are also useful. So that when coal is short the coal-miner will be granted special rations and other perquisites. But other groups in the community will think that their work is as hard, as unpleasant or as necessary as that of the coal-miner and feel a sense of injustice. Each group, therefore, will have a direct interest in keeping down its production, in making its product the crucial bottleneck in the economy. For in that way the power of the group will be increased and the bounty of the planners' largesse made more certain.

Thirdly, in an atmosphere of black markets and lawlessness each man's hand is set against another's. Those who have inherited habits of honesty from life in a liberal society become first indignant at, and ultimately covetous of, the profits going to the law-breakers. The common informer comes into his own and the free-and-easy contacts between individuals are spoilt.

Fourthly, vested interests must organise themselves and clash because, once the market economy is destroyed, that is the form taken by social competition. In allocating the national resources the planners can follow no guiding principles. Since the price system can no longer pass back messages concerning the proper allocation of goods and services, the planners must either organise production without regard for consumers' needs or turn themselves into a gigantic listening-post through which they seek to record in other ways the demands of the people. If the Government is listening, it clearly pays organised groups to shout hard to establish their claims to some sort of priority and to belittle the claims of others. New class rivalries are, thereby, created.

Finally, comprehensive national planning sets one nation against another and engenders frictions which result in the distintegration of the world economy and the danger of war. This subject will be referred to in the next chapter.

* * *

The Destruction of Independent Thought and Criticism

In the long run the planned economy destroys the independent habits and attitudes through which alone freedom can be preserved. As private property diminishes in importance through penal taxation, the lowering of the rate of interest and the growing relative importance of State property, fewer and fewer people are in the independent position in which they can fearlessly criticise Government policy without risking their livelihood and the security of their family. The number of people grows whose incomes wholly or partly depend upon keeping their mouths shut and their thoughts private. The planned economy always involves a great increase in the number of Government officials who can hardly criticise their employer without risking their chances of promotion. Business men operating in what is left of the free economy know only too well that there are innumerable ways in which outspoken critics of official muddles can be penalised. They may tell in private their stories of planning inefficiency but, in self-defence, they dare go no further. And some professional classes, such as accountants and lawyers, often stand to gain, at least for a time, out of the conditions which exist under extensive Government intervention.

Independence is further undermined by the deliberate destruction or the progressive atrophy of voluntary organisations and associations. These forms of co-operation are not "plannable instruments" and must, therefore, be frowned upon in the planned system. Voluntary associations are the life-blood of free society; they have in the past led to much of our progress in education, social insurance and health services because they have left the way open for groups of like-minded people to experiment with new ideas and to criticise existing methods by showing the way to do better. They are hardly likely to survive in an environment in which it is assumed that the State has taken upon itself the responsibility, often to the deliberate exclusion of private effort, for all social services.

The planned economy must finally destroy the very instruments of free speech. The burden thrown upon the legislature by the enormous mass of work involved in a planned economy inevitably drives the executive to restrict the freedom of debate in the Houses of Representatives. When resources have to be allocated between rival uses, the claims of the instruments of free speech will be relegated to second or third place. Harassed by the interminable complexities of their own system, the planners must finally be driven, in order to keep economic life in operation at all, to cut through their knots by making arbitrary decisions and stifling unwelcome criticism.

Perhaps, however, for the mass of the people the whole atmosphere of independence and freedom is most insidiously destroyed by the proliferation of minor officials, essential for the working of the plan, each of whom is charged with certain powers over our everyday actions. These officials are no better or worse than any of us. Most of them may be conscientiously anxious to carry out their duties and to use their powers with discretion and understanding. But the system which brings them into existence is dangerous. They are conscious of their power, they (and those who are subject to them) recognise the inconvenience of recourse to appeal against the exercise of that power. These are the conditions which may multiply petty tyranny of the most obnoxious kind. The network of power may extend quietly without it being remarked. The Prime Minister revealed in February 1947 that seventeen Ministries have power to authorise inspections involving the entry into private houses and premises without a search warrant. It later was admitted that 10,916 Government officials were authorised to carry out inspections and investigations without a search warrant. The "snooping" called for in enforcing regulations leads to the creation of a new body of plain-clothed police whose work may differ little from that of the *agent provocateur*. This is the sordid atmosphere which breeds the anonymous informer and everywhere sets one man against another.

The modern planning movement sets out, with good will and noble intentions, to control things and invariably ends up by controlling men.

*   *   *

THE OBSESSION WITH MATERIAL ENDS

At some periods throughout the vicissitudinous history of socialist ideas, spiritual values have been highly rated and at all times the solid support for socialist policy has come from men of good will who dreamed of a finer and more humane society. It is the more tragic that the contemporary efforts to fulfil the socialist purpose through the central direction of the economy is destined to drag down these fine aspirations to an over-preoccupation with material things and physical satisfactions.

The symptoms are always the same. Public discussion centres almost wholly on economic affairs; the community lives in a distracting hullabaloo, momentarily stimulating but ultimately exhausting; the leaders harangue and exhort in ever more strident tones in an effort to picture economic effort as a struggle for survival in which luxuries and refinements must be cut off and individual liberty must temporarily go to the wall; there is an anxious straining for more and more effort, higher and higher targets; the public sadly yearns for the promised land which steadily recedes.

This immitigable struggle leaves less room for the refinements of life such as the delights of leisure, the pleasures of solitude, the search for knowledge, the satisfaction of craftsmanship. So the local soviets in Russia gather together to applaud last month's steel output and pledge themselves to ever greater effort. So the British citizen submits to bombardment from cinema, newspaper, radio and hoarding urging him to work harder and accept more sacrifices. In this there is nothing which satisfies the spirit. The harvest festivals of the past did at least confer a sense of a task well done, a purpose fulfilled. But the industrial festivals of the planning age seem to provide nothing but the occasion for once again laying the lash on the backs of workers with the endless cry for more. The keen and stimulating buoyancy of an expanding free economy may at times be fretful and wearing but, at least, it leaves wide individual horizons, opportunity and the right to withdraw from the race at any time. In the planned economy the anxiety neurosis is that of individuals who watch the circle of their initiative slowly shrinking.

The absence of an inner tranquillity in the planned economy is commonly observed but the many and variable reasons for it are perhaps not so well understood. The first is that since planned economies will be poverty-stricken, the minds of the people are much taken up with meeting elementary physical needs. The second is that the planners, in order to cover up the deficiencies of the system and to achieve this target or that programme, will seek to attach some mystical value to work for its own sake and will overlook the elementary truth that work is for leisure and the means to make leisure purposeful. The choice between work and leisure is not a choice between good and evil but between different ways of gaining satisfaction. The third is that the planning crises tend to be sharper, more unpredictable and more catastrophic than any known in other economic systems, and the sense of ever-impending disaster is as crippling as the prospects, to an invalid, of the onset of some dread disease, such as thrombosis or haemophilia.

But the most deep-rooted sickness of the planned economy is that it seeks to bind together the community by an appeal to an end which cannot provide any lasting social cohesion—the pursuit of wealth. It is ultimately disastrous to expect men to enjoy the communion of their common brotherhood, their sense of playing their part in some satisfying joint effort, their feeling of the unfolding of the full potentialities of their personality by putting before them a target (incidentally fixed by someone else) for the output of steel, coal, electrical switches or paper bags. Yet this is precisely the religion that is preached. Thus Lenin:

> We need a plan at once to give the masses a shining unimpeded example to work for.

So Sir Oliver Franks:

> The plans must become the plans of the nation and animate the constructive endeavour of the managements and workers. . . . Import and Export programmes must become symbols of the life the people wills to achieve. . . . It is at once the task and the miracle of statesmanship to translate them into terms which have meaning and inspiration to ordinary men in ordinary circumstances.

So Sir Stafford Cripps:

> We have got to engender in the people the same spirit of determination to see this programme through that they have displayed in winning victory in the war.

The planners seem to dig themselves out of one pit only by digging themselves into another. They recognise, and rightly, that the plan stands no chance of success unless the economic affairs of the community are placed in the very forefront of every mind in the group. Work, sacrifice and the achievement of targets must be hammered into the public sleeping and waking, eating and drinking. The statesman must adopt every trick and device to mould the ideal economic man for the purpose. Cupidity ("the golden age is just round the corner"); narrow patriotism ("our community must stand on its own feet"); fear ("the struggle is one for survival") and hatred ("the laggards must be run to earth"); the use of all these are now well-established methods of the planned economy.

Let us assume that the miracle of statesmanship is performed (which I submit is impossible in a free society) and the life of the people is firmly centred on material objectives. Let us further assume that the economic objectives are reached (which I submit are unachievable). Then the community must distintegrate. For the pursuit of wealth cannot bind men together, it is a centrifugal not a centripetal force. The vow of poverty can bring social cohesion. Trappists, Hindus, Christians, Buddhists—history is full of cases where groups have voluntarily and willingly submitted themselves to deprivation because they believed their cause was good. But not so the vow of plenty. There is never in this the threads out of which can be woven the mutual respect and comradeship constituting the stuff of stable and effective communities.

So is destroyed the last hope of the philosophers of planning. For when all else fails—when the promise of plenty is not fulfilled, when security and stability is not achieved, when the claims of the plan to be scientific prove hollow, when the effective employment of the resources of the community is not reached, when the targets prove to be will-o'-the-wisps—it is still argued that the plan justifies itself because, woeful as may be its economic consequences, it still makes it possible for each member of the group to feel himself "part of a united community . . . moving purposefully towards known objectives." But in the last analysis the spiritual content of planning proves to be a sham.

These, of course, are precisely the charges which have been laid against the free market economy. But in that economy no one need ever claim that economic activity is the highest form of activity or that the first aim of an individual or a community is to become rich. The market economy is simply a device for creating automatic regulations which will enable us to provide for physical needs by the most economical route, of pushing economic problems into a corner to be forgotten, like the thermostat in a house, so that we can get on as uninterruptedly as possible with the development of the real art of living and the discovery of those forms of human relations which will bring us the ideal society.

9 VON HAYEK

True and False Individualism

Few scholars of this century have made as many or as varied contributions to the fields of politics, philosophy, economics, psychology, and law as has Friedrich A. von Hayek (1899–   ). Formerly a professor of economics in the London School of Economics and Political Science, he is also an emeritus member of the Committee on Social Thought of the University of Chicago. An Austrian by birth and a British subject, he now holds the emeritus chair of economics policy at the University of Freiburg in Germany. He is the founder and honorary president of the Mont Pelerin Society, an international association of scholars and statesmen who share a common tradition which might broadly be called classical liberalism. His best-known works are *The Road to Serfdom* (Chicago, 1944) and *The Constitution of Liberty* (Chicago, 1960), which includes an epilogue entitled "Why I Am Not a Conservative." The selection is from the first chapter of his *Individualism and Economic Order,** "Individualism: True and False."

The title which I have chosen for this chapter shows that to me there still seems to exist such a philosophy—a set of principles which, indeed, is implicit in most of Western or Christian political tradition but which can no longer be unambiguously described by any readily understood term. It is therefore necessary to restate these principles fully before we can decide whether they can still serve us as practical guides.

The difficulty which we encounter is not merely the familiar fact that the current political terms are notoriously ambiguous or even that the same term often means nearly the opposite to different groups.

* (Chicago: University of Chicago Press, 1948.) By permission.

There is the much more serious fact that the same word frequently appears to unite people who in fact believe in contradictory and irreconcilable ideals. Terms like "liberalism" or "democracy," "capitalism" or "socialism," today no longer stand for coherent systems of ideas. They have come to describe aggregations of quite heterogeneous principles and facts which historical accident has associated with these words but which have little in common beyond having been advocated at different times by the same people or even merely under the same name.

No political term has suffered worse in this respect than "individualism." It not only has been distorted by its opponents into an unrecognizable caricature—and we should always remember that the political concepts which are today out of fashion are known to most of our contemporaries only through the picture drawn of them by their enemies—but has been used to describe several attitudes toward society which have as little in common among themselves as they have with those traditionally regarded as their opposites. Indeed, when in the preparation of this paper I examined some of the standard descriptions of "individualism," I almost began to regret that I had ever connected the ideals in which I believe with a term which has been so abused and so misunderstood. Yet, whatever else "individualism" may have come to mean in addition to these ideals, there are two good reasons for retaining the term for the view I mean to defend: this view has always been known by that term, whatever else it may also have meant at different times, and the term has the distinction that the word "socialism" was deliberately coined to express its opposition to individualism.* It is with the system which forms the alternative to socialism that I shall be concerned.

Before I explain what I mean by true individualism, it may be useful if I give some indication of the intellectual tradition to which it belongs. The true individualism which I shall try to defend began its modern development with John Locke, and particularly with Bernard Mandeville and David Hume, and achieved full stature for the first

---

* Both the term "individualism" and the term "socialism" are originally the creation of the Saint-Simonians, the founders of modern socialism. They first coined the term "individualism" to describe the competitive society to which they were opposed and then invented the word "socialism" to describe the centrally planned society in which all activity was directed on the same principle that applied within a single factory.

time in the work of Josiah Tucker, Adam Ferguson, and Adam Smith and in that of their great contemporary, Edmund Burke—the man whom Smith described as the only person he ever knew who thought on economic subjects exactly as he did without any previous communication having passed between them. In the nineteenth century I find it represented most perfectly in the work of two of its greatest historians and political philosophers: Alexis de Tocqueville and Lord Acton. These two men seem to me to have more successfully developed what was best in the political philosophy of the Scottish philosophers, Burke, and the English Whigs than any other writers I know; while the classical economists of the nineteenth century, or at least the Benthamites or philosophical radicals among them, came increasingly under the influence of another kind of individualism of different origin.

This second and altogether different strand of thought, also known as individualism, is represented mainly by French and other Continental writers—a fact due, I believe, to the dominant role which Cartesian rationalism plays in its composition. The outstanding representatives of this tradition are the Encyclopedists, Rousseau, and the physiocrats; and, for reasons we shall presently consider, this rationalistic individualism always tends to develop into the opposite of individualism, namely, socialism or collectivism. It is because only the first kind of individualism is consistent that I claim for it the name of true individualism, while the second kind must probably be regarded as a source of modern socialism as important as the properly collectivist theories.

I can give no better illustration of the prevailing confusion about the meaning of individualism than the fact that the man who to me seems to be one of the greatest representatives of true individualism, Edmund Burke, is commonly (and rightly) represented as the main opponent of the so-called "individualism" of Rousseau, whose theories he feared would rapidly dissolve the commonwealth "into the dust and powder of individuality," and that the term "individualism" itself was first introduced into the English language through the translation of one of the works of another of the great representatives of true individualism, De Tocqueville, who uses it in his *Democracy in America* to describe an attitude which he deplores and rejects. Yet there can be no doubt that both Burke and De Tocqueville stand in all essentials close to Adam Smith, to whom nobody will deny the title of individualist, and that the "individualism" to which they are opposed is something altogether different from that of Smith.

What, then, are the essential characteristics of true individualism? The first thing that should be said is that it is primarily a theory of society, an attempt to understand the forces which determine the social life of man, and only in the second instance a set of political maxims derived from this view of society. This fact should by itself be sufficient to refute the silliest of the common misunderstandings: the belief that individualism postulates (or bases its arguments on the assumption of) the existence of isolated or self-contained individuals, instead of starting from men whose whole nature and character is determined by their existence in society. If that were true, it would indeed have nothing to contribute to our understanding of society. But its basic contention is quite a different one; it is that there is no other way toward an understanding of social phenomena but through our understanding of individual actions directed toward other people and guided by their expected behavior. This argument is directed primarily against the properly collectivist theories of society which pretend to be able directly to comprehend social wholes like society, etc., as entities *sui generis* which exist independently of the individuals which compose them. The next step in the individualistic analysis of society, however, is directed against the rationalistic pseudo-individualism which also leads to practical collectivism. It is the contention that, by tracing the combined effects of individual actions, we discover that many of the institutions on which human achievements rest have arisen and are functioning without a designing and directing mind; that, as Adam Ferguson expressed it, "nations stumble upon establishments, which are indeed the result of human action but not the result of human design"; and that the spontaneous collaboration of free men often creates things which are greater than their individual minds can ever fully comprehend. This is the great theme of Josiah Tucker and Adam Smith, of Adam Ferguson and Edmund Burke, the great discovery of classical political economy which has become the basis of our understanding not only of economic life but of most truly social phenomena.

The difference between this view, which accounts for most of the order which we find in human affairs as the unforeseen result of individual actions, and the view which traces all discoverable order to deliberate design is the first great contrast between the true individualism of the British thinkers of the eighteenth century and the so-called "individualism" of the Cartesian school. But it is merely one aspect of an even wider difference between a view which in general rates rather low the place which reason plays in human affairs, which contends that man has achieved what he has in spite of the fact that he is only partly guided by reason, and that his individual reason is very limited and imperfect, and a view which assumes that Reason, with a capital *R*, is always fully and equally available to all humans and that everything which man achieves is the direct result of, and therefore subject to, the control of individual reason. One might even say that the former is a product of an acute consciousness of the limitations of the individual mind which induces an attitude of humility toward the impersonal and anonymous social processes by which individuals help to create things greater than they know, while the latter is the product of an exaggerated belief in the powers of individual reason and of a consequent contempt for anything which has not been consciously designed by it or is not fully intelligible to it. . . .

However that may be, the main point about which there can be little doubt is that Smith's chief concern was not so much with what man might occasionally achieve when he was at his best but that he should have as little opportunity as possible to do harm when he was at his worst. It would scarcely be too much to claim that the main merit of the individualism which he and his contemporaries advocated is that it is a system under which bad men can do least harm. It is a social system which does not depend for its functioning on our finding good men for running it, or on all men becoming better than they now are, but which makes use of men in all their given variety and complexity, sometimes good and sometimes bad, sometimes intelligent and more often stupid. Their aim was a system under which it should be possible to grant freedom to all, instead of restricting it, as their French contemporaries wished, to "the good and the wise."

The chief concern of the great individualist writers was indeed to find a set of institutions by which man could be induced, by his own choice and from the motives which determined his ordinary conduct, to contribute as much as possible to the need of all others; and their discovery was that the system of private property did provide such inducements to a much greater extent than had yet been understood. They did not contend, however, that this system was incapable of further improvement and, still less, as another of the current distortions of their arguments will have it, that there existed a "natural harmony of interests" irrespective of the positive institutions. They were more than merely aware of the conflicts of individual interests and stressed the necessity of "well-constructed institutions" where the "rules and principles of contending interests and compromised advantages" would reconcile conflicting interests without giving any one group power to make their views and interests always prevail over those of all others.

There is one point in these basic psychological assumptions which it is necessary to consider somewhat more fully. As the belief that individualism approves and encourages human selfishness is one of the main reasons why so many people dislike it, and as the confusion which exists in this respect is caused by a real intellectual difficulty, we must carefully examine the meaning of the assumption it makes. There can be no doubt, of course, that in the language of the great writers of the eighteenth century it was man's "self-love," or even his "selfish interests," which they represented as the "universal mover," and that by these terms they were referring primarily to a moral attitude, which they thought to be widely prevalent. These terms, however, did not mean egotism in the narrow sense of concern with only the immediate needs of one's proper person. The "self," for which alone people were supposed to care, did as a matter of course include their family and friends; and it would have made no difference to the argument if it had included anything for which people in fact did care.

Far more important than this moral attitude, which might be regarded as changeable, is an indisputable intellectual fact which nobody can hope to alter and which by itself is a sufficient basis for the conclusions which the individualist philosophers drew. This is the constitutional limitation of man's knowledge and interests, the fact that he *cannot* know more than a tiny part of the whole of society and that therefore all that can enter into his motives are the immediate effects which his actions will have in the sphere he knows. All the possible differences in men's moral attitudes amount to little, so far as their significance for social organization is concerned, compared with the fact that all man's mind can effectively comprehend are the facts of the narrow circle of which he is the center; that, whether he is completely selfish or the most perfect altruist, the human needs for which he *can* effectively care are an almost negligible fraction of the needs of all members of society. The real question, therefore, is not whether man is, or ought to be, guided by selfish motives but whether we can allow him to be guided in his actions by those immediate consequences which he can know and care for or whether he ought to be made to do what seems appropriate to somebody else who is supposed to possess a fuller comprehension of the significance of these actions to society as a whole.

To the accepted Christian tradition that man must be free to follow *his* conscience in moral matters if his actions are to be of any merit, the economists added the further argument that he should be free to make full use of *his* knowledge and skill, that he must be allowed to be guided by his concern for the particular things of which *he* knows and for which *he* cares, if he is to make as great a contribution to the common purposes of society as he is capable of making. Their main problem was how these limited concerns, which did in fact determine people's actions, could be made effective inducements to cause them voluntarily to contribute as much as possible to needs which lay outside the range of their vision. What the economists understood for the first time was that the market as it had grown up was an effective way of making man take part in a process more complex and extended than he could comprehend and that it was through the market that he was made to contribute "to ends which were no part of his purpose."

It was almost inevitable that the classical writers in explaining their contention should use language which was bound to be misunderstood and that they thus earned the reputation of having extolled selfishness. We rapidly discover the reason when we try to restate the correct argument in simple language. If we put it concisely by saying that people are and ought to be guided in their actions by *their* interests and desires, this will at once be misunderstood or distorted into the false contention that they are or ought to be exclusively guided by their personal needs or selfish interests, while what we mean is that they ought to be allowed to strive for whatever *they* think desirable.

Another misleading phrase, used to stress an important point, is the famous presumption that each man knows his interests best. In this form the contention is neither plausible nor necessary for the individualist's conclusions. The true basis of his argument is that nobody can know *who* knows best and that the only way by which we can find out is through a social process in which everybody is allowed to try and see what he can do. The fundamental assumption, here as elsewhere, is the unlimited variety of human gifts and skills and the consequent ignorance of any single individual of most of what is known to all the other members of society taken together. Or, to put this fundamental contention differently, human Reason, with a capital R, does not exist in the singular, as given or available to any particular person, as the rationalist approach seems to assume, but must be conceived as an interpersonal process in which anyone's contribution is tested and corrected by others. This argument does not assume that all men are equal in their natural endowments and capacities but only that no man is qualified to pass final judgment on the capacities which another possesses or is to be allowed to exercise.

Here I may perhaps mention that only because men are in fact unequal can we treat them equally. If all men were completely equal in their gifts and inclinations, we should have to treat them differently in order to achieve any sort of social organization. Fortunately, they are not equal; and it is only owing to this that the differentiation of functions need not be determined by the arbitrary decision of some organizing will but that, after creating formal equality of the rules applying in the same manner to all, we can leave each individual to find his own level.

There is all the difference in the world between treating people equally and attempting to make them equal. While the first is the condition of a free society, the second means, as De Tocqueville described it, "a new form of servitude.". . .

That true individualism affirms the value of the family and all the common efforts of the small community and group, that it believes in local autonomy and voluntary associations, and that indeed its case rests largely on the contention that much for which the coercive action of the state is usually invoked can be done better by voluntary collaboration need not be stressed further. There can be no greater contrast to this than the false individualism which wants to dissolve all these smaller groups into atoms which have no cohesion other than the coercive rules imposed by the state, and which tries to make all social ties prescriptive, instead of using the state mainly as a protection of the individual against the arrogation of coercive powers by the smaller groups.

Quite as important for the functioning of an individualist society as these smaller groupings of men are the traditions and conventions which evolve in a free society and which, without being enforceable, establish flexible but normally observed rules that make the behavior of other people predictable in a high degree. The willingness to submit to such rules, not merely so long as one understands the reason for them but so long as one has no definite reasons to the contrary, is an essential condition for the gradual evolution and improvement of rules of social intercourse; and the readiness ordinarily to submit to the products of a social process which nobody has designed and the reasons for which nobody may understand is also an indispensable condition if it is to be possible to dispense with compulsion. That the existence of common conventions and traditions among a group of people will enable them to work together smoothly and efficiently with much less formal organization and compulsion than a group without such common background, is, of course, a commonplace. But the reverse of this, while less familiar, is probably not less true: that coercion can probably only be kept to a minimum in a society where conventions and tradition have made the behavior of man to a large extent predictable.* . . .

The unwillingness to tolerate or respect any social forces which are not recognizable as the product of intelligent design, which is so important a cause of the present desire for comprehensive economic planning, is indeed only one aspect of a more general movement. We meet the same tendency in the field of morals and conventions, in the desire to substitute an artificial for the existing languages, and in the whole modern attitude toward processes which govern the growth of knowledge. The belief that only a synthetic system of morals, an artificial language, or even an artificial society can be justified in an age of science, as well as the increasing unwillingness to bow before any moral rules whose utility is not rationally demonstrated, or to

* Is it necessary to quote Edmund Burke once more to remind the reader how essential a condition for the possibility of a free society was to him the strength of moral rules? "Men are qualified for civil liberty," he wrote, "in exact proportion to their disposition to put moral chains upon their own appetites; in proportion as their love of justice is above their rapacity; in proportion as their own soundness and sobriety of understanding is above their vanity and presumption; in proportion as they are more disposed to listen to the councils of the wise and good, in preference to the flattery of knaves" (*A Letter to a Member of the National Assembly* [1791], in *Works* [World's Classics ed.], IV, 319).

conform with conventions whose rationale is not known, are all manifestations of the same basic view which wants all social activity to be recognizably part of a single coherent plan. They are the results of that same rationalistic "individualism" which wants to see in everything the product of conscious individual reason. They are certainly not, however, a result of true individualism and may even make the working of a free and truly individualistic system difficult or impossible. Indeed, the great lesson which the individualist philosophy teaches us on this score is that, while it may not be difficult to destroy the spontaneous formations which are the indispensable bases of a free civilization, it may be beyond our power deliberately to reconstruct such a civilization once these foundations are destroyed. . . .

The attitude of individualism to nationalism, which intellectually is but a twin brother of socialism, would deserve special discussion. Here I can only point out that the fundamental difference between what in the nineteenth century was regarded as liberalism in the English-speaking world and what was so called on the Continent is closely connected with their descent from true individualism and the false rationalistic individualism, respectively. It was only liberalism in the English sense that was generally opposed to centralization, to nationalism and to socialism, while the liberalism prevalent on the Continent favored all three. I should add, however, that, in this as in so many other respects, John Stuart Mill, and the later English liberalism derived from him, belong at least as much to the Continental as to the English tradition; and I know no discussion more illuminating of these basic differences than Lord Acton's criticism of the concessions Mill had made to the nationalistic tendencies of Continental liberalism.

There are two more points of difference between the two kinds of individualism which are also best illustrated by the stand taken by Lord Acton and De Tocqueville by their views on democracy and equality toward trends which became prominent in their time. True individualism not only believes in democracy but can claim that democratic ideals spring from the basic principles of individualism. Yet, while individualism affirms that all government should be democratic, it has no superstitious belief in the omnicompetence of majority decisions, and in particular it refuses to admit that "absolute power may, by the hypothesis of popular origin, be as legitimate as constitutional freedom." It believes that under a democracy, no less than under any other form of government, "the sphere of enforced command ought to be restricted within fixed limits"; and it is particularly opposed to the most fateful and dangerous of all current misconceptions of democracy—the belief that we must accept as true and binding for future development the views of the majority. While democracy is founded on the convention that the majority view decides on common action, it does not mean that what is today the majority view ought to become the generally accepted view—even if that were necessary to achieve the aims of the majority. On the contrary, the whole justification of democracy rests on the fact that in course of time what is today the view of a small minority may become the majority view. I believe, indeed, that one of the most important questions on which political theory will have to discover an answer in the near future is that of finding a line of demarcation between the fields in which the majority views must be binding for all and the fields in which, on the contrary, the minority view ought to be allowed to prevail if it can produce results which better satisfy a demand of the public. I am, above all, convinced that, where the interests of a particular branch of trade are concerned, the majority view will always be the reactionary, stationary view and that the merit of competition is precisely that it gives the minority a chance to prevail. Where it can do so without any coercive powers, it ought always to have the right.

I cannot better sum up this attitude of true individualism toward democracy than by once more quoting Lord Acton: "The true democratic principle," he wrote, "that none shall have power over the people, is taken to mean that none shall be able to restrain or to elude its power. The true democratic principle, that the people shall not be made to do what it does not like, is taken to mean that it shall never be required to tolerate what it does not like. The true democratic principle, that every man's will shall be as unfettered as possible, is taken to mean that the free will of the collective people shall be fettered in nothing."

When we turn to equality, however, it should be said at once that true individualism is not equalitarian in the modern sense of the word. It can see no reason for trying to make people equal as distinct from treating them equally. While individualism is profoundly opposed to all prescriptive privilege, to all protection, by law or force, of any rights not based on rules equally applicable to all persons, it also denies government the right to limit what the able or fortunate may achieve. It is equally opposed to any rigid limitation of the position individuals may achieve, whether this power is used to perpetuate inequality or to create equality. Its main principle is that no man or group of men should have power to decide what another man's status ought to be, and it regards this as a condition of freedom so essential that it must not be sacrificed to the gratification of our sense of justice or of our envy.

From the point of view of individualism there would not appear to exist even any justification for making all individuals start on the same level by preventing them from profiting by advantages which they have in no way earned, such as being born to parents who are more intelligent or more conscientious than the average. Here individualism is indeed less "individualistic" than socialism, because it recognizes the family as a legitimate unit as much as the individual; and the same is true with respect to other groups, such as linguistic or religious communities, which by their common efforts may succeed for long periods in preserving for their members material or moral standards different from those of the rest of the population. De Tocqueville and Lord Acton speak with one voice on this subject. "Democracy and socialism," De Tocqueville wrote, "have nothing in common but one word, equality. But notice the difference: while democracy seeks equality in liberty, socialism seeks equality in restraint and servitude." And Acton joined him in believing that "the deepest cause which made the French revolution so disastrous to liberty was its theory of equality" and that "the finest opportunity ever given to the world was thrown away, because the passion for equality made vain the hope for freedom."

10 OAKESHOTT

The Conservative Mode of Thought

Michael Oakeshott (1901–   ), who succeeded Harold Laski in the chair of politics at the London School of Economics and Political Science, is probably the most eminent contemporary practitioner of the British traditionalist approach to conservative thought. His essay "Rationalism in Politics" was an incisive critique of the extreme reliance on rationalism of many anticonservative thinkers. He has tried to show that a reasonable man will know the limits of his reason and not misuse his intellectual gifts. The selection comprises most of his essay "On Being Conservative," followed by a short excerpt from "Rationalism in Politics." *

To be conservative is to be disposed to think and behave in certain manners; it is to prefer certain kinds of conduct and certain conditions of human circumstances to others; it is to be disposed to make certain kinds of choices. And my design here is to construe this disposition as it appears in contemporary character, rather than to transpose it into the idiom of general principles.

The general characteristics of this disposition are not difficult to discern, although they have often been mistaken. They centre upon a propensity to use and to enjoy what is available rather than to wish for or to look for something else; to delight in what is present rather than what was or what may be. Reflection may bring to light an appropriate gratefulness for what is available, and consequently there is no mere idolizing of what is past and gone. What is esteemed is the

* Michael Oakeshott, *Rationalism in Politics and Other Essays* (New York: Basic Books, 1962). By permission.

acknowledgment of a gift or an inheritance from the past; but there present; and it is esteemed not on account of its connections with a remote antiquity, nor because it is recognized to be more admirable than any possible alternative, but on account of its familiarity: not, *Verweile doch, du bist so schön,* but, *Stay with me because I am attached to you.* . . .

To be conservative, then, is to prefer the familiar to the unknown, to prefer the tried to the untried, fact to mystery, the actual to the possible, the limited to the unbounded, the near to the distant, the sufficient to the superabundant, the convenient to the perfect, present laughter to utopian bliss. Familiar relationships and loyalties will be preferred to the allure of more profitable attachments; to acquire and to enlarge will be less important than to keep, to cultivate and to enjoy; the grief of loss will be more acute than the excitement of novelty or promise. It is to be equal to one's own fortune, to live at the level of one's own means, to be content with the want of greater perfection which belongs alike to oneself and one's circumstances. With some people this is itself a choice; in others it is a disposition which appears, frequently or less frequently, in their preferences and aversions, and is not itself chosen or specifically cultivated. . . .

Changes are without effect only upon those who notice nothing, who are ignorant of what they possess and apathetic to their circumstances; and they can be welcomed indiscriminately only by those who esteem nothing, whose attachments are fleeting and who are strangers to love and affection. The conservative disposition provokes neither of these conditions: the inclination to enjoy what is present and available is the opposite of ignorance and apathy and it breeds attachment and affection. Consequently, it is averse from change, which appears always, in the first place, as deprivation. A storm which sweeps away a copse and transforms a favourite view, the death of friends, the sleep of friendship, the desuetude of customs of behaviour, the retirement of a favourite clown, involuntary exile, reversals of fortune, the loss of abilities enjoyed and their replacement by others— these are changes, none perhaps without its compensations, which the man of conservative temperament unavoidably regrets. But he has difficulty in reconciling himself to them, not because what he has lost in them was intrinsically better than any alternative might have been or was incapable of improvement, nor because what takes its place is inherently incapable of being enjoyed, but because what he has lost was something he actually enjoyed and had learned how to enjoy and what takes its place is something to which he has acquired no attachment. Consequently, he will find small and slow changes more tolerable than large and sudden; and he will value highly every appearance of continuity. Some changes, indeed, will present no difficulty; but, again, this is not because they are manifest improvements but merely because they are easily assimilated: the changes of the seasons are mediated by their recurrence and the growing up of children by its continuousness. And, in general, he will accommodate himself more readily to changes which do not offend expectation than to the destruction of what seems to have no ground of dissolution within itself.

Moreover, to be conservative is not merely to be averse from change (which may be an idiosyncrasy); it is also a manner of accommodating ourselves to changes, an activity imposed upon all men. For, change is a threat to identity, and every change is an emblem of extinction. But a man's identity (or that of a community) is nothing more than an unbroken rehearsal of contingencies, each at the mercy of circumstance and each significant in proportion to its familiarity. It is not a fortress into which we may retire, and the only means we have of defending it (that is, ourselves) against the hostile forces of change is in the open field of our experience; by throwing our weight upon the foot which for the time being is most firmly placed, by cleaving to whatever familiarities are not immediately threatened and thus assimilating what is new without becoming unrecognizable to ourselves. The Masai, when they were moved from their old country to the present Masai reserve in Kenya, took with them the names of their hills and plains and rivers and gave them to the hills and plains and rivers of the new country. And it is by some such subterfuge of conservatism that every man or people compelled to suffer a notable change avoids the shame of extinction.

Changes, then, have to be suffered; and a man of conservative temperament (that is, one strongly disposed to preserve his identity) cannot be indifferent to them. In the main, he judges them by the disturbance they entail and, like everyone else, deploys his resources to meet them. The idea of innovation, on the other hand, is improvement. Nevertheless, a man of this temperament will not himself be an ardent innovator. In the first place, he is not inclined to think that nothing is happening unless great changes are afoot and therefore he is not worried by the absence of innovation: the use and enjoyment of things as they are occupies most of his attention. Further, he is aware that not all innovation is, in fact, improvement; and he will think that to innovate without improving is either designed or inadvertent folly. Moreover, even when an innovation commends itself as a convincing improvement, he will look twice at its claims before accepting them. From his point of view, because every improvement involves change, the disruption entailed has always to be set against the benefit anticipated. But when he has satisfied himself about this, there will be other considerations to be taken into the account. Innovating is always an equivocal enterprise, in which gain and loss (even excluding the loss of familiarity) are so closely interwoven that it is exceedingly difficult to forecast the final upshot: there is no such thing as an unqualified improvement. For, innovating is an activity which generates not only the 'improvement' sought, but a new and complex situation of which this is only one of the components. The total change is always more extensive than the change designed; and the whole of what is entailed can neither be foreseen nor circumscribed. Thus, whenever there is innovation there is the certainty that the change will be greater than was intended, that there will be loss as well as gain and that the loss and the gain will not be equally distributed among the people affected; there is the chance that the benefits derived will be greater than those which were designed; and there is the risk that they will be off-set by changes for the worse.

From all this the man of conservative temperament draws some appropriate conclusions. First, innovation entails certain loss and possible gain, therefore, the onus of proof, to show that the proposed change may be expected to be on the whole beneficial, rests with the would-be innovator. Secondly, he believes that the more closely an innovation resembles growth (that is, the more clearly it is intimated in and not merely imposed upon the situation) the less likely it is to result in a preponderance of loss. Thirdly, he thinks that an innovation which is a response to some specific defect, one designed to redress some specific disequilibrium, is more desirable than one which springs from a notion of a generally improved condition of human circumstances, and is far more desirable than one generated by a vision of perfection. Consequently, he prefers small and limited innovations to large and indefinite. Fourthly, he favours a slow rather than a rapid pace, and pauses to observe current consequences and make appropriate adjustments. And lastly, he believes the occasion to be important; and, other things being equal, he considers the most favourable occasion for innovation to be when the projected change is most likely to be limited to what is intended and least likely to be corrupted by undesired and unmanageable consequences.

The disposition to be conservative is, then, warm and positive in respect of enjoyment, and correspondingly cool and critical in respect of change and innovation: these two inclinations support and elucidate one another. The man of conservative temperament believes that a known good is not lightly to be surrendered for an unknown better. He is not in love with what is dangerous and difficult; he is unadventurous; he has no impulse to sail uncharted seas; for him there is no magic in being lost, bewildered or shipwrecked. If he is forced to navigate the unknown, he sees virtue in heaving the lead every inch of the way. What others plausibly identify as timidity, he recognizes in himself as rational prudence; what others interpret as inactivity, he recognizes as a disposition to enjoy rather than to exploit. He is cautious, and he is disposed to indicate his assent or dissent, not in absolute, but in graduated terms. He eyes the situation in terms of its propensity to disrupt the familiarity of the features of his world.

How, then, are we to construe the disposition to be conservative in respect of politics? And in making this inquiry what I am interested in is not merely the intelligibility of this disposition in any set of circumstances, but its intelligibility in our own contemporary circumstances. . . .

Let us begin at what I believe to be the proper starting-place; not in the empyrean, but with ourselves as we have come to be. I and my neighbours, my associates, my compatriots, my friends, my enemies and those who I am indifferent about, are people engaged in a great variety of activities. We are apt to entertain a multiplicity of opinions on every conceivable subject and are disposed to change these beliefs as we grow tired of them or as they prove unserviceable. Each of us is pursuing a course of his own; and there is no project so unlikely that somebody will not be found to engage in it, no enterprise so foolish that somebody will not undertake it. There are those who spend their lives trying to sell copies of the Anglican Catechism to the Jews. And one half of the world is engaged in trying to make the other half want what it has hitherto never felt the lack of. We are all inclined to be passionate about our own concerns, whether it is making things or selling them, whether it is business or sport, religion or learning, poetry, drink or drugs. Each of us has preferences of his own. For some, the opportunities of making choices (which are numerous) are invitations readily accepted; others welcome them less eagerly or even find them burdensome. Some dream dreams of new and better worlds: others are more inclined to move in familiar paths or even to be idle. Some are apt to deplore the rapidity of change, others delight in it; all recognize it. At times we grow tired and fall asleep: it is a blessed relief to gaze in a shop window and see nothing we want; we are grateful for ugliness merely because it repels attention. But, for the most part, we pursue happiness by seeking the satisfaction of desires which spring from one another inexhaustably. We enter into relationships of interest and of emotion, of competition, partnership, guardianship, love, friendship, jealousy and hatred, some of which are more durable than others. We make agreements with one another; we have expectations about one another's conduct; we approve, we are indifferent and we disapprove. This multiplicity of activity and variety of opinion is apt to produce collisions: we pursue courses which cut across those of others, and we do not all approve the same sort of conduct. But, in the main, we get along with one another, sometimes by giving way, sometimes by standing fast, sometimes in a compromise. Our conduct consists of activity assimilated to that of others in small, and for the most part unconsidered and unobtrusive, adjustments.

Why all this should be so, does not matter. It is not necessarily so. A different condition of human circumstance can easily be imagined, and we know that elsewhere and at other times activity is, or has been, far less multifarious and changeful and opinion far less diverse and far less likely to provoke collision; but, by and large, we recognize this to be our condition. It is an acquired condition, though nobody designed or specifically chose it in preference to all others. It is the product, not of 'human nature' let loose, but of human beings impelled by an acquired love of making choices for themselves. And we know as little and as much about where it is leading us as we know about the fashion in hats of twenty years' time or the design of motor-cars.

Surveying the scene, some people are provoked by the absence of order and coherence which appears to them to be its dominant feature; its wastefulness, its frustration, its dissipation of human energy, its lack not merely of a premeditated destination but even of any discernible direction of movement. It provides an excitement similar to that of a stock-car race; but it has none of the satisfaction of a well-conducted business enterprise. Such people are apt to exaggerate the current disorder; the absence of plan is so conspicuous that the small adjustments, and even the more massive arrangements, which restrain the chaos seem to them nugatory; they have no feeling for the warmth of untidiness but only for its inconvenience. But what is significant is not the limitations of their powers of observation, but the turn of their thoughts. They feel that there ought to be something that ought to be done to convert this so-called chaos into order, for this is no way for rational human beings to be spending their lives. Like Apollo when he saw Daphne with her hair hung carelessly about her neck, they sigh and say to themselves: 'What if it were properly arranged.' Moreover, they tell us that they have seen in a dream the glorious, collisionless manner of living proper to all mankind, and this dream they understand as their warrant for seeking to remove the diversities and occasions of conflict which distinguish our current manner of living. Of course, their dreams are not all exactly alike; but they have this in common: each is a vision of a condition of human circumstance from which the occasion of conflict has been removed, a vision of human activity co-ordinated and set going in a single direction and of every resource being used to the full. And such people appropriately understand the office of government to be the imposition upon its subjects of the condition of human circumstances of their dream. To govern is to turn a private dream into a public and compulsory manner of living. Thus, politics becomes an encounter of dreams and the activity in which government is held to this understanding of its office and provided with the appropriate instruments. . . .

By one road or another, by conviction, by its supposed inevitability, by its alleged success, or even quite unreflectively, almost all politics today have become Rationalist or near-Rationalist.

The general character and disposition of the Rationalist are, I think, not difficult to identify. At bottom he stands (he always *stands*) for independence of mind on all occasions, for thought free from obligation to any authority save the authority of 'reason'. His circumstances in the modern world have made him contentious: he is the *enemy* of authority, of prejudice, of the merely traditional, customary or habitual. His mental attitude is at once sceptical and optimistic:

sceptical, because there is no opinion, no habit, no belief, nothing so firmly rooted or so widely held that he hesitates to question it and to judge it by what he calls his 'reason'; optimistic, because the Rationalist never doubts the power of his 'reason' (when properly applied) to determine the worth of a thing, the truth of an opinion or the propriety of an action. Moreover, he is fortified by a belief in a 'reason' common to all mankind, a common power of rational consideration, which is the ground and inspiration of argument: set up on his door is the precept of Parmenides—judge by rational argument. But besides this, which gives the Rationalist a touch of intellectual equalitarianism, he is something also of an individualist, finding it difficult to believe that anyone who can think honestly and clearly will think differently from himself. . . .

Now, of all worlds, the world of politics might seem the least amenable to rationalist treatment—politics, always so deeply veined with both the traditional, the circumstantial and the transitory. And, indeed, some convinced Rationalists have admitted defeat here: Clemenceau, intellectually a child of the modern Rationalist tradition (in his treatment of morals and religion, for example), was anything but a Rationalist in politics. But not all have admitted defeat. If we except religion, the greatest apparent victories of Rationalism have been in politics: it is not to be expected that whoever is prepared to carry his rationalism into the conduct of life will hesitate to carry it into the conduct of public affairs. . . .

The conduct of affairs, for the Rationalist, is a matter of solving problems, and in this no man can hope to be successful whose reason has become inflexible by surrender to habit or is clouded by the fumes of tradition. In this activity the character which the Rationalist claims for himself is the character of the engineer, whose mind (it is supposed) is controlled throughout by the appropriate technique and whose first step is to dismiss from his attention everything not directly related to his specific intentions. This assimilation of politics to engineering is, indeed, what may be called the myth of rationalist politics. And it is, of course, a recurring theme in the literature of Rationalism. The politics it inspires may be called the politics of the felt need; for the Rationalist, politics are always charged with the feeling of the moment. He waits upon circumstance to provide him with his problems, but rejects its aid in their solution. That anything should be allowed to stand between a society and the satisfaction of the felt needs of each moment in its history must appear to the Rationalist a piece of mysticism and nonsense. And his politics are, in fact, the rational solution of those practical conundrums which the recognition of the sovereignty of the felt need perpetually creates in the life of a society. Thus, political life is resolved into a succession of crises, each to be surmounted by the application of 'reason'. Each generation, indeed, each administration, should see unrolled before it the blank sheet of infinite possibility. And if by chance this *tabula rasa* has been defaced by the irrational scribblings of tradition-ridden ancestors, then the first task of the Rationalist must be to scrub it clean; as Voltaire remarked, the only way to have good laws is to burn all existing laws and to start afresh.*

Two other general characteristics of rationalist politics may be observed. They are the politics of perfection, and they are the politics of uniformity; either of these characteristics without the other denotes a different style of politics, the essence of rationalism is their combination. The evanescence of imperfection may be said to be the first item of the creed of the Rationalist. He is not devoid of humility; he can imagine a problem which would remain impervious to the onslaught of his own reason. But what he cannot imagine is politics which do not consist in solving problems, or a political problem of which there is no 'rational' solution at all. Such a problem must be counterfeit. And the 'rational' solution of any problem is, in its nature, the perfect solution. There is no place in his scheme for a 'best in the circumstances', only a place for 'the best'; because the function of reason is precisely to surmount circumstances. Of course, the Rationalist is not always a perfectionist in general, his mind governed in each occasion by a comprehensive Utopia; but invariably he is a perfectionist in detail. And from this politics of perfection springs the politics of uniformity; a scheme which does not recognize circumstance can have no place for variety. 'There must in the nature of things be one best form of government which all intellects, sufficiently roused from the slumber of savage ignorance, will be irresistibly incited to approve,' writes Godwin. This intrepid Rationalist states in general what a more modest believer might prefer to assert only in detail; but the principle holds—there may not be one universal remedy for all

* Cf. Plato, *Republic,* 501A. The idea that you can get rid of a law by burning it is characteristic of the Rationalist, who can think of a law only as something written down.

political ills, but the remedy for any particular ill is as universal in its application as it is rational in its conception. If the rational solution for one of the problems of a society has been determined, to permit any relevant part of the society to escape from the solution is, *ex hypothesi*, to countenance irrationality. There can be no place for preference that is not rational preference, and all rational preferences necessarily coincide. Political activity is recognized as the imposition of a uniform condition of perfection upon human conduct. . . .

I do not propose to criticize this jump to glory style of politics in which governing is understood as a perpetual take-over bid for the purchase of the resources of human energy in order to concentrate them in a single direction; it is not at all unintelligible, and there is much in our circumstances to provoke it. My purpose is merely to point out that there is another quite different understanding of government, and that it is no less intelligible and in some respects perhaps more appropriate to our circumstances.

The spring of this other disposition in respect of governing and the instruments of government—a conservative disposition—is to be found in the acceptance of the current condition of human circumstances as I have described it: the propensity to make our own choices and to find happiness in doing so, the variety of enterprises each pursued with passion, the diversity of beliefs each held with the conviction of its exclusive truth; the inventiveness, the changefulness and the absence of any large design; the excess, the over-activity and the informal compromise. And the office of government is not to impose other beliefs and activities upon its subjects, not to tutor or to educate them, not to make them better or happier in another way, not to direct them, to galvanize them into action, to lead them or to coordinate their activities so that no occasion of conflict shall occur; the office of government is merely to rule. This is a specific and limited activity, easily corrupted when it is combined with any other, and, in the circumstances, indispensable. The image of the ruler is the umpire whose business is to administer the rules of the game, or the chairman who governs the debate according to known rules but does not himself participate in it.

Now people of this disposition commonly defend their belief that the proper attitude of government towards the current condition of human circumstance is one of acceptance by appealing to certain general ideas. They contend that there is absolute value in the free play of human choice, that private property (the emblem of choice) is a natural right, that it is only in the enjoyment of diversity of opinion and activity that true belief and good conduct can be expected to disclose themselves. But I do not think that this disposition requires these or any similar beliefs in order to make it intelligible. Something much smaller and less pretentious will do: the observation that this condition of human circumstance is, in fact, current, and that we have learned to enjoy it and how to manage it; that we are not children *in statu pupillari* but adults who do not consider themselves under any obligation to justify their preference for making their own choices; and that it is beyond human experience to suppose that those who rule are endowed with a superior wisdom which discloses to them a better range of beliefs and activities and which gives them authority to impose upon their subjects a quite different manner of life. In short, if the man of this disposition is asked: Why ought governments to accept the current diversity of opinion and activity in preference to imposing upon their subjects a dream of their own? it is enough for him to reply: Why not? Their dreams are no different from those of anyone else; and if it is boring to have to listen to dreams of others being recounted, it is insufferable to be forced to re-enact them. We tolerate monomaniacs, it is our habit to do so; but why should we be *ruled* by them? Is it not (the man of conservative disposition asks) an intelligible task for a government to protect its subjects against the nuisance of those who spend their energy and their wealth in the service of some pet indignation, endeavouring to impose it upon everybody, not by suppressing their activities in favour of others of a similar kind, but by setting a limit to the amount of noise anyone may emit?

Nevertheless, if this acceptance is the spring of the conservative's disposition in respect of government, he does not suppose that the office of government is to do nothing. As he understands it, there is work to be done which can be done only in virtue of a genuine acceptance of current beliefs simply because they are current and current activities simply because they are afoot. And, briefly, the office he attributes to government is to resolve some of the collisions which this variety of beliefs and activities generates; to preserve peace, not by placing an interdict upon choice and upon the diversity that springs from the exercise of preference, not by imposing substantive uniformity, but by enforcing general rules of procedure upon all subjects alike. . . .

To some people, 'government' appears as a vast reservoir of power which inspires them to dream of what use might be made of it. They have favourite projects, of various dimensions, which they sincerely believe are for the benefit of mankind, and to capture this source of power, if necessary to increase it, and to use it for imposing their favourite projects upon their fellows is what they understand as the adventure of governing men. They are, thus, disposed to recognize government as an instrument of passion; the art of politics is to inflame and direct desire. In short, governing is understood to be just like any other activity—making and selling a brand of soap, exploiting the resources of a locality, or developing a housing estate—only the power here is (for the most part) already mobilized, and the enterprise is remarkable only because it aims at monopoly and because of its promise of success once the source of power has been captured. Of course a private enterprise politician of this sort would get nowhere in these days unless there were people with wants so vague that they can be prompted to ask for what he has to offer, or with wants so servile that they prefer the promise of a provided abundance to the opportunity of choice and activity on their own account. And it is not all as plain sailing as it might appear: often a politician of this sort misjudges the situation; and then, briefly, even in democratic politics, we become aware of what the camel thinks of the camel driver. . . .

It is not, then, mere stupid prejudice which disposes a conservative to take this view of the activity of governing; nor are any highfalutin metaphysical beliefs necessary to provoke it or make it intelligible. It is connected merely with the observation that where activity is bent upon enterprise the indispensable counterpart is another order of activity, bent upon restraint, which is unavoidably corrupted (indeed, altogether abrogated) when the power assigned to it is used for advancing favourite projects. An 'umpire' who at the same time is one of the players is no umpire; 'rules' about which we are not disposed to be conservative are not rules but incitements to disorder; the conjunction of dreaming and ruling generates tyranny.

Political conservatism is, then, not at all unintelligible in a people disposed to be adventurous and enterprising, a people in love with change and apt to rationalize their affections in terms of 'progress'. And one does not need to think that the belief in 'progress' is the most cruel and unprofitable of all beliefs, arousing cupidity without satisfying it, in order to think it inappropriate for a government to be conspicuously 'progressive'. Indeed, a disposition to be conservative in respect of government would seem to be pre-eminently appropriate to men who have something to do and something to think about on their own account, who have a skill to practise or an intellectual fortune to make, to people whose passions do not need to be inflamed, whose desires do not need to be provoked and whose dreams of a better world need no prompting. Such people know the value of a rule which imposes orderliness without directing enterprise, a rule which concentrates duty so that room is left for delight. They might even be prepared to suffer a legally established ecclesiastical order; but it would not be because they believed it to represent some unassailable religious truth, but merely because it restrained the indecent competition of sects and (as Hume said) moderated 'the plague of a too diligent clergy'.

Now, whether or not these beliefs recommend themselves as reasonable and appropriate to our circumstances and to the abilities we are likely to find in those who rule us, they and their like are in my view what make intelligible a conservative disposition in respect of politics. What would be the appropriateness of this disposition in circumstances other than our own, whether to be conservative in respect of government would have the same relevance in the circumstances of an unadventurous, a slothful or a spiritless people, is a question we need not try to answer: we are concerned with ourselves as we are. I myself think that it would occupy an important place in any set of circumstances. But what I hope I have made clear is that it is not at all inconsistent to be conservative in respect of government and radical in respect of almost every other activity. And, in my opinion, there is more to be learnt about this disposition from Montaigne, Pascal, Hobbes and Hume than from Burke or Bentham.

Of the many entailments of this view of things that might be pointed to, I will notice one, namely, that politics is an activity unsuited to the young, not on account of their vices but on account of what I at least consider to be their virtues.

Nobody pretends that it is easy to acquire or to sustain the mood of indifference which this manner of politics calls for. To rein-in one's own beliefs and desires, to acknowledge the current shape of things, to feel the balance of things in one's hand, to tolerate what is abominable, to distinguish between crime and sin, to respect formality even when it appears to be leading to error, these are difficult achievements; and they are achievements not to be looked for in the young.

Everybody's young days are a dream, a delightful insanity, a sweet solipsism. Nothing in them has a fixed shape, nothing a fixed price; everything is a possibility, and we live happily on credit. There are no obligations to be observed; there are no accounts to be kept. Nothing is specified in advance; everything is what can be made of it. The world is a mirror in which we seek the reflection of our own desires. The allure of violent emotions is irresistible. When we are young we are not disposed to make concessions to the world; we never feel the balance of a thing in our hands—unless it be a cricket bat. We are not apt to distinguish between our liking and our esteem; urgency is our criterion of importance; and we do not easily understand that what is humdrum need not be despicable. We are impatient of restraint; and we readily believe, like Shelley, that to have contracted a habit is to have failed. These, in my opinion, are among our virtues when we are young; but how remote they are from the disposition appropriate for participating in the style of government I have been describing. Since life is a dream, we argue (with plausible but erroneous logic) that politics must be an encounter of dreams, in which we hope to impose our own. Some unfortunate people, like Pitt (laughably called 'the Younger'), are born old, and are eligible to engage in politics almost in their cradles; others, perhaps more fortunate, belie the saying that one is young only once, they never grow up. But these are exceptions. For most there is what Conrad called the 'shadow line' which, when we pass it, discloses a solid world of things, each with its fixed shape, each with its own point of balance, each with its price; a world of fact, not poetic image, in which what we have spent on one thing we cannot spend on another; a world inhabited by others besides ourselves who cannot be reduced to mere reflections of our own emotions. And coming to be at home in this commonplace world qualifies us (as no knowledge of 'political science' can ever qualify us), if we are so inclined and have nothing better to think about, to engage in what the man of conservative disposition understands to be political activity.

II

Nature, Law, and History

Some kind of a belief in a higher law of nature which is above the ordinary man-made laws holds an important place in the thought of many, perhaps most, conservatives. There is, however, a minority tradition which is possibly a majority in the English-speaking world: the empiricist branch of conservatism, represented by Peel and Salisbury certainly and at least in great measure by Burke himself.

Although conservatives have had different views on the many varieties and nuances of natural law theories, they would all agree on the great principle that will, anyone's will, does not sanction law, does not compel us to obedience. As Burke told the electors of Bristol in 1774, "If government were a matter of will upon any side, yours, without question, ought to be superior. But government and legislation are matters of reason and judgment, and not inclination."

The idea that reason, rightly used within a moral tradition, must be our guide in matters of high politics—not the number of votes, the strength of armies, or the lineage of a king—was taught to the West by Cicero.

"There is in fact a true law," he wrote in the most famous single statement of the natural law philosophy, "—namely, right reason—which is in accordance with nature, applies to all men, and is unchangeable and eternal. By its commands, this law summons men to the performance of their duties; by its prohibitions it restrains them from doing wrong."

Cicero's great contribution to political thought is that he transmitted the theory of natural law of the Roman Stoic philosophers, together with its assumption that all men are equal in its light, to the Fathers of the Church, from whence it was carried through the Middle Ages into our own time.

Thomas Aquinas, the most influential of medieval thinkers, refined the notion of a higher law and applied it to the problems of his own age. Richard Hooker, writing three centuries later, interpreted the doctrine anew for an England troubled by disunity and civil disobedience. Hooker taught that man may recognize the rules of reason by the general assent of mankind. "That which all men have at all times learned, nature herself must needs have taught."

In the eighteenth century both Adam Smith and Edmund Burke spoke

118

often of the "laws of natural liberty." Burke rested his case against a British governor in India, Warren Hastings, on the principle that while Hastings might have been legally awarded arbitrary power he was nevertheless subject to the same higher law as all men. A few decades later, G. F. W. Hegel, in his monumental *Philosophy of Right,* was to offer a profound reinterpretation of natural law and of history which has influenced all political thought, conservative and liberal (as well as Marxist), ever since.

In our own century, such scholars as A. P. d'Entrèves (*Natural Law,* London, 1951) and Jacques Maritain (*True Humanism,* London, 1938) have continued the tradition of Cicero, Aquinas, and (in some of their moods) Locke and Burke. Leo Strauss, who taught for many years in German universities before he came to the United States, is certainly one of the most distinguished of these contemporary scholars. His *Natural Right and History* (Chicago, 1953) was immediately recognized as a most illuminating work on the importance of a belief in a natural law for the history of the West. He has had a preeminent influence on the contemporary development of political philosophy in North America as well as in Europe.

Although there had been a trend away from natural law concepts among most contemporary philosophers, it is interesting to note a new movement, in just the last few years, toward a reformulation of the old doctrines. H. L. A. Hart, for instance, has advanced the notion of a "minimum concept of natural law" in his study *The Concept of Law* (London, 1961). Stephen Toulmin in his *The Place of Reason in Ethics* (Cambridge, 1950) makes a compelling case that we should not abandon reason or surrender our judgment to a moral relativism just because we cannot fully accept the objectivist position in ethics.

Conservatism and liberalism, at their best, merge at this point (as they do at many points); so long as there is some outside standard of judgment—an individual's reason or conscience, an independent church or judiciary—no government can ever be absolute and no citizen can ever surrender *all* of his rights.

11 CICERO

True Law Is Right Reason

Marcus Tullius Cicero (106–43 B.C.) was the most prominent political philosopher of the Roman Republic. In the Stoic tradition, Cicero taught that all men are equal in their capacity to distinguish virtue from vice, that there is an eternal law of nature, a constitution of the universe, to which all men are equally subject, and that a "mixed government" is, on the whole, best. Although he was not an original thinker, his influence was great, both in his own time and in later ages. The selections here are from his two chief works; from Books I and II of the *Laws* and from Book III of the *Republic* (*Of The Commonwealth*).*

MARCUS. Once more, then, before we come to the individual laws, let us look at the character and nature of Law for fear that, though it must be the standard to which we refer everything, we may now and then be led astray by an incorrect use of terms, and forget the rational principles on which our laws must be based.

QUINTUS. Quite so, that is the correct method of exposition.

MARCUS. Well, then, I find that it has been the opinion of the wisest men that Law is not a product of human thought, nor is it any enactment of peoples, but something eternal which rules the whole universe by its wisdom in command and prohibition. Thus they have been accustomed to say that Law is the primal and ultimate mind of God, whose reason directs all things either by compulsion or restraint. Wherefore that Law, which the gods have given to the human race has been justly praised; for it is the reason and mind of a wise lawgiver applied to command and prohibition.

* From the English translation of Clinton Keyes (New York: G. P. Putnam's Sons, 1928).

QUINTUS. You have touched upon this subject several times before. But before you come to the laws of peoples please make the character of this heavenly Law clear to us, so that the waves of habit may not carry us away and sweep us into the common mode of speech on such subjects.

MARCUS. Ever since we were children, Quintus, we have learned to call, "If one summon another to court," and other rules of the same kind, laws. But we must come to the true understanding of the matter, which is as follows: this and other commands and prohibitions of nations have the power to summon to righteousness and away from wrongdoing; but this power is not merely older than the existence of nations and States, it is coeval with that God who guards and rules heaven and earth. For the divine mind cannot exist without reason, and divine reason cannot but have this power to establish right and wrong. No written law commanded that a man should take his stand on a bridge alone, against the full force of the enemy, and order the bridge broken down behind him; yet we shall not for that reason suppose that the heroic Cocles was not obeying the law of bravery and following its decrees in doing so noble a deed. Even if there was no written law against rape at Rome in the reign of Lucius Tarquinius, we cannot say on that account that Sextus Tarquinius did not break that eternal Law by violating Lucretia, the daughter of Tricipitinus. For reason did exist, derived from the Nature of the universe, urging men to right conduct and diverting them from wrongdoing, and this reason did not first become Law when it was written down, but when it first came into existence; and it came into existence simultaneously with the divine mind. Wherefore the true and primal Law, applied to command and prohibition, is the right reason of supreme Jupiter.

QUINTUS. I agree with you, brother, that what is right and true is also eternal, and does not begin or end with written statutes.

MARCUS. Therefore, just as that divine mind is the supreme Law, so, when (reason) is perfected in man (that also is Law; and this perfected reason exists) in the mind of the wise man; but those rules which, in varying forms and for the need of the moment, have been formulated for the guidance of nations, bear the title of laws rather by favour than because they are really such. For every law which really deserves that name is truly praiseworthy, as they prove by approximately the following arguments. It is agreed, of course, that laws were invented for the safety of citizens, the preservation of

States and the tranquillity and happiness of human life, and that those who first put statutes of this kind in force convinced their people that it was their intention to write down and put into effect such rules as, once accepted and adopted, would make possible for them an honourable and happy life; and when such rules were drawn up and put into force, it is clear that men called them 'laws.' From this point of view it can be readily understood that those who formulated wicked and unjust statutes for nations, thereby breaking their promises and agreements, put into effect anything but 'laws.' It may thus be clear that in the very definition of the term 'law' there inheres the idea and principle of choosing what is just and true. I ask you then, Quintus, according to the custom of the philosophers: if there is a certain thing, the lack of which in a State compels us to consider it no State at all, must we consider this thing a good?

QUINTUS. One of the greatest goods, certainly.

MARCUS. And if a State lacks Law, must it for that reason be considered no State at all?

QUINTUS. It cannot be denied.

MARCUS. Then Law must necessarily be considered one of the greatest goods.

QUINTUS. I agree with you entirely.

MARCUS. What of the many deadly, the many pestilential statutes which nations put into force? These no more deserve to be called laws than the rules a band of robbers might pass in their assembly. For if ignorant and unskilful men have prescribed deadly poisons instead of healing drugs, these cannot possibly be called physicians' prescriptions; neither in a nation can a statute of any sort be called a law, even though the nation, in spite of its being a ruinous regulation, has accepted it. Therefore Law is the distinction between things just and unjust, made in agreement with that primal and most ancient of all things, Nature; and in conformity to Nature's standard are framed those human laws which inflict punishment upon the wicked but defend and protect the good.

QUINTUS. I understand you completely and believe that from now on we must not consider or even call anything else a law. . . .

*　　*　　*

MARCUS. Now, let us investigate the origins of Justice.

Well, then, the most learned men have determined to begin with Law and it would seem that they are right, if, according to their definition, Law is the highest reason, implanted in Nature, which commands what ought to be done and forbids the opposite. This reason, when firmly fixed and fully developed in the human mind, is Law. And so they believe that Law is intelligence, whose natural function it is to command right conduct and forbid wrongdoing. They think that this quality has derived its name in Greek from the idea of granting to every man his own, and in our language I believe it has been named from the idea of choosing. For as they have attributed the idea of fairness to the word law, so we have given it that of selection, though both ideas properly belong to Law. Now if this is correct, as I think it to be in general, then the origin of Justice is to be found in Law, for Law is a natural force; it is the mind and reason of the intelligent man, the standard by which Justice and Injustice are measured. But, since our whole discussion has to do with the reasoning of the populace it will sometimes be necessary to speak in the popular manner and give the name of law to that which in written form decrees whatever it wishes, either by command or prohibition. For such is the crowd's definition of law. But, in determining what Justice is, let us begin with that supreme Law which had its origin ages before any written law existed or any State had been established.

QUINTUS. Indeed that will be preferable and more suitable to the character of the conversation we have begun.

MARCUS. Well, then, shall we seek the origin of Justice itself at its fountain-head? For, when that is discovered, we shall undoubtedly have a standard by which the things we are seeking may be tested.

QUINTUS. I think that is certainly what we must do.

ATTICUS. Put me down also as agreeing with your brother's opinion.

MARCUS. Since, then, we must retain and preserve that constitution of the State which Scipio proved to be the best in the six books devoted to the subject, and all our laws must be fitted to that type of State, and since we must also inculcate good morals, and not prescribe everything in writing, I shall seek the root of Justice in Nature, under whose guidance our whole discussion must be conducted.

ATTICUS. Quite right. Surely with her as our guide, it will be impossible for us to go astray.

MARCUS. Do you grant us, then, Pomponius (for I am aware of what Quintus thinks), that it is by the might of the immortal gods, or by their nature, reason, power, mind, will, or any other term which may make my meaning clearer, that all Nature is governed? For if you do not admit it, we must begin our argument with this problem before taking up anything else.

ATTICUS. Surely I will grant it, if you insist upon it, for the singing of the birds about us and the babbling of the streams relieve me from all fear that I may be overheard by any of my comrades in the school.

MARCUS. Yet you must be careful; for it is their way to become very angry at times, as virtuous men will; and they will not tolerate your treason, if they hear of it, to the opening passage of that excellent book, in which the author has written, "God troubles himself about nothing, neither his own concerns nor those of others."

ATTICUS. Continue, if you please, for I am eager to learn what my admission will lead to.

MARCUS. I will not make the argument long. Your admission leads us to this: that animal which we call man, endowed with foresight and quick intelligence, complex, keen, possessing memory, full of reason and prudence, has been given a certain distinguished status by the supreme God who created him; for he is the only one among so many different kinds and varieties of living beings who has a share in reason and thought, while all the rest are deprived of it. But what is more divine, I will not say in man only but in all heaven and earth, than reason? And reason when it is full grown and perfected is rightly called wisdom. Therefore, since there is nothing better than reason, and since it exists both in man and God, the first common possession of man and God is reason. But those who have reason in common must also have right reason in common. And since right reason is Law, we must believe that men have Law also in common with the gods. Further, those who share Law must also share Justice; and those who share these are to be regarded as members of the same commonwealth. If, indeed, they obey the same authorities and powers, this is true in a far greater degree; but as a matter of fact they do obey this celestial system, the divine mind, and the God of transcendent power. Hence we must now conceive of this whole universe as one commonwealth of which both gods and men are members. . . .

MARCUS. The points which are now being briefly touched upon are certainly important; but out of all the material of the philosophers' discussions, surely there comes nothing more valuable than the full realization that we were born for Justice, and that right is based, not upon men's opinions, but upon Nature. This fact will immediately be plain if you once get a clear conception of man's fellowship and union with his fellow-men. For no single thing is so like another, so exactly its counterpart, as all of us are to one another. Nay, if bad habits and false beliefs did not twist the weaker minds and turn them in whatever direction they are inclined, no one would be so like his own self as all men would be like all others. And so, however we may define man, a single definition will apply to all. This is sufficient proof that there is no difference in kind between man and man; for if there were, one definition could not be applicable to all men; and indeed reason, which alone raises us above the level of the beasts and enables us to draw inferences, to prove and disprove, to discuss and solve problems, and to come to conclusions, is certainly common to us all, and, though varying in what it learns, at least in the capacity to learn it is invariable. For the same things are invariably perceived by the senses, and those things which stimulate the senses, stimulate them the same way in all men; and those rudimentary beginnings of intelligence to which I have referred, which are imprinted on our minds, are imprinted on all minds alike; and speech, the mind's inter-preter, though differing in the choice of words, agrees in the senti-ments expressed. In fact, there is no human being of any race who, if he finds a guide, cannot attain to virtue.

The similarity of the human race is clearly marked in its evil tend-encies as well as in its goodness, for pleasure also attracts all men; and even though it is an enticement to vice, yet it has some likeness to what is naturally good. For it delights us by its lightness and agree-ableness; and for this reason, by an error of thought, it is embraced as something wholesome. It is through a similar misconception that we shun death as though it were a dissolution of nature, and cling to life because it keeps us in the sphere in which we were born; and that we look upon pain as one of the greatest of evils, not only because of its cruelty, but also because it seems to lead to the des-truction of nature. In the same way, on account of the similarity be-tween moral worth and renown, those who are publicly honoured are considered happy, while those who do not attain fame are thought miserable. Troubles, joys, desires, and fears haunt the minds of all men without distinction, and even if different men have different beliefs, that does not prove, for example, that it is not the same quality of superstition that besets those races which worship dogs and cats as gods, as that which torments other races. But what nation does not love courtesy, kindliness, gratitude, and remembrance of favours bestowed? What people does not hate and despise the haughty, the wicked, the cruel, and the ungrateful? Inasmuch as these considerations prove to us that the whole human race is bound together in unity, it follows, finally, that knowledge of the principles of right living is what makes men better.

If you approve of what has been said, I will go on to what follows. But if there is anything that you care to have explained, we will take that up first.

ATTICUS. We have no questions, if I may speak for both of us.

MARCUS. The next point, then, is that we are so constituted by Nature as to share the sense of Justice with one another and to pass it on to all men. And in this whole discussion I want it understood that what I shall call Nature is (that which is implanted in us by Nature); that, however, the corruption caused by bad habits is so great that the sparks of fire, so to speak, which Nature has kindled in us are extinguished by this corruption, and the vices which are their opposites spring up and are established. But, if the judgments of men were in agreement with Nature, so that, as the poet says, they considered "nothing alien to them which concerns mankind," then Justice would be equally observed by all. For those creatures who have received the gift of reason from Nature have also received right reason, and therefore they have also received the gift of Law, which is right reason applied to command and prohibition. And if they have received Law, they have received Justice also. Now all men have received reason; therefore all men have received Justice. . . .

Now, all this is really a preface to what remains to be said in our discussion, and its purpose is to make it more easily understood that Justice is inherent in Nature. After I have said a few words more on this topic, I shall go on to the civil law, the subject which gives rise to all this discourse.

QUINTUS. You certainly need to say very little more on that head, for from what you have already said, Atticus is convinced, and certainly I am, that Nature is the source of Justice.

ATTICUS. How can I help being convinced, when it has just been proved to us, first, that we have been provided and equipped with what we may call the gifts of the gods; next, that there is only one principle by which men may live with one another, and that this is the same for all, and possessed equally by all; and, finally, that all men are bound together by a certain natural feeling of kindliness and good-will, and also by a partnership in Justice? Now that we have admitted the truth of these conclusions, and rightly, I think, how can we separate Law and Justice from Nature?

*   *   *

. . . True law is right reason in agreement with nature; it is of universal application, unchanging and everlasting; it summons to duty by its commands, and averts from wrongdoing by its prohibitions. And it does not lay its commands or prohibitions upon good men in vain, though neither have any effect on the wicked. It is a sin to try and alter this law, nor is it allowable to attempt to repeal any part of it, and it is impossible to abolish it entirely. We cannot be freed from its obligations by senate or people, and we need not look outside ourselves for an expounder or interpreter of it. And there will not be different laws at Rome and at Athens, or different laws now and in the future, but one eternal and unchangeable law will be valid for all nations and all times, and there will be one master and ruler, that is, God, over us all, for he is the author of this law, its promulgator, and its enforcing judge. Whoever is disobedient is fleeing from himself and denying his human nature, and by reason of this very fact he will suffer the worst penalties, even if he escapes what is commonly considered punishment. . . .

12 HOOKER

The Doctrine of Natural Law

Richard Hooker (1554–1600) studied at Corpus Christi College, Oxford, became a minister of the Church of England, and for many years taught theology at his old college. In 1594 he published the first book of his *The Laws of Ecclesiastical Polity**, often cited by John Locke, who called him "the judicious Hooker." Hooker's work is important as one of the last statements of the medieval tradition in English political thought; he carried forth the tradition of Cicero and Aquinas, applying philosophy of the natural law to the problems of his own time.

I am not ignorant that by law eternal the learned for the most part do understand the order, not which God hath eternally purposed himself in all his works to observe, but rather that which with himself he hath set down as expedient to be kept by all his creatures, according to the several condition wherewith he hath endued them. They who thus are accustomed to speak apply the name of *Law* unto that only rule of working which superior authority imposeth; whereas we somewhat more enlarging the sense thereof term any kind of rule or canon, whereby actions are framed, a law. Now that law which, as it is laid up in the bosom of God, they call *eternal*, receiveth according unto the different kinds of things which are subject unto it different and sundry kinds of names. That part of it which ordereth natural agents we call usually *nature's* law; that which Angels do clearly behold and without any swerving observe is a law *celestial* and heavenly; the law of *reason*, that which bindeth creatures reasonable in this world, and with which by reason they may most plainly perceive themselves bound; that which bindeth them, and is not known

---

* Ed. by R. Church (Oxford: Clarendon Press, 1882).

but by special revelation from God, *Divine* law; *human* law, that
which out of the law either of reason or of God men probably gathering to be expedient, they make it a law. All things therefore, which
are as they ought to be, are conformed unto *this second law eternal;*
and even those things which to this eternal law are not conformable,
are notwithstanding in some sort ordered by *the first eternal law.* For
what good or evil is there under the sun, what action correspondent
or repugnant unto the law which God hath imposed upon his creatures, but in or upon it God doth work according to the law which
himself hath eternally purposed to keep; that is to say, the *first law
eternal?* So that a twofold law eternal being thus made, it is not hard
to conceive how they both take place in all things. . . .

To take away all such mutual grievances, injuries, and wrongs,
there was no way but only by growing unto composition and agreement amongst themselves, by ordaining some kind of government
public, and by yielding themselves subject thereunto; that unto whom
they granted authority to rule and govern, by them the peace, tranquillity, and happy estate of the rest might be procured. Men always
knew that when force and injury was offered they might be defenders
of themselves; they knew that howsoever men may seek their own
commodity, yet if this were done with injury unto others it was not to
be suffered, but by all men and by all good means to be withstood;
finally they knew that no man might in reason take upon him to
determine his own right, and according to his own determination proceed in maintenance thereof, inasmuch as every man is towards himself and them whom he greatly affecteth partial; and therefore that
strifes and troubles would be endless, except they gave their common
consent all to be ordered by some whom they should agree upon:
without which consent there was no reason that one man should take
upon him to be lord or judge over another; because, although there
be according to the opinion of some very great and judicious men a
kind of natural right in the noble, wise, and virtuous, to govern them
which are of servile disposition; nevertheless for manifestation of this
their right, and men's more peaceable contentment on both sides, the
assent of them who are to be governed seemeth necessary.

To fathers within their private families nature hath given a supreme
power; for which cause we see throughout the world even from the
foundation thereof, all men have ever been taken as lords and lawful
kings in their own houses. Howbeit over a whole grand multitude

having no such dependency upon any one, and consisting of so many families as every politic society in the world doth, impossible it is that any should have complete lawful power, but by consent of men, or immediate appointment of God; because not having the natural superiority of fathers, their power must needs be either usurped, and then unlawful; or, if lawful, then either granted or consented unto by them over whom they exercise the same, or else given extraordinarily from God, unto whom all the world is subject. It is no improbable opinion therefore which the Arch-philosopher was of, that as the chiefest person in every household was always as it were a king, so when numbers of households joined themselves in civil society together, kings were the first kind of governors amongst them. Which is also (as it seemeth) the reason why the name of *Father* continued still in them, who of fathers were made rulers; as also the ancient custom of governors to do as Melchisedec, and being kings to exercise the office of priests, which fathers did at the first, grew perhaps by the same occasion.

Howbeit not this the only kind of regiment that hath been received in the world. The inconveniences of one kind have caused sundry other to be devised. So that in a word all public regiment of what kind soever seemeth evidently to have risen from deliberate advice, consultation, and composition between men, judging it convenient and behoveful; there being no impossibility in nature considered by itself, but that men might have lived without any public regiment. Howbeit, the corruption of our nature being presupposed, we may not deny but that the law of nature doth now require of necessity some kind of regiment; so that to bring things unto the first course they were in, and utterly to take away all kind of public government in the world, were apparently to overturn the whole world.

The case of man's nature standing therefore as it doth, some kind of regiment the law of nature doth require; yet the kinds thereof being many, nature tieth not to any one, but leaveth the choice as a thing arbitrary. At the first when some certain kind of regiment was once approved, it may be that nothing was then further thought upon for the manner of governing, but all permitted unto their wisdom and discretion which were to rule; till by experience they found this for all parts very inconvenient, so as the thing which they had devised for a remedy did indeed but increase the sore which it should have cured. They saw that to live by one man's will became the cause of all men's misery. This constrained them to come unto laws, wherein all men might see their duties beforehand, and know the penalties of transgressing them. If things be simply good or evil, and withal universally so acknowledged there needs no new law to be made for such things. The first kind therefore of things appointed by laws human containeth whatsoever being in itself naturally good or evil, is notwithstanding more secret than that it can be discerned by every man's present conceit, without some deeper discourse and judgment. In which discourse because there is difficulty and possibility many ways to err, unless such things were set down by laws, many would be ignorant of their duties which now are not, and many that know what they should do would nevertheless dissemble it, and to excuse themselves pretend ignorance and simplicity, which now they cannot.

And because the greatest part of men are such as prefer their own private good before all things, even that good which is sensual before whatsoever is most divine; and for that the labour of doing good, together with the pleasure arising from the contrary, doth make men for the most part slower to the one and proner to the other, than that duty prescribed them by law can prevail sufficiently with them: therefore unto laws that men do make for the benefit of men it hath seemed always needful to add rewards, which may more allure unto good than any hardness deterreth from it, and punishments, which may more deter from evil than any sweetness thereto allureth. Wherein as the generality is natural, *Virtue rewardable and vice punishable;* so the particular determination of the reward or punishment belongeth unto them by whom laws are made. Theft is naturally punishable, but the kind of punishment is positive, and such lawful as men shall think with discretion convenient by law to appoint.

In laws, that which is natural bindeth universally, that which is positive not so. To let go those kind of positive laws which men impose upon themselves, as by vow unto God, contract with men, or such like; somewhat it will make unto our purpose, a little more fully to consider what things are incident into the making of the positive laws for the government of them that live united in public society. Laws do not only teach what is good, but they enjoin it, they have in them a certain constraining force. And to constrain men unto any thing inconvenient doth seem unreasonable. Most requisite therefore it is that to devise laws which all men shall be forced to obey none but wise men be admitted. Laws are matters of principal consequence; men of common capacity and but ordinary judgment are not able (for how should they?) to discern what things are fittest for each kind and state of regiment. We cannot be ignorant how much our obedience unto laws dependeth upon this point. Let a man though never so justly oppose himself unto them that are disordered in their ways, and what one amongst them commonly doth not stomach at such contradiction, storm at reproof, and hate such as would reform them? Notwithstanding even they which brook it worst that men should tell them of their duties, when they are told the same by a law, think very well and reasonably of it. For why? They presume that the law doth speak with all indifferency; that the law hath no side-respect to their persons; that the law is as it were an oracle proceeded from wisdom and understanding.

Howbeit laws do not take their constraining force from the quality of such as devise them, but from that power which doth give them the strength of laws. That which we spake before concerning the power of government must here be applied unto the power of making laws whereby to govern; which power God hath over all: and by the natural law, whereunto he hath made all subject, the lawful power of making laws to command whole politic societies of men belongeth so properly unto the same entire societies, that for any prince or potentate of what kind soever upon earth to exercise the same of himself, and not either by express commission immediately and personally received from God, or else by authority derived at the first from their consent upon whose persons they impose laws, it is no better than mere tyranny.

Laws they are not therefore which public approbation hath not made so. But approbation not only they give who personally declare their assent by voice, sign, or act, but also when others do it in their names by right originally at the least derived from them. As in parliaments, councils, and the like assemblies, although we be not personally ourselves present, notwithstanding our assent is, by reason of others, agents there in our behalf. And what we do by others, no reason but that it should stand as our deed, no less effectually to bind us than if ourselves had done it in person. In many things assent is given, they that give it not imagining they do so, because the manner of their assenting is not apparent. As for example, when an absolute monarch commandeth his subjects that which seemeth good in his own discretion, hath not his edict the force of a law whether they approve or dislike it? Again, that which hath been received long sithence and is by custom now established, we keep as a law which we may not transgress; yet what consent was ever thereunto sought or required at our hands?

Of this point therefore we are to note, that sith men naturally have no full and perfect power to command whole politic multitudes of men, therefore utterly without our consent we could in such sort be at no man's commandment living. And to be commanded we do consent, when that society whereof we are part hath at any time before consented, without revoking the same after by the like universal agreement. Wherefore as any man's deed past is good as long as himself continueth; so the act of a public society of men done five hundred years sithence standeth as theirs who presently are of the same societies, because corporations are immortal; we were then alive in our predecessors, and they in their successors do live still. Laws therefore human, of what kind soever, are available by consent.

If here it be demanded how it cometh to pass that this being common unto all laws which are made, there should be found even in good laws so great variety as there is; we must note the reason hereof to be the sundry particular ends, whereunto the different disposition of that subject or matter, for which laws are provided, causeth them to have especial respect in making laws. A law there is mentioned amongst the Grecians whereof Pittacus is reported to have been author; and by that law it was agreed, that he which being overcome with drink did then strike any man, should suffer punishment double as much as if he had done the same being sober. No man could ever have thought this reasonable, that had intended thereby only to punish the injury committed according to the gravity of the fact: for who knoweth not that harm advisedly done is naturally less pardonable, and therefore worthy of the sharper punishment? But forasmuch as none did so usually this way offend as men in that case, which they wittingly fell into, even because they would be so much the more freely outrageous; it was for their public good, where such disorder was grown, to frame a positive law for remedy thereof accordingly. To this appertain those known laws of making laws; as that lawmakers must have an eye to the place where, and to the men amongst whom: that one kind of laws cannot serve for all kinds of regiment: that where the multitude beareth sway, laws that shall tend unto preservation of that state must make common smaller offices to go

by lot, for fear of strife and division likely to arise, by reason that
ordinary qualities sufficing for discharge of such offices, they could
not but by many be desired, and so with danger contended for, and
not missed without grudge and discontentment, whereas at an uncertain lot none can find themselves grieved, on whomsoever it
lighteth; contrariwise the greatest, whereof but few are capable, to
pass by popular election, that neither the people may envy such as
have those honours, inasmuch as themselves bestow them, and that
the chiefest may be kindled with desire to exercise all parts of rare
and beneficial virtue, knowing they shall not lose their labour by
growing in fame and estimation amongst the people: if the helm of
chief government be in the hands of a few of the wealthiest, that then
laws providing for continuance thereof must make the punishment of
contumely and wrong offered unto any of the common sort sharp
and grievous, that so the evil may be prevented whereby the rich are
most likely to bring themselves into hatred with the people, who are
not wont to take so great an offence when they are excluded from
honours and offices, as when their persons are contumeliously trodden
upon. In other kinds of regiment the like is observed concerning the
difference of positive laws, which to be every where the same is impossible and against their nature.

Now as the learned in the laws of this land observe, that our statutes
sometimes are only the affirmation or ratification of that which by
common law was held before; so here it is not to be omitted that
generally all laws human, which are made for the ordering of politic
societies, be either such as establish some duty whereunto all men
by the law of reason did before stand bound; or else such as make
that a duty now which before was none. The one sort we may for
distinction's sake call *mixedly*, and the other *merely* human. That
which plain or necessary reason bindeth men unto may be in sundry
considerations expedient to be ratified by human law. For example,
if confusion of blood in marriage, the liberty of having many wives
at once, or any other the like corrupt and unreasonable custom doth
happen to have prevailed far, and to have gotten the upper hand of
right reason with the greatest part, so that no way is left to rectify
such foul disorder without prescribing by law the same things which
reason necessarily *doth* enforce but is not *perceived* that so it doth;
or if many be grown unto that which the Apostle did lament in some,
concerning whom he writeth, saying, that *Even what things they natur-*

ally know, in those very things as beasts void of reason they corrupted themselves; or if there be no such special accident, yet forasmuch as the common sort are led by the sway of their sensual desires, and therefore do more shun sin for the sensible evils which follow it amongst men, than for any kind of sentence which reason doth pronounce against it; this very thing is cause sufficient why duties belonging unto each kind of virtue, albeit the law of reason teach them, should notwithstanding be prescribed even by human law. Which law in this case we term *mixed,* because the matter whereunto it bindeth is the same which reason necessarily doth require at our hands, and from the law of reason it differeth in the manner of binding only. For whereas men before stood bound in conscience to do as the law of reason teacheth, they are now by virtue of human law become constrainable, and if they outwardly transgress, punishable. As for laws which are *merely* human, the matter of them is any thing which reason doth but probably teach to be fit and convenient; so that till such time as law hath passed amongst men about it, of itself it bindeth no man. One example whereof may be this. Lands are by human law in some places after the owner's decease divided unto all his children, in some all descendeth to the eldest son. If the law of reason did necessarily require but the one of these two to be done, they which by law have received the other should be subject to that heavy sentence, which denounceth against all that decree wicked, unjust, and unreasonable things *woe*. Whereas now whichsoever be received there is no law of reason transgressed; because there is probable reason why either of them may be expedient, and for either of them more than probable reason there is not to be found.

Laws whether mixedly or merely human are made by politic societies: some, only as those societies are civilly united; some, as they are spiritually joined and make such a body as we call the Church. Of laws human in this later kind we are to speak in the third book following. Let it therefore suffice thus far to have touched the force wherewith almighty God hath graciously endued our nature, and thereby enabled the same to find out both those laws which all men generally are for ever bound to observe, and also such as are most fit for their behoof, who lead their lives in any ordered state of government.

Now besides that law which simply concerneth men as men, and that which belongeth unto them as they are men linked with others in some form of politic society, there is a third kind of law which toucheth all such several bodies politic, so far forth as one of them hath public commerce with another. And this third is the *law of nations*. Between men and beasts there is no possibility of sociable communion; because the well-spring of that communion is a natural delight which man hath to transfuse from himself into others, and to receive from others into himself, especially those things wherein the excellency of his kind doth most consist. The chiefest instrument of human communion therefore is speech, because thereby we impart mutually one to another the conceits of our reasonable understanding. And for that cause seeing beasts are not hereof capable, forasmuch as with them we can use no such conference, they being in degree, although above other creatures on earth to whom nature hath denied sense, yet lower than to be sociable companions of man to whom nature hath given reason; it is of Adam said that amongst the beasts *He found not for himself any meet companion*. Civil society doth more content the nature of man than any private kind of solitary living, because in society this good of mutual participation is so much larger than otherwise. Herewith notwithstanding we are not satisfied, but we covet (if it might be) to have a kind of society and fellowship even with all mankind. Which thing Socrates intending to signify professed himself a citizen, not of this or that commonwealth, but of the world. And an effect of that very natural desire in us, (a manifest token that we wish after a sort an universal fellowship with all men,) appeareth by the wonderful delight men have, some to visit foreign countries, some to discover nations not heard of in former ages, we all to know the affairs and dealings of other people, yea to be in league of amity with them: and this not only for traffic's sake, or to the end that when many are confederated each may make other the more strong, but for such cause also as moved the Queen of Saba to visit Salomon; and in a word, because nature doth presume that how many men there are in the world, so many Gods as it were there are, or at leastwise such they should be towards men.

Touching laws which are to serve men in this behalf; even as those laws of reason, which (man retaining his original integrity) had been sufficient to direct each particular person in all his affairs and duties, are not sufficient but require the access of other laws, now that man and his offspring are grown thus corrupt and sinful; again, as those laws of polity and regiment, which would have served men living in public society together with that harmless disposition which then they should have had, are not able now to serve, when men's iniquity is so hardly restrained within any tolerable bounds: in like manner, the national laws of mutual commerce between societies of that former and better quality might have been other than now, when nations are so prone to offer violence, injury, and wrong. Hereupon hath grown in every of these three kinds that distinction between *Primary* and *Secondary* laws; the one grounded upon sincere, the other built upon depraved nature. Primary laws of nations are such as concern embassage, such as belong to the courteous entertainment of foreigners and strangers, such as serve for commodious traffic, and the like. Secondary laws in the same kind are such as this present unquiet world is most familiarly acquainted with; I means laws of arms, which yet are much better known than kept. But what matter the law of nations doth contain I omit to search.

The strength and virtue of that law is such that no particular nation can lawfully prejudice the same by any their several laws and ordinances, more than a man by his private resolutions the law of the whole commonwealth or state wherein he liveth. For as civil law, being the act of the whole body politic, doth therefore overrule each several part of the same body; so there is no reason that any one commonwealth of itself should to the prejudice of another annihilate that whereupon the whole world hath agreed. For which cause, the Lacedemonians forbidding all access of strangers into their coasts are in that respect both by Josephus and Theodoret deservedly blamed, as being enemies to that hospitality which for common humanity's sake all the nations on earth should embrace. . . .

13 HEGEL

The State as Ethical Will

Georg W. F. Hegel (1770–1831) attempted to establish what Burke had taken for granted. He was convinced that general laws of society were discoverable by the use of reason; that the method of dialectic reason would also fruitfully apply to philosophy and the social sciences.

Unity and harmony held a high place in Hegel's system of values. His first important book, *The Phenomenology of Spirit,* was completed as Napoleon's troops entered the city of Jena, where Hegel was living; keenly aware of the significance of the historic events around him, he came to regard history as of crucial philosophic importance and indicative of laws of social development. A strong proponent of German unification in the post-Napoleonic period, he dominated German intellectual life as a professor of philosophy at the University of Berlin, where he was often called the leader of the intellectual bodyguard of the House of Hohenzollern. His scorn of paper constitutions and his emphasis on tradition and custom in opposition to liberal utilitarianism place him in the great tradition of Hume, Rousseau, and Burke as a profound conservative thinker.

The selection is taken from Chapters 1, 2, 3, and 4 of his chief political work, *The Philosophy of Right.** It is important to bear in mind in reading the selection that Hegel's use of the word "state" does not refer merely to the political structure of the government but to the entire organization of society which, in his view, finds its comprehensive organization in its political government.

The state is the realized ethical idea or ethical spirit. It is the will

* From the translation by S. W. Dyde (London: George Bell & Sons, 1821, 1896).

which manifests itself, makes itself clear and visible, substantiates itself. It is the will which thinks and knows itself, and carries out what it knows, and in so far as it knows. The state finds in ethical custom its direct and unreflected existence, and its indirect and reflected existence in the self-consciousness of the individual and in his knowledge and activity. Self-consciousness in the form of social disposition has its substantive freedom in the state, as the essence, purpose, and product of its activity. . . .

The state, which is the realized substantive will, having its reality in the particular self-consciousness raised to the plane of the universal, is absolutely rational. This substantive unity is its own motive and absolute end. In this end freedom attains its highest right. This end has the highest right over the individual, whose highest duty in turn is to be a member of the state.

Were the state to be considered as exchangeable with the civic society, and were its decisive features to be regarded as the security and protection of property and personal freedom, the interest of the individual as such would be the ultimate purpose of the social union. It would then be at one's option to be a member of the state.—But the state has a totally different relation to the individual. It is the objective spirit, and he has his truth, real existence, and ethical status only in being a member of it. Union, as such, is itself the true content and end, since the individual is intended to pass a universal life. His particular satisfactions, activities, and way of life have in this authenticated substantive principle their origin and result. . . .

The state as a completed reality is the ethical whole and the actualization of freedom. It is the absolute purpose of reason that freedom should be actualized. The state is the spirit, which abides in the world and there realizes itself consciously; while in nature it is realized only as the other of itself or the sleeping spirit. Only when it is present in consciousness, knowing itself as an existing object, is it the state. In thinking of freedom we must not take our departure from individuality or the individual's self-consciousness, but from the essence of self-consciousness. Let man be aware of it or not, this essence realizes itself as an independent power, in which particular persons are only phases. The state is the march of God in the world; its ground or cause is the power of reason realizing itself as will. When thinking of the idea of the state, we must not have in our mind any particular state, or particular institution, but must rather contemplate the idea, this actual God, by itself. Although a state may be declared to violate right principles and to be defective in various ways, it always contains the essential moments of its existence, if, that is to say, it belongs to the full formed states of our own time. But as it is more easy to detect short-comings than to grasp the positive meaning, one easily falls into the mistake of dwelling so much upon special aspects of the state as to overlook its inner organic being. The state is not a work of art. It is in the world, in the sphere of caprice, accident, and error. Evil behaviour can doubtless disfigure it in many ways, but the ugliest man, the criminal, the invalid, the cripple, are living men. The positive thing, the life, is present in spite of defects, and it is with this affirmative that we have here to deal. . . .

The state is the embodiment of concrete freedom. In this concrete freedom, personal individuality and its particular interests, as found in the family and civic community, have their complete development. In this concrete freedom, too, the rights of personal individuality receive adequate recognition. These interests and rights pass partly of their own accord into the interest of the universal. Partly, also, do the individuals recognize by their own knowledge and will the universal as their own substantive spirit, and work for it as their own end. Hence, neither is the universal completed without the assistance of the particular interest, knowledge, and will, nor, on the other hand, do individuals, as private persons, live merely for their own special concern. They regard the general end, and are in all their activities conscious of this end. The modern state has enormous strength and depth, in that it allows the principle of subjectivity to complete itself to an independent extreme of personal particularity, and yet at the same time brings it back into the substantive unity, and thus preserves particularity in the principle of the state. . . .

The political state is divided into three substantive branches:

(a) The power to fix and establish the universal. This is legislation.

(b) The power, which brings particular spheres and individual cases under the universal. This is the function of government.

(c) The function of the prince, as the subjectivity with which rests the final decision. In this function the other two are brought into an individual unity. It is at once the culmination and beginning of the whole. This is constitutional monarchy. . . .

The function of the prince contains of itself the three elements of the totality, (1) the universality of the constitution and the laws;

(2) counsel, or reference of the particular to the universal; and (3) the final decision, or the self-determination, into which all else returns and from which it receives the beginning of its actuality. This absolute self-determination, constituting the distinguishing principle of the princely function, as such, must be the first to be considered.

We begin with the princely function or the factor of individuality, because in it the three phases of the state are interrelated as a totality. The I is at once the most individual and the most universal. The individual occurs also in nature, but there reality is equal to non-ideality, and its parts exist externally to one another. Hence it is not self-complete existence; in it the different individualities subsist side by side. In spirit, on the other hand, all differences exist only as ideal or as a unity. The state as spiritual is the interpretation of all its elements, but individuality is at the same time the soul, the vital and sovereign principle, which embraces all differences.

The basal principle of the political state is the substantive unity, which is the ideality of its elements. In this ideality the particular functions and offices of the state are just as much dissolved as retained. Indeed, they are retained only as having no independent authority, but such and so extensive an authority as is yielded them in the idea of the whole. They proceed, therefore, from the power of the state, and are the flexible limbs of the state as of their own simplified self.

This ideality of elements is like the life of an organized body. Life exists in every part. There is but one life in all points, and there is no opposition to it. Any part separated from it is dead. Such is also the ideality of all individual occupations, functions, and corporations, great as may be their impulse to subsist and do for themselves. It is as in the organism, where the stomach assumes independence, and yet is at the same time superseded and sacrificed by becoming a member of one whole.

The particular offices and agencies of the state, being its essential elements, are intimately connected with it. To the individuals, who manage and control them, they are attached in virtue not of their direct personality but of their objective and universal qualities. With particular personality, as such, they are joined only externally and accidentally. The business and functions of the state cannot therefore be private property.

The agencies of the state are attached to individuals, who nevertheless are not authorized to discharge their offices through natural fitness, but by reason of their objective qualification. Capacity, skill, character, belong to the particularity of the individual, who must, however, be adapted to his special business by education and training. An office can, therefore, be neither sold nor bequeathed. Formerly in France seats in parliament were saleable, and this is still the case with any position of officer in the English army below a certain grade. These facts depended, or depend, upon the mediaeval constitution of certain states, and are now gradually vanishing.

These two characteristics, namely that the particular offices and functions of the state have independent and firm footing neither in themselves, nor in the particular will of individuals, but ultimately in the unity of the state as in their simple self, constitute the sovereignty of the state. . . .

Sovereignty, at first only the universal thought of this ideality, exists merely as a subjectivity assured of itself, and as the abstract and so far groundless self-direction and ultimate decision of the will; by virtue of this quality the state is individual and one. But in the next place subjectivity exists in its truth only as a subject, and personality as a person. In the constitution, which has matured into rational reality, each of the three elements of the conception has its own independent, real, and separate embodiment. Hence, the element which implies absolute decision is not individuality in general but one individual, the monarch.

The internal development of a science, whose whole content is deduced out of the simple conception—the only method which is deserving of the name philosophic,— reveals the peculiarity that one and the same conception, here the will, which at the beginning is abstract because it is the beginning, yet contains itself, condenses of itself its own characteristics, and in this way acquires a concrete content. Thus it is fundamental in the personality, which is at first in simple right abstract. It then develops itself through the different forms of subjectivity, and at last in absolute right, the state or the complete, concrete objectivity of the will, attains to the personality of the state and its conscious assurance of itself. This final term gives to all particularities a new form by taking them up into its pure self. It ceases to hesitate between reasons *pro* and *con,* and deciding by an "I will," initiates all action and reality.

Personality, further, or subjectivity generally, as infinite and self-referring, has truth only as a person or independent subject. This independent existence must be one, and the truth which it has is of the most direct or immediate kind. The personality of the state is actualized only as a person, the monarch.—Personality expresses the conception as such, while person contains also the actuality of the conception. Hence the conception becomes the idea or truth, only when it receives this additional character.—A so-called moral person, a society, congregation, or family, be it as concrete as it may, possesses personality only as an element and abstractly. It has not reached the truth of its existence. But the state is this very totality, in which the moments of the conception gain reality in accordance with their peculiar truth.—All these phases of the idea have been already explained, both in their abstract and in their concrete forms, in the course of this treatise. Here, however, they need to be repeated, because we, while easily admitting them piecemeal in their particular forms, do not so readily recognise and apprehend them in their true place as elements of the idea.

The conception of monarch offers great difficulty to abstract reasonings and to the reflective methods of the understanding. The understanding never gets beyond isolated determinations, and ascribes merit to mere reasons, or finite points of view and what can be derived from them. Thus the dignity of the monarch is represented as something derivative not only in its form but also in its essential character. But the conception of the monarch is not derivative, but purely self-originated. Akin to this mistaken notion is the idea that the right of the monarch is based upon and receives its unconditional nature from divine authority. The misconceptions that are allied to this idea are well-known; besides, philosophy sets itself the task of conceiving the divine.

The phrase "sovereignty of the people," can be used in the sense that a people is in general self-dependent in its foreign relations, and constitutes its own state. Such are the people of Great Britain, for example. But the people of England, Scotland, Ireland, Venice, Genoa, or Ceylon, have ceased to be a sovereign people, since they no longer have independent princes, and the chief government is not exclusively their own. Further, it may be said that internal sovereignty resides in the people if, as was already pointed out, we speak in general terms, and mean that sovereignty accrues to the whole state. But the sovereignty of the people is usually in modern times opposed to the sovereignty of the monarch. This view of the sovereignty of the people may be traced to a confused idea of what is meant by "the people." The people apart from their monarch, and the common membership necessarily and directly associated with him, is a formless mass. It is no longer a state. In it occur none of the characteristic features of an equipped whole, such as sovereignty, government, law-courts, magistrates, professions, etc., etc. When these elements of an organized national life make their appearance in a people, it ceases to be that undefined abstraction, which is indicated by the mere general notion "people." . . .

In the organization of the state, that is to say, in constitutional monarchy, we must have before us nothing except the inner necessity of the idea. Every other point of view must disappear. The state must be regarded as a great architectonic building, or the hieroglyph of reason, presenting itself in actuality. Everything referring merely to utility, externality, etc., must be excluded from a philosophic treatment. It is easy for one to grasp the notion that the state is the self-determining and completely sovereign will, whose judgment is final. It is more difficult to apprehend this "I will" as a person. By this is not meant that the monarch can be wilful in his acts. Rather is he bound to the concrete content of the advice of his councillors, and, when the constitution is established, he has often nothing to do but sign his name. But this name is weighty. It is the summit, over which nothing can climb. It may be said that an articulated organization has already existed in the beautiful democracy of Athens. Yet we see that the Greeks extracted the ultimate judgment from quite external phenomena, such as oracles, entrails of sacrificial animals, and the flight of birds, and that to nature they held as to a power, which in these ways made known and gave expression to what was good for mankind. Self-consciousness had at that time not yet risen to the abstraction of subjectivity, or to the fact that concerning the matter to be judged upon must be spoken a human "I will." This "I will" constitutes the greatest distinction between the ancient and the modern world, and so must have its peculiar niche in the great building of state. It is to be deplored that this characteristic should be viewed as something merely external, to be set aside or used at pleasure.

This ultimate self of the state's will is in this its abstraction an individuality, which is simple and direct. Hence its very conception implies that it is natural. Thus the monarch as a specific individual is abstracted from all other content, and is appointed to the dignity of monarch in a directly natural way, by natural birth. . . .

It is often maintained that the position of monarch gives to the affairs of state a haphazard character. It is said that the monarch may be ill-educated, and unworthy to stand at the helm of state, and that it is absurd for such a condition of things to exist under the name of reason. It must be replied that the assumption on which these objections proceed is of no value, since there is here no reference to particularity of character. In a completed organization we have to do with nothing but the extreme of formal decision, and that for this office is needed only a man who says "Yes," and so puts the dot upon the "i." The pinnacle of state must be such that the private character of its occupant shall be of no significance. What beyond this final judgment belongs to the monarch devolves upon particularity, with which we have no concern. There may indeed arise circumstances, in which this particularity alone has prominence, but in that case the state is not yet fully, or else badly constructed. In a well-ordered monarchy only the objective side of law comes to hand, and to this the monarch subjoins merely the subjective "I will."

Both elements, the final motiveless self of the will, and the like motiveless existence on the side of nature, indissolubly unite in the idea of that which is beyond the reach of caprice, and constitute the majesty of the monarch. In this unity lies the actualized unity of the state. Only by means of its unmotived directness on both its external and its internal side is the unity taken beyond the possibility of degradation to the wilfulness, ends, and views of particularity. It is thus removed also from the enfeeblement and overthrow of the functions of state and from the struggle of faction against faction around the throne.

Right of birth and right of inheritance constitute the basis of legitimacy, not as regards positive right merely, but likewise in the idea.— Through the self-determined or natural succession to the vacant throne all factious disputes are avoided. This has rightly been reckoned as one of the advantages of inheritance. However, it is only a consequence, and to assign it as a motive is to drag majesty down into the sphere of mere reasonings. The character of majesty is unmotived directness, and final self-involved existence. To speak of grounds is to propound as its basis not the idea of the state, which is internal to it, but something external in its nature and alien, such as the thought of the well-being of the state or of the people. By such a method inheritance can indeed be deduced through *medii termini;* but there might be other *medii termini* with quite other consequences. And it is only too well known what consequences may be drawn from the well-being of the people (*salut du peuple*).—Hence, philosophy ventures to contemplate majesty only in the medium of thought. Every other method of inquiry, except the speculative method of the infinite self-grounded idea, absolutely annuls the nature of majesty.

Freely to elect the monarch is readily taken as the most natural way. It is closely allied to the following shallow thought: —"Because it is the concern and interest of the people which the monarch has to provide for, it must be left to the people to choose whom it will depute to provide for them, and only out of such a commission arises the right of governing." This view, as well as the idea that the monarch is chief-officer of state, and also the idea of a contract between him and the people, proceed from the will of the multitude, in the form of inclination, opinion, and caprice. These views, as we long ago remarked, first make themselves good, or rather seek to do so, in the civic community. They can make no headway against the principle of the family, still less that of the state, or, in general, the idea of the ethical system.—That the election of a monarch is the worst of proceedings may be even by ratiocination detected in the consequences, which to it appear only as something possible or probable, but are in fact inevitable. Through the relation involved in free choice the particular will gives the ultimate decision, and the constitution becomes a free-capitulation, that is, the abandonment of the functions of state to the discretion of the particular will. The specific functions of state are thus transformed into private property, and there ensue the enfeeblement and injury of the sovereignty of the state, its internal dissolution and external overthrow.

If we are to apprehend the idea of the monarch, it is not sufficient for us to say that God has established kings, since God has made everything, even the worst of things. Nor can we proceed very far under the guidance of the principle of utility, since it is always open to point out disadvantages. Just as little are we helped by regarding monarchy as positive right. That I should have property is necessary, but this specific possession is accidental. Accidental also appears to be the right that one man should stand at the helm of state, if this right, too, be regarded as abstract and positive. But this right is present absolutely, both as a felt want and as a need of the thing itself. A monarch is not remarkable for bodily strength or intellect, and yet millions permit themselves to be ruled by him. To say that men permit themselves to be governed contrary to their interests, ends, and intentions is preposterous, since men are not so stupid. It is their need and the inner power of the idea which urge them to this in opposition to their seeming consciousness, and retain them in this relation. . . .

Decision is to be distinguished from its execution and application, and in general from the prosecution and preservation of what has been already resolved, namely, the existing laws, regulations, establishments for common ends, and the like. This business of subsumption or application is undertaken by the executive, including the judiciary and police. It is their duty directly to care for each particular thing in the civic community, and in these private ends make to prevail the universal interest. . . .

To secure the universal interest of the state and to preserve the law in the province of particular rights, and also to lead these rights back to the universal interest, require the attention of subordinates of the executive. These subordinates are on one side executive officers and on the other a college of advisers. These two meet together in the highest offices of all, which are in contact with the monarch. . . .

In the business of the executive also there is a division of labour. The organized executive officers have therefore a formal though difficult task before them. The lower concrete civil life must be governed from below in a concrete way. And yet the work must be divided into its abstract branches, specially officered by middlemen, whose activity in connection with those below them must from the lowest to the highest executive offices take the form of a continuous concrete oversight.

The main point which crops up in connection with the executive is the division of offices. This division is concerned with the transition from the universal to the particular and singular; and the business is to be divided according to the different branches. The difficulty is that the different functions, the inferior and superior, must work in harmony. The police and the judiciary proceed each on its own course, it is true, but they yet in some office or other meet again. The means used to effect this conjunction often consists in appointing the chancellor of state and the prime minister, ministers in council. The matter is thus simplified on its upper side. In this way also everything issues from above out of the ministerial power, and business is, as they say, centralized. . . . For some time past the chief task has been that of organization carried on from above: while the lower and bulky part of the whole was readily left more or less unorganized. Yet it is of high importance that it also should be organized, because only as an organism is it a power or force. Otherwise it is a mere heap or mass of broken bits. An authoritative power is found only in the organic condition of the particular spheres.

The offices of the executive are of an objective nature, which is already independently marked out in accordance with their substance. They are at the same time conducted by individuals. Between the objective element and individuals there is no direct, natural connecting tie. Hence individuals are not set aside for these offices by natural personality or by birth. There is required in them the objective element, namely, knowledge and proof of fitness. This proof guarantees to the state what it needs, and, as it is the sole condition, makes it possible for any citizen to devote himself to the universal class.

The subjective side is found in this, that out of many one individual must be chosen, and empowered to discharge the office. Since in this case the objective element does not lie in genius, as it does in art, the number of persons from whom the selection may be made is necessarily indefinite, and whom finally to prefer is beyond the possibility of absolute determination. The junction of individual and office, two phases whose relation is always accidental, devolves upon the princely power as decisive and sovereign.

The particular state-business, which monarchy transfers to executive officers, constitutes the objective side of the sovereignty inherent in the monarch. The distinguishing feature of this state-business is found in the nature of its matter. Just as the activity of the authorities is the discharge of a duty, so their office is not subject to chance but a right.

The individual, who by the act of the sovereign is given an official vocation, holds it on the condition that he discharges his duty, which is the substantive factor in his relation. By virtue of this factor the individual finds in his official employment his livelihood and the assured satisfaction of his particularity, and in his external surroundings and official activity is free from subjective dependence and influences. . . .

Security for the state and its subjects against misuse of power by the authorities and their officers is found directly in their responsibility arising out of their nature as a hierarchy. But it is also found in the legitimate societies and corporations. They hold in check the inflow of subjective wilfulness into the power of the officers. They also supplement from below the control from above, which cannot reach down to the conduct of individuals. . . .

Whether or no integrity of conduct, gentleness, and freedom from passion pass into social custom depends upon the nature of the direct ethical life and thought. These phases of character maintain the spiritual balance over against the merely mental acquisition of the so-called sciences, dealing with the objects of these spheres of government, against also the necessary practice of business, and the actual labour or mechanical and other trades. The greatness of the state is also a controlling element, by virtue of which the importance of family relations and other private ties is diminished, and revenge, hate, and the like passions become inoperative and powerless. In concern for the great interests of a large state, these subjective elements sink out of sight, and there is produced an habitual regard for universal interests and affairs.

The members of the executive and the state officials constitute the main part of the middle class, in which are found the educated intelligence and the consciousness of right of the mass of a people. The institutions of sovereignty operating from above and the rights of corporations from below prevent this class from occupying the position of an exclusive aristocracy and using their education and skill wilfully and despotically.

At one time the administration of justice, whose object is the peculiar interest of all individuals, had been converted into an instrument of gain and despotism. The knowledge of law was concealed under a pedantic or foreign speech, and the knowledge of legal procedure under an involved formalism.

The state's consciousness and the most conspicuous education are found in the middle class, to which the state officials belong. The members of this class, therefore, form the pillars of the state in regard to rectitude and intelligence. The state, if it has no middle class, is still at a low stage of development. In Russia, for example, there is a multitude of serfs and a host of rulers. It is of great concern to the state that a middle class should be formed, but this can be effected only in an organization such as we have described, namely, by the legalization of particular circles, which are relatively independent, and by a force of officials, whose wilfulness has no power over these legalized circles. Action in accordance with universal right, and the habit of such action, are consequences of the opposition produced by these self-reliant independent circles.

The legislature interprets the laws and also those internal affairs of the state whose content is universal. This function is itself a part of the constitution. In it the constitution is presupposed, and so far lies absolutely beyond direct delimitation. Yet it receives development in the improvement of the laws, and the progressive character of the universal affairs of government. . . .

These objects are defined in reference to individuals more precisely in two ways, (a) what of good comes to individuals to enjoy at the hands of the state, and (b) what they must perform for the state. The first division embraces the laws of private right in general, also the rights of societies and corporations. To these must be added universal institutions, and indirectly the whole of the constitution. But that which, on the other hand, is to be performed, is reduced to money as the existing universal value of things and services. Hence, it can be determined only in so equitable a way that the particular tasks and services, which the individual can perform, may be effected by his private will. . . .

In the legislative function in its totality are active both the monarchical element and the executive. The monarchical gives the final decision, and the executive element advises. The executive element has concrete knowledge and oversight of the whole in its many sides and in the actual principles firmly rooted in them. It has also acquaintance with the wants of the offices of state. In the legislature are at last represented the different classes or estates.

It proceeds from a wrong view of the state to exclude the members of the executive from the legislature, as was at one time done by the constituent assembly. In England the ministers are rightly members of parliament, since those who share in the executive should stand in connection with and not in opposition to the legislature. The idea that the functions of government should be independent contains the fundamental error that they should check one another. But this independence is apt to usurp the unity of the state, and unity is above all things to be desired.

By admitting the classes the legislature gives not simply implicit but actual existence to matters of general concern. The element of subjective formal freedom, the public consciousness, or the empirical universality of the views and thoughts of the many, here becomes a reality. . . .

There are found in current opinion so unspeakably many perverted and false notions and sayings concerning the people, the constitution, and the classes, that it would be a vain task to specify, explain, and correct them. When it is argued that an assembly of estates is necessary and advantageous, it is meant that the people's deputies, or, indeed, the people itself, must best understand their own interest, and that it has undoubtedly the truest desire to secure this interest. But it is rather true that the people, in so far as this term signifies a special part of the citizens, does not know what it wills. To know what we will, and further what the absolute will, namely reason, wills, is the fruit of deep knowledge and insight, and is therefore not the property of the people.

It requires but little reflection to see that the services performed by the classes in behalf of the general well-being and public liberty cannot be traced to an insight special to these classes. The highest state officials have necessarily deeper and more comprehensive insight into the workings and needs of the state, and also greater skill and wider practical experience. They are able without the classes to secure the best results, just as it is they who must continually do this when the classes are in actual assembly. General well-being does not therefore depend upon the particular insight of the classes, but is rather the achievement of the official deputies. They can inspect the work of the officers who are farthest removed from the observation of the chief functionaries of state. They, too, have a concrete perception of the more urgent special needs and defects. But to this intelligent oversight must be added the possibility of public censure. This possibility has the effect of calling out the best insight upon public affairs and projects, and also the purest motives; its influence is felt by the members of the classes themselves. As for the conspicuously good will, which is said to be shown by the classes towards the general interest, it has already been remarked that the masses, who in general adopt a negative standpoint, take for granted that the will of the government is evil or but little good. If this assumption were replied to in kind, it would lead to the recrimination that the classes, since they originate in individuality, the private standpoint and particular interests, are apt to pursue these things at the expense of the universal interest; while the other elements of the state, being already at the point of view of the state, are devoted to universal ends. As for the pledge to respect the public welfare and rational freedom, it should be given especially by the classes, but is shared in by all the other institutions of state. This guarantee is present in such institutions as the sovereignty of the monarch, hereditary succession, and the constitution of the law-courts, much more pronouncedly than in the classes. The classes, therefore, are specially marked out by their containing the subjective element of universal liberty. In them the peculiar insight and peculiar will of the sphere, which in this treatise has been called the civic community, is actualized in relation to the state. It is here as elsewhere by means of the philosophic point of view that this element is discerned to be a mark of the idea when developed to a totality. This inner necessity is not to be confounded with the external necessities and utilities of this phase of state activity.

The attitude of the government to the classes must not be in its essence hostile. The belief in the necessity of this hostile relation is a sad mistake. The government is not one party which stands over against another, in such a way that each is seeking to wrest something from the other. If the state should find itself in such a situation, it must be regarded as a misfortune and not as a sign of health. Further, the taxes, to which the classes give their consent, are not to be looked upon as a gift to the state, but are contributed for the interest of the contributors. The peculiar significance of the classes or estates is this, that through them the state enters into and begins to share in the subjective consciousness of the people. . . .

Of the classes of the civic community one contains the principle, which is really capable of filling this political position. This is the class, whose ethical character is natural. As its basis it has family life, and as regards subsistence it has the possession of the soil. As regards its particularity it has a will, which rests upon itself, and, in common with the princely function, it bears the mark of nature.

In its political position and significance this class becomes more clearly defined, when its means are made as independent of the wealth of the state as they are of the uncertainty of trade, the desire for gain. and the fluctuations of property. It is secure from the favour at once of the executive and of the multitude. It is further secured even from its own caprice, since the members of this class, who are called to this office, do without the rights exercised by the other citizens. They do not freely dispose of their property, nor do they divide it equally among their children, whom they love equally. This wealth becomes an inalienable inheritance burdened by primogeniture. . . .

The right of this part of the substantive class is based upon the nature-principle of the family. But through heavy sacrifices for the state this principle is transformed, and by the transformation this class is set apart for political activity. Hence it is called and entitled to this sphere by birth, without the accident of choice. It thus receives a stable substantive situation intermediate between the subjective caprice and the accidents of the two extremes. While it resembles the princely function, it participates in the wants and rights of the other extreme. It thus becomes a support at once to the throne and to the community.

Under the other part of the general class element is found the fluctuating side of the civic community, which externally because of its numerous membership, and necessarily because of its nature and occupation, takes part in legislation only through deputies. If the civic community appoints these deputies, it does so in accordance with its real nature. It is not a number of atoms gathering together merely for a particular and momentary act without any further bond of union, but a body systematically composed of constituted societies, communities, and corporations. These various circles receive in this way political unity. Through the just claim of this part to be repre- sented by a deputation to be summoned by the princely power, and also through the claim of the first part to make an appearance, the existence of the classes and of their assembly finds its peculiar con- stitutional guarantee. . . .

Counsels and decisions upon universal concerns require delegates, who are chosen under the belief that they have a better understanding of state business than the electors themselves. They are trusted to prosecute not the particular interest of a community or a corporation in opposition to the universal, but the universal only. Hence, to the deputies are not committed specific mandates or explicit instructions. But just as little has the assembly the character merely of a lively gathering of persons, each of whom is bent upon instructing, convinc- ing, and advising the rest. . . .

Deputies from the civic community should be acquainted with the particular needs and interests of the body which they represent, and also with the special obstacles which ought to be removed. They should therefore be chosen from amongst themselves. Such a delegation is naturally appointed by the different corporations of the civic community by a simple process, which is not disturbed by abstractions and atomistic notions. Thus they fulfil the point of view of the community directly, and either an election is altogether superfluous, or the play of opinion and caprice is reduced to a minimum.

It is a manifest advantage to have amongst the delegates individuals who represent every considerable special branch of the community, such as trade, manufacture, etc. These individuals must be thoroughly acquainted with their branch and belong to it. In the idea of a loose, indefinite election this important circumstance is given over to accident. Every branch, however, has an equal right to be represented. To regard the deputies as representatives has a significance that is organic and rational, only if they are not representatives of mere separate individuals or of a mere multitude, but of one of the essential spheres of the community and of its larger interests. Representation no longer means that one person should take the place of another. Rather is the interest itself actually present in the person of the representative, since he is there in behalf of his own objective nature. . . .

Of the two elements comprised under the classes, each brings into council a particular modification. As one of these elements has within the sphere of the classes the peculiar function of mediation, and that, too, between two things which both exist, it has a separate existence. The assembly of the classes is thus divided into two chambers.

By this separation the number of courts is increased, and there is a greater certainty of mature judgment. Moreover, an accidental decision, secured on the spur of the moment by a simple majority of the votes, is rendered much less probable. But these are not the main advantages. There is, besides, smaller opportunity or occasion for direct opposition to arise between the class element and the government. Or in the case when the mediating element is also found on the side of the lower chamber, the insight of this lower house becomes all the stronger, since it in this case appears to be more unpartisan and its opposition to be neutralized.

The classes are not the sole investigators of the affairs of state and sole judges of the general interest. Rather do they form merely an addition. Their distinctive trait is that, as they represent the members of the civic community who have no share in the government, it is through their co-operating knowledge, counsel, and judgment that the element of formal freedom attains its right. Besides, a general acquaintance with state affairs is more widely extended through the publicity given to the transactions of the classes.

By means of this avenue to knowledge public opinion first attains to true thoughts, and to an insight into the condition and conception of the state and its concerns. It thus first reaches the capacity of judging rationally concerning them. It learns, besides, to know and esteem the management, talents, virtues, and skill of the different officers of state. While these talents by receiving publicity are given a strong impulse towards development and an honourable field for exhibiting their worth, they are also an antidote for the pride of individuals and of the multitude, and are one of the best means for their education. . . .

Formal subjective freedom, implying that individuals as such should have and express their own judgment, opinion, and advice concerning affairs of state, makes its appearance in that aggregate, which is called public opinion. In it what is absolutely universal, substantive, and true is joined with its opposite, the independent, peculiar, and particular opinions of the many. This phase of existence is therefore the actual contradiction of itself; knowledge is appearance, the essential exists directly as the unessential. . . .

Public opinion deserves, therefore, to be esteemed and despised; to be despised in its concrete consciousness and expression, to be esteemed in its essential basis. At best, its inner nature makes merely an appearance in its concrete expression, and that, too, in a more or less troubled shape. Since it has not within itself the means of drawing distinctions, nor the capacity to raise its substantive side into definite knowledge, independence of it is the first formal condition of anything great and reasonable, whether in actuality or in science. Of any reasonable end we may be sure that public opinion will ultimately be pleased with it, recognize it, and constitute it one of its prepossessions.

In public opinion all is false and true, but to find out the truth in it is the affair of the great man. He who tells the time what it wills and means, and then brings it to completion, is the great man of the time. In his act the inner significance and essence of the time is actualized. Who does not learn to despise public opinion, which is one thing in one place and another in another, will never produce anything great. . . .

14 STRAUSS

Natural Rights, Reason, and History

Leo Strauss (1899–) was born in Hesse, Germany, received a PhD from the University of Hamburg, and taught political philosophy in German universities until 1938, when he accepted a professorship at the New School for Social Research in New York City. From there and from the University of Chicago, Strauss trained generations of graduate students in the thoughtful and careful reading of political texts until his recent semiretirement to a chair in the Claremont Graduate School in California. Few would dispute that any one of his books would have secured him a place among eminent political theorists, and many would say that he is the greatest teacher of politics of our time. His first major work was *The Political Philosophy of Hobbes* (1936), followed by *Natural Right and History* (1953) and *What Is Political Philosophy?* (1959). With Joseph Cropsey he has also edited *A History of Political Philosophy* (1963). The selection here is taken from Chapters 1, 3, and 4 of *Natural Right and History**, in which Strauss provides us with a contemporary defense of the Ciceronian tradition of natural law and a critique of recent trends toward a "value-free" social science.

Natural Right and the Historical Approach

The attack on natural right in the name of history takes, in most cases, the following form: natural right claims to be a right that is discernible by human reason and is universally acknowledged; but history (including anthropology) teaches us that no such right exists; instead of the supposed uniformity, we find an indefinite variety of

* (Chicago: The University of Chicago Press, 1953.) By permission.

notions of right or justice. Or, in other words, there cannot be natural right if there are no immutable principles of justice, but history shows us that all principles of justice are mutable. One cannot understand the meaning of the attack on natural right in the name of history before one has realized the utter irrelevance of this argument. In the first place, "consent of all mankind" is by no means a necessary condition of the existence of natural right. Some of the greatest natural right teachers have argued that, precisely if natural right is rational, its discovery presupposes the cultivation of reason, and therefore natural right will not be known universally: one ought not even to expect any real knowledge of natural right among savages.[1] In other words, by proving that there is no principle of justice that has not been denied somewhere or at some time, one has not yet proved that any given denial was justified or reasonable. Furthermore, it has always been known that different notions of justice obtain at different times and in different nations. It is absurd to claim that the discovery of a still greater number of such notions by modern students has in any way affected the fundamental issue. Above all, knowledge of the indefinitely large variety of notions of right and wrong is so far from being incompatible with the idea of natural right that it is the essential condition for the emergence of that idea: realization of the variety of notions of right is *the* incentive for the quest for natural right. If the rejection of natural right in the name of history is to have any significance, it must have a basis other than historical evidence. Its basis must be a philosophic critique of the possibility, or of the knowability, of natural right—a critique somehow connected with "history."

The conclusion from the variety of notions of right to the non-existence of natural right is as old as political philosophy itself. Political philosophy seems to begin with the contention that the variety of notions of right proves the nonexistence of natural right or the conventional character of all right.[2] We shall call this view "conventionalism." To clarify the meaning of the present-day rejection of natural right in the name of history, we must first grasp the specific

[1] Consider Plato *Republic* 456b12–c2, 452a7–8 and c6–d1; *Laches* 184d1–185a3; Hobbes, *De cive*, II, 1; Locke, *Two Treatises of Civil Government*, Book II, sec. 12, in conjunction with *An Essay on the Human Understanding*, Book I, chap. iii. Compare Rousseau, *Discours sur l'origine de l'inégalité*, Preface; Montesquieu, *De l'esprit des lois*, I, 1–2; also Marsilius *Defensor pacis* ii. 12. 8.

[2] Aristotle *Eth. Nic.* 1134b24–27.

difference between conventionalism, on the one hand, and "the historical sense" or "the historical consciousness" characteristic of nineteenth- and twentieth-century thought, on the other.[3]

Conventionalism presupposed that the distinction between nature and convention is the most fundamental of all distinctions. It implied that nature is of incomparably higher dignity than convention or the fiat of society, or that nature is the norm. The thesis that right and justice are conventional meant that right and justice have no basis in nature, that they are ultimately against nature, and that they have their ground in arbitrary decisions, explicit or implicit, of communities: they have no basis but some kind of agreement, and agreement may produce peace but it cannot produce truth. The adherents of the modern historical view, on the other hand, reject as mythical the premise that nature is the norm; they reject the premise that nature is of higher dignity than any works of man. On the contrary, either they conceive of man and his works, his varying notions of justice included, as equally natural as all other real things, or else they assert a basic dualism between the realm of nature and the realm of freedom or history. In the latter case they imply that the world of man, of human creativity, is exalted far above nature. Accordingly, they do not conceive of the notions of right and wrong as fundamentally arbitrary. They try to discover their causes; they try to make intelligible their variety and sequence; in tracing them to acts of freedom, they insist on the fundamental difference between freedom and arbitrariness.

What is the significance of the difference between the old and the modern view? Conventionalism is a particular form of classical philosophy. There are obviously profound differences between conven-

---

3 The legal positivism of the nineteenth and twentieth centuries cannot be simply identified with either conventionalism or historicism. It seems, however, that it derives its strength ultimately from the generally accepted historicist premise (see particularly Karl Bergbohm, *Jurisprudenz und Rechtsphilosophie*, I [Leipzig, 1892], 409 ff.). Bergbohm's strict argument against the possibility of natural right (as distinguished from the argument that is meant merely to show the disastrous consequences of natural right for the positive legal order) is based on "the undeniable truth that nothing eternal and absolute exists except the One Whom man cannot comprehend, but only divine in a spirit of faith" (p. 416 n.), that is, on the assumption that "the standards with reference to which we pass judgment on the historical, positive law . . . are themselves absolutely the progeny of their time and are always historical and relative" (p. 450 n.).

tionalism and the position taken by Plato, for example. But the classical opponents agree in regard to the most fundamental point: both admit that the distinction between nature and convention is fundamental. For this distinction is implied in the idea of philosophy. Philosophizing means to ascend from the cave to the light of the sun, that is, to the truth. The cave is the world of opinion as opposed to knowledge. Opinion is essentially variable. Men cannot live, that is, they cannot live together, if opinions are not stabilized by social fiat. Opinion thus becomes authoritative opinion or public dogma or Weltanschauung. Philosophizing means, then, to ascend from public dogma to essentially private knowledge. The public dogma is originally an inadequate attempt to answer the question of the all-comprehensive truth or of the eternal order.[4] Any inadequate view of the eternal order is, from the point of view of the eternal order, accidental or arbitrary; it owes its validity not to its intrinsic truth but to social fiat or convention. The fundamental premise of conventionalism is, then, nothing other than the idea of philosophy as the attempt to grasp the eternal. The modern opponents of natural right reject precisely this idea. According to them, all human thought is historical and hence unable ever to grasp anything eternal. Whereas, according to the ancients, philosophizing means to leave the cave, according to our contemporaries all philosophizing essentially belongs to a "historical world," "culture," "civilization," "Weltanschauung," that is, to what Plato had called the cave. We shall call this view "historicism."

We have noted before that the contemporary rejection of natural right in the name of history is based, not on historical evidence, but on a philosophic critique of the possibility or knowability of natural right. We note now that the philosophic critique in question is not particularly a critique of natural right or of moral principles in general. It is a critique of human thought as such. Nevertheless, the critique of natural right played an important role in the formation of historicism.

Historicism emerged in the nineteenth century under the protection of the belief that knowledge, or at least divination, of the eternal is possible. But it gradually undermined the belief which had sheltered it in its infancy. It suddenly appeared within our lifetime in its mature form. The genesis of historicism is inadequately understood. In the present state of our knowledge, it is difficult to say at what point in

[4] Plato *Minos* 314b10–315b2.

the modern development the decisive break occurred with the "unhistorical" approach that prevailed in all earlier philosophy. For the purpose of a summary orientation it is convenient to start with the moment when the previously subterranean movement came to the surface and began to dominate the social sciences in broad daylight. That moment was the emergence of the historical school. . . .

*   *   *

All natural right doctrines claim that the fundamentals of justice are, in principle, accessible to man as man. They presuppose, therefore, that a most important truth can, in principle, be accessible to man as man. Denying this presupposition, radical historicism asserts that the basic insight into the essential limitation of all human thought is not accessible to man as man, or that it is not the result of the progress or the labor of human thought, but that it is an unforeseeable gift of unfathomable fate. It is due to fate that the essential dependence of thought on fate is realized now, and was not realized in earlier times. Historicism has this in common with all other thought, that it depends on fate. It differs from all other thought in this, that, thanks to fate, it has been given to realize the radical dependence of thought on fate. We are absolutely ignorant of the surprises which fate may have in store for later generations, and fate may in the future again conceal what it has revealed to us; but this does not impair the truth of that revelation. One does not have to transcend history in order to see the historical character of all thought: there is a privileged moment, an absolute moment in the historical process, a moment in which the essential character of all thought becomes transparent. In exempting itself from its own verdict, historicism claims merely to mirror the character of historical reality or to be true to the facts; the self-contradictory character of the historicist thesis should be charged not to historicism but to reality.

The assumption of an absolute moment in history is essential to historicism. In this, historicism surreptitiously follows the precedent set in a classic manner by Hegel. Hegel had taught that every philosophy is the conceptual expression of the spirit of its time, and yet he maintained the absolute truth of his own system of philosophy by ascribing absolute character to his own time; he assumed that his own time was the end of history and hence the absolute moment. Historicism explicitly denies that the end of history has come, but it implicitly asserts the opposite: no possible future change of orientation can legitimately make doubtful the decisive insight into the inescapable dependence of thought on fate, and therewith into the essential character of human life; in the decisive respect the end of history, that is, of the history of thought, has come. But one cannot simply assume that one lives or thinks in the absolute moment; one must show, somehow, how the absolute moment can be recognized as such. According to Hegel, the absolute moment is the one in which philosophy, or quest for wisdom, has been transformed into wisdom, that is, the moment in which the fundamental riddles have been fully solved. Historicism, however, stands or falls by the denial of the possibility of theoretical metaphysics and of philosophic ethics or natural right; it stands or falls by the denial of the solubility of the fundamental riddles. According to historicism, therefore, the absolute moment must be the moment in which the insoluble character of the fundamental riddles has become fully manifest or in which the fundamental delusion of the human mind has been dispelled. . . .

The Origin of the Idea of Natural Right

To understand the problem of natural right, one must start, not from the "scientific" understanding of political things but from their "natural" understanding, i.e., from the way in which they present themselves in political life, in action, when they are our business, when we have to make decisions. This does not mean that political life necessarily knows of natural right. Natural right had to be discovered, and there was political life prior to that discovery. It means merely that political life in all its forms necessarily points toward natural right as an inevitable problem. Awareness of this problem is not older than political science but coeval with it. Hence a political life that does not know of the idea of natural right is necessarily unaware of the possibility of political science and, indeed, of the possibility of science as such, just as a political life that is aware of the possibility of science necessarily knows natural right as a problem.

The idea of natural right must be unkown as long as the idea of nature is unknown. The discovery of nature is the work of philosophy. Where there is no philosophy, there is no knowledge of natural right as such. The Old Testament, whose basic premise may be said to be the implicit rejection of philosophy, does not know "nature": the Hebrew term for "nature" is unknown to the Hebrew Bible. It goes without saying that "heaven and earth," for example, is not the same thing as "nature." There is, then, no knowledge of natural right as such in the Old Testament. The discovery of nature necessarily precedes the discovery of natural right. Philosophy is older than political philosophy.

Philosophy is the quest for the "principles" of all things, and this means primarily the quest for the "beginnings" of all things or for "the first things." In this, philosophy is at one with myth. But the *philosophos* ("lover of wisdom") is not identical with the *philomythos* ("lover of myth"). Aristotle calls the first philosophers simply "men who discoursed on nature" and distinguishes them from the men who preceded them and "who discoursed on gods." [5] Philosophy as distinguished from myth came into being when nature was discovered, or the first philosopher was the first man who discovered nature. The whole history of philosophy is nothing but the record of the ever repeated attempts to grasp fully what was implied in that crucial discovery which was made by some Greek twenty-six hundred years ago or before. To understand the meaning of that discovery in however provisional a manner, one must return from the idea of nature to its prephilosophic equivalent.

The purport of the discovery of nature cannot be grasped if one understands by nature "the totality of phenomena." For the discovery of nature consists precisely in the splitting-up of that totality into phenomena which are natural and phenomena which are not natural: "nature" is a term of distinction. Prior to the discovery of nature, the characteristic behavior of any thing or any class of things was conceived of as its custom or its way. That is to say, no fundamental distinction was made between customs or ways which are always and everywhere the same and customs or ways which differ from tribe to tribe. Barking and wagging the tail is the way of dogs, menstruation is the way of women, the crazy things done by madmen are the way of madmen, just as not eating pork is the way of Jews and not drinking wine is the way of Moslems. "Custom" or "way" is the prephilosophic equivalent of "nature."

While every thing or every class of things has its custom or way, there is a particular custom or way which is of paramount importance: "our" way, the way of "us" living "here," the way of life of the

---

[5] Aristotle *Metaphysics* 981b27–29, 982b18 (cf. *Nicomachean Ethics* 1117b33–35), 983b7 ff., 1071b26–27; Plato *Laws* 891c, 892c2–7; 896a5–b3.

independent group to which a man belongs. We may call it the "paramount" custom or way. Not all members of the group remain always in that way, but they mostly return to it if they are properly reminded of it: the paramount way is the right path. Its rightness is guaranteed by its oldness: "There is a sort of presumption against novelty, drawn out of a deep consideration of human nature and human affairs; and the maxim of jurisprudence is well laid down, *Vetustas pro lege semper habetur.*" But not everything old everywhere is right. "Our" way is the right way because it is both old and "our own" or because it is both "home-bred and prescriptive." [6] Just as "old and one's own" originally was identical with right or good, so "new and strange" originally stood for bad. The notion connecting "old" and "one's own" is "ancestral." Prephilosophic life is characterized by the primeval identification of the good with the ancestral. Therefore, the right way necessarily implies thoughts about the ancestors and hence about the first things simply.[7]

For one cannot reasonably identify the good with the ancestral if one does not assume that the ancestors were absolutely superior to "us," and this means that they were superior to all ordinary mortals; one is driven to believe that the ancestors, or those who established the ancestral way, were gods or sons of gods or at least "dwelling near the gods." The identification of the good with the ancestral leads to the view that the right way was established by gods or sons of gods or pupils of gods: the right way must be a divine law. Seeing that the ancestors are ancestors of a distinct group, one is led to believe that there is a variety of divine laws or codes, each of which is the work of a divine or semidivine being.[8]

Originally, the questions concerning the first things and the right way

[6] Burke, *Letters on a Regicide Peace,* i and iv; cf. Herodotus iii. 38 and i. 8.

[7] "The right way" would seem to be the link between "way" (or "custom") in general and "the first things," i.e., between the roots of the two most important meanings of "nature": "nature" as essential character of a thing or a group of things and "nature" as "the first things." For the second meaning see Plato's *Laws* 891c1–4 and 892c2–7. For the first meaning, consider Aristotle's as well as the Stoic's reference to "way" in their definitions of nature (Aristotle *Physics* 193b13–19, 194a27–30, and 199a9–10; Cicero *De natura deorum* ii. 57 and 81). When "nature" is denied, "custom" is restored to its original place. Compare Maimonides *Guide of the Perplexed* i. 71 and 73; and Pascal, *Pensées,* ed. Brunschvicg, Frags. 222, 233, 92.

[8] Plato *Laws* 624a1–6, 634e1–2, 662c7, d7–e7; *Minos* 318c1–3; Cicero *Laws* ii. 27; cf. Fustel de Coulanges, *La Cité antique,* Part III, chap. xi.

are answered before they are raised. They are answered by authority. For authority as the right of human beings to be obeyed is essentially derivative from law, and law is originally nothing other than the way of life of the community. The first things and the right way cannot become questionable or the object of a quest, or philosophy cannot emerge, or nature cannot be discovered, if authority as such is not doubted or as long as at least any general statement of any being whatsoever is accepted on trust.[9] The emergence of the idea of natural right presupposes, therefore, the doubt of authority.

Plato has indicated by the conversational settings of his *Republic* and his *Laws* rather than by explicit statements how indispensable doubt of authority or freedom from authority is for the discovery of natural right. In the *Republic* the discussion of natural right starts long after the aged Cephalus, *the* father, the head of the house, has left to take care of the sacred offerings to the gods: the absence of Cephalus, or of what he stands for, is indispensable for the quest for natural right. Or, if you wish, men like Cephalus do not need to know of natural right. Besides, the discussion makes the participants wholly oblivious of a torch race in honor of a goddess which they were supposed to watch—the quest for natural right replaces that torch race. The discussion recorded in the *Laws* takes place while the participants, treading in the footsteps of Minos, who, being the son and pupil of Zeus, had brought the Cretans their divine laws, are walking from a Cretan city to the cave of Zeus. Whereas their conversation is recorded in its entirety, nothing is said of whether they arrived at their initial goal. The end of the *Laws* is devoted to the central theme of the *Republic:* natural right, or political philosophy and the culmination of political philosophy, replace the cave of Zeus. If we take Socrates as the representative of the quest for natural right, we may illustrate the relation of that quest to authority as follows: in a community governed by divine laws, it is strictly forbidden to subject these laws to genuine discussion, i.e., to critical examination, in the presence of young men; Socrates, however, discusses natural right—a subject whose discovery presupposes doubt of the ancestral or divine code—not only in the presence of young men but in conversation with them. Some time before Plato, Hero-

---

[9] Cf. Plato *Charmides* 161c3–8 and *Phaedrus* 275c1–3 with *Apology of Socrates* 21b6–c2; cf. also Xenophon *Apology of Socrates* 14–15 with *Cyropaedia* vii. 2. 15–17.

dotus had indicated this state of things by the place of the only debate which he recorded concerning the principles of politics: he tells us that the free discussion took place in truth-loving Persia after the slaughter of the Magi.[10] This is not to deny that, once the idea of natural right has emerged and become a matter of course, it can easily be adjusted to the belief in the existence of divinely revealed law. We merely contend that the predominance of that belief prevents the emergence of the idea of natural right or makes the quest for natural right infinitely unimportant: if man knows by divine revelation what the right path is, he does not have to discover that path by his unassisted efforts.

The original form of the doubt of authority and therefore the direction which philosophy originally took or the perspective in which nature was discovered were determined by the original character of authority. The assumption that there is a variety of divine codes leads to difficulties, since the various codes contradict one another. One code absolutely praises actions which another code absolutely condemns. One code demands the sacrifice of one's first-born son, whereas another code forbids all human sacrifices as an abomination. The burial rites of one tribe provoke the horror of another. But what is decisive is the fact that the various codes contradict one another in what they suggest regarding the first things. The view that the gods were born of the earth cannot be reconciled with the view that the earth was made by the gods. Thus the question arises as to which code is the right code and which account of the first things is the true account. The right way is now no longer guaranteed by authority; it becomes a question or the object of a quest. The primeval identification of the good with the ancestral is replaced by the fundamental distinction between the good and the ancestral; the quest for the right way or for the first things is the quest for the good as distinguished from the ancestral.[11] It will prove to be the quest for what is good by nature as distinguished from what is good merely by convention.

The quest for the first things is guided by two fundamental distinctions which antedate the distinction between the good and the ancestral. Men must always have distinguished (e.g., in judicial matters)

---

[10] Plato *Laws* 634d7–635a5; cf. *Apology of Socrates* 23c2 ff. with *Republic* 538c5–e6; Herodotus iii. 76 (cf. i. 132).

[11] Plato *Republic* 538d3–4 and e5–6; *Statesman* 296c8–9; *Laws* 702c5–8; Xenophon *Cyropaedia* ii. 2. 26; Aristotle *Politics* 1269a3–8, 1271b23–24.

between hearsay and seeing with one's own eyes and have preferred what one has seen to what he has merely heard from others. But the use of this distinction was originally limited to particular or subordinate matters. As regards the most weighty matters—the first things and the right way—the only source of knowledge was hearsay. Confronted with the contradiction between the many sacred codes, someone—a traveler, a man who had seen the cities of many men and recognized the diversity of their thoughts and customs—suggested that one apply the distinction between seeing with one's own eyes and hearsay to all matters, and especially to the most weighty matters. Judgment on, or assent to, the divine or venerable character of any code or account is suspended until the facts upon which the claims are based have been made manifest or demonstrated. They must be made manifest—manifest to all, in broad daylight. Thus man becomes alive to the crucial difference between what his group considers unquestionable and what he himself observes; it is thus that the I is enabled to oppose itself to the We without any sense of guilt. But it is not the I as I that acquires that right. Dreams and visions had been of decisive importance for establishing the claims of the divine code or of the sacred account of the first things. By virtue of the universal application of the distinction between hearsay and seeing with one's own eyes, a distinction is now made between the one true and common world perceived in waking and the many untrue and private worlds of dreams and visions. Thus it appears that neither the We of any particular group or a unique I, but man as man, is the measure of truth and untruth, of the being or nonbeing of all things. Finally, man thus learns to distinguish between the names of things which he knows through hearsay and which differ from group to group and the things themselves which he, as well as any other human being, can see with his own eyes. He thus can start to replace the arbitrary distinctions of things which differ from group to group by their "natural" distinctions.

The divine codes and the sacred accounts of the first things were said to be known not from hearsay but by way of superhuman information. When it was demanded that the distinction between hearsay and seeing with one's own eyes be applied to the most weighty matters, it was demanded that the superhuman origin of all alleged superhuman information must be proved by examination in the light, not, for example, of traditional criteria used for distinguishing between true and false oracles, but of such criteria as ultimately derive in an evident manner from the rules which guide us in matters fully accessible to human knowledge. The highest kind of human knowledge that existed prior to the emergence of philosophy or science was the arts. The second prephilosophic distinction that originally guided the quest for the first things was the distinction between artificial or man-made things and things that are not man-made. Nature was discovered when man embarked on the quest for the first things in the light of the fundamental distinctions between hearsay and seeing with one's own eyes, on the one hand, and between things made by man and things not made by man, on the other. The first of these two distinctions motivated the demand that the first things must be brought to light by starting from what all men can see now. But not all visible things are an equally adequate starting point for the discovery of the first things. The man-made things lead to no other first things than man, who certainly is not the first thing simply. The artificial things are seen to be inferior in every respect to, or to be later than, the things that are not made but found or discovered by man. The artificial things are seen to owe their being to human contrivance or to forethought. If one suspends one's judgment regarding the truth of the sacred accounts of the first things, one does not know whether the things that are not man-made owe their being to forethought of any kind, i.e., whether the first things originate all other things by way of forethought, or otherwise. Thus one realizes the possibility that the first things originate all other things in a manner fundamentally different from all origination by way of forethought. The assertion that all visible things have been produced by thinking beings or that there are any superhuman thinking beings requires henceforth a demonstration: a demonstration that starts from what all can see now.[12]

In brief, then, it can be said that the discovery of nature is identical with the actualization of a human possibility which, at least according to its own interpretation, is trans-historical, trans-social, trans-moral, and trans-religious.[13] . . .

[12] Plato *Laws* 888c–889c, 891 c1–9, 892c2–7, 966d6–967e1. Aristotle *Metaphysics* 989b29–990a5, 1000a9–20, 1042a3 ff.; *De caelo* 298b13–24. Thomas Aquinas *Summa theologica* i. qu. 2, *a.* 3.

[13] This view is still immediately intelligible, as can be seen, to a certain extent, from the following remark of A. N. Whitehead: "After Aristotle, ethical and religious interests began to influence metaphysical conclusion. . . .

Classic Natural Right

Man is by nature a social being. He is so constituted that he cannot live, or live well, except by living with others. Since it is reason or speech that distinguishes him from the other animals, and speech is communication, man is social in a more radical sense than any other social animal: humanity itself is sociality. Man refers himself to others, or rather he is referred to others, in every human act, regardless of whether that act is "social" or "antisocial." His sociality does not proceed, then, from a calculation of the pleasures which he expects from association, but he derives pleasure from association because he is by nature social. Love, affection, friendship, pity, are as natural to him as concern with his own good and calculation of what is conducive to his own good. It is man's natural sociality that is the basis of natural right in the narrow or strict sense of right. Because man is by nature social, the perfection of his nature includes the social virtue par excellence, justice; justice and right are natural. All members of the same species are akin to one another. This natural kinship is deepened and transfigured in the case of man as a consequence of his radical sociality. In the case of man the individual's concern with procreation is only a part of his concern with the preservation of the species. There is no relation of man to man in which man is absolutely free to act as he pleases or as it suits him. And all men are somehow aware of this fact. Every ideology is an attempt to justify before one's self or others such courses of action as are somehow felt to be in need of justification, i.e., as are not obviously right. Why did the Athenians believe in their autochthony, except because they knew that robbing others of their land is not just and because they felt that a self-respecting society cannot become reconciled to the notion that its foundation was laid in crime? [14]   Why do the Hindus believe in

It may be doubted whether any properly general metaphysics can ever, without the illicit introduction of other considerations, get much further than Aristotle" (*Science and the Modern World* [Mentor Books ed.], pp. 173–74). Cf. Thomas Aquinas *Summa theologica* i. 2. qu. 58, *a*. 4–5, and qu. 104, *a*. 1; ii. 2, qu. 19, *a*. 7, and qu. 45, *a* 3 (on the relation of philosophy to morality and religion).

[14] Plato *Republic* 369b5–370b2; *Symposium* 207a6–c1; *Laws* 776d5–778a6; Aristotle *Politics* 125a7–18, 1278b18–25; *Nicomachean Ethics* 1161b1–8 (cf. Plato *Republic* 395e5) and 1170b10–14; *Rhetoric* 1373b6–9; Isocrates *Panegyricus* 23–24;; Cicero *Republic* i. 1, 38–41; iii. 1–3, 25; iv. 3; *Laws* i. 30, 33–35, 43; *De finibus* ii. 45, 78, 109–10; iii. 62–71; iv. 17–18; Grotius *De jure belli*, Prolegomena, §§ 6–8.

their *karma* doctrine if not because they know that otherwise their caste system would be indefensible? By virtue of his rationality, man has a latitude of alternatives such as no other earthly being has. The sense of this latitude, of this freedom, is accompanied by a sense that the full and unrestrained exercise of that freedom is not right. Man's freedom is accompanied by a sacred awe, by a kind of divination that not everything is permitted.[15]   We may call this awe-inspired fear "man's natural conscience." Restraint is therefore as natural or as primeval as freedom. As long as man has not cultivated his reason properly, he will have all sorts of fantastic notions as to the limits set to his freedom; he will elaborate absurd taboos. But what prompts the savages in their savage doings is not savagery but the divination of right.

Man cannot reach his perfection except in society or, more precisely, in civil society. Civil society, or the city as the classics conceived of it, is a closed society and is, in addition, what today would be called a "small society." A city, one may say, is a community in which everyone knows, not indeed every other member, but at least an acquaintance of every other member. A society meant to make man's perfection possible must be kept together by mutual trust, and trust presupposes acquaintance. Without such trust, the classics thought, there cannot be freedom; the alternative to the city, or a federation of cities, was the despotically ruled empire (headed, if possible, by a deified ruler) or a condition approaching anarchy. A city is a community commensurate with man's natural powers of firsthand or direct knowledge. It is a community which can be taken in in one view, or in which a mature man can find his bearings through his own observation, without having to rely habitually on indirect information in matters of vital importance. For direct knowledge of men can safely be replaced by indirect knowledge only so far as the individuals who make up the political multitude are uniform or "mass-men." Only a society small enough to permit mutual trust is small enough to permit mutual responsibility or supervision—the supervision of actions or manners which is indispensable for a society concerned with the perfection of its members; in a very large city, in "Babylon," everyone can live more or less as he lists. Just as man's natural power of firsthand knowledge, so his power of love or of active concern, is by nature limited; the limits of the city coincide with the range of man's

15 Cicero *Republic* v. 6; *Laws* i. 24, 40; *De finibus* iv. 18.

active concern for nonanonymous individuals. Furthermore, political freedom, and especially that political freedom that justifies itself by the pursuit of human excellence, is not a gift of heaven; it becomes actual only through the efforts of many generations, and its preservation always requires the highest degree of vigilance. The probability that all human societies should be capable of genuine freedom at the same time is exceedingly small. For all precious things are exceedingly rare. An open or all-comprehensive society would consist of many societies which are on vastly different levels of political maturity, and the chances are overwhelming that the lower societies would drag down the higher ones. An open or all-comprehensive society will exist on a lower level of humanity than a closed society, which, through generations, has made a supreme effort toward human perfection. The prospects for the existence of a good society are therefore greater if there is a multitude of independent societies than if there is only one independent society. If the society in which man can reach the perfection of his nature is necessarily a closed society, the distinction of the human race into a number of independent groups is according to nature. This distinction is not natural in the sense that the members of one civil society are by nature different from the members of others. Cities do not grow like plants. They are not simply based on common descent. They come into being through human actions. There is an element of choice and even of arbitrariness involved in the "settling together" of these particular human beings to the exclusion of others. This would be unjust only if the condition of those excluded were impaired by their exclusion. But the condition of people who have not yet made any serious effort toward the perfection of human nature is, of necessity, bad in the decisive respect; it cannot possibly be impaired by the mere fact that those among them whose souls have been stirred by the call to perfection do make such efforts. Besides, there is no necessary reason why those excluded should not form a civil society of their own. Civil society as a closed society is possible and necessary in accordance with justice, because it is in accordance with nature.[16]

If restraint is as natural to man as is freedom, and restraint must

---

[16] Plato *Republic* 423a5–c5; *Laws* 681c4–d5, 708b1–d7, 738d6–e3 ff.; Aristotle *Nicomachean Ethics* 1158a10–18, 1170b20–1171a20; *Politics* 1253a30–31, 1276a27 –34 (cf. Thomas Aquinas, *ad loc.*), 1326a9–b26; Isocrates *Antidosis* 171–72; Cicero *Laws* ii. 5; cf. Thomas, *Summa theologica* i. qu. 65, a. 2, ad 3.

in many cases be forcible restraint in order to be effective, one cannot say that the city is conventional or against nature because it is coercive society. Man is so built that he cannot achieve the perfection of his humanity except by keeping down his lower impulses. He cannot rule his body by persuasion. This fact alone shows that even despotic rule is not per se against nature. What is true of self-restraint, self-coercion, and power over one's self applies in principle to the restraint and co-ercion of others and to power over others. To take the extreme case, despotic rule is unjust only if it is applied to beings who can be ruled by persuasion or whose understanding is sufficient: Prospero's rule over Caliban is by nature just. Justice and coercion are not mutually exclusive; in fact, it is not altogether wrong to describe justice as a kind of benevolent coercion. Justice and virtue in general are neces-sarily a kind of power. To say that power as such is evil or corrupting would therefore amount to saying that virtue is evil or corrupting. While some men are corrupted by wielding power, others are improved by it: "power will show a man." [17]

The full actualization of humanity would then seem to consist, not in some sort of passive membership in civil society, but in the proper-ly directed activity of the statesman, the legislator, or the founder. Serious concern for the perfection of a community requires a higher degree of virtue than serious concern for the perfection of an indi-vidual. The judge and ruler has larger and nobler opportunities to act justly than the ordinary man. The good man is not identical simply with the good citizen but with the good citizen who exercises the function of a ruler in a good society. It is then something more solid than the dazzling splendor and clamor that attends high office and something more noble than the concern with the well-being of their bodies which induces men to pay homage to political greatness. Being sensitive to mankind's great objects, freedom and empire, they sense somehow that politics is the field on which human excellence can show itself in its full growth and on whose proper cultivation every form of excellence is in a way dependent. Freedom and empire are desired as elements or conditions of happiness. But the feelings which are stirred by the very words "freedom" and "empire" point to a more adequate understanding of happiness than that which underlies the

[17] Plato *Republic* 372b7–8 and 607a4, 519e4–520a5, 561d5–7; *Laws* 689e ff.; Aristotle *Nicomachean Ethics* 1130a1–2, 1180a14–22; *Politics* 1254a18–20, b5–6; 1255a3–22, 1325b7 ff.

identification of happiness with the well-being of the body or the gratification of vanity; they point to the view that happiness or the core
of happiness consists in human excellence. Political activity is then
properly directed if it is directed toward human perfection or virtue.
The city has therefore ultimately no other end than the individual.
The morality of civil society or of the state is the same as the morality
of the individual. The city is essentially different from a gang of robbers because it is not merely an organ, or an expression, of collective
selfishness. Since the ultimate end of the city is the same as that of the
individual, the end of the city is peaceful activity in accordance with
the dignity of man, and not war and conquest.[18]

Since the classics viewed moral and political matters in the light
of man's perfection, they were not egalitarians. Not all men are equally
equipped by nature for progress toward perfection, or not all
"natures" are "good natures." While all men, i.e., all normal men,
have the capacity for virtue, some need guidance by others, whereas
others do not at all or to a much lesser degree. Besides, regardless of
differences of natural capacity, not all men strive for virtue with
equal earnestness. However great an influence must be ascribed to the
way in which men are brought up, the difference between good and
bad upbringing is partly due to the difference between a favorable
and an unfavorable natural "environment." Since men are then unequal in regard to human perfection, i.e., in the decisive respect, equal
rights for all appeared to the classics as most unjust. They contended
that some men are by nature superior to others and therefore, according to natural right, the rulers of others. It is sometimes suggested
that the view of the classics was rejected by the Stoics and especially
by Cicero and that this change marks an epoch in the development
of natural right doctrine or a radical break with the natural right
doctrine of Socrates, Plato, and Aristotle. But Cicero himself, who
must be supposed to have known what he was talking about, was
wholly unaware of a radical difference between Plato's teaching and
his own. The crucial passage in Cicero's *Laws*, which according to a
common view is meant to establish egalitarian natural right, is, in
fact, meant to prove man's natural sociality. In order to prove man's

18 Thucydides iii. 45. 6; Plato *Gorgias* 464b3–c3, 478a1–b5, 521d6–e1; *Clitopho*
408b2–5; *Laws* 628b6–e1, 645b1–8; Xenophon *Memorabilia* ii. 1. 17; iii. 2. 4;
iv. 2. 11; Aristotle *Nicomachean Ethics* 1094b7–10, 1129b25–1130a8; *Politics*
1278b1–5; 1324b23–41, 1333b39 ff.; Cicero *Republic* i. 1; iii. 10–11, 34–41; vi.
13, 16; Thomas Aquinas, *De regimine principum* i. 9.

natural sociality, Cicero speaks of all men being similar to one another, i.e., akin to one another. He presents the similarity in question as the natural basis of man's benevolence to man: *simile simili gaudet.* It is a comparatively unimportant question whether an expression used by Cicero in this context might not be indicative of a slight bias in favor of egalitarian conceptions. It suffices to remark that Cicero's writings abound with statements which reaffirm the classical view that men are unequal in the decisive respect and which reaffirm the political implications of that view.[19]

In order to reach his highest stature, man must live in the best kind of society, in the kind of society that is most conducive to human excellence. The classics called the best society the best *politeia.* By this expression they indicated, first of all, that, in order to be good, society must be civil or political society, a society in which there exists government of men and not merely administration of things. *Politeia* is ordinarily translated by "constitution." But when using the term "constitution" in a political context, modern men almost inevitably mean a legal phenomenon, something like the fundamental law of the land, and not something like the constitution of the body or of the soul. Yet *politeia* is not a legal phenomenon. The classics used *politeia* in contradistinction to "laws." The *politeia* is more fundamental than any laws; it is the source of all laws. The *politeia* is rather the factual distribution of power within the community than what constitutional law stipulates in regard to political power. The *politeia* may be defined by laws, but it need not be. The laws regarding a *politeia* may be deceptive, unintentionally and even intentionally, as to the true character of the *politeia.* No law, and hence no constitution, can be the fundamental political fact, because all laws depend on human beings. Laws have to be adopted, preserved, and administered by men. The human beings making up a political community may be "arranged" in greatly different ways in regard to the control of communal affairs. It is primarily the factual "arrangement" of human beings in regard to political power that is meant by *politeia.*

The American Constitution is not the same thing as the American

[19] Plato *Republic* 374e4–376c6, 431c5–7, 485a4–487a5; Xenophon *Memorabilia* iv. 1. 2; *Hiero* 7. 3; Aristotle *Nicomachean Ethics* 1099b18–20, 1095b 10–13, 1179b7–1180a10, 1114a31–b25; *Politics* 1254a29–31, 1267b7, 1327b18–39; Cicero *Laws* i. 28–35; *Republic* i. 49, 52; iii. 4, 37–38; *De finibus* iv. 21, 56; v. 69; *Tusc. Disp.* ii. 11, 13; iv. 31–32; v. 68; *Offices* i. 105, 107. Thomas Aquinas, *Summa theologica* i. qu. 96, *a.* 3 and 4.

way of life. *Politeia* means the way of life of a society rather than its constitution. Yet it is no accident that the unsatisfactory translation "constitution" is generally preferred to the translation "way of life of a society." When speaking of constitution, we think of government; we do not necessarily think of government when speaking of the way of life of a community. When speaking of *politeia,* the classics thought of the way of life of a community as essentially determined by its "form of government." We shall translate *politeia* by "regime," taking regime in the broad sense in which we sometimes take it when speaking, e.g., of the Ancien Régime of France. The thought connecting "way of life of a society" and "form of government" can provisionally be stated as follows: The character, or tone, of a society depends on what the society regards as most respectable or most worthy of admiration. But by regarding certain habits or attitudes as most respectable, a society admits the superiority, the superior dignity, of those human beings who most perfectly embody the habits or attitudes in question. That is to say, every society regards a specific human type (or a specific mixture of human types) as authoritative. When the authoritative type is the common man, everything has to justify itself before the tribunal of the common man; everything which cannot be justified before the tribunal becomes, at best, merely tolerated, if not despised or suspect. And even those who do not recognize that tribunal are, willy-nilly, molded by its verdicts. What is true of the society ruled by the common man applies also to societies ruled by the priest, the wealthy merchant, the war lord, the gentleman, and so on. In order to be truly authoritative, the human beings who embody the admired habits or attitudes must have the decisive say within the community in broad daylight: they must form the regime. When the classics were chiefly concerned with the different regimes, and especially with the best regime, they implied that the paramount social phenomenon, or that social phenomenon than which only the natural phenomena are more fundamental, is the regime.[20]

[20] Plato *Republic* 497a3–5, 544d6–7; *Laws* 711c5–8. Xenophon *Ways and Means* 1. 1; *Cyropaedia* i. 2. 15; Isocrates *To Nicocles* 31; *Nicocles* 37; *Areopagiticus* 14; Aristotle *Nicomachean Ethics* 1181b12–23; *Politics* 1273a40 ff., 1278b11–13, 1288a23–24, 1289a12–20, 1292b11–18, 1295b1, 1297a14 ff.; Cicero *Republic* i. 47; v. 5–7; *Laws* i. 14–15, 17, 19; iii. 2.

III

The Distribution of Power

Although most conservatives have shared a skeptical view of human nature and a belief in some kind of higher law, they have long been divided over what form of government best promotes conservative values.

From the time of Plato, many thinkers concerned with social stability, harmony, and virtue have been convinced their ideals would best be encouraged by the straightforward rule of the wisest and best—in Plato's phrase, by philosopher-kings. Others, including Plato's most distinguished pupil, Aristotle, have maintained that many groups and interests must be involved in the governing of a healthy state and that some kind of balance of forces must be the goal of statesmanship.

There is, of course, an underlying philosophical conflict in these two approaches to government. Plato and his followers (which include many modern-day liberals as well as conservatives) are convinced that there are right answers to political questions, and they are pretty certain that they themselves have the right answers. It is natural, therefore, for Platonists to favor benevolent dictatorship to enforce virtue. On the other hand, those who are not so sure that they are right are inclined to a system of compromise and moderation ; the conciliation of the major points of view of a community is their goal. It would be fair to say that the majority of conservatives, especially in the English-speaking world, have taken their lead from Aristotle rather than from Plato and have favored mixed government over rule by an elite.

Within this basic framework, conservatives from the ancients to our time have worked out their own responses to the perpetual question: Who should govern? In nineteenth-century Britain and France respectively, Benjamin Disraeli and Alexis de Tocqueville defended the ideal of a balanced government with all levels of society represented. De Tocqueville, of course, was more inclined to the democratic element than was Disraeli, who preferred to place his trust in the "gentlemen of England," as he liked to call them. Both men agreed that all governments should be limited in their powers and that the rights of minorities should be respected. De Tocqueville foresaw the coming triumph of democracy. He also foresaw the great paradox that would result if the people were in power : it would be necessary for the people to restrain themselves against themselves. Democracy, he believed, could only work in a mature nation with a people accustomed to self-denial as well as self-reliance. Disraeli also saw that almost all of the people would one day be electors, and he looked forward to the day when "Tory Democracy" (an alliance of the country gentlemen and the urban workers) would be the alternative to a party led by businessmen and "rootless intellectuals." Unlike De Tocqueville, who saw the need for the people themselves to be their own guardians, Disraeli remained a paternalist. Most conservatives today would subscribe to one or another variation of these two basic approaches to the problem of the distribution of political power.

In our own century, many conservative writers, schooled by Burke, have argued for the permanence of traditional values. Dr. Otto von Habsburg is one of these scholars; the essential problems of government, he believes, have not changed much since Burke's time. A constitutional monarchy, supported by both popular and aristocratic institutions, he maintains, will best safeguard the rights of individuals and secure the wisest and most stable government. Like De Tocqueville and Disraeli, he places great reliance on a system of checks and balances. Gaetano Mosca, on the other hand, has emphasized the role of modern technology in producing a new class of governors, a technocracy. The great problem of our century, he would say, is to reconcile the conflicting requirements of technical expertise and popular control in the distribution of power. Obviously, the people cannot govern directly; their best hope of guiding their own destinies must lie in a pluralistic society where power alliances are shifting and no one concentrated bloc is able to gain permanent command in the seat of government.

The division of power among a broad range of classes in order to ensure both a limited and a stable government has been the preoccupation of most conservative thinkers. How best to achieve this object has been a point of contention among them since the time of Plato and Aristotle.

15 PLATO

Until Philosophers Are Kings

The Greek philosopher Plato (*c.* 427–347 B.C.) advocated rule by specially trained "philosopher-kings" as the ideal form of government. This high-minded paternalism has inspired both liberals and conservatives from Plato's time to our own ; at the same time, many other conservatives and liberals have preferred to be wrong with freedom than to be right with Plato. The first selection is from Chapters V, VI, and VII of *The Republic ;* the second selection is from *Crito.** In the latter, Socrates-Plato argues that an individual citizen has an obligation to obey the laws of his community ; if in conscience he cannot obey them, he must accept whatever punishment the community which nurtured him is pleased to award.

Socrates speaks to Glaucon:

Would a painter be any the worse because, after having delineated with consummate art an ideal of a perfectly beautiful man, he was unable to show that any such man could ever have existed?

He would be none the worse.

Well, and were we not creating an ideal of a perfect state?

To be sure.

And is our theory a worse theory because we are unable to prove the possibility of a city being ordered in the manner described?

Surely not, he replied.

That is the truth, I said. But if, at your request, I am to try and show how and under what conditions the possibility is highest, I must ask you, having this in view, to repeat your former admissions.

* These two selections are taken from the standard translations of Benjamin Jowett.

What admissions?

I want to know whether ideals are ever fully realized in language? Does not the word express more than the fact, and must not the actual, whatever a man may think, always, in the nature of things, fall short of the truth? What do you say?

I agree.

Then you must not insist on my proving that the actual state will in every respect coincide with the ideal: if we are only able to discover how a city may be governed nearly as we proposed, you will admit that we have discovered the possibility which you demand; and will be contented. I am sure that I should be contented—will not you? . . .

Now then, I said, I go to meet that which I liken to the greatest of the waves; yet shall the word be spoken, even though the wave break and drown me in laughter and dishonor; and do you mark my words.

Proceed.

I said: *Until philosophers are kings, or the kings and princes of this world have the spirit and power of philosophy, and political greatness and wisdom meet in one, and those commoner natures who pursue either to the exclusion of the other are compelled to stand aside, cities will never have rest from their evils,—no, nor the human race, as I believe,—and then only will this our state have a possibility of life and behold the light of day.* Such was the thought, my dear Glaucon, which I would fain have uttered if it had not seemed too extravagant; for to be convinced that in no other state can there be happiness private or public is indeed a hard thing. . . .

*   *   *

The pilot should not humbly beg the sailors to be commanded by him—that is not the order of nature; neither are "the wise to go to the doors of the rich"—the ingenious author of this saying told a lie—but the truth is, that, when a man is ill, whether he be rich or poor, to the physician he must go, and he who wants to be governed, to him who is able to govern. The ruler who is good for anything ought not to beg his subjects to be ruled by him; although the present governors of mankind are of a different stamp; they may be justly compared to the mutinous sailors, and the true helmsmen to those who are called by them good-for-nothings and star-gazers. . . .

Yes, my friend, I said, and I then shrank from hazarding the bold word; but now let me dare to say—that the perfect guardian must be a philosopher.

Yes, he said, let that be affirmed.

And do not suppose that there will be many of them; for the gifts which were deemed by us to be essential rarely grow together; they are mostly found in shreds and patches.

What do you mean? he said.

You are aware, I replied, that quick intelligence, memory, sagacity, cleverness, and similar qualities, do not often grow together, and that persons who possess them and are at the same time high-spirited and magnanimous are not so constituted by nature as to live orderly and in a peaceful and settled manner; they are driven any way by their impulses, and all solid principle goes out of them.

Very true, he said.

On the other hand, those steadfast natures which can better be depended upon, which in a battle are impregnable to fear and immovable, are equally immovable when there is anything to be learned; they are always in a torpid state, and are apt to yawn and go to sleep over any intellectual toil.

Quite true.

And yet we were saying that both qualities were necessary in those to whom the higher education is to be imparted, and who are to share in any office or command.

Certainly, he said.

And will they be a class which is rarely found?

Yes, indeed.

Then the aspirant must not only be tested in those labors and dangers and pleasures which we mentioned before, but there is another kind of probation which we did not mention—he must be exercised also in many kinds of knowledge, to see whether the soul will be able to endure the highest of all, or will faint under them as in any other studies and exercises.

Observe, Glaucon, that there will be no injustice in compelling our philosophers to have a care and providence of others; we shall explain to them that in other states, men of their class are not obliged to share in the toils of politics: and this is reasonable, for they grow up at their own sweet will, and the government would rather not have them. Being self-taught, they cannot be expected to show any gratitude for a culture which they have never received. But we have brought you into the world to be rulers of the hive, kings of yourselves and of the other citizens, and have educated you far better and more perfectly than they have been educated, and you are better able to share in the double duty. Wherefore each of you, when his turn comes, must go down to the general underground abode, and get the habit of seeing in the dark. When you have acquired the habit, you will see ten thousand times better than the inhabitants of the den, and you will know what the several images are, and what they represent, because you have seen the beautiful and just and good in their truth. And thus our state, which is also yours, will be a reality, and not a dream only, and will be administered in a spirit unlike that of other states, in which men fight with one another about shadows only and are distracted in the struggle for power, which in their eyes is a great good. Whereas the truth is that the state in which the rulers are most reluctant to govern is always the best and most quietly governed, and the state in which they are most eager, the worst.

Quite true, he replied.

And will our pupils, when they hear this, refuse to take their turn at the toils of state, when they are allowed to spend the greater part of their time with one another in the heavenly light?

Impossible, he answered; for they are just men, and the commands which we impose upon them are just; there can be no doubt that every one of them will take office as a stern necessity, and not after the fashion of our present rulers of state.

Yes, my friend, I said; and there lies the point. You must contrive for your future rulers another and a better life than that of a ruler, and then you may have a well-ordered state; for only in the state which offers this will they rule who are truly rich, not in silver and gold, but in virtue and wisdom, which are the true blessings of life. Whereas if they go to the administration of public affairs, poor and hungering after their own private advantage, thinking that hence they are to snatch the chief good, order there can never be; for they will be fighting about office, and the civil and domestic broils which thus arise will be the ruin of the rulers themselves and of the whole state.

Most true, he replied.

And the only life which looks down upon the life of political ambition is that of true philosophy. Do you know of any other?

Indeed, I do not, he said.

And those who govern ought not to be lovers of the task? For, if they are, there will be rival lovers, and they will fight.

No question.

Who then are those whom we shall compel to be guardians? Surely they will be the men who are wisest about affairs of state, and by whom the state is administered, and who at the same time have other honors and another and better life than that of politics?

They are the men, and I will choose them, he replied.

And now let me remind you that, although in our former selection we chose old men, we must not do so in this. Solon was under a delusion when he said that a man when he grows old may learn many things—for he can no more learn much than he can run much; youth is the time for any extraordinary toil.

Of course.

And, therefore, calculation and geometry and all the other elements of instruction, which are a preparation for dialectic, should be presented to the mind in childhood; not, however, under any notion of forcing our system of education.

Why not?

Because a freeman ought not to be a slave in the acquisition of knowledge of any kind. Bodily exercise, when compulsory, does no harm to the body; but knowledge which is acquired under compulsion obtains no hold on the mind.

Very true.

Then, my good friend, I said, do not use compulsion, but let early education be a sort of amusement; you will then be better able to find out the natural bent.

That is a very rational notion, he said.

Do you remember that the children, too, were to be taken to see the battle on horseback; and that if there were no danger they were to be brought close up and, like young hounds, have a taste of blood given them?

Yes, I remember.

The same practice may be followed, I said, in all these things— labors, lessons, dangers—and he who is most at home in all of them ought to be enrolled in a select number.

At what age?

At the age when the necessary gymnastics are over: the period whether of two or three years which passes in this sort of training is useless for any other purpose; for sleep and exercise are unpropitious to learning; and the trial of who is first in gymnastic exercises is one of the most important tests to which our youth are subjected.

Certainly, he replied.

After that time those who are selected from the class of twenty years old will be promoted to higher honor, and the sciences which they learned without any order in their early education will now be brought together, and they will be able to see the natural relationship of them to one another and to true being.

Yes, he said, that is the only kind of knowledge which takes lasting root.

Yes, I said; and the capacity for such knowledge is the great criterion of dialectical talent: the comprehensive mind is always the dialectical.

I agree with you, he said.

These, I said, are the points which you must consider; and those who have most of this comprehension, and who are most steadfast in their learning, and in their military and other appointed duties, when they have arrived at the age of thirty will have to be chosen by you out of the select class, and elevated to higher honor; and you will have to prove them by the help of dialectic, in order to learn which of them is able to give up the use of sight and the other senses, and in company with truth to attain absolute being. . . .

Suppose, I said, the study of philosophy to take the place of gymnastics and to be continued diligently and earnestly and exclusively for twice the number of years which were passed in bodily exercise— will that be enough?

Would you say six or four years? he asked.

Say five years, I replied; at the end of the time they must be sent down again into the den and compelled to hold any military or other office which young men are qualified to hold: in this way they will get their experience of life, and there will be an opportunity of trying whether, when they are drawn all manner of ways by temptation, they will stand firm or flinch.

And how long is this stage of their lives to last?

Fifteen years, I answered; and when they have reached fifty years of age, then let those who still survive and have distinguished themselves in every action of their lives and in every branch of knowledge come at last to their consummation: the time has now arrived at which they must raise the eye of the soul to the universal light which lightens all things, and behold the absolute good; for that is the pattern according to which they are to order the state and the lives of individuals, and the remainder of their own lives also; making philosophy their chief pursuit, but, when their turn comes, toiling also at politics and ruling for the public good, not as though they were performing some heroic action, but simply as a matter of duty; and when they have brought up in each generation others like themselves and left them in their place to be governors of the state, then they will depart to the Islands of the Blest and dwell there; and the city will give them public memorials and sacrifices and honor them, if the Pythian oracle consent, as demigods, but if not, as in any case blessed and divine.

You are a sculptor, Socrates, and have made statues of our governors faultless in beauty.

Yes, I said, Glaucon, and of our governesses too; for you must not suppose that what I have been saying applies to men only and not to women as far as their natures can go.

There you are right, he said, since we have made them to share in all things like the men.

Well, I said, and you would agree (would you not?) that what has been said about the state and the government is not a mere dream, and although difficult not impossible, but only possible in the way which has been supposed; that is to say, when the true philosopher kings are born in a state, one or more of them, despising the honors of this present world which they deem mean and worthless, esteeming above all things right and the honor that springs from right, and regarding justice as the greatest and most necessary of all things, whose ministers they are, and whose principles will be exalted by them when they set in order their own city?

How will they proceed?

They will begin by sending out into the country all the inhabitants of the city who are more than ten years old, and will take possession of their children, who will be unaffected by the habits of their parents; these they will train in their own habits and laws, I mean in the laws which we have given them: and in this way the state and constitution of which we were speaking will soonest and most easily attain happiness, and the nation which has such a constitution will gain most.

Yes, that will be the best way. And I think, Socrates, that you have very well described how, if ever, such a constitution might come into being.

Enough then of the perfect state, and of the man who bears its image—there is no difficulty in seeing how we shall describe him.

There is no difficulty, he replied; and I agree with you in thinking that nothing more need be said.

16 PLATO

Society and the Individual *

Soc. And I should like to know whether I may say the same of
another proposition—that not life, but a good life, is to be chiefly
valued?

Cr. Yes, that also remains unshaken.

Soc. And a good life is equivalent to a just and honourable one—
that holds also?

Cr. Yes, it does.

Soc. From these premises I proceed to argue the question whether
I ought or ought not to try and escape without the consent of the
Athenians: and if I am clearly right in escaping, then I will make the
attempt; but if not, I will abstain. The other considerations which you
mention, of money and loss of character and the duty of educating
one's children, are, I fear, only the doctrines of the multitude, who
would be as ready to restore people to life, if they were able, as they
are to put them to death—and with as little reason. But now, since
the argument has thus far prevailed, the only question which remains
to be considered is, whether we shall do rightly either in escaping or
in suffering others to aid in our escape and paying them in money
and thanks, or whether in reality we shall not do rightly; and if the
latter, then death or any other calamity which may ensue on my
remaining here must not be allowed to enter into the calculation.

Cr. I think that you are right, Socrates; how then shall we proceed?

Soc. Let us consider the matter together, and do you either refute
me if you can, and I will be convinced; or else cease, my dear friend,

* See introductory remarks to Selection 15.

from repeating to me that I ought to escape against the wishes of the Athenians: for I highly value your attempts to persuade me to do so, but I may not be persuaded against my own better judgment. And now please to consider my first position, and try how you can best answer me.

Cr. I will.

Soc. Are we to say that we are never intentionally to do wrong, or that in one way we ought and in another way we ought not to do wrong, or is doing wrong always evil and dishonourable, as I was just now saying, and as has been already acknowledged by us? Are all our former admissions which were made within a few days to be thrown away? And have we, at our age, been earnestly discoursing with one another all our life long only to discover that we are no better than children? Or, in spite of the opinion of the many, and in spite of consequences whether better or worse, shall we insist on the truth of what was then said, that injustice is always an evil and dishonour to him who acts unjustly? Shall we say or not?

Cr. Yes.

Soc. Then we must do no wrong?

Cr. Certainly not.

Soc. Nor when injured injure in return, as the many imagine; for we must injure no one at all?

Cr. Clearly not.

Soc. Again, Crito, may we do evil?

Cr. Surely not, Socrates.

Soc. And what of doing evil in return for evil, which is the morality of the many—is that just or not?

Cr. Not just.

Soc. For doing evil to another is the same as injuring him?

Cr. Very true.

Soc. Then we ought not to retaliate or render evil for evil to any one, whatever evil we may have suffered from him. But I would have you consider, Crito, whether you really mean what you are saying. For this opinion has never been held, and never will be held, by any considerable number of persons; and those who are agreed and those who are not agreed upon this point have no common ground, and can only despise one another when they see how widely they differ. Tell me, then, whether you agree with and assent to my first principle, that neither injury nor retaliation nor warding off evil by evil is ever right.

And shall that be the premise of our argument? Or do you decline and dissent from this? For so I have ever thought, and continue to think; but, if you are of another opinion, let me hear what you have to say. If, however, you remain of the same mind as formerly, I will proceed to the next step.

Cr. You may proceed, for I have not changed my mind.

Soc. Then I will go on to the next point, which may be put in the form of a question:— Ought a man to do what he admits to be right, or ought he to betray the right?

Cr. He ought to do what he thinks right.

Soc. But if this is true, what is the application? In leaving the prison against the will of the Athenians, do I wrong any? or rather do I not wrong those whom I ought least to wrong? Do I not desert the principles which were acknowledged by us to be just—what do you say?

Cr. I cannot tell, Socrates; for I do not know.

Soc. Then consider the matter in this way:—Imagine that I am about to play truant (you may call the proceeding by any name which you like), and the laws and the government come and interrogate me: 'Tell us, Socrates,' they say; 'what are you about? are you not going by an act of yours to overturn us—the laws, and the whole state, as far as in you lies? Do you imagine that a state can subsist and not be overthrown, in which the decisions of law have no power, but are set aside and trampled upon by individuals?' What will be our answer, Crito, to these and the like words? Any one, and especially a rhetorician, will have a good deal to say on behalf of the law which requires a sentence to be carried out. He will argue that this law should not be set aside; and shall we reply, 'Yes; but the state has injured us and given an unjust sentence.' Suppose I say that?

Cr. Very good, Socrates.

Soc. 'And was that our agreement with you?' the law would answer; 'or were you to abide by the sentence of the state?' And if I were to express my astonishment at their words, the law would probably add: 'Answer, Socrates, instead of opening your eyes—you are in the habit of asking and answering questions. Tell us,—What complaint have you to make against us which justifies you in attempting to destroy us and the state? In the first place did we not bring you into existence? Your father married your mother by our aid and begat you. Say whether you have any objection to urge against those of us who regulate marriage?' None, I should reply. 'Or against those of us who after birth regulate the nurture and education of children, in which you also were trained? Were not the laws, which have the charge of education, right in commanding your father to train you in music and gymnastic? ' Right, I should reply. 'Well then, since you were brought into the world and nurtured and educated by us, can you deny in the first place that you are our child and slave, as your fathers were before you? And if this is true you are not on equal terms with us; nor can you think that you have a right to do to us what we are doing to you. Would you have any right to strike or revile or do other evil to your father or your master, if you had one, because you have been struck or reviled by him, or received some other evil at his hands?—you would not say this? And because we think right to destroy you, do you think that you have any right to destroy us in return, and your country as far as in you lies? Will you, O professor of true virtue, pretend that you are justified in this? Has a philosopher like you failed to discover that our country is more to be valued and higher and holier far than mother or father or any ancestor, and more to be regarded in the eyes of the gods and of men of understanding? also to be soothed, and gently and reverently entreated when angry, even more than a father, and either to be persuaded, or if not persuaded, to be obeyed? And when we are punished by her, whether with imprisonment or stripes, the punishment is to be endured in silence; and if she leads us to wounds or death in battle, thither we follow as is right; neither may any one yield or retreat or leave his rank, but whether in battle or in a court of law, or in any other place, he must do what his city and his country order him; or he must change their view of what is just: and if he may do no violence to his father or mother, much less may he do violence to his country.' What answer shall we make to this, Crito? Do the laws speak truly, or do they not?

Cr. I think that they do.

Soc. Then the laws will say: 'Consider, Socrates, if we are speaking truly that in your present attempt you are going to do us an injury. For, having brought you into the world, and nurtured and educated you, and given you and every other citizen a share in every good which we had to give, we further proclaim to any Athenian by the liberty which we allow him, that if he does not like us when he has become of age and has seen the ways of the city, and made our acquaintance, he may go where he pleases and take his goods with him.

None of us laws will forbid him or interfere with him. Any one who does not like us and the city, and who wants to emigrate to a colony or to any other city, may go where he likes, retaining his property. But he who has experience of the manner in which we order justice and administer the state, and still remains, has entered into an implied contract that he will do as we command him. And he who disobeys us is, as we maintain, thrice wrong; first, because in disobeying us he is disobeying his parents; secondly, because we are the authors of his education; thirdly, because he has made an agreement with us that he will duly obey our commands; and he neither obeys them nor convinces us that our commands are unjust; and we do not rudely impose them, but give him the alternative of obeying or convincing us;—that is what we offer, and he does neither.

'These are the sort of accusations to which, as we were saying, you, Socrates, will be exposed if you accomplish your intentions; you, above all other Athenians.' Suppose now I ask, why I rather than anybody else? they will justly retort upon me that I above all other men have acknowledged the agreement. 'There is clear proof,' they will say, 'Socrates, that we and the city were not displeasing to you. Of all Athenians you have been the most constant resident in the city, which, as you never leave, you may be supposed to love. For you never went out of the city either to see the games, except once when you went to the Isthmus, or to any other place unless when you were on military service; nor did you travel as other men do. Nor had you any curiosity to know other states or their laws: your affections did not go beyond us and our state; we were your special favourites, and you acquiesced in our government of you; and here in this city you begat your children, which is a proof of your satisfaction. Moreover, you might in the course of the trial, if you had liked, have fixed the penalty at banishment; the state which refuses to let you go now would have let you go then. But you pretended that you preferred death to exile, and that you were not unwilling to die. And now you have forgotten these fine sentiments, and pay no respect to us the laws, of whom you are the destroyer; and are doing what only a miserable slave would do, running away and turning your back upon the compacts and agreements which you made as a citizen. And first of all answer this very question: Are we right in saying that you agreed to be governed according to us in deed, and not in word only? Is that true or not?' How shall we answer, Crito? Must we not assent?

Cr. We cannot help it, Socrates,

Soc. Then will they not say: 'You, Socrates, are breaking the covenants and agreements which you made with us at your leisure, not in any haste or under any compulsion or deception, but after you have had seventy years to think of them, during which time you were at liberty to leave the city, if we were not to your mind, or if our covenants appeared to you to be unfair. . . .

'Listen, then, Socrates, to us who have brought you up. Think not of life and children first, and of justice afterwards, but of justice first, that you may be justified before the princes of the world below. For neither will you nor any that belong to you be happier or holier or juster in this life, or happier in another, if you do as Crito bids. Now you depart in innocence, a sufferer and not a doer of evil; a victim, not of the laws but of men. But if you go forth, returning evil for evil, and injury for injury, breaking the covenants and agreements which you have made with us, and wronging those whom you ought least of all to wrong, that is to say, yourself, your friends, your country, and us, we shall be angry with you while you live, and our brethren, the laws in the world below, will receive you as an enemy; for they will know that you have done your best to destroy us. Listen, then, to us and not to Crito.'

This, dear Crito, is the voice which I seem to hear murmuring in my ears, like the sound of the flute in the ears of the mystic; that voice, I say, is humming in my ears, and prevents me from hearing any other. And I know that anything more which you may say will be vain. Yet speak, if you have anything to say.

Cr. I have nothing to say, Socrates.

Soc. Leave me then, Crito, to fulfil the will of God, and to follow whither he leads.

17 ARISTOTLE

On Mixed Government

Aristotle (384–322 B.C.) was Plato's foremost pupil, the tutor of Alexander the Great, the most persistent student of constitutional arrangements in the ancient Greek world, and the father of the democratic theory. From his study of governmental systems he concluded that a mixed government is most conducive to the development and maintenance of a free society; it is this Aristotelian concept that Montesquieu was to redevelop in the eighteenth century into the theory of checks and balances which became the basis of the American Constitution. Aristotle argued in his *Politics* that the purpose of government is to further the good life of its citizens, and doing this requires that the government include all elements of the society in a predetermined "mixture," not merely an oppressive minority or an oppressive majority. The selection is taken from Books I, III, and IV.*

As we see that every state is a society, and that every society is established for the sake of some good end; (for an apparent good is the spring of all human actions;) it is evident that all societies aim at some good or other: and this is more especially true of that which aims at the highest possible end, and is itself the most excellent, and embraces all the rest. Now this is that which is called a state, and forms a political society. For those are greatly at fault, who think that the principles of a political, a regal, a domestic, and a despotic government are the same; inasmuch as they suppose that each of these differ merely in point of number, and not in kind: so that with them a despotic government is one composed of a very few, a domestic of

* *The Politics of Aristotle,* from the text of I. Bekker (Oxford: Oxford University Press, 1855).

more, a civil and a regal of still more, as if there were no difference between a large family and a small city; and they hold that a regal and political government are the same things; only that in the one, a single person is continually at the head of affairs, while in the other, each individual in his turn becomes a magistrate and again a private person, according to the rules of political science. Now this is not true; and what we say will be evident to any one who will consider this question after the approved method. For as, in every other subject, it is necessary to separate its component nature, till we arrive at its first elements, which are the most minute parts thereof; so by viewing the first elements of which a state is composed, we shall see wherein states differ from each other, and whether it is possible to arrive at any systematic knowledge concerning each of the points above mentioned.

Now if any one would watch the parts of a state from the very first as they rise into existence, as in other matters, so here he would gain the truest view of the subject. In the first place, then, it is requisite that those should be joined together, which cannot exist without each other, as the male and the female, for the business of propagation; and this not through deliberate choice, but by that natural impulse which acts both in plants and in animals, namely, the desire of leaving behind them others like themselves. By nature too some beings command, and others obey, for the sake of mutual safety; for a being endowed with discernment and forethought is by nature the superior and governor; whereas he who is merely able to execute by bodily labour, is the inferior and a natural slave; and hence the interest of master and slave is identical. But there is a natural difference between the female and the slave; for nature does nothing meanly, like artists who make the Delphic swords; but she has one instrument for one end; for thus her instruments are most likely to be brought to perfection, being made to contribute to one end, and not to many. Yet, among Barbarians, the female and the slave are upon a level in the community; the reason for which is, that they are not fitted by nature to rule; and so their relationship becomes merely that between slaves of different sexes. For which reason the poets say,

"'Tis meet that barbarous tribes to Greeks should bow,"

as if a barbarian and a slave were by nature one and the same. Now

of these two societies the domestic tie is the first, and Hesiod is right
when he says,

"First house, then wife, then oxen for the plough ;"

for the ox is to the poor man in the place of a household slave. That
society, then, which nature has established for daily support, is a
family. . , . But the society of many families, which was instituted
for lasting and mutual advantage, is called a village . . . and a village
is most naturally composed of the emigrant members of one family,
. . . the children and the children's children. And hence, by the
way, states were originally governed by kings, as the Barbarians now
are; for they were composed of those who always were under kingly
government. For every family is governed by the elder, as are its
branches, on account of their relationship; and this is what Homer
says,

"Then each his wife and child doth rule,"

for in this scattered manner they formerly lived. And the general
opinion which makes the gods themselves subject to kingly government, arises from the fact that most men formerly were, and many
are so now; and as they hold the gods to be like themselves in form,
so they suppose their manner of life must needs be the same. But
when many villages join themselves perfectly together into one society,
that society is a state, . . . and contains in itself, if I may so
speak, the perfection of independence; and it is first founded that
men may live, but continued that they may live happily. For which
reason every state is the work of nature, since the first social ties are
such; for to this they all tend as to an end, and the nature of a thing
is judged by its tendency. For what every being is in its perfect state,
that certainly is the nature of that being, whether it be a man, a
horse, or a house; besides, its own final cause and its end must be
the perfection of any thing; but a government complete in itself constitutes a final cause and what is best. Hence it is evident, that a state
is one of the works of nature, and that man is naturally a political
animal, and that whosoever is naturally, and not accidentally, unfit
for society, must be either inferior or superior to man; just as the
person reviled in Homer,

"No tribe, nor state, nor home hath he."

For he whose nature is such as this, must needs be a lover of strife, and as solitary as a bird of prey. It is clear, then, that man is truly a more social animal than bees, or any of the herding cattle; for nature, as we say, does nothing in vain, and man is the only animal who has reason. Speech, indeed, as being the token of pleasure and pain, is imparted to other beings also, and thus far their nature extends; they can perceive pleasure and pain, and can impart these sensations to others; but speech is given to us to express what is useful or hurtful to us, and also what is just and unjust; for in this particular man differs from other animals, that he alone has a perception of good and evil, of justice and injustice, and it is the interchange of these common sentiments which forms a family and a city. And further, in the order of nature, the state is prior to the family or the individual; for the whole must necessarily be prior to the parts; for if you take away the whole body, you cannot say a foot or a hand remains, unless by equivocation, as if any one should call a hand made of stone, a hand; for such only can it have when mutilated. But every thing is defined according to its effects and inherent powers, so that when these no longer remain such as they were, it cannot be said to be the same, but something of the same name. It is plain, then, that the state is prior to the individual, for if an individual is not complete in himself, he bears the same relation to the state as other parts do to a whole; but he that is incapable of society, or so complete in himself as not to want it, makes no part of a state, but is either a beast or a god. There is then in all persons a natural impetus to associate with each other in this manner, and he who first established civil society was the cause of the greatest benefit; for as man, thus perfected, is the most excellent of all living beings, so without law and justice he would be the worst of all; for nothing is so savage as injustice in arms; but man is born with a faculty of gaining himself arms by prudence and virtue; arms which yet he may apply to the most opposite purposes. And hence he who is devoid of virtue will be the most wicked and cruel, the most lustful and gluttonous being imaginable. Now justice is a social virtue; for it is the rule of the social state, and the very criterion of what is right.

Having established these particulars, the next point is to consider how many different kinds of governments there are, and what they are; and first we must review those of them which are correct; for when we have determined this their deflections will be evident enough.

It is evident that every form of government or administration, (for the words are of the same import,) must contain the supreme power over the whole state, and that this supreme power must necessarily be in the hands of one person, or of a few, or of the many; and that when the one, the few, or the many direct their policy to the common good, such states are well governed : but when the interest of the one, the few, or the many who are in office, is alone consulted, a perversion takes place; for we must either affirm that those who share in the community are not citizens, or else let these share in the advantages of government. Now we usually call a state which is governed by one person for the common good, a kingdom; one that is governed by more than one, but by a few only, an aristocracy; either because the government is in the hands of the most worthy citizens, or because it is the best form for the city, and its inhabitants. But when the citizens at large direct their policy to the public good, it is called simply a polity; a name which is common to all other governments. And this distinction is consonant to reason; for it will be easy to find one person, or a very few, of very distinguished abilities, but most difficult to meet with the majority of a people eminent for every virtue; but if there is one common to a whole nation it is valour; for this exists among numbers : for which reason, in this state the military have most power, and those who possess arms will have their share in the government. Now the perversions attending each of these governments are these; a kingdom may degenerate into a tyranny, an aristocracy into an oligarchy, and a state into a democracy. Now a tyranny is a monarchy where the good of one man only is the object of government, an oligarchy considers only the rich, and a democracy only the poor; but neither of them have the common good of all in view.

. . . It is evident, then, that a state is not a mere community of place, nor established for the sake of mutual safety or traffic; but that these things are the necessary consequences of a state, although they may all exist where there is no state; but a state is a society of people joining together with their families, and their children, to live well, for the sake of a perfect and independent life; and for this purpose it is necessary that they should live in one place, and intermarry with each other. Hence in all cities there are family meetings, clubs, sacrifices, and public entertainments, to promote friendship; for a love of sociability is friendship itself; so that the end for which a state is established is that the inhabitants of it may live happily; and these things are conducive to that end; for it is a community of families and villages, formed for the sake of a perfect independent life; that is, as we have already said, for the sake of living well and happily. The political state therefore is founded not for the purpose of men's merely living together, but for their living as men ought; for which reason those who contribute most to this end deserve to have greater power in the state than either those who are their equals in family and freedom, but their inferiors in civil virtue, or those who excel them in wealth, but are below them in worth. It is evident from what has been said, that in all disputes upon forms of government each party says something that is just.

There may also be a doubt as to who should possess the supreme power of the state. Shall it be the majority, or the wealthy, or a number of proper persons, or one better than the rest, or a tyrant? But whichever of these we prefer, some difficulty will arise. For what? if the poor, because they are the majority, may divide among themselves what belongs to the rich, is not this unjust? In sooth, by heaven, it will have been judged just enough by the multitude when they gain the supreme power. What therefore is the extremity of injustice, if this is not? Again, if the many seize into their own hands every thing which belongs to the few, it is evident that the state will be at an end. But virtue never tends to destroy what is itself virtuous; nor can what is right be the ruin of the state. Therefore such a law can never be right; nor can the acts of a tyrant ever be wrong, for of necessity they must all be just; for, from his unlimited power, he compels every one to obey his command, as the multitude oppress the rich. Is it right then that the rich and few should have the supreme power? and what if they be guilty of the same rapine, and plunder the possessions of the majority, will this be just? It will be the same as in the other case; but it is evident that all things of this sort are wrong and unjust. Well then, suppose that those of the better sort shall have the supreme power, must not then all the other citizens live unhonoured, without sharing the offices of the state? for the offices of a state we call honours, and if one set of men are always in power, it is evident that the rest must be without honours. Then, will it be better that the supreme power be in the hands of that one person who is fittest for it? but by this means the power will be still more confined, for a greater number than before will continue unhonoured. But some one may say, that, in short, it is wrong that man should have the supreme power rather than the law, as his soul is subject to so many passions. But if this law appoints an aristocracy, or a democracy, how will it help us in our present doubts? for those things will happen which we have already mentioned.

Of other particulars, then, let us treat hereafter; but as to the fact that the supreme power ought to be lodged with the many, rather than with those of the better sort, who are few, there would seem to be some doubt, though also some truth as well. Now, though each individual of the many may himself be unfit for the supreme power, yet, when these many are joined together, it is possible that they may be better qualified for it, than the others; and this not separately, but as a collective body. So the public suppers exceed those which are given at one person's private expense: for, as they are many, each person brings in his share of virtue and wisdom; and thus, coming together, they are like one man made up of a multitude, with many feet, many hands, and many senses. Thus is it with respect to the character and understanding. And for this reason the many are the best judges of music and poetry; for some understand one part, some another, and all collectively the whole. And in this particular men of consequence differ from each of the many; as they say those who are beautiful differ from those who are not so, and as fine pictures excel any natural objects, by collecting into one the several beautiful parts which were dispersed among different originals, although the separate parts of individuals, as the eye or any other part, may be handsomer than in the picture. But it is not clear whether it is possible that this distinction should exist between every people and general assembly, and some few men of consequence; but, by heaven, doubtless it is clear enough that, with respect to a few, it is impossible; since the same conclusion might be applied even to brutes: and indeed, so to say, wherein do some men differ from brutes? But nothing prevents what I have said being true of the people in some states. The doubt, then, which we have lately proposed, with that which is its consequence, may be settled in this manner; it is necessary that the freemen and the bulk of the people should have absolute power in some things; but these are such as are not men of property, nor have they any reputation for virtue. And so it is not safe to trust them with the first offices in the state, both on account of their injustice and their ignorance; from the one of which they are likely to do what is wrong, from the other to make mistakes. And yet it is dangerous to allow them no power or share in the government; for when there are many poor people who are excluded from office, the state must necessarily have very many enemies in it. It remains, then, that they should have a place in the public assemblies, and in determining causes. And for this reason Socrates and some other legislators give them the power of electing the officers of the state, and also of inquiring into their conduct after their term of office, but do not allow them to act as magistrates by themselves. For the multitude, when they are collected together, have all of them sufficient understanding for these purposes, and by mixing among those of higher rank are serviceable to the state; as some things which alone are improper for food, when mixed with others, make the whole more wholesome than a few of them would be; though each individual is unfit to form a judgment by himself. But there is a difficulty attending this form of government; for it seems that the same person, who himself was capable of curing any one who was then sick, must be the best judge who to employ as a physician; but such a one must be himself a physician. And the same holds true in every other practice and art: and as a physician ought to give an account of his practice to physicians, so ought it to be in other arts. But physicians are of three sorts; the first makes up the medicines; the second prescribes; the third understands the science, but never practises it. Now these three distinctions may be found in those who understand all other arts; and we have no less opinion of their judgment who are only instructed in the principles of the art, than of those who practise it. And with respect to elections the same would seem to hold true; for to elect a proper person in any line, is the business of those who are skilled in it; as in geometry, it is the part of geometricians, and of steersmen in the art of steering. But even if some individuals do know something of particular arts and works, they do not know more than the professors of them; so that, even upon this principle, neither the election of magistrates, nor the censure of their conduct, should be intrusted to the many. But possibly much that has been here said may not be right; for, to resume the argument lately used, if the people are not very brutal indeed, although we allow that each individual knows less of these affairs than those who have given particular attention to them, yet when they come together they will know them better, or at least not worse: besides, in some particular arts it is not the workman only who is the best judge, as in those the works of which are understood by those who do not profess them. Thus he who builds a house is not the only judge of it, (for the master of the family who inhabits it is a better one;) thus also a steersman is a better judge of a tiller than he who made it, and he who gives an entertainment than the cook. What has been said seems a sufficient solution of this difficulty; but there is another that follows it: for it seems absurd that greater power in the state should be lodged with the bad than with the good. Now the power of election and censure are of the very utmost consequence, and this, as has been said, in some states they intrust to the people; for the general assembly is the supreme court of all. And yet they have a voice in this court, and deliberate on all public affairs, and try all causes, without any objection to the meanness of their circumstances, and at any age: but their quæstors, generals, and other great officers of state are taken from men of high condition. This difficulty, then, may be solved upon the same principle; and here too they may be right. For the power is not in the man who is member of the assembly or council, but in the assembly itself, and in the council and people, of which each individual of the whole community forms a part, as senator, adviser, or judge. And for this reason it is very right that the many should have the greatest powers in their own hands; for the people, the council, and the judges are composed of them, and the property of all these collectively is more than the property of any person, or of a few who fill the great offices of the state: and thus let us determine these points.

But the first question that we stated shows nothing besides so plainly, as that the supreme power should be lodged in laws duly made, and that the magistrate, or magistrates, (either one or more,) should be authorized to determine those cases on which the laws cannot define particularly; as it is impossible for them, in general language, to explain themselves upon every thing that may arise. But what these laws are, which are established upon the best foundations, has not been yet explained, but still remains a matter of some question: but the laws of every state will necessarily be like the state itself, either trifling or excellent, just or unjust; for it is evident, that the laws which are framed, must correspond to the constitution of the government; and, if so, it is plain, that a well-formed government will have good laws, a bad one, bad ones.

It follows next in order to consider the absolute monarch whom we have just mentioned, who does every thing according to his own will; for a king governing under the direction of laws does not of himself constitute any particular species of government, as we have already said; for in every state whatsoever, whether an aristocracy or a democracy, it is easy to appoint a general for life; and there are many who intrust the administration of affairs to one person only; such is the government at Dyrrachium, and the same at Opus though in a less degree. As for an absolute monarchy, as it is called, (that is to say, when the whole state is wholly subject to the will of one person, namely the king,) it seems to many to be unnatural that one man should have the entire rule over his fellow-citizens, when the state consists of equals; for nature requires that the same right, and the same rank, should necessarily exist amongst all those who are equal by nature; for as it would be hurtful to the body, for those who are of different constitutions to observe the same regimen, either of diet, or clothing; so with respect to the honours of the state, it is as hurtful that those who are equal in merit should be unequal in rank. And for this reason it is as much a man's duty to submit to command, as to assume it, and this also by rotation; for this is law, for order is law; and it is more proper that the law should govern, than any one of the citizens. Upon the same principle, if it is advantageous to place the supreme power in some particular persons, they should be appointed to be only guardians and servants of the laws, for the supreme power must be placed somewhere; but they say, that it is unjust that where all are equal, one person should continually enjoy it. But man would scarcely be able to adjust that which the law cannot determine. It may be replied, that the law having purposely laid down the best rules, leaves the rest to be adjusted by the most fair decision, and to be regulated by the magistrates; besides, it allows any thing to be altered, which experience proves may be better established. Moreover, he who bids the law to be supreme, makes God supreme, [and the laws;] but he who intrusts man with supreme power, gives it to a wild beast, for such his appetites sometimes make him; passion, too, influences those who are in power, even the very best of men; for which reason the law is intel-

lect free from appetite. The instance taken from the arts seems falla-
cious: wherein it is said to be wrong for a sick person to apply for
a remedy to books, but that it would be far more eligible to employ
those who are skilful in physic; for these are not biassed by any feeling towards their patient to act contrary to the principles of their art;
but when the cure is performed, they receive a pecuniary recompence:
whereas those who have the management of public affairs, do many
things through hatred or favour. And, as a proof of what we have advanced, it may be observed, that whenever a sick person suspects that
his physician has been persuaded by his enemies to be guilty of any
foul practice to him in his profession, he then chooses rather to apply
to books for his cure. And not only this, but even physicians themselves, when they are ill, call in other physicians: and those who
teach others the gymnastic exercises practise with those of the same
profession, as being incapable from self-partiality to form a proper
judgment of what concerns themselves.   From whence it is evident,
that those who seek for what is just, seek for a mean; now the law is
a mean. Moreover, the moral law is far superior to the written law,
and is conversant with far superior objects; for the supreme magistrate is safer to be trusted to than the written one, though he is inferior to the moral law. . . .

We ought not, however, to define a democracy as some do now-a-
days, who say simply that it is a government where the supreme power
is lodged in the people; for even in oligarchies every where the supreme
power is in the majority.   Nor should we define an oligarchy as a
government where the supreme power is in the hands of a few: for let
us suppose the number of a people to be thirteen hundred, and that of
these, one thousand were rich, who would not permit the three hundred poor to have any share in the government, although they were
free, and their equals in every thing else; no one would say that this
government was a democracy. In like manner, if the poor, when few in
number, should acquire the power over the rich, though more than
themselves, no one would say that this formed an oligarchy; nor would
any one call such a state an oligarchy, when the poor, though few in
number, are superior in power to the rich, who have a majority.   We
should rather say that the state is a democracy, when the supreme
power is in the hands of the freemen; an oligarchy, when it is in the
hands of the rich. It happens indeed that in the one case the many

will possess it, in the other the few; because there are many poor, and few rich. And if the offices of state were to be distributed according to the size of the citizens, as they say it is in Æthiopia, or according to their beauty, then it would be an oligarchy: for the number of those who are tall or beautiful is small. Nor withal are those things which we have already mentioned, alone sufficient to describe these states; for since there are many species both of a democracy and an oligarchy, the matter requires that further distinction be made; as we cannot admit, that if a few freemen possess the supreme power over the many who are not free, this government is a democracy: as in Apollonia upon the Ionian Sea, and in Thera; for in each of these cities the honours of the state were in the hands of some few distinguished families who first founded the colonies. Nor would the rich, because they are superior in numbers, form a democracy, as formerly at Colophon; for there the majority had large possessions before the Lydian war. But a democracy is a state where the freemen and the poor, being the majority, are invested with the power of the state; and an oligarchy is a state where the rich and those of noble family, being few, possess it. We have now proved that there are various forms of government, and we have assigned a reason for it; and shall proceed to show, that there are even more than these, and what they are, and why; starting from the first principle which we have already laid down. We admit that every state consists not of one, but of many parts. For example, if it should be our purpose to comprehend the different species of animals, we should first of all note those parts which every animal must have, as certain of the organs of sense, as also what is fitted to receive and retain its food, as a mouth and a belly; and besides, certain parts to enable it to move from place to place. If, then, these are the only parts of an animal, and there are differences between them, namely, in their various sorts of mouths, and bellies, and organs of sense, and besides these in their powers of motion; the number of all these combined together must necessarily make up different species of animals. For it is not possible that the same kind of animal should have any very great deal of difference in its mouth or ears; so that when all these possible combinations are collected together, they will make up various species of animals, which will be as many kinds as there are of these general combinations of necessary parts. Now the same thing is true of what are called polities; for a state is not made up of one, but of many parts, as has already been often said; one of which is those who supply provisions, called husbandmen; another called mechanics, whose employment is in the manual arts, without which the city could not be inhabited; of these some are busied about what is absolutely necessary, others about things which contribute to the elegancies and pleasures of life; the third sort are hucksters, I mean by these buyers, sellers, petty traffickers, and retail dealers; the fourth are hired labourers, or workmen; the fifth are the men-at-arms, a rank not less useful than the other, unless the community choose to be the slaves of every invader. For doubtless a state which is naturally a slave, is unworthy of the name of a city; for a city is self-sufficient, but a slave is not. So that when Socrates says that a city is necessarily composed of four sorts of people, weavers, husbandmen, shoemakers, and builders; he then adds, as if these were not sufficient, smiths, herdsmen for what cattle are necessary, and also merchants and victuallers, and these are by way of appendix to his first list; as if a city was established for necessity, and not for the sake of perfect life, or as if it was equally in need of shoemakers and husbandmen. Also he does not reckon the military as a part of the state, before its territory increases and brings about war, by touching on the borders of the neighbouring powers. And even amongst them who compose his four divisions, or whoever have any connexion with each other, it will be necessary to have some one to distribute justice, and to determine between man and man. Since, then, any one would hold that the mind is more truly a part of man than his body, one would regard such things as more properly belonging to his city than matters of every-day necessity: such things are the portion devoted to war and the administration of forensic justice; to which may be added those who are members of the council, which is the business of political sagacity. Nor is it of any consequence, whether these different employments are filled by different persons, or by one, as the same man is oftentimes both a soldier and a husbandman. So that if both the judge and the senator are parts of the city, it necessarily follows that the soldier must be so also. The seventh sort are those who serve the public in expensive employments at their own charge; and these are called the opulent. The eighth are those who in like manner execute the different offices of the state, and without these it could not possibly subsist: it is therefore necessary that there should be some persons capable of governing and of filling the places in the city; and this either for life, or in rotation. The office of a senator, and of him who administers justice to litigants, alone now remain; and these we have already sufficiently defined. Since, then, these things are necessary for a state, to the end that it may be happy and just, it follows that citizens who engage in public affairs should be men of abilities therein. Many persons think it possible that different employments may be allotted to the same person, as that of a soldier, a husbandman, and an artificer; as also, that others may be both senators and judges: but all men lay claim to political ability, and think themselves qualified for almost every department in the state. But the same person cannot at once be poor and rich: for which reason the most obvious division of the city is into two parts, the poor and rich. Moreover, since in general the one are few, the other many, they seem of all the parts of a city most clearly contrary to each other; so that as the one or the other prevail, they form different polities, and these two forms of polity are democracy and oligarchy. It has been already mentioned that there are many different states, and from what causes they arise; let us therefore now show that there are also different kinds both of democracy and oligarchy. Though this indeed is evident from what we have already said: for there are many different sorts of common people, and also of those who are called the upper classes. Of the different sorts of the first are the husbandmen, artificers, and hucksters, who are employed in buying and selling; seamen, of whom some are engaged in war, some in traffic, some in carrying goods and passengers, others in fishing;—(and of each of these there are often many, as fishermen at Tarentum and Byzantium, masters of galleys at Athens, merchants at Ægina and Chios, those who carry passengers at Tenedos;)—to these we may add those who live by their manual labour, and have so little property that they cannot live without some employ; and also those who are not free-born from citizens on both sides, and whatever other sort of common people there may be. That which marks the upper classes, is their fortune, their birth, their abilities, or their education, or any such like excellence which is attributed to them. The most pure democracy is that which is called so principally from the equality which prevails in it: for this is what the law in that state directs, that the poor shall be in no greater subjection than the rich; and that the supreme power shall be not lodged with either of these, but that both shall share it alike. For if liberty and equality, as some persons suppose, are chiefly to be found in a democracy, it must be most so, by every department of government being alike open to all; but as the people are the majority, and what they vote is law, it follows that such a state must be a democracy. This then is one species of a democratic government. Another is, when the magistrates are elected by a certain census, the standard of which is low; and where every one who possesses property ought to have a share in the government, but as soon as he has lost that property, he ought no longer. Another sort is, that in which every man who is not under ban has a share in the government, but where the government is in the law. Another, where every one, provided he be a citizen, has this right, but where the government is in the law. Another is the same with these in other particulars, but allows the people and not the law to be supreme; and this takes place when every thing is determined by a majority of votes, and not by a law; a thing which happens by reason of the demagogues. For where a democracy is governed by stated laws, there is no room for a demagogue, but men of worth fill the first offices in the state; but where the power is not vested in the laws, there demagogues abound. For there the people's voice becomes that of a king, the whole composing one body; for they are supreme, not as individuals, but in their collective capacity. Homer also says,

"Ill fares it, where the multitude hath sway ;"

but whether he means this kind of democracy, or one where the many are individually supreme, is uncertain. Now, when the people possess this power, they desire to be altogether absolute, that they may not be under the control of the law, and they grow despotical, so that flatterers are held in repute; and such a people become analogous to tyranny among the forms of monarchy; for their manners are the same, and they both hold a despotic power over better persons than themselves. For their decrees are like the others' edict; and a demagogue with them is like a flatterer among the others; but both these two classes abound with each, flatterers with tyrants, and demagogues among such a people. And to them it is owing that the supreme power is lodged in the votes of the people, and not in written laws; for they bring every thing before them. And this they do because they have influence, on account of the supreme power being lodged in the people; for these are they whom the multitude obey. Besides, those who inveigh against rulers are wont to say that the people ought to be the judges of their conduct; and the people gladly receive their complaints as the means of destroying all their offices. Any one therefore may with great justice blame such a government by calling it a democracy, and not a free state; for where the government is not vested in the laws, then there is no free state, for the law ought to be supreme over all things; and particular incidents which arise, should be determined by the magistrates or by the state. If, therefore, a democracy is to be reckoned as one among free states, it is evident that any such establishment which centres all power in the votes of the people cannot, properly speaking, be a democracy; for their decrees cannot be general in their extent. Let this, then, be our description of the several species of democracies.

18 DE TOCQUEVILLE

Dangers of Democratic Despotism

Alexis de Tocqueville (1805–1859) was a French liberal of noble family who was thoroughly aware of all the many dangers of democracy but who nevertheless saw it as the best hope of the future. He had faith in the ability of the people to educate themselves and to limit their own power by moral restraint. Politicians, he thought, would try to use democracy as a means of gaining power for themselves; he saw the chief peril to be the increasing centralization of government. In the fourth book of his *Democracy in America* (from which the selection is taken)* De Tocqueville warned against the mild despotism of well-meaning paternalists who wish to manipulate the lives of people for their own good.

The principle of equality, which makes men independent of each other, gives them a habit and a taste for following, in their private actions, no other guide but their own will. This complete independence, which they constantly enjoy towards their equals and in the intercourse of private life, tends to make them look upon all authority with a jealous eye, and speedily suggests to them the notion and the love of political freedom. Men living at such times have a natural bias to free institutions. Take any one of them at a venture, and search if you can his most deep-seated instincts; you will find that of all governments he will soonest conceive and most highly value that government, whose head he has himself elected, and whose administration he may control.

Of all the political effects produced by the equality of conditions, this love of independence is the first to strike the observing, and to

* Trans. by Henry Reeve (London, 1840).

alarm the timid; nor can it be said that their alarm is wholly misplaced, for anarchy has a more formidable aspect in democratic countries than elsewhere. As the citizens have no direct influence on each other, as soon as the supreme power of the nation fails, which kept them all in their several stations, it would seem that disorder must instantly reach its utmost pitch, and that, every man drawing aside in a different direction, the fabric of society must at once crumble away.

I am however persuaded that anarchy is not the principal evil which democratic ages have to fear, but the least. For the principle of equality begets two tendencies; the one leads men straight to independence, and may suddenly drive them into anarchy; the other conducts them by a longer, more secret, but more certain road, to servitude. Nations readily discern the former tendency, and are prepared to resist it; they are led away by the latter, without perceiving its drift; hence it is peculiarly important to point it out.

For myself, I am so far from urging as a reproach to the principle of equality that it renders men untractable, that this very circumstance principally calls forth my approbation. I admire to see how it deposits in the mind and heart of man the dim conception and instinctive love of political independence, thus preparing the remedy for the evil which it engenders: it is on this very account that I am attached to it.

The notion of secondary powers, placed between the sovereign and his subjects, occurred naturally to the imagination of aristocratic nations, because those communities contained individuals or families raised above the common level, and apparently destined to command by their birth, their education, and their wealth. This same notion is naturally wanting in the minds of men in democratic ages, for converse reasons; it can only be introduced artificially, it can only be kept there with difficulty; whereas they conceive, as it were without thinking upon the subject, the notion of a sole and central power which governs the whole community by its direct influence. Moreover in politics, as well as in philosophy and in religion, the intellect of democratic nations is peculiarly open to simple and general notions. Complicated systems are repugnant to it, and its favourite conception is that of a great nation composed of citizens all resembling the same pattern, and all governed by a single power.

The very next notion to that of a sole and central power, which presents itself to the minds of men in the ages of equality, is the notion of uniformity of legislation. As every man sees that he differs but little from those about him, he cannot understand why a rule which is applicable to one man should not be equally applicable to all others. Hence the slightest privileges are repugnant to his reason; the faintest dissimilarities in the political institutions of the same people offend him, and uniformity of legislation appears to him to be the first condition of good government.

I find, on the contrary, that this same notion of a uniform rule, equally binding on all the members of the community, was almost unknown to the human mind in aristocratic ages; it was either never entertained, or it was rejected.

These contrary tendencies of opinion ultimately turn on either side to such blind instincts and such ungovernable habits, that they still direct the actions of men, in spite of particular exceptions. Notwithstanding the immense variety of conditions in the middle ages, a certain number of persons existed at that period in precisely similar circumstances; but this did not prevent the laws then in force from assigning to each of them distinct duties and different rights. On the contrary, at the present time all the powers of government are exerted to impose the same customs and the same laws on populations which have as yet but few points of resemblance.

As the conditions of men become equal amongst a people, individuals seem of less importance, and society of greater dimensions; or rather, every citizen, being assimilated to all the rest, is lost in the crowd, and nothing stands conspicuous but the great and imposing image of the people at large. This naturally gives the men of democratic periods a lofty opinion of the privileges of society, and a very humble notion of the rights of individuals; they are ready to admit that the interests of the former are everything, and those of the latter nothing. They are willing to acknowledge that the power which represents the community has far more information and wisdom than any of the members of that community; and that it is the duty, as well as the right, of that power to guide as well as govern each private citizen.

If we closely scrutinize our contemporaries, and penetrate to the root of their political opinions, we shall detect some of the notions which I have just pointed out, and we shall perhaps be surprised to find so much accordance between men who are so often at variance.

The Americans hold, that in every state the supreme power ought to emanate from the people; but when once that power is constituted, they can conceive, as it were, no limits to it, and they are ready to admit that it has the right to do whatever it pleases. They have not the slightest notion of peculiar privileges granted to cities, families, or persons; their minds appear never to have foreseen that it might be possible not to apply with strict uniformity the same laws to every part, and to all the inhabitants.

These same opinions are more and more diffused in Europe; they even insinuate themselves amongst those nations which most vehemently reject the principle of the sovereignty of the people. Such nations assign a different origin to the supreme power, but they ascribe to that power the same characteristics. Amongst them all, the idea of intermediate powers is weakened and obliterated: the idea of rights inherent in certain individuals is rapidly disappearing from the minds of men; the idea of the omnipotence and sole authority of society at large rises to fill its place. These ideas take root and spread in proportion as social conditions become more equal, and men more alike; they are engendered by equality, and in turn they hasten the progress of equality. . . .

As in ages of equality no man is compelled to lend his assistance to his fellow-men, and none has any right to expect much support from them, every one is at once independent and powerless. These two conditions, which must never be either separately considered or confounded together, inspire the citizen of a democratic country with very contrary propensities. His independence fills him with self-reliance and pride amongst his equals; his debility makes him feel from time to time the want of some outward assistance, which he cannot expect from any of them, because they are all impotent and unsympathizing. In this predicament he naturally turns his eyes to that imposing power which alone rises above the level of universal depression. Of that power his wants and especially his desires continually remind him, until he ultimately views it as the sole and necessary support of his own weakness.

This may more completely explain what frequently takes place in democratic countries, where the very men who are so impatient of superiors patiently submit to a master, exhibiting at once their pride and their servility.

The hatred which men bear to privilege increases in proportion as privileges become more scarce and less considerable, so that democratic passions would seem to burn most fiercely at the very time when they have least fuel. I have already given the reason of this phenomenon. When all conditions are unequal, no inequality is so great as to offend the eye; whereas the slightest dissimilarity is odious in the midst of general uniformity: the more complete is this uniformity, the more insupportable does the sight of such a difference become. Hence it is natural that the love of equality should constantly increase together with equality itself, and that it should grow by what it feeds upon.

This never-dying ever-kindling hatred, which sets a democratic people against the smallest privileges, is peculiarly favourable to the gradual concentration of all political rights in the hands of the representative of the state alone. The sovereign, being necessarily and incontestably above all the citizens, excites not their envy, and each of them thinks that he strips his equals of the prerogative which he concedes to the crown.

The man of a democratic age is extremely reluctant to obey his neighbour who is his equal; he refuses to acknowledge in such a person ability superior to his own; he mistrusts his justice, and is jealous of his power; he fears and he contemns him; and he loves continually to remind him of the common dependence in which both of them stand to the same master.

Every central power which follows its natural tendencies courts and encourages the principle of equality; for equality singularly facilitates, extends, and secures the influence of a central power.

In like manner it may be said that every central government worships uniformity: uniformity relieves it from inquiry into an infinite number of small details which must be attended to if rules were to be adapted to men, instead of indiscriminately subjecting men to rules: thus the government likes what the citizens like, and naturally hates what they hate. These common sentiments, which, in democratic nations, constantly unite the sovereign and every member of the community in one and the same conviction, establish a secret and lasting sympathy between them. The faults of the government are pardoned for the sake of its tastes; public confidence is only reluctantly withdrawn in the midst even of its excesses and its errors, and it is restored at the first call. Democratic nations often hate those in whose hands the central power is vested; but they always love that power itself.

Thus, by two separate paths, I have reached the same conclusion.

I have shown that the principle of equality suggests to men the notion of a sole, uniform, and strong government: I have now shown that the principle of equality imparts to them a taste for it. To governments of this kind the nations of our age are therefore tending. They are drawn thither by the natural inclination of mind and heart; and in order to reach that result, it is enough that they do not check themselves in their course.

I am of opinion, that, in the democratic ages which are opening upon us, individual independence and local liberties will ever be the produce of artificial contrivance; that centralization will be the natural form of government.

*　*　*

As long as the democratic revolution was glowing with heat, the men who were bent upon the destruction of old aristocratic powers hostile to that revolution, displayed a strong spirit of independence; but as the victory of the principle of equality became more complete, they gradually surrendered themselves to the propensities natural to that condition of equality, and they strengthened and centralized their governments. They had sought to be free in order to make themselves equal; but in proportion as equality was more established by the aid of freedom, freedom itself was thereby rendered of more difficult attainment. . . .

In our days men see that constituted powers are dilapidated on every side—they see all ancient authority gasping away, all ancient barriers tottering to their fall, and the judgement of the wisest is troubled at the sight: they attend only to the amazing revolution which is taking place before their eyes, and they imagine that mankind is about to fall into perpetual anarchy: if they looked to the final consequences of this revolution, their fears would perhaps assume a different shape. For myself, I confess that I put no trust in the spirit of freedom which appears to animate my contemporaries: I see well enough that the nations of this age are turbulent, but I do not clearly perceive that they are liberal; and I fear lest, at the close of those perturbations which rock the base of thrones, the domination of sovereigns may prove more powerful than it ever was before. . . .

No sovereign ever lived in former ages so absolute or so powerful as to undertake to administer by his own agency, and without the assistance of intermediate powers, all the parts of a great empire: none ever attempted to subject all his subjects indiscriminately to strict uniformity of regulation, and personally to tutor and direct every member of the community. The notion of such an undertaking never occurred to the human mind; and if any man had conceived it, the want of information, the imperfection of the administrative system, and above all, the natural obstacles caused by the inequality of conditions, would speedily have checked the execution of so vast a design.

When the Roman emperors were at the height of their power, the different nations of the empire still preserved manners and customs of great diversity; although they were subject to the same monarch, most of the provinces were separately administered; they abounded in powerful and active municipalities; and although the whole government of the empire was centred in the hands of the emperor alone, and he always remained, upon occasions, the supreme arbiter in all matters, yet the details of social life and private occupations lay for the most part beyond his control. The emperors possessed, it is true, an immense and unchecked power, which allowed them to gratify all their whimsical tastes, and to employ for that purpose the whole strength of the State. They frequently abused that power arbitrarily to deprive their subjects of property or of life: their tyranny was extremely onerous to the few, but it did not reach the greater number; it was fixed to some few main objects, and neglected the rest; it was violent, but its range was limited.

But it would seem that if despotism were to be established amongst the democratic nations of our days, it might assume a different character; it would be more extensive and more mild; it would degrade men without tormenting them. I do not question, that in an age of instruction and equality like our own, sovereigns might more easily succeed in collecting all political power into their own hands, and might interfere more habitually and decidedly within the circle of private interests, than any sovereign of antiquity could ever do. But this same principle of equality which facilitates despotism, tempers its rigour. We have seen how the manners of society become more humane and gentle in proportion as men become more equal and alike. When no member of the community has much power or much wealth, tyranny is, as it were, without opportunities and a field of action. As all fortunes are scanty, the passions of men are naturally circumscribed,—their imagination limited, their pleasures simple. This universal moderation moderates the sovereign himself, and checks within certain limits the inordinate stretch of his desires. . . .

Democratic governments may become violent and even cruel at certain periods of extreme effervescence or of great danger; but these crises will be rare and brief. When I consider the petty passions of our contemporaries, the mildness of their manners, the extent of their education, the purity of their religion, the gentleness of their morality, their regular and industrious habits, and the restraint which they almost all observe in their vices no less than in their virtues, I have no fear that they will meet with tyrants in their rulers, but rather guardians.

I think then that the species of oppression by which democratic nations are menaced is unlike anything which ever before existed in the world: our contemporaries will find no prototype of it in their memories. I am trying myself to choose an expression which will accurately convey the whole of the idea I have formed of it, but in vain; the old words despotism and tyranny are inappropriate: the thing itself is new; and since I cannot name it, I must attempt to define it.

I seek to trace the novel features under which despotism may appear in the world. The first thing that strikes the observation is an innumerable multitude of men all equal and alike, incessantly endeavouring to procure the petty and paltry pleasures with which they glut their lives. Each of them, living apart, is as a stranger to the fate of all the rest,—his children and his private friends constitute to him the whole of mankind; as for the rest of his fellow-citizens, he is close to them, but he sees them not;—he touches them, but he feels them not; he exists but in himself and for himself alone; and if his kindred still remain to him, he may be said at any rate to have lost his country.

Above this race of men stands an immense and tutelary power, which takes upon itself alone to secure their gratifications, and to watch over their fate. That power is absolute, minute, regular, provident, and mild. It would be like the authority of a parent, if, like that authority, its object was to prepare men for manhood; but it seeks on the contrary to keep them in perpetual childhood: it is well content that the people should rejoice, provided they think of nothing but rejoicing. For their happiness such a government willingly labours, but it chooses to be the sole agent and the only arbiter of that happiness: it provides for their security, foresees and supplies their necessities, facilitates their pleasures, manages their principal concerns, directs their industry, regulates the descent of property, and subdivides their inheritances—what remains, but to spare them all the care of thinking and all the trouble of living?

Thus it every day renders the exercise of the free agency of man less useful and less frequent; it circumscribes the will within a narrower range, and gradually robs a man of all the uses of himself. The principle of equality has prepared men for these things: it has predisposed men to endure them, and oftentimes to look on them as benefits.

After having thus successively taken each member of the community in its powerful grasp, and fashioned them at will, the supreme power then extends its arm over the whole community. It covers the surface of society with a net-work of small complicated rules, minute and uniform, through which the most original minds and the most energetic characters cannot penetrate, to rise above the crowd. The will of man is not shattered, but softened, bent, and guided: men are seldom forced by it to act, but they are constantly restrained from acting: such a power does not destroy, but it prevents existence; it does not tyrannize, but it compresses, enervates, extinguishes, and stupefies a people, till each nation is reduced to be nothing better than a flock of timid and industrious animals, of which the government is the shepherd.

I have always thought that servitude of the regular, quiet, and gentle kind which I have just described, might be combined more easily than is commonly believed with some of the outward forms of freedom; and that it might even establish itself under the wing of the sovereignty of the people.

Our contemporaries are constantly excited by two conflicting passions; they want to be led, and they wish to remain free: as they cannot destroy either one or the other of these contrary propensities, they strive to satisfy them both at once. They devise a sole, tutelary, and all-powerful form of government, but elected by the people. They combine the principle of centralization and that of popular sovereignty; this gives them a respite: they console themselves for being in tutelage by the reflection that they have chosen their own guardians. Every man allows himself to be put in leading-strings, because he sees that it is not a person or a class of persons, but the people at large that holds the end of his chain.

By this system the people shake off their state of dependence just long enough to select their master, and then relapse into it again. A great many persons at the present day are quite contented with this sort of compromise between administrative despotism and the sovereignty of the people; and they think they have done enough for the protection of individual freedom when they have surrendered it to the power of the nation at large. This does not satisfy me: the nature of him I am to obey signifies less to me than the fact of extorted obedience.

I believe that it is easier to establish an absolute and despotic government amongst a people in which the conditions of society are equal, than amongst any other; and I think that if such a government were once established amongst such a people, it would not only oppress men, but would eventually strip each of them of several of the highest qualities of humanity. Despotism therefore appears to me peculiarly to be dreaded in democratic ages. I should have loved freedom, I believe, at all times, but in the time in which we live I am ready to worship it.

On the other hand, I am persuaded that all who shall attempt, in the ages upon which we are entering, to base freedom upon aristocratic privilege, will fail;—that all who shall attempt to draw and to retain authority within a single class, will fail. At the present day no ruler is skilful or strong enough to found a despotism, by re-establishing permanent distinctions of rank amongst his subjects: no legislator is wise or powerful enough to preserve free institutions, if he does not take equality for his first principle and his watchword. All those of our contemporaries who would establish or secure the independence and the dignity of their fellow-men, must show themselves the friends of equality; and the only worthy means of showing themselves as such, is to be so: upon this depends the success of their holy enterprize. Thus the question is not how to reconstruct aristocratic society, but how to make liberty proceed out of that democratic state of society in which God has placed us.

These two truths appear to me simple, clear, and fertile in consequences; and they naturally lead me to consider what kind of free government can be established amongst a people in which social conditions are equal.

It results from the very constitution of democratic nations and from their necessities, that the power of government amongst them must be more uniform, more centralized, more extensive, more searching, and more efficient than in other countries. Society at large is naturally stronger and more active, individuals more subordinate and weak; the former does more, the latter less; and this is inevitably the case.

It is not therefore to be expected that the range of private independence will ever be as extensive in democratic as in aristocratic countries;—nor is this to be desired; for, amongst aristocrat nations, the mass is often sacrificed to the individual, and the prosperity of the greater number to the greatness of the few. It is both necessary and desirable that the government of a democratic people should be active and powerful: and our object should not be to render it weak or indolent, but solely to prevent it from abusing its aptitude and its strength.

The circumstance which most contributed to secure the independence of private persons in aristocratic ages, was, that the supreme power did not affect to take upon itself alone the government and administration of the community; those functions were necessarily partially left to the members of the aristocracy: so that as the supreme power was always divided, it never weighed with its whole weight and in the same manner on each individual.

Not only did the government not perform everything by its immediate agency; but as most of the agents who discharged its duties derived their power not from the State, but from the circumstance of their birth, they were not perpetually under its control. The government could not make or unmake them in an instant, at pleasure, nor bend them in strict uniformity to its slightest caprice—this was an additional guarantee of private independence.

I readily admit that recourse cannot be had to the same means at the present time; but I discover certain democratic expedients which may be substituted for them. Instead of vesting in the government alone all the administrative powers of which corporations and nobles have been deprived, a portion of them may be entrusted to secondary public bodies, temporarily composed of private citizens: thus the liberty of private persons will be more secure, and their equality will not be diminished. . . .

In periods of aristocracy every man is always bound so closely to many of his fellow-citizens, that he cannot be assailed without their coming to his assistance. In ages of equality every man naturally stands alone; he has no hereditary friends whose co-operation he may demand,—no class upon whose sympathy he may rely: he is easily got rid of, and he is trampled on with impunity. At the present time, an oppressed member of the community has therefore only one method of self-defence,—he may appeal to the whole nation; and if the whole nation is deaf to his complaint, he may appeal to mankind: the only means he has of making this appeal is by the press. Thus the liberty of the press is infinitely more valuable amongst democratic nations than amongst all others; it is the only cure for the evils which equality may produce. Equality sets men apart and weakens them; but the press places a powerful weapon within every man's reach, which the weakest and loneliest of them all may use. Equality deprives a man of the support of his connexions; but the press enables him to summon all his fellow-countrymen and all his fellow-men to his assistance. Printing has accelerated the progress of equality, and it is also one of its best correctives.

I think that men living in aristocracies may, strictly speaking, do without the liberty of the press: but such is not the case with those who live in democratic countries. To protect their personal independence I trust not to great political assemblies, to parliamentary privilege, or to the assertion of popular sovereignty. All these things may, to a certain extent, be reconciled with personal servitude—but that servitude cannot be complete if the press is free: the press is the chiefest democratic instrument of freedom.

Something analogous may be said of the judicial power. It is a part of the essence of judicial power to attend to private interests, and to fix itself with predilection on minute objects submitted to its observation: another essential quality of judicial power is never to volunteer its assistance to the oppressed, but always to be at the disposal of the humblest of those who solicit it; their complaint, however feeble they may themselves be, will force itself upon the ear of justice and claim redress, for this is inherent in the very constitution of the courts of justice.

A power of this kind is therefore peculiarly adapted to the wants of freedom, at a time when the eye and finger of the government are constantly intruding into the minutest details of human actions, and when private persons are at once too weak to protect themselves, and too much isolated for them to reckon upon the assistance of their fellows. The strength of the courts of law has ever been the greatest security which can be offered to personal independence; but this is more especially the case in democratic ages: private rights and interests are in constant danger, if the judicial power does not grow more extensive and more strong to keep pace with the growing equality of conditions. . . .

Another tendency, which is extremely natural to democratic nations and extremely dangerous, is that which leads them to despise and undervalue the rights of private persons. The attachment which men feel to a right, and the respect which they display for it, is generally proportioned to its importance, or to the length of time during which they have enjoyed it. The rights of private persons amongst democratic nations are commonly of small importance, of recent growth, and extremely precarious,—the consequence is that they are often sacrificed without regret, and almost always violated without remorse.

But it happens that at the same period and amongst the same nations in which men conceive a natural contempt for the rights of private persons, the rights of society at large are naturally extended and consolidated: in other words, men become less attached to private rights at the very time at which it would be most necessary to retain and to defend what little remains of them. It is therefore most especially in the present democratic ages, that the true friends of the liberty and the greatness of man ought constantly to be on the alert to prevent the power of government from lightly sacrificing the private rights of individuals to the general execution of its designs. At such times no citizen is so obscure that it is not very dangerous to allow him to be oppressed—no private rights are so unimportant that they can be surrendered with impunity to the caprices of a government. The reason is plain:—if the private right of an individual is violated at a time when the human mind is fully impressed with the importance and the sanctity of such rights, the injury done is confined to the individual whose right is infringed; but to violate such a right, at the present day, is deeply to corrupt the manners of the nation and to put the whole community in jeopardy, because the very notion of this kind of right constantly tends amongst us to be impaired and lost. . . .

I know of no countries in which revolutions are more dangerous than in democratic countries; because, independently of the accidental and transient evils which must always attend them, they may always create some evils which are permanent and unending.

I believe that there are such things as justifiable resistance and legitimate rebellion: I do not therefore assert, as an absolute proposition, that the men of democratic ages ought never to make revolutions; but I think that they have especial reason to hesitate before they embark in them, and that it is far better to endure many grievances in their present condition than to have recourse to so perilous a remedy. . . .

In olden society everything was different: unity and uniformity were nowhere to be met with. In modern society everything threatens to become so much alike, that the peculiar characteristics of each individual will soon be entirely lost in the general aspect of the world. Our forefathers were ever prone to make an improper use of the notion, that private rights ought to be respected; and we are naturally prone on the other hand to exaggerate the idea that the interest of a private individual ought always to bend to the interest of the many.

The political world is metamorphosed: new remedies must henceforth be sought for new disorders. To lay down extensive, but distinct and settled limits, to the action of the government; to confer certain rights on private persons, and to secure to them the undisputed enjoyment of those rights; to enable individual man to maintain whatever independence, strength, and original power he still possesses; to raise him by the side of society at large, and uphold him in that position,— these appear to me the main objects of legislators in the ages upon which we are now entering.

It would seem as if the rulers of our time sought only to use men in order to make things great; I wish that they would try a little more to make great men; that they would set less value on the work, and more upon the workman; that they would never forget that a nation cannot long remain strong when every man belonging to it is individually weak, and that no form or combination of social polity has yet been devised, to make an energetic people out of a community of pusillanimous and enfeebled citizens.

I trace amongst our contemporaries two contrary notions which are equally injurious. One set of men can perceive nothing in the principle of equality but the anarchical tendencies which it engenders: they dread their own free agency—they fear themselves. Other thinkers, less numerous but more enlightened, take a different view: beside that track which starts from the principle of equality to terminate in anarchy, they have at last discovered the road which seems to lead men to inevitable servitude. They shape their souls beforehand to this necessary condition; and, despairing of remaining free, they already do obeisance in their hearts to the master who is soon to appear. The former abandon freedom, because they think it dangerous; the latter, because they hold it to be impossible.

If I had entertained the latter conviction, I should not have written this book, but I should have confined myself to deploring in secret the destiny of mankind. I have sought to point out the dangers to which the principle of equality exposes the independence of man, because I firmly believe that these dangers are the most formidable, as well as the least foreseen, of all those which futurity holds in store; but I do not think that they are insurmountable.

The men who live in the democratic ages upon which we are entering have naturally a taste for independence: they are naturally impatient of regulation, and they are wearied by the permanence even of the condition they themselves prefer. They are fond of power; but they are prone to despise and hate those who wield it, and they easily elude its grasp by their own mobility and insignificance.

These propensities will always manifest themselves, because they originate in the groundwork of society, which will undergo no change: for a long time they will prevent the establishment of any despotism, and they will furnish fresh weapons to each succeeding generation which shall struggle in favour of the liberty of mankind. Let us then look forward to the future with that salutary fear which makes men keep watch and ward for freedom, not with that faint and idle terror which depresses and enervates the heart. . . .

If I endeavour to find out the most general and the most prominent of all these different characteristics, I shall have occasion to perceive, that what is taking place in men's fortunes manifests itself under a thousand other forms. Almost all extremes are softened or blunted: all that was most prominent is superseded by some mean term, at once less lofty and less low, less brilliant and less obscure, than what before existed in the world.

When I survey this countless multitude of beings, shaped in each other's likeness, amidst whom nothing rises and nothing falls, the sight of such universal uniformity saddens and chills me, and I am tempted to regret that state of society which has ceased to be. When the world was full of men of great importance and extreme insignificance, of great wealth and extreme poverty, of great learning and extreme ignorance, I turned aside from the latter to fix my observation on the former alone, who gratified my sympathies. But I admit that this gratification arose from my own weakness: it is because I am unable to see at once all that is around me, that I am allowed thus to select and separate the objects of my predilection from among so many others. Such is not the case with that Almighty and Eternal Being, whose gaze necessarily includes the whole of created things, and who surveys distinctly, though at once, mankind and man.

We may naturally believe that it is not the singular prosperity of the few, but the greater well-being of all, which is most pleasing in the sight of the Creator and Preserver of men. What appears to me to be man's decline, is to His eye advancement; what afflicts me is acceptable to Him. A state of equality is perhaps less elevated, but it is more just; and its justice constitutes its greatness and its beauty. I would strive then to raise myself to this point of the Divine contemplation, and thence to view and to judge the concerns of men.

No man, upon the earth, can as yet affirm absolutely and generally, that the new state of the world is better than its former one; but it is already easy to perceive that this state is different. Some vices and some virtues were so inherent in the constitution of an aristocratic nation, and are so opposite to the character of a modern people, that they can never be infused into it; some good tendencies and some bad propensities which were unknown to the former, are natural to the latter; some ideas suggest themselves spontaneously to the imagination of the one, which are utterly repugnant to the mind of the other. They are like two distinct orders of human beings, each of which has its own merits and defects, its own advantages and its own evils. Care must therefore be taken not to judge the state of society, which is now coming into existence, by notions derived from a state of society which no longer exists; for as these states of society are exceedingly different in their structure, they cannot be submitted to a just or fair comparison.

It would be scarcely more reasonable to require of our own contemporaries the peculiar virtues which originated in the social condition of their forefathers, since that social condition is itself fallen, and has drawn into one promiscuous ruin the good and evil which belonged to it.

But as yet these things are imperfectly understood. I find that a great number of my contemporaries undertake to make a certain selection from amongst the institutions, the opinions, and the ideas which originated in the aristocratic constitution of society as it was: a portion of these elements they would willingly relinquish, but they would keep the remainder and transplant them into their new world. I apprehend that such men are wasting their time and their strength in virtuous but unprofitable efforts.

The object is not to retain the peculiar advantages which the inequality of conditions bestows upon mankind, but to secure the new benefits which equality may supply. We have not to seek to make ourselves like our progenitors, but to strive to work out that species of greatness and happiness which is our own.

For myself, who now look back from this extreme limit of my task, and discover from afar, but at once, the various objects which have attracted my more attentive investigation upon my way, I am full of apprehensions and of hopes. I perceive mighty dangers which it is possible to ward off,—mighty evils which may be avoided or alleviated; and I cling with a firmer hold to the belief, that for democratic nations to be virtuous and prosperous they require but to will it.

I am aware that many of my contemporaries maintain that nations are never their own masters here below, and that they necessarily obey some insurmountable and unintelligent power, arising from anterior events, from their race, or from the soil and climate of their country. Such principles are false and cowardly; such principles can never produce aught but feeble men and pusillanimous nations. Providence has not created mankind entirely independent or entirely free. It is true that around every man a fatal circle is traced, beyond which he cannot pass; but within the wide verge of that circle he is powerful and free: as it is with man, so with communities. The nations of our time cannot prevent the conditions of men from becoming equal; but it depends upon themselves whether the principle of equality is to lead them to servitude or freedom, to knowledge or barbarism, to prosperity or to wretchedness.

19 DISRAELI

The Conservative Concept of Equality

Benjamin Disraeli (1804–1881), later the Earl of Beaconsfield, was twice Prime Minister of Great Britain and the leader of the
Conservative Party during the latter part of the nineteenth century. He
saw himself as the defender of the British way of life against the intrusions
of cosmopolitanism and liberalism from the European continent. In his
political program he forged an alliance of "the gentlemen of England,"
the landed aristocracy, and the new urban working class to whom he extended the franchise in his Reform Bill of 1867. The selections are taken
from the last part of his *Vindication of the English Constitution* (written
at the start of his career in 1835) and several subsequent public addresses.

If we take a superficial view of the nature of the English constitution, we shall perceive that the government of the country is carried
on by a king and two limited orders of his subjects: but if we indulge in a more profound and comprehensive survey—if we examine
not only the political constitution, but the political condition of the
country, we shall in truth discover that the state of our society is that
of a complete democracy, headed by an hereditary chief, the executive
and legislative functions performed by two privileged classes of the
community, but the whole body of the nation entitled, if duly qualified, to participate in the exercise of those functions, and constantly
participating in them.

The basis of English society is Equality. But here let us distinguish:
there are two kinds of equality; there is the equality that levels and
destroys, and the equality that elevates and creates. It is this last, this
sublime, this celestial equality, that animates the laws of England. The

principle of the first equality, base, terrestrial, Gallic, and grovelling, is that no one should be privileged: the principle of English equality is that every one should be privileged. Thus the meanest subject of our King is born to great and important privileges; an Englishman, however humble may be his birth, whether he be doomed to the plough or destined to the loom, is born to the noblest of all inheritances, the equality of civil rights; he is born to freedom, he is born to justice, and he is born to property. There is no station to which he may not aspire; there is no master whom he is obliged to serve; there is no magistrate who dares imprison him against the law; and the soil on which he labours must supply him with an honest and decorous maintenance. These are rights and privileges as valuable as King, Lords, and Commons; and it is only a nation thus schooled and cradled in the principles and practice of freedom, which, indeed, could maintain such institutions. Thus the English in politics are as the old Hebrews in religion, "a favoured and peculiar people." As Equality is the basis, so Gradation is the superstructure; and the English nation is essentially a nation of classes, but not of castes. Hence that admirable order, which is the characteristic of our society; for in England every man knows or finds his place; the law has supplied every man with a position, and nature has a liberal charter to amend the arrangement of the law. Our equality is the safety valve of tumultuous spirits; our gradation the security of the humble and the meek. The latter take refuge in their order; the former seek relief in emancipating themselves from its rank. English equality calls upon the subject to aspire; French equality summons him to abase himself. In England the subject is invited to become an object of admiration or respect; in France he is warned lest he become an object of envy or of ridicule. The law of England has invested the subject with equality in order that if entitled to eminence, he should rise superior to the mass. The law of France has invested the subject with equality, on condition that he prevent the elevation of his fellow. English equality blends every man's ambition with the perpetuity of the state; French equality, which has reduced the subject into a mere individual, has degraded the state into a mere society. English equality governs the subject by the united and mingled influences of reason and imagination; French equality having rejected imagination and aspiring to reason, has in reality, only resolved itself into a barren fantasy. The constitution of England is founded not only on a profound knowledge of human nature, but of human nature in England; the political scheme of France originates not only in a profound ignorance of human nature in general, but of French human nature in particular: thus in England, however vast and violent may be our revolutions, the Constitution ever becomes more firm and vigorous, while in France a riot oversets the government, and after half a century of political experiments, one of the most intellectual of human races has succeeded in losing every attribute of a nation, and has sought refuge from anarchy in a despotism without lustre, which contradicts all its theories, and violates all the principles for which it has ever affected to struggle.

The English nation, to obtain the convenience of monarchy, have established a popular throne, and to enjoy the security of aristocracy, have invested certain orders of their fellow subjects with legislative functions: but these estates, however highly privileged, are invested with no quality of exclusion; and the Peers and the Commons of England are the trustees of the nation, not its masters. The country where the legislative and even the executive office may be constitutionally obtained by every subject of the land, is a democracy, and a democracy of the noblest order.

20 DISRAELI

English Democracy *

. . . It is quite impossible that a whole people can be a branch of a legislature. If a whole people have the power of making laws, it is folly to suppose that they will allow an assembly of 300 or 400 individuals, or a solitary being on a throne, to thwart their sovereign will and pleasure. But I deny that a people can govern itself. Self-government is a contradiction in terms. Whatever form a government may assume, power must be exercised by a minority of numbers. I shall, perhaps, be reminded of the ancient republics. I answer, that the ancient republics were as aristocratic communities as any that flourished in the middle ages. The Demos of Athens was an oligarchy living upon slaves. There is a great slave population even in the United States, if a society of yesterday is to illustrate an argument on our ancient civilisation.

But it is useless to argue the question abstractedly. The phrase 'the people' is sheer nonsense. It is not a political term. It is a phrase of natural history. A people is a species; a civilised community is a nation. Now, a nation is a work of art and a work of time. A nation is gradually created by a variety of influences—the influence of original organisation, of climate, soil, religion, laws, customs, manners, extraordinary accidents and incidents in their history, and the individual character of their illustrious citizens. These influences create the nation—these form the national mind, and produce in the course of centuries a high degree of civilisation. If you destroy the political in-

* Benjamin Disraeli, *The Runneymede Letters* (London: Richard Bentley & Sons, 1885; first published, 1836), "The Spirit of Whiggism," from Chapters IV and V. See introductory remarks to Selection 19.

stitutions which these influences have called into force, and which are
the machinery by which they constantly act, you destroy the nation.
The nation, in a state of anarchy and dissolution, then becomes a
people; and after experiencing all the consequent misery, like a company of bees spoiled of their queen and rifled of their hive, they set
to again and establish themselves into a society.

Although all society is artificial, the most artificial society in the
world is unquestionably the English nation. Our insular situation and
our foreign empire, our immense accumulated wealth and our industrious character, our peculiar religious state, which secures alike ortho-
doxy and toleration, our church and our sects, our agriculture and
our manufactures, our military services, our statute law, and supplementary equity, our adventurous commerce, landed tenure, and un-
precedented system of credit, form, among many others, such a variety
of interests, and apparently so conflicting, that I do not think even
the Abbé Sieyès himself could devise a scheme by which this nation
could be absolutely and definitely represented.

The framers of the English constitution were fortunately not of the
school of Abbé Sieyès. Their first object was to make us free; their
next to keep us so. While, therefore, they selected equality as the basis
of their social order, they took care to blend every man's ambition
with the perpetuity of the State. Unlike the levelling equality of modern days, the ancient equality of England elevates and creates. Learned
in human nature, the English constitution holds out privilege to every
subject as the inducement to do his duty. As it has secured freedom,
justice, and even property to the humblest of the commonwealth, so,
pursuing the same system of privileges, it has confided the legislature
of the realm to two orders of the subjects—orders, however, in which
every English citizen may be constitutionally enrolled—the Lords and
the Commons. The two estates of the Peers are personally summoned
to meet in their chamber: the more extensive and single estate of the
Commons meets by its representatives.   Both are political orders,
complete in their character, independent in their authority, legally irresponsible for the exercise of their power. But they are the trustees
of the nation, not its masters; and there is a High Court of Chancery
in the public opinion of the nation at large, which exercises a vigilant
control over these privileged classes of the community, and to which
they are equitably and morally amenable. Estimating, therefore, the
moral responsibility of our political estates, it may fairly be main-

tained that, instead of being irresponsible, the responsibility of the Lords exceeds that of the Commons. The House of Commons itself not being an estate of the realm, but only the representatives of an estate, owes to the nation a responsibility neither legal nor moral. The House of Commons is responsible only to that privileged order who are its constituents. Between the Lords and the Commons themselves there is this prime difference—that the Lords are known, and seen, and marked; the Commons are unknown, invisible, and unobserved. The Lords meet in a particular spot; the Commons are scattered over the kingdom. The eye of the nation rests upon the Lords, few in number, and notable in position; the eye of the nation wanders in vain for the Commons, far more numerous, but far less remarkable. As a substitute the nation appeals to the House of Commons, but sometimes appeals in vain; for if the majority of the Commons choose to support their representatives in a course of conduct adverse to the opinion of the nation, the House of Commons will set the nation at defiance. They have done so once; may they never repeat that destructive career! Such are our two Houses of Parliament—the most illustrious assemblies since the Roman Senate and Grecian Areopagus; neither of them is the 'House of the People,' but both alike represent the 'Nation.'

There are two propositions, which, however at the first glance they may appear to contradict the popular opinions of the day, are nevertheless, as I believe, just and true. And they are these:—

First. That there is no probability of ever establishing a more democratic form of government than the present English constitution.

Second. That the recent political changes of the Whigs are, in fact, a departure from the democratic spirit of that constitution.

Whatever form a government may assume, its spirit must be determined by the laws which regulate the property of the country. You may have a Senate and Consuls, you may have no hereditary titles, and you may dub each householder or inhabitant a citizen; but if the spirit of your laws preserves masses of property in a particular class, the government of the country will follow the disposition of the property. So also you may have an apparent despotism without any formal popular control, and with no aristocracy, either natural or artificial, and the spirit of the government may nevertheless be republican. Thus the ancient polity of Rome, in its best days, was an aristocracy, and the government of Constantinople is the nearest approach to a democracy on a great scale, and maintained during a great period, that history offers. . . .

The disposition of property in England throws the government of the country into the hands of its natural aristocracy. I do not believe that any scheme of the suffrage, or any method of election, could divert that power into other quarters. It is the necessary consequence of our present social state. I believe, the wider the popular suffrage, the more powerful would be the natural aristocracy. This seems to me an inevitable consequence; but I admit this proposition on the clear understanding that such an extension should be established on a fair, and not a factious, basis. Here, then, arises the question of the ballot, into the merits of which I shall take another opportunity of entering, recording only now my opinion, that in the present arrangement of the constituencies, even the ballot would favour the power of the natural aristocracy, and that, if the ballot were simultaneously introduced with a fair and not a factious extension of the suffrage, it would produce no difference whatever in the ultimate result.

Quitting, then, these considerations, let us arrive at the important point. Is there any probability of a different disposition of property in England—a disposition of property which, by producing a very general similarity of condition, would throw the government of the country into the hands of any individuals whom popular esteem or fancy might select?

It appears to me that this question can only be decided by ascertaining the genius of the English nation. What is the prime characteristic of the English mind? I apprehend I may safely decide upon its being industry. Taking a general but not a superficial survey of the English character since the Reformation, a thousand circumstances convince me that the salient point in our national psychology is the passion for accumulating wealth, of which industry is the chief instrument. We value our freedom principally because it leaves us unrestricted in our pursuits; and that reverence for law and all that is established, which also eminently distinguishes the English nation, is occasioned by the conviction that, next to liberty, order is the most efficacious assistant of industry.

And thus we see that those great revolutions which must occur in the history of all nations, when they happen here produce no permanent effects upon our social state. Our revolutions are brought about by the passions of creative minds taking advantage, for their own aggrandisement, of peculiar circumstances in our national progress. They are never called for by the great body of the nation. Churches are plundered, long rebellions maintained, dynasties changed, parliaments abolished; but when the storm is passed, the features of the social landscape remain unimpaired; there are no traces of the hurricane, the earthquake, or the volcano; it has been but a tumult of the atmosphere, that has neither toppled down our old spires and palaces nor swallowed up our cities and seats of learning, nor blasted our ancient woods, nor swept away our ports and harbours. The English nation ever recurs to its ancient institutions—the institutions that have alike secured freedom and order; and after all their ebullitions, we find them, when the sky is clear, again at work, and toiling on at their eternal task of accumulation.

There is this difference between the revolutions of England and the revolutions of the Continent—the European revolution is a struggle against privilege; an English revolution is a struggle for it. If a new class rises in the State, it becomes uneasy to take its place in the natural aristocracy of the land: a desperate faction or a wily leader takes advantage of this desire, and a revolution is the consequence. Thus the Whigs in the present day have risen to power on the shoulders of the manufacturing interest. To secure themselves in their posts, the Whigs have given the new interest an undue preponderance; but the new interest, having obtained its object, is content. The manufacturer, like every other Englishman, is as aristocratic as the landlord. The manufacturer begins to lack in movement. Under Walpole the Whigs played the same game with the commercial interest; a century has passed, and the commercial interest are all as devoted to the constitution as the manufacturers soon will be. . . .

When passions have a little subsided, the industrious ten-pounder, who has struggled into the privileged order of the Commons, proud of having obtained the first step of aristocracy, will be the last man to assist in destroying the other gradations of the scale which he or his posterity may yet ascend; the new member of a manufacturing district has his eye already upon a neighbouring park, avails himself of his political position to become a county magistrate, meditates upon a baronetcy, and dreams of a coroneted descendant.

The nation that esteems wealth as the great object of existence will submit to no laws that do not secure the enjoyment of wealth. Now, we deprive wealth of its greatest source of enjoyment, as well as of its best security, if we deprive it of power. The English nation, therefore, insists that property shall be the qualification for power, and the whole scope of its laws and customs is to promote and favour the accumulation of wealth and the perpetuation of property. We cannot alter, therefore, the disposition of property in this country without we change the national character. Far from the present age being hostile to the supremacy of property, there has been no period of our history where property has been more esteemed, because there has been no period when the nation has been so industrious.

Believing, therefore, that no change will occur in the disposition of property in this country, I cannot comprehend how our government can become more democratic. The consequence of our wealth is an aristocratic constitution; the consequence of our love of liberty is an aristocratic constitution founded on an equality of civil rights. And who can deny that an aristocratic constitution resting on such a basis, where the legislative, and even the executive office may be obtained by every subject of the realm, is, in fact, a noble democracy? The English constitution, faithful to the national character, secures to all the enjoyment of property and the delights of freedom. Its honours are a perpetual reward of industry; every Englishman is toiling to obtain them; and this is the constitution to which every Englishman will always be devoted, except he is a Whig.

21 DISRAELI

Popular Principles vs. Liberal Opinion *

In the great struggle between popular principles and liberal opinions, which is the characteristic of our age, I hope ever to be found on the side of the people, and of the Institutions of England. . . . Liberal opinions are the opinions of those who would be free from certain constraints and regulations, from a certain dependence and duty which are deemed necessary for the general and popular welfare. Liberal opinions are very convenient opinions for the rich and the powerful. They ensure enjoyment and are opposed to self-sacrifice. The holder of Liberal opinions, for example, maintains that the possession of land is to be considered in a commercial light and no other. He looks to the income which it will afford him. It is not a Liberal principle that the holder of land should incur the duty of executing justice and maintaining truth among the multitude for nothing. That, gentlemen, is a popular principle, a principle of government for the benefit of the people, not a Liberal opinion. A poor law is founded upon a popular principle: Liberal opinions are entirely averse to its enactments. . . .

---

* Quoted in William F. Monypenny and G. E. Buckle, *The Life of Benjamin Disraeli,* Vol. III (London: John Murray, 1914). [Address to the electors of Buckingham County, May 25, 1847.] See introductory remarks to Selection 19.

22 DISRAELI

Tory Democracy *

You want in this House every element that obtains respect and engages the interest of the country. You must have lineage and great territorial property; you must have manufacturing enterprise of the highest character; you must have commercial weight; you must have professional ability in all its forms; but you want something more— you want a body of men not too ultimately connected either with agriculture, or with manufactures, or with commerce; not too much wedded to professional thought and professional habits; you want a body of men representing the vast variety of the English character: men who would arbitrate between the claims of those great predominant interests, who would temper the acerbity of their controversies. You want a body of men to represent that immense portion of the community who cannot be ranked under any of those striking and powerful classes to which I have referred, but who are in aggregate equally important and valuable, and perhaps as numerous. . . .

* Benjamin Disraeli, *Parliamentary Reform,* ed. by Montagu Corry (London: Longmans Green, 1867). [Speech in the House of Commons, February 28, 1859.] See introductory remarks to Selection 19.

23   DISRAELI

The Danger of Democracy *

And now, Sir, how are we met upon this question? An hon. Gentleman, a friend of mine . . . says that he is not afraid of the people of England; whereupon there is great cheering from hon. Gentlemen opposite; and I doubt not that if the sentiment had been uttered so well and so forcibly at any of the minor theatres it would have been received with applause still more enthusiastic. My hon. Friend might have stopped and made two enquiries. He might have asked, What are the people? and why should I fear? Why, Sir, I have no apprehension myself that, if you had manhood suffrage to-morrow, the honest, brave, and good-natured people of England would resort to pillage, incendiarism, and massacre. Who expects that? But—though I would do as much justice to the qualities of our countrymen as any Gentleman in this House—though I may not indulge in high-flown and far-fetched expressions with respect to them like those we have listened to, for the people may have their parasites as well as monarchs and aristocracies—yet I have no doubt that, whatever may be their high qualities, our countrymen are subject to the same political laws that affect the condition of all other communities and nations. If you establish a democracy you must in due season reap the fruits of a democracy. You will in due season have great impatience of the public burdens combined in due season with great increase of the public expenditure. You will in due season reap the fruits of such united influence. You will in due season have wars entered into from passion

* Benjamin Disraeli, *Parliamentary Reform,* ed. by Montagu Corry (London: Longmans Green, 1867). [Speech in the House of Commons, March 31, 1859.] See introductory remarks to Selection 19.

and not from reason; and you will in due season submit to peace ignominiously sought and ignominiously obtained, which will diminish your authority and perhaps endanger your independence. You will in due season, with a democracy, find that your property is less valuable, and that your freedom is less complete. I doubt not when there has been realised a sufficient quantity of disaffection and dismay, the good sense of this country will come to the rally, and that you will obtain some remedy for your grievances, and some redress for your wrongs, by the process through which alone it can be obtained—by that process which may render your property more secure, but which will not render your liberty more eminent.

24 DISRAELI

The Three Chief Tory Goals *

Now, I have always been of opinion that the Tory party has three great objects. The first is to maintain the institutions of the country—not from any sentiment of political supersition, but because we believe that they embody the principles upon which a community like England can alone safely rest. The principles of liberty, of order, of law, and of religion ought not to be entrusted to individual opinion or to the caprice and passion of multitudes, but should be embodied in a form of permanence and power. We associate with the Monarchy the ideas which it represents—the majesty of law, the administration of justice, the fountain of mercy and of honour. We know that in the Estates of the Realm and the privileges they enjoy, is the best security for public liberty and good government. We believe that a national profession of faith can only be maintained by an Established Church, and that no society is safe unless there is a public recognition of the Providential government of the world, and of the future responsibility of man. Well, it is a curious circumstance that during all these same forty years of triumphant Liberalism, every one of these institutions has been attacked and assailed—I say, continuously attacked and assailed. And what, gentlemen, has been the result? For the last forty years the most depreciating comparisons have been instituted between the Sovereignty of England and the Sovereignty of a great Republic. We have been called upon in every way, in Parliament, in the Press,

---

* Benjamin Disraeli, *Selected Speeches of the Earl of Beaconsfield,* Vol. II, ed. by T. E. Kebbel (London: Longmans Green, 1882) ["Speech on Conservative and Liberal Principles, June, 1872.] See introductory remarks to Selection 19.

by articles in newspapers, by pamphlets, by every means which can influence opinion, to contrast the simplicity and economy of the Sovereignty of the United States with the cumbrous cost of the Sovereignty of England.

Gentlemen, I need not in this company enter into any vindication of the Sovereignty of England on that head. I have recently enjoyed the opportunity, before a great assemblage of my countrymen, of speaking upon that subject. I have made statements with respect to it which have not been answered either on this side of the Atlantic or the other. Only six months ago the advanced guard of Liberalism, acting in entire unison with that spirit of assault upon the Monarchy which the literature and the political confederacies of Liberalism have for forty years encouraged, flatly announced itself as Republican, and appealed to the people of England on that distinct issue. Gentlemen, what was the answer? I need not dwell upon it. It is fresh in your memories and hearts. The people of England have expressed, in a manner which cannot be mistaken, that they will uphold the ancient Monarchy of England, the Constitutional Monarchy of England, limited by the co-ordinate authority of the Estates of the Realm, but limited by nothing else. Now, if you consider the state of public opinion with regard to those Estates of the Realm, what do you find? Take the case of the House of Lords. The House of Lords has been assailed during this reign of Liberalism in every manner and un-ceasingly. Its constitution has been denounced as anomalous, its influence declared pernicious; but what has been the result of this assault and criticism of forty years? Why, the people of England, in my opinion, have discovered that the existence of a second Chamber is necessary to Constitutional Government; and, while necessary to Constitutional Government, is, at the same time, of all political inventions the most difficult. Therefore, the people of this country have congratulated themselves that, by the aid of an ancient and famous history, there has been developed in this country an Assembly which possesses all the virtues which a Senate should possess—independence, great local influence, eloquence, all the accomplishments of political life, and a public training which no theory could supply.

The assault of Liberalism upon the House of Lords has been mainly occasioned by the prejudice of Liberalism against the land laws of this country. But in my opinion, and in the opinion of wiser men than myself, and of men in other countries beside this, the liberty of

England depends much upon the landed tenure of England—upon the fact that there is a class which can alike defy despots and mobs, around which the people may always rally, and which must be patriotic from its intimate connection with the soil. Well, gentlemen, so far as these institutions of the country—the Monarchy and the Lords Spiritual and Temporal—are concerned, I think we may fairly say, without exaggeration, that public opinion is in favour of those institutions, the maintenance of which is one of the principal tenets of the Tory party, and the existence of which has been unceasingly criticised for forty years by the Liberal party. Now, let me say a word about the other Estate of the Realm, which was first attacked by Liberalism.

One of the most distinguishing features of the great change effected in 1832 was that those who brought it about at once abolished all the franchises of the working classes. They were franchises as ancient as those of the Baronage of England; and, while they abolished them, they proposed no substitute. The discontent upon the subject of the representation which has from that time more or less pervaded our society dates from that period, and that discontent, all will admit, has now ceased. It was terminated by the Act of Parliamentary Reform of 1867–8. That Act was founded on a confidence that the great body of the people of this country were 'Conservative.' When I say 'Conservative,' I use the word in its purest and loftiest sense. I mean that the people of England, and especially the working classes of England, are proud of belonging to a great country, and wish to maintain its greatness—that they are proud of belonging to an Imperial country, and are resolved to maintain, if they can, their empire—that they believe, on the whole, that the greatness and the empire of England are to be attributed to the ancient institutions of the land. . . .

I say with confidence that the great body of the working class of England utterly repudiate such sentiments. They have no sympathy with them. They are English to the core. They repudiate cosmopolitan principles. They adhere to national principles. They are for maintaining the greatness of the kingdom and the empire, and they are proud of being subjects of our Sovereign and members of such an Empire. Well, then, as regards the political institutions of this country, the maintenance of which is one of the chief tenets of the Tory party, so far as I can read public opinion, the feeling of the nation is in accordance with the Tory party. It was not always so. There was a time when the institutions of this country were decried. They have passed through a scathing criticism of forty years; they have passed through that criticism when their political upholders have, generally speaking, been always in opposition. They have been upheld by us when we were unable to exercise any of the lures of power to attract force to us, and the people of this country have arrived at these conclusions from their own thought and their own experience.

Let me say one word upon another institution, the position of which is most interesting at this time. No institution of England, since the advent of Liberalism, has been so systematically, so continuously assailed as the Established Church. Gentlemen, we were first told that the Church was asleep, and it is very possible, as everybody, civil and spiritual, was asleep forty years ago, that that might have been the case. Now we are told that the Church is too active, and that it will be destroyed by its internal restlessness and energy. I see in all these efforts of the Church to represent every mood of the spiritual mind of man, no evidence that it will fall, no proof that any fatal disruption is at hand. I see in the Church, as I believe I see in England, an immense effort to rise to national feelings and recur to national principles. The Church of England, like all our institutions, feels it must be national, and it knows that, to be national, it must be comprehensive. Gentlemen, I have referred to what I look upon as the first object of the Tory party—namely, to maintain the institutions of the country, and reviewing what has occurred, and referring to the present temper of the times upon these subjects, I think that the Tory party, or, as I will venture to call it, the National party, has everything to encourage it. I think that the nation, tested by many and severe trials, has arrived at the conclusion which we have always maintained, that it is the first duty of England to maintain its institutions, because to them we principally ascribe the power and prosperity of the country.

Gentlemen, there is another and second great object of the Tory party. If the first is to maintain the institutions of the country, the second is, in my opinion, to uphold the Empire of England. If you look to the history of this country since the advent of Liberalism—forty years ago—you will find that there has been no effort so continuous, so subtle, supported by so much energy, and carried on with so much ability and acumen, as the attempts of Liberalism to effect the disintegration of the Empire of England. . . .

Gentlemen, another great object of the Tory party, and one not inferior to the maintenance of the Empire, or the upholding of our institutions, is the elevation of the condition of the people. Let us see in this great struggle between Toryism and Liberalism that has prevailed in this country during the last forty years what are the salient features. It must be obvious to all who consider the condition of the multitude with a desire to improve and elevate it, that no important step can be gained unless you can effect some reduction of their hours of labour and humanise their toil. The great problem is to be able to achieve such results without violating those principles of economic truth upon which the prosperity of all States depends. You recollect well that many years ago the Tory party believed that these two results might be obtained—that you might elevate the condition of the people by the reduction of their toil and the mitigation of their labour, and at the same time inflict no injury on the wealth of the nation. You know how that effort was encountered—how these views and principles were met by the triumphant statesmen of Liberalism. They told you that the inevitable consequence of your policy was to diminish capital, that this, again, would lead to the lowering of wages, to a great diminution of the employment of the people, and ultimately to the impoverishment of the kingdom.

These were not merely the opinions of Ministers of State, but those of the most blatant and loud-mouthed leaders of the Liberal party. And what has been the result? Those measures were carried, but carried, as I can bear witness, with great difficulty and after much labour and a long struggle. Yet they were carried; and what do we now find? That capital was never accumulated so quickly, that wages were never higher, that the employment of the people was never greater, and the country never wealthier. I ventured to say a short time ago, speaking in one of the great cities of this country, that the health of the people was the most important question for a statesman. It is, gentlemen, a large subject. It has many branches. It involves the state of the dwellings of the people, the moral consequences of which are not less considerable than the physical. It involves their enjoyment of some of the chief elements of nature—air, light, and water. It involves the regulation of their industry, the inspection of their toil. It involves the purity of their provisions, and it touches upon all the means by which you may wean them from habits of excess and of brutality. Now, what is the feeling upon these subjects of the Liberal party—that Liberal party who opposed the Tory party when, even in their weakness, they advocated a diminution of the toil of the people, and introduced and supported those Factory Laws, the principles of which they extended, in the brief period when they possessed power, to every other trade in the country? What is the opinion of the great Liberal party—the party that seeks to substitute cosmopolitan for national principles in the government of this country —on this subject? Why, the views which I expressed in the great capital of the county of Lancaster have been held up to derision by the Liberal Press. A leading member—a very rising member, at least, among the new Liberal members—denounced them the other day as the 'policy of sewage.'

Well, it may be the 'policy of sewage' to a Liberal member of Parliament. But to one of the labouring multitude of England, who has found fever always to be one of the inmates of his household—who has, year after year, seen stricken down the children of his loins, on whose sympathy and material support he has looked with hope and confidence, it is not a 'policy of sewage,' but a question of life and death. And I can tell you this, gentlemen, from personal conversation with some of the most intelligent of the labouring class—and I think there are many of them in this room who can bear witness to what I say—that the policy of the Tory party—the hereditary, the traditionary policy of the Tory party, that would improve the condition of the people—is more appreciated by the people than the ineffable mysteries and all the pains and penalties of the Ballot Bill. Gentlemen, is that wonderful? Consider the condition of the great body of the working classes of this country. They are in possession of personal privileges— of personal rights and liberties—which are not enjoyed by the aristocracies of other countries. Recently they have obtained—and wisely obtained—a great extension of political rights; and when the people of England see that under the constitution of this country, by means of the constitutional cause which my right honourable friend the Lord Mayor has proposed, they possess every personal right of freedom, and, according to the conviction of the whole country, also an adequate concession of political rights, is it at all wonderful that they should wish to elevate and improve their condition, and is it unreasonable that they should ask the Legislature to assist them in that behest as far as it is consistent with the general welfare of the realm?

Why, the people of England would be greater idiots than the Jacobinical leaders of London even suppose, if, with their experience and acuteness, they should not long have seen that the time had arrived when social, and not political improvement is the object which they ought to pursue. I have touched, gentlemen, on the three great objects of the Tory party. I told you I would try to ascertain what was the position of the Tory party with reference to the country now. I have told you also with frankness what I believe the position of the Liberal party to be. Notwithstanding their proud position, I believe they are viewed by the country with mistrust and repugnance. But on all the three great objects which are sought by Toryism—the maintenance of our institutions, the preservation of our Empire, and the improvement of the condition of the people—I find a rising opinion in the country sympathising with our tenets, and prepared, I believe, if the opportunity offers, to uphold them until they prevail. . . .

25 MOSCA

Pluralism and Democracy

Gaetano Mosca (1858–1941) was an eminent Italian scholar in politics and sociology. His chief work, *Elementi di Scienza Politica,* appeared in 1895; in 1939 a revised version was published in English translation under the title *The Ruling Class.* Mosca was concerned to demonstrate that any government, no matter how democratic, is directed by a relatively small ruling or political class. The object of those who favor a free society must be to keep any permanent alliance of interests, any permanent majority class, from gaining absolute control. To this end, pluralism, a shifting alliance of minority interests, ought to be encouraged. It will be seen that Mosca's advocacy of mixed government puts him in the tradition of Aristotle and of most modern conservatives. The selections below are taken from Chapters II, V, XV, and XVIII of *The Ruling Class.**

Among the constant facts and tendencies that are to be found in all political organisms, one is so obvious that it is apparent to the most casual eye. In all societies—from societies that are very meagerly developed and have barely attained the dawnings of civilization, down to the most advanced and powerful societies—two classes of people appear—a class that rules and a class that is ruled. The first class, always the less numerous, performs all political functions, monopolizes power and enjoys the advantages that power brings, whereas the second, the more numerous class, is directed and controlled by the first, in a manner that is now more or less legal, now more or less arbitrary and violent, and supplies the first, in appearance at least, with material means of subsistence and with the instrumentalities that are essential to the vitality of the political organism.

In practical life we all recognize the existence of this ruling class (or political class, as we have elsewhere chosen to define it). We all know that, in our own country, whichever it may be, the management of public affairs is in the hands of a minority of influential persons, to which management, willingly or unwillingly, the majority defer. We know that the same thing goes on in neighbouring countries, and in fact we should be put to it to conceive of a real world otherwise organized—a world in which all men would be directly subject to a single person without relationships of superiority or subordination, or in which all men would share equally in the direction of political affairs. If we reason otherwise in theory, that is due partly to inveterate habits that we follow in our thinking and partly to the exaggerated importance that we attach to two political facts that loom far larger in appearance than they are in reality.

The first of these facts—and one has only to open one's eyes to see it—is that in every political organism there is one individual who is chief among the leaders of the ruling class as a whole and stands, as we say, at the helm of the state. That person is not always the person who holds supreme power according to law. At times, along-side of the hereditary king or emperor there is a prime minister or a major-domo who wields an actual power that is greater than the sovereign's. At other times, in place of the elected president the influential politician who has procured the president's election will govern. Under special circumstances there may be, instead of a single person, two or three who discharge the functions of supreme control.

The second fact, too, is readily discernible. Whatever the type of political organization, pressures arising from the discontent of the masses who are governed, from the passions by which they are swayed, exert a certain amount of influence on the policies of the ruling, the political, class.

But the man who is at the head of the state would certainly not be able to govern without the support of a numerous class to enforce respect for his orders and to have them carried out; and granting that he can make one individual, or indeed many individuals, in the ruling class feel the weight of his power, he certainly cannot be at odds with the class as a whole or do away with it. Even if that were possible, he would at once be forced to create another class, without the support

of which action on his part would be completely paralyzed. On the
other hand, granting that the discontent of the masses might succeed
in deposing a ruling class, inevitably, as we shall later show, there
would have to be another organized minority within the masses themselves to discharge the functions of a ruling class. Otherwise all organization, and the whole social structure, would be destroyed.

From the point of view of scientific research the real superiority of
the concept of the ruling, or political, class lies in the fact that the
varying structure of ruling classes has a preponderant importance in
determining the political type, and also the level of civilization, of the
different peoples. . . .

. . . The classification mentioned above, which divides governments
into absolute monarchies, limited monarchies and republics, was devised by Montesquieu and was intended to replace the classical categories of Aristotle, who divided governments into monarchies, aristocracies and democracies. What Aristotle called a democracy was simply an aristocracy of fairly broad membership. Aristotle himself was in
a position to observe that in every Greek state, whether aristocratic
or democratic, there was always one person or more who had a preponderant influence. Between the day of Polybius and the day of
Montesquieu, many writers perfected Aristotle's classification by introducing into it the concept of "mixed" governments. Later on the
modern democratic theory, which had its source in Rousseau, took its
stand upon the concept that the majority of the citizens in any state
can participate, and in fact *ought* to participate, in its political life,
and the doctrine of popular sovereignty still holds sway over many
minds in spite of the fact that modern scholarship is making it increasingly clear that democratic, monarchical and aristocratic principles function side by side in every political organism. We shall not
stop to refute this democratic theory here, since that is a task of this
work as a whole. . . .

The absolute preponderance of a single political force, the predominance of any over-simplified concept in the organization of the
state, the strictly logical application of any single principle in all
public law are the essential elements in any type of despotism, whether
it be a despotism based upon divine right or a despotism based ostensibly on popular sovereignty; for they enable anyone who is in power
to exploit the advantages of a superior position more thoroughly for

the benefit of his own interests and passions. When the leaders of the governing class are the exclusive interpreters of the will of God or of the will of the people and exercise sovereignty in the name of those abstractions on societies that are deeply imbued with religious beliefs or with democratic fanaticism, and when no other organized social forces exist apart from those which represent the principle on which sovereignty over the nation is based, then there can be no resistance, no effective control, to restrain a natural tendency in those who stand at the head of the social order to abuse their powers.

When a governing class can permit itself anything in the name of a sovereign who can do anything, it undergoes a real moral degeneration, the degeneration that is common to all men whose acts are exempt from the restraint that the opinion and the conscience of their fellows ordinarily impose. When responsibility in subordinates in the end is one with irresponsibility and omnipotence in the man or in the little group of men standing at the head of the official hierarchy as a whole—call that man czar or sultan, or that group Committee of Public Safety—the vices that absolutism generates in its leaders are communicated downward to the whole political structure. Anything may be ventured when one is interpreting the will, real or imaginary, of a person who thinks he has the right to bend everything to his will, but who cannot possibly see everything and who does not have free and disinterested consciences about him to control his passions and correct his mistakes. . . .

If a political organism is to progress in the direction of attaining greater and greater improvement in juridical defense, the prime and most essential requisite is that the secular and ecclesiastical powers shall be separated, or, better, that the principle on which the exercise of temporal authority is based shall have nothing sacred and immutable about it. When power rests on a system of ideas and beliefs outside of which it is felt that there can be neither truth nor justice, it is almost impossible that its acts should be debated and moderated in practice. Social progress can hardly reach a point where, in such a case, the different powers will harmonize with each other and check each other effectively enough to prevent absolute control by the individual, or individuals, who stand at the head of the social order. The relative immobility of certain social types must be ascribed to failures in the respects here suggested. The sacred character of the caste has for many centuries prevented any social progress in Hindu civilization. In its beginnings that civilization must have had very brilliant possibilities. Otherwise there would be no way to account for the great material and artistic progress which it actually did achieve. That leads to a supposition, which seems, for that matter, to be confirmed by recent studies, that the division of the Hindu population into castes, and the isolation of the various castes, cannot always have been as thoroughgoing and extreme as we find them today. It seems that Brahminism did not become altogether rigid, stationary and formalistic until after its victorious struggle with Buddhism in India. . . .

Christian peoples have managed to avoid the dangerous confusion that Leroy-Beaulieu refers to, and so, as the result of a number of favoring circumstances, they have been able to create the secular state. In the first place the Bible luckily contains very few maxims that can be directly applied to political life. In the second place, though the Catholic Church has always aspired to a preponderant share in political power, it has never been able to monopolize it entirely, because of two traits, chiefly, that are basic in its structure. Celibacy has generally been required of the clergy and of monks. Therefore no real dynasties of abbots and bishops have ever been able to establish themselves. On this score the western world owes Gregory VII a great debt of gratitude. Secondly, in spite of numerous examples to the contrary supplied by the warlike Middle Ages, the ecclesiastical calling has by its very nature never been strictly compatible with the bearing of arms. The precept that exhorts the Church to abhor bloodshed has never dropped completely out of sight, and in relatively tranquil and orderly times it has always been very much to the fore. In the period between the eleventh and the fourteenth century even Guelph writers had to recognize that side by side with papal supremacy an emperor existed as a secular sovereign who functioned as the instrument and secular arm of the Church. The most complete despotisms to which Christian peoples have ever been subject arose in Byzantium and in Russia, where the secular rulers succeeded most completely in bringing ecclesiastical authority under their direct control. The English, on the other hand, are greatly indebted for their liberties to the Puritans and to other nonconformists.

Next after the separation of secular and ecclesiastical authority, the most essential requisites for a more or less advanced type of juridical defense are to be found in the way in which wealth is distributed in a society and in the way in which military forces are organized. . . .

A society is best placed to develop a relatively perfect political organization when it contains a large class of people whose economic position is virtually independent of those who hold supreme power and who have sufficient means to be able to devote a portion of their time to perfecting their culture and acquiring that interest in the public weal—that aristocratic spirit, we are almost tempted to say—which alone can induce people to serve their country with no other satisfactions than those that come from individual pride and self-respect. In all countries that ever have been, or now are, in the lead as regards juridical defense—or liberty, as it is commonly called—such a class has been prominent. There was such a class in Rome, when Rome had a teeming plebs of small property owners who, the times being modest ones, managed to be self-sufficient and to win step by step, with amazing persistence, the rights of full citizenship. There was such a class in England in the seventeenth century, and there is one there now. England's numerous gentry, which was made up in those days chiefly of moderately rich landowners and is now chiefly made up of moderately rich businessmen, is now supplying, as it then supplied, the best elements to the ruling class. There has been and there still is such a class in the United States of America, and such a class has existed in most of the countries of central and western Europe. Where the class is inadequate to its task because of deficiencies in cultivation or in education or in wealth, parliamentary government bears its worst fruits, as would any other political system. . . .

The democratic tendency—the tendency to replenish ruling classes from below—is constantly at work with greater or lesser intensity in all human societies. . . .

If it is confined within moderate limits, the democratic tendency is in a sense indispensable to what is called "progress" in human societies. If all aristocracies had remained steadfastly closed and stationary, the world would never have changed, and mankind would have stopped developing at the stage that it had attained at the time of the Homeric monarchies, or the old Near Eastern empires. The struggle between those who are at the top and those who are born at the bottom but aspire to climb has been, is and will ever be the ferment that forces individuals and classes to widen their horizons and seek the new roads that have brought the world to the degree of civilization that it attained in the nineteenth century. That high level of civilization made it possible to create in the political field the great modern representative state, which . . . is of all political organisms the one that has succeeded in coordinating the largest sum of individual energies and activities and applying them to purposes that are related to the collective interest.

When the democratic tendency does not exert too great an influence, to the exclusion of other tendencies, it represents a conservative force. It enables ruling classes to be continually replenished through the admission of new elements who have inborn talents for leadership and a will to lead, and so prevents that exhaustion of aristocracies of birth which usually paves the way for great social cataclysms. . . .

In his dialogue on the Laws Plato sets forth the thought of his maturer years, and it is significant that he there maintains that the best form of government is one in which autocracy and democracy are fused and balanced. As we have already seen, aristocracy and democracy were, for Plato, the two typical forms of government. In his *Politics*, Aristotle gives an objective description of his three fundamental forms of government, monarchy, aristocracy and democracy, and then goes on to show his preference for a modified aristocracy or, better still, for a modified democracy, in which not even the working classes, let alone slaves and metics, would be admitted to public office. Almost two centuries later, Polybius considered the political organization of Rome the best, because he thought that the three fundamental types of Aristotle found simultaneous application in it. About a century after Polybius, Cicero set forth a somewhat similar view in *De Republica*, and more than twelve centuries after Cicero, at a time when political science was beginning to show signs of new life, St. Thomas also expressed a preference for mixed governments. Montesquieu freed himself of Aristotle's classification and divided governments into despotic, monarchical and republican. His preference lay with a modified monarchy, in which the three fundamental powers, the legislative, executive and judiciary, were entrusted to separate organs, all independent of one another. In that, evidently, Montesquieu was groping toward the concept of a necessary balance between the various political forces and influences. One might add that Cavour, too, declared that in politics he was a believer in the *juste milieu*, which would involve balance and mutual control between the many political forces or doctrines.

All these great thinkers or statesmen, then, would seem to have had one common feeling: that the soundness of political institutions depends upon an appropriate fusing and balancing of the differing but constant principles and tendencies which are at work in all political organisms. It would be premature in the present state of political science to attempt to formulate a law, but some such hypothesis as the following might be ventured: that violent political upheavals, such as occurred at the fall of the Roman Empire and are today occurring in Russia, entailing unutterable suffering for large portions of humanity and interrupting the progress of civilization for long years and perhaps centuries, arise primarily from the virtually absolute predominance of one of the two principles, or one of the two tendencies, that we have been studying; whereas the stability of state, the infrequency of such catastrophes, depends on a proper balancing of the two principles, the two tendencies.

This hypothesis could be corroborated by historical experiences in considerable numbers. But it rests primarily upon the assumption that only the opposition—one might almost say only the competition—of these contrary principles and tendencies can prevent an overaccentuation of the vices that are congenital to each of them.

This conclusion would correspond very closely to the old doctrine of the golden mean, which judged mixed governments best. In fact, we would only be reviving that doctrine, though on the basis of the more exact and profound knowledge that our times have attained as to the natural laws that influence and control the political organization of society. To be sure, there would still be the difficulty of determining just where the golden mean lies, and that difficulty would be so great that each of us could feel quite free to locate it as best suits his passions and interests.

But one practical method has occurred to us for helping wellmeaning persons, whose exclusive aim is the general welfare and prosperity quite apart from any personal interest, or any systematic preconception. It would be to watch for—so to say—atmospheric changes in the times and in the peoples who live about us.

When, for instance, a glacial calm prevails, when we can feel no breath of political discussion blowing, when everybody is raising hymns of praise to some great restorer of order and peace, then we may rest assured that the autocratic principle is prevailing too strongly over the liberal, and vice versa when everybody is cursing tyrants and championing liberty. So too, when the novelists and poets are vaunting the glories of great families and uttering imprecations upon the common herd, we may safely consider that the aristocratic tendency is becoming too strong; and when a wild wind of social equality is howling and all men are voicing their tenderness for the interests of the humble, it is evident that the democratic tendency is strongly on the upgrade and approaching the danger point. To put the matter in two words, it is just a question of following a rule that is the opposite of the one that climbers have consciously or unconsciously followed at all times in all countries. If we do that, the little nucleus of sound minds and choice spirits that keep mankind from going to the dogs every other generation may on occasion be able to render a service to its contemporaries, and especially to the children of its contemporaries. For in political life, the mistakes of one generation are almost always paid for by the generation that follows. . . .

[I]n modern Europe, and in all countries of European civilization in general, the conception of political liberty has not been applied solely by instituting representative government. Almost everywhere the latter has been supplemented to a greater or lesser extent by a series of institutions that assure individuals and groups of individuals not a few effective guarantees as against holders of public power. In countries that have so far rightly been reputed free, private property cannot be violated arbitrarily. A citizen cannot be arrested and condemned unless specified rules are observed. Each person can follow the religion of his choice without forfeiture of his civil and political rights. The press cannot be subjected to censorship and is free to discuss and criticize acts of government. Finally, if they conform with certain rules, citizens can meet to engage in discussions of a political character, and they can form associations for the attainment of moral, political or professional ends.

These liberties, and others like them, may be looked upon as real limitations which the state has imposed upon its own sovereign powers in its relations to individual citizens. They are largely imitations of laws that England had adopted at the end of the seventeenth century, after the "Glorious Revolution," or even at later dates. They are necessary complements to representative systems, which would function very badly if all free political activity on the part of individuals were suppressed, and if individuals were not fairly well protected against arbitrary acts on the part of the executive and judiciary powers. At the same time, those liberties find their maximum guarantee in the existence of the representative system, which provides that legislative power, which alone has the right to remove or restrict them, should emanate from the same political forces that are interested in conserving them.

Far harder to put into practice has been the concept of equality, for equality is contrary to the nature of things, and is also less real, less concrete, than liberty in the sense just mentioned.

Naturally, the class privileges that still remained at the end of the eighteenth century were abolished as a matter of law at that time, since it was to the interest of the bourgeoisie to abolish them. All citizens were solemnly proclaimed equal before the law. But little could be done with natural inequalities, or with those artificial inequalities, so to speak, which result from family inheritance—disparities in wealth, upbringing and education, for instance.

Now equality ought to imply the disappearance of social classes as one of its necessary implications, and equality has in fact been officially proclaimed. But the gap between the various social classes in ways of thinking, in manners of feeling and in tastes and inclinations has perhaps never been more marked than it is in twentieth century European society; and never, perhaps, have classes been less comprehensible to each other. That is not due altogether to inequalities in wealth. The intelligence and the psychology of a man of the lower middle class, who has managed to win a university degree or even a secondary school diploma, are almost always closer to those of a millionaire than to those of a workingman, though from an economic standpoint a man of the lower middle class stands closer to the workingman than he does to the millionaire. All that is a result of progress in culture, in what Italians call "civility," whereby those who devote themselves to intellectual pursuits, and sometimes to the refinements of leisure, necessarily become more and more differentiated from the social strata that are devoted exclusively to manual pursuits and are fitted for no other. . . .

But, as early as the day of Aristotle, when the majority of manual laborers were still excluded from citizenship and therefore from suffrage, people were aware of the difficulty of reconciling political equality, which gave the poor predominance over the rich, with economic inequality. It is not surprising, then, that the European and American ruling classes should have found themselves facing the same difficulty after granting universal suffrage. They were able to meet that difficulty with relative ease before the World War, and to overcome it up to a certain point. That was due partly to the political unpreparedness of the masses, which, in many countries, readily allowed themselves to be regimented within the framework of bourgeois parties. But it was also due in part to the great powers of resistance that the modern state has; and in larger part still to the great economic prosperity that prevailed in the second half of the nineteenth century and which even increased during the twenty or thirty years prior to 1914. Prosperity made it possible in many countries to grant very considerable concessions of an economic nature to the more populous classes, without preventing increases in private savings, without impairing the inviolability of private property too seriously and without laying unbearable burdens upon large and moderate fortunes. Among these concessions one might mention shorter working hours, insurance against old age, illness, unemployment and accidents, and restrictions on labor by women and children. Such provisions are all acceptable when they are not carried too far, and when industry, agriculture and public finance are able to carry them. Unfortunately they almost always serve to justify creating large bureaucracies, which regularly become drags and nuisances. The best and the most welcome of all these concessions was a rapid raising of wages, which was made possible by increased production in industry and agriculture, especially in the last decades before 1914.

As matters turned out, these improvements in the status of the lower classes were of no little service to agitators too, for they could boast of wresting them from the bourgeoisie through their organization of labor and through the activity of their representatives in parliament. In such claims, as all economists know, there is a small amount of truth and a large amount of falsehood. Certainly improved economic conditions have on the whole made the laboring classes less prone to resort to desperate and violent acts. . . .

. . . Our political system must necessarily have made its contribution to all these scientific and ecnomic achievements. Confining oneself to the political field, one has to admit thc great benefits which constitute the undying glory of the nineteenth century as a result of the very illusions that guided it. To be sure, majority government and absolute political equality, two of the mottos that the century inscribed on its banners, were not achieved, because they could not be achieved, and the same may be said of fraternity. But the ranks of the ruling classes have been held open. The barriers that kept individuals of the lower classes from entering the higher have been either removed or lowered, and the development of the old absolutist state into the modern representative state has made it possible for almost all political forces, almost all social values, to participate in the political management of society.

This development, it should be noted, has divided the political class into two distinct branches, one issuing from popular suffrage, and the other from bureaucratic appointment. This has not only permitted a better utilization of individual capacities; it has also made it possible to distribute the sovereign functions, or powers, of the state, and that distribution, whenever social conditions are such as to make it effective, constitutes the chief virtue of representative systems. It is the chief reason why they have given better results than any of the many others that have so far been applied to great political organizations. Rousseau set himself an unattainable goal when he tried to show that the only form of legitimate government was one that was founded upon the express consent of the majority of citizens. Montesquieu stated a much more practical and profound idea when he maintained that if a nation is to be free, in other words governed according to law and not according to the arbitrary will of its rulers, it must have a political organization in which authority arrests and limits authority, and in which, therefore, no individual and no assembly has the power to make laws and at the same time the power to apply them. To make that doctrine complete, one need add that a controlling and limiting political institution can be effective only when it represents a section of the political class that is different from the section represented by the institution to be limited and controlled.

If, again, we take due account of the individual liberties that protect the citizen from possible arbitrary acts on the part of any or all of the powers of the state, especially of liberty of the press, which, along with liberty of parliamentary debate, serves to call public attention to all possible abuses on the part of those who govern, one readily sees the great superiority of the representative system. That system has permitted the establishment of a strong state, which has been able to canalize immense sums of individual energies toward purposes related to the collective interest. At the same time it has not trampled on those energies or suppressed them. It has left them with sufficient vitality to achieve remarkable results in other fields, notably in the scientific, literary and economic fields. If, therefore, the nations of European civilization have succeeded in maintaining their primacy in the world during the age that is now closing, the fact has been due in large part to the beneficent effects of their political system. . . .

26   VON HABSBURG

Monarchy or Republic

The Archduke Otto von Habsburg (1912–   ) was the last crown prince of the Austro-Hungarian monarchy and is the present head of the House of Habsburg. He is the author of several books and of many essays which appeared in scholarly journals in Europe and America ; he holds a doctorate in philosophy from the University of Louvain. One of his chief interests has been the idea of Pan-Europeanism, and he has lectured and written a good deal on the need for Contintental unity. In his *The Social Order of Tomorrow,** he asserts that today, more than ever, monarchy has a place in the modern world. The selection is taken from the chapter "The State in the Twentieth Century" ; he weighs the differing advantages and disadvantages of the monarchical and republican forms of governments.

We come here to the formal aspect of the State—the question of monarchy versus republic—which is mostly discussed from a highly emotional rather than a rational point of view.

The debate proceeds by arguments *ad hominem.* A few undignified occupants of royal thrones are enumerated, and are then presented as examples of monarchy as such. The defenders of monarchy are no better. They point to corrupt professional politicians, of whom there exist a sufficient number, and claim that this is the necessary consequence of a republican constitution. Neither is a rational argument.   There have been good and bad monarchies—good republics (like Switzerland), and others which are far from living up to the same standard.

Every human institution, after all, has its good and bad sides. As

---

* Trans. by Iuo Jarosy (London: Oswald Wolff, 1958). Reprinted by permission of Paulist Press/Newman Press, New York.

long as this world is inhabited by men and not by angels, crimes and mistakes will continue to occur. . . .

Republicans are fond of claiming that a monarchial régime means the rule of the aristocracy. Monarchists, on the other hand, point to the economic difficulties, the tax burdens and State interference in private life in present-day republics, and compare this state of affairs with the freedom and economic well-being under the pre-1914 monarchies. Both arguments are unconvincing. They use the old propagandist trick of comparing results brought about by entirely dissimilar causes. Anyone who is honest will compare present-day monarchies with present-day republics. It will then be apparent that the aristocracy of birth occupies no greater share of leading positions in monarchies than in republics, and that all states, whatever their form of government, are equally affected by the serious economic problems of the present day.

Republicans frequently claim, in addition, that monarchy is a form of government belonging to the past, while republicanism is that of the future. Even a slight knowledge of history is enough to disprove this. Both forms have been in existence since the earliest times (though the monarchial periods have usually lasted considerably longer than the republican ones). In any case, it is misleading to call an institution which we already find in ancient Greece, Rome and Carthage, the form of government of the future.

In any objective discussion, we must also assign this question its proper place in our hierarchy of values.

It is not an accident that we speak of the "form" of government. There is a great difference between the "form" and the "content"— or purpose—of the State. The latter is its essential *raison d'être*, its very soul. The former corresponds to the bodily form of a living being. The one can certainly not exist without the other; but in any sane hierarchy of values the soul occupies a higher place than the body.

The essential purpose of the State, its "content," is rooted in natural law. The State is not an end in itself; it exists for the sake of its citizens. It is therefore not the source of all law (a claim that is still far too widely accepted), nor is it all-powerful. Its authority is circumscribed by the rights of its citizens. It is only free to act in those fields that are outside their free initiative. The State is therefore at all times the servant of natural law. Its task is to give practical effect to this law; nothing more.

If the mission of the State is the practical realisation of natural law, the form of government is a means by which the community attempts to achieve this aim. It is not an end in itself.

This explains the relatively subordinate importance of this whole question. Undoubtedly a great deal of importance attaches to the choice of the right means, since this choice will determine whether or not the end is attained. But what is lasting in political life is only natural law. The attempt to realise this law in practice will always have to take account of current conditions. To speak of an eternally valid form of government, right under all circumstances, shows ignorance and presumption.

From this it would seem to follow that it is fruitless to try to determine—mostly from the wrong philosophical premises—the objective value of one or the other form of government. The discussion will only become fruitful if we keep in mind the end which every such form is intended to serve. It is therefore not a question of investigating what value we are to attach to monarchies or republics as such. What we must ask ourselves is which form offers the best chances of safeguarding natural law under present-day conditions.

Once this point has been clarified, we can pass on to two other problems, which have frequently been dragged into this discussion and are threatening to poison the whole atmosphere.

There is constant controversy about the relation between monarchism, republicanism and democracy. Here again we encounter the blurred thinking characteristic of our era of slogans and propaganda. The concept of democracy has become infinitely elastic. In Russia it is compatible with mass liquidations, secret police and labour camps. In America, on the other hand—and occasionally in Europe—even political theorists are frequently unable to distinguish between republicanism and democracy. Furthermore, both words are used to designate conceptions and characteristics that go far beyond the political field, and belong to the economic or sociological sphere. It must therefore be clearly stated that, generally speaking, democracy means the right of the people to participate in determining their own development and future.

If we accept this definition, we shall see that neither of the two classical forms of government is by nature linked with democracy. Democracy can exist under both forms, just as there exist authoritarian republics as well as monarchies. Monarchists, in fact, frequently claim that democracy functions better under a monarchy than under a republic. If we look at present-day Europe, there is certainly some truth in this argument, though its validity may be restricted in time and space. At the same time, it is necessary to point out that in small states which are strongly rooted in their traditions, like Switzerland, democracy and republicanism can coexist successfully.

Still more hotly discussed is the question of monarchism and socialism, and republicanism and socialism. The reason for this is largely that in German-speaking countries the great majority of the official socialist parties are republican in outlook. Hence we find there among narrow and uneducated minds the belief that socialism and monarchism are incompatible.

This belief is due to a basic confusion. Socialism—at least in its present-day form—is essentially an economic and social programme. It has nothing to do with the form of government. The republicanism of some socialist parties does not arise from their actual programmes, but is due to the personal beliefs of their leaders. This is shown by the fact that the majority of the really powerful European socialist parties are not republican but monarchist. This is the case in Britain, in Scandinavia and in Holland. In all these countries we not only find excellent relations existing between the Crown and the socialists, but one cannot escape the impression that a monarchy provides a better soil for working-class parties than a republic. In any case, experience shows that socialism remains longer in power under a monarchy than under a republic. One of the great leaders of the British Labour Party explained this by the moderating and balancing influence of the Crown, which enabled socialists to carry through their programme more slowly, more reasonably, and hence also more successfully. At the same time, a ruler standing above the parties represented a sufficient safeguard to the opposition, so that it need not have recourse to extreme measures in order to regain power. It could watch developments more calmly.

Whether or not this is true, the facts prove that it is unjustified to draw an artificial dividing-line between monarchism and socialism, or between monarchism and classical democracy. The same applies to republicanism.

One other point must be mentioned. This is the frequent confusion, particularly among those not trained in political science, between monarchy as a form of government and one or other monarchical dynasty; in other words, the confusion between monarchism and legitimism.

Legitimism, a special tie with one person or one dynasty, is something that can hardly ever be discussed in reasonable and objective terms. It is matter of subjective feeling, and is therefore advocated or opposed by arguments *ad hominem*. Any rational discussion of current problems must therefore make a clear distinction between monarchism and dynastic legitimism. The form of government of a State is a political problem. It must therefore be discussed independently of the family or person who stand, or stood, at the head of the State. Even in monarchies dynastic changes take place. In any case, the institution is of greater importance than its representative; the latter is mortal while the former is, historically speaking, immortal.

To look at a form of government merely with an eye to its present representative leads to grotesque results. For in that case republics, too, would have to be judged not on political grounds, but according to the characters of their presidents. This would, of course, be the height of unfairness.

It should be added that among the protagonists of monarchism in republican Europe, there are relatively few legitimists. King Alfonso XIII of Spain once remarked that legitimism cannot survive one generation. It is valuable where there exists a strongly established, traditional form of government, with which most of the citizens are satisfied. But this kind of legitimism can be found in republics as well as in monarchies. One can speak of republican legitimism in Switzerland and the United States just as one can speak of monarchist legitimism in Britain and Holland. In most countries of Europe, of course, there have been so many profound changes in the course of the centuries that legitimism is less frequently encountered. Under such conditions, it is particularly dangerous to have recourse to emotional arguments.

We are now in a position to define what we understand by a monarchy and a republic. Monarchy is that form of government in which the head of State is not elected, but bases his office on a higher law, with the claim that all power derives from a transcendental source. In a republic, the highest officer of State is elected, and hence derives his authority from his electors, that is, from the particular group which elected him.

Leaving aside purely emotional considerations, there are good arguments for both of these basic forms of government.

The most important arguments in favour of republicanism can be summarised as follows:

In the first place, republics are, with few exceptions, secular. They require no appeal to God in order to justify their authority. Their sovereignty, the source of their authority, derives from the people. In our time, which turns increasingly away from religious concepts, or at least refers them into the realm of metaphysics, secular constitutional concepts and a secular form of government are more easily acceptable than a form rooted, in the last resort, in theocratic ideas. It is, therefore, also easier for a republic to embrace a secular version of the Rights of Man. The advantage this form of government offers would therefore seem to be that it is in closer touch with the spirit of our time, and hence with the great mass of the population.

In addition, the choice of the head of State depends not on an accident of birth, but on the will of the people or of an *élite*. The president's term of office is limited. He can be removed, and if he is incapable it is easy to replace him. Himself an ordinary citizen, he is in closer touch with real life. And it is to be hoped that, with better education, the masses will become increasingly capable of choosing the right man. In a monarchy, on the other hand, once a bad ruler has ascended the throne, it is almost impossible to remove him without overthrowing the whole régime.

And lastly it is claimed that the fact that every citizen can, at least theoretically, become president, encourages a sense of political responsibility and helps the population to attain political maturity. The patriarchal character of a monarchy, on the other hand, leads the citizens to rely on their ruler, and to shift all political responsibility on to his shoulders.

In favour of monarchism, the following arguments are put forward:

Experience shows that kings mostly rule better, not worse, than presidents. There is a practical reason for this. A king is born to his office. He grows up in it. He is, in the truest sense of the word, a "professional," an expert in the field of statecraft. In all walks of life, the fully qualified expert is rated higher than the amateur, however brilliant. For particularly in a difficult, highly technical subject—and what is more difficult than the modern State?—knowledge and experience outweigh sheer brilliance. The danger certainly exists that an incompetent may succeed to the throne. But was not a Hitler chosen as leader, and a Warren Harding elected president? In the classical monarchies of the Middle Ages, it was almost always possible to replace an obviously incapable successor to the throne by a more suitable one. It was only with the decadence of monarchism, in the age of the courtly despotism of Versailles, that this corrective was discarded. Nothing would be more appropriate in a modern monarchy than the institution of a judicial tribunal, which could, if necessary, intervene to change the order of succession to the throne.

Even more important than the king's "professional" qualifications is the fact that he is not tied to any party. He does not owe his position to a body of voters or the support of powerful interests. A president, on the other hand, is always indebted to someone. Elections are expensive and difficult to fight. The power of money and the great mass organisations always makes itself felt. Without their help, it is almost impossible to become the head of State of a republic. Such support is not, however, given for nothing. The head of State remains dependent on those who helped him into the saddle. It follows that the president is mostly not the president of the whole people, but only of those groups that helped him to attain office. In this way, political parties or groups of economic interests can take over the highest command positions of the State, which then no longer belongs to the whole people, but, temporarily or permanently, becomes the privileged domain of one or another group of citizens. The danger exists therefore that a republic will cease to be the guardian of the rights of all its citizens. This, it is stressed by monarchists, is particularly dangerous at the present time. For today the rights of the individual and of minority groups are in greater danger than ever before. Financial power-concentrations and large, powerful organisations generally are everywhere threatening the "little man." Particularly in a democracy, it is extremely difficult for the latter to make himself heard, since this section of the population cannot easily be organised and is of no great economic importance. If even the topmost pinnacle of the State is handed over to political parties, there will be no one to whom the weak can turn for help. A monarchical ruler, on the other hand—so it is claimed—is independent, and is there for all citizens equally. His hands are not tied in the face of the powerful, and he can protect the rights of the weak. Particularly in an age of profound economic and social transformations, it is of the highest importance that the head of State should stand above the parties. . . .

And, finally, the Crown contributes to political life that stability without which no great problems can be solved. In a republic, the firm foundation is lacking. Whoever is in power must achieve a positive success in the shortest possible time, otherwise he will not be re-elected. This leads to short-term policies, which will not be able to cope successfully with problems of world-historical scope.

There is one more point we must consider before we can answer the question of which form of government will best serve the community in the future.

Generally speaking, democratic republics represent a régime dominated by the legislature, while authoritarian régimes are dominated by the executive. The judicial power has not had the primacy for a long time, as we have shown above. It found its earlier expression in the Christian monarchies. It is frequently forgotten that the true ruler has always been the guardian of law and justice. The most ancient monarchs—the kings of the Bible—came from the ranks of the judges. St. Louis of France regarded the administration of justice as his noblest task. The same principle can be seen in the many German "Palatinates," since the Count Palatine (*Palatinus*) was the guardian of law and justice delegated by the King-Emperor. The history of the great medieval monarchies shows that the legislative power of the king—even of a king as powerful as Charles V—was severely limited by local autonomies. The same is true of the ruler's executive function. He was not, in the first place, a law-giver or head of the executive; he was a judge. All other functions were subordinate, and were only exercised to the extent necessary to make his judicial function effective.

The reason for this institutional arrangement is clear. The judge must interpret the meaning of law and justice, and to do this he must be independent. It is essential that he should not owe his position, his function, to any man. The highest judge, at least, must be in this position. This is only possible under a monarchy. For in a republic, even the highest guardian of the law derives his position from some other source, to which he is responsible and on which he remains dependent to some extent. This is not a satisfactory state of affairs. His most important task is not to pass judgment in actual legal disputes, but to stand guard over the purpose of the State and natural law. Above all, it is the task of the supreme judge to see that all legislation is in accordance with the State's fundamental principles, that is, with natural law. The monarch's right to veto legislation passed by parliament is a remnant of this ancient function. . . .

The future form of the State will be something entirely new, something which will represent principles of eternal validity in a form appropriate to the future, without the errors of the past. . . .

The hereditary character of the monarchial function finds its justification not merely in the "professional" upbringing of the heir to the throne. Nor is it merely a question of continuity at the summit of the political hierarchy, though such continuity is highly desirable when it is a question of planning for generations to come. Its deepest justification lies in the fact that the hereditary ruler owes his position not to one or another social group, but to the will of God alone. That is the true meaning of the frequently misunderstood words "by the grace of God," which always signify a duty and a task. It would be wrong for the ruler by the grace of God to regard himself as an exceptional being. On the contrary, the words "by the grace of God" should remind him that he does not owe his position to his own merits, but must prove his fitness by ceaseless efforts in the cause of justice.

While there is thus much to be said for a hereditary transmission of the supreme position of the State, there is also one serious drawback, which has already been mentioned. If the succession occurs automatically, there is the possibility that the throne will be occupied by an incompetent. This is the greatest danger of the monarchial system. On the other hand, this danger only dates from the period when the inflexible legitimism of Versailles came into being, and the safeguards present in one form or another in most classical monarchies disappeared. Such safeguards would therefore have to be built into any future monarchical constitution. It would be wrong to hand this task over to political bodies, as that would open the door to private interests. The decision should be left to a judicial tribunal. The king, as the highest constitutional judge of the State, cannot exercise his function in a vacuum. He will have to be assisted by a body representing the highest judicial authority, of which he forms the head. It is this body which should pronounce on whether a law or a regulation is constitutional, that is, in accordance with the purpose of the State. When the ruler dies, the other judges will continue in office.

It should be their duty to pronounce on the suitability of the heir presumptive, and, if necessary, to replace him by the next in succession.

The activity of the head of State will undoubtedly go beyond the purely judicial field. He will have to control the executive, since it is his duty to see that the decisions of the judicial power are carried out in practice. Nevertheless, all these tasks will remain of secondary importance. It is in his judicial function that a twentieth-century monarch will find his primary justification.

IV
Liberty, Equality, and Authority

Liberty and authority, conservatives have always known, are the two prime principles of government, which must be defined anew every day in accordance with a particular time and place. Their object has been to steer a steady course, avoiding the Scylla of despotism and the Charybdis of anarchy. When the threat to civilized values has come from too much government, conservatives have stressed their libertarian heritage. When the danger has come from the opposite direction, they have stood for stability and order.

In the same way, there is no doubt that equality before the law is a prerequisite for ordered liberty; there are times, however, when a misconceived idea of equality can endanger both just authority and secure liberty. The conservative instinct has been to approach these twin ideals with a certain caution—to ask what the exact circumstances are, what the practical results are likely to be. Many would hold this questioning of abstract principles to be the essence of conservatism, an essence never better expressed than it was in these words of Edmund Burke's: "I flatter myself that I love a manly, moral, regulated liberty as well as any gentleman. . . . But I cannot . . . give praise or blame to anything which relates to human actions and human concerns on a simple view of the object, as it stands stripped of every relation, in all the nakedness and solitude of metaphysical abstraction." It is the circumstances, Burke stressed, which render political principles or plans "beneficial or noxious to mankind." Common sense would dictate that no sane man would congratulate the French, let us say, on their government under a monarchy or under a republic until he had inquired into exactly what kind of a government it was and how it was administered. Burke concluded his argument by asking another pointed question: "Is it because liberty in the abstract may be classed amongst the blessings of mankind, that I am to seriously felicitate a madman who has escaped from the protecting restraint . . . of his cell on his restoration to the enjoyment of . . . liberty? "

Following in the path marked out by Burke, Joseph de Maistre in Italy and Juan Donoso-Cortés in Spain upheld the principle of authority as being most in need of protection in their own time from the assaults of an unrealistic and misplaced liberalism. They saw clearly that revolutions like the French were all too likely to produce alternate kinds of equality: either a state of near anarchy without that hierarchy of authority necessary for civilized society or else one despot with everyone else equally unimportant compared to him.

Lord Acton, a few decades later, devoted himself to defending the liberty of the individual, especially in matters of the mind and conscience, against the increasing power of the state and of the majority of the people. He was always aware of the important role of a just and wise authority, but he was resolute in his conviction that, while authority should be respected, each person's conscience must ultimately be independent and supreme.

Acton's contemporary, Sir James Fitzjames Stephen, was, like Acton, a member of the British Liberal Party; like Acton, he always supported the rights of minorities to freedom of conscience against those who would stifle dissent. Both shared a common fear of the growing power of the state and the increasing intolerance of the majority; in this respect they were to ally themselves on many occasions with those conservatives who stood for ordered liberty and equality under the law. Stephen, in particular, was suspicious of abstract theorizing about human rights without taking into consideration the practical effect that each claimed right might have on society. His classic answer to John Stuart Mill's *On Liberty* was a model of argument in the style of Edmund Burke (who also, it must never be forgotten, was a member of the liberal party of his time, the Whigs).

Just as conservatives have usually striven to balance power between groups and interests, to absorb the new without abandoning the old, so they have never committed themselves to one overriding goal or principle. At various times and in diverse ways they have been moderate libertarians, moderate equalitarians, and moderate authoritarians. In the name of authentic balance and a reverence for the Aristotelian principle of moderation, the conservative tradition has always warned against slavery to any particular ideological principle or special pleading; it has commended flexibility of approach, the necessity of balancing liberty, equality, and authority. In the conflict among these three social values the conservative who is true to his tradition will focus his attention on whichever of these values is being denied.

27   DE MAISTRE

The Authority of Custom

Count Joseph de Maistre (1753–1821) was the leading spokesman for the forces of reaction in Europe against the years of the French
Revolution. His service as Sardinian ambassador to the Court of the
Czar gave De Maistre time to reflect and write on the events of his
youth. His essays, especially *On the Generative Principle of Political
Constitutions** (first published in 1814), are fascinating for their insights
into human psychology and the workings of society. In the selection
(parts of the first two chapters of his essay) De Maistre argued against
the reliance on abstract reason in the fashioning of constitutions. If a
structure of society is to last, he argued, it must be founded not on an
ivory-tower notion of utopian ideals but on the customs and prejudices
of people.

The Fallacy of the Written Constitution

One of the grand errors of an age, which professed them all, was,
to believe that a political constitution could be written and created
à priori; whilst reason and experience unite in establishing, that a
constitution is a Divine work, and that that which is most fundamental,
and most essentially constitutional, in the laws of a nation, is precisely
what cannot be written.

It has often been supposed to be an excellent piece of pleasantry
upon Frenchmen, to ask them *in what book the Salic law was written?*
But Jérôme Bignon answered, very apropos, and probably without
knowing the full truth of what he said, *that it was written* IN *the hearts
of Frenchmen.* Let us suppose, in effect, that a law of so much import-

* Trans. anonymous (Boston: Little, Brown, 1847).

ance existed only because it was written; it is certain that any authority whatsoever which may have written it, will have the right of annulling it; the law will not then have that character of sacredness and immutability which distinguishes laws truly constitutional. The essence of a fundamental law, is, that no one has the right to abolish it: now, how can it be above *all*, if *any one* has made it? The agreement of the people is impossible; and even if it should be otherwise, a compact is not a law, and binds nobody, unless there is a superior authority by which it is guarantied.

Hence it is that the good sense of antiquity, happily anterior to sophisms, has sought, on every side, the sanction of laws, in a power above man, either in recognizing that sovereignty comes from God, or in revering certain unwritten laws as proceeding from him.

Ask Roman history what was precisely the power of the Senate: she is silent, at least as to the exact limits of that power. We see, indeed, in general, that the power of the people and that of the Senate mutually balanced each other, and that the opposition was unceasing; we observe also that patriotism or weariness, weakness or violence, terminated these dangerous struggles: but we know no more about it.

The English Constitution is an example nearer to us, and, therefore, more striking. Whoever examines it with attention, will see *that it goes only in not going* (if this play upon words is permissible). It is maintained only by the exceptions. The *habeas corpus*, for example, has been so often and for so long time suspended, that it is doubted whether the exception has not become the rule. Suppose for a moment that the authors of this famous act had undertaken to fix the cases in which it should be suspended; they would *ipso facto* have annihilated it.

At the sitting of the House of Commons, June 26, 1807, a lord cited the authority of a great statesman to show that the King had no right to dissolve Parliament during the session; but this opinion was contradicted: Where is the law? Attempt to make a law, and to fix exclusively *by writing* the case where the King has this right, and you will produce a revolution. *The King*, said one of the members, *has this right when the occasion is important;* but what is an *important* occasion? Try to decide this too by writing.

Towards the end of the last century, a great outcry was made against a Minister, who had conceived the project of introducing this same English Constitution (or what was called by that name) into a kingdom which was convulsed, and which demanded a constitution of some kind, with a sort of frenzy. He was wrong, if you please, so far at least as one can be wrong when he acts in good faith. But who at that time had the right of condemning him? If the principle is granted, *that man can create a constitution,* this Minister had the same right to make his own as well as another. Were the doctrines on this point doubted? Was it not believed, on all sides, that a constitution was the work of intelligence, like an ode or tragedy? Had not *Thomas Paine* declared, with a profoundness that charmed the Universities, *that a constitution does not exist, so long as one cannot put it into his pocket?* The eighteenth century, which distrusted itself in nothing, hesitated at nothing.

The more we examine the influence of human agency in the formation of political constitutions, the greater will be our conviction that it enters there only in a manner infinitely subordinate, or as a simple instrument; and I do not believe there remains the least doubt of the incontestable truth of the following propositions: —

1. That the fundamental principles of political constitutions exist before all written law.

2. That a constitutional law is, and can only be, the development or sanction of an unwritten pre-existing right.

3. That which is most essential, most intrinsically constitutional, and truly fundamental, is never written, and could not be, without endangering the state.

4. That the weakness and fragility of a constitution are actually in direct proportion to the multiplicity of written constitutional articles.

We are deceived on this point by a sophism so natural, that it entirely escapes our attention. Because man acts, he thinks he acts alone; and because he has the consciousness of his liberty, he forgets his dependence. In the physical order, he listens to reason; for although he can, for example, plant an acorn, water it, etc., he is convinced that he does not make the oaks, because he witnesses their growth and perfection without the aid of human power; and moreover, that he does not make the acorn; but in the social order, where he is present, and acts, he fully believes that he is really the sole author of all that is done by himself. This is, in a sense, as if the trowel should believe itself the architect. Man is a free, intelligent, and noble being: without doubt; but he is not less an *instrument of God*. . . .

Let us now consider some one political constitution, that of England, for example. It certainly was not made *à priori*. Her Statesmen never assembled themselves together and said, *Let us create three powers, balancing them in such a manner, etc.* No one of them ever thought of such a thing. The Constitution is the work of circumstances, and the number of these is infinite. Roman laws, ecclesiastical laws, feudal laws; Saxon, Norman, and Danish customs; the privileges, prejudices, and claims of all orders; wars, revolts, revolutions, the Conquest, Crusades; virtues of every kind, and all vices; knowledge of every sort, and all errors and passions;—all these elements, in short, acting together, and forming, by their admixture and reciprocal action, combinations multiplied by myriads of millions, have produced at length, after many centuries, the most complex unity, and happy equilibrium of political powers that the world has ever seen.

Now since these elements, thus projected into space, have arranged themselves in such beautiful order, without a single man, among the innumerable multitude who have acted in this vast field, having ever known what he had done relatively to the whole, nor foreseen what would happen, it follows, inevitably, that these elements were guided in their fall by an infallible hand, superior to man. The greatest folly, perhaps, in an age of follies, was in believing that fundamental laws could be written *à priori*, whilst they are evidently the work of a power above man; and whilst the very committing them to writing, long after, is the most certain sign of their nullity. . . .

These ideas (taken in their general sense) were not unknown to the ancient philosophers: they keenly felt the impotency, I had almost said the nothingness, of writing, in great institutions; but no one of them has seen this truth more clearly, or expressed it more happily, than Plato, whom we always find the first upon the track of all great truths. According to him, "the man who is wholly indebted to writing for his instruction, *will only possess the appearance of wisdom.* The word is to writing, what the man is to his portrait. The productions of the pencil present themselves to our eyes as living things; but *if we interrogate them, they maintain a dignified silence.* It is the same with writing, *which knows not what to say to one man, nor what to conceal from another.* If you attack it or insult it without a cause, it cannot defend itself; *for its author is never present to sustain it.* So that he who imagines himself capable of establishing, clearly and permanently, one single doctrine, by writing alone, IS A GREAT BLOCK-HEAD. If he really possessed the true germs of truth, he would not indulge the thought, that *with a little black liquid and a pen* he could cause them to germinate in the world, defend them from the inclemency of the season, and communicate to them the necessary efficacy. As for the man who undertakes to write *laws or civil constitutions,* and who fancies that, because he has written them, he is able to give them adequate evidence and stability, whoever he may be, a private man or legislator, he disgraces himself, whether we say it or not; for he has proved thereby that he is equally ignorant of the nature of inspiration and delirium, right and wrong, good and evil. Now, this ignorance is a reproach, though the entire mass of the vulgar should unite in its praise."

After having heard the *wisdom of the Gentiles,* it will not be useless to listen further to Christian Philosophy.

"It were indeed desirable for us," says one of the most eloquent of the Greek fathers [St. Chrysostom], "never to have required the aid of the written word, but to have had the Divine precepts written only in our hearts, by grace, as they are written with ink in our books; but since we have lost this grace by our own fault, let us then, as it is necessary, seize *a plank instead of the vessel,* without however forgetting the pre-eminence of the first state. God never revealed any thing in writing to the elect of the old Testament: He always spoke to them directly, because He saw the purity of their hearts; but the Hebrew people having fallen into the very abyss of wickedness, books and laws became necessary. The same proceeding is repeated under the empire of the New Revelation; for Christ did not leave a single writing to his Apostles. Instead of books, he promised to them the Holy Spirit: *It is He,* saith our Lord to them, *who shall teach you what you shall speak.* But because, in process of time, sinful men rebelled against the faith and against morality, it was necessary to have recourse to books."

The Necessity for Reliance upon God

If the desires of a mere mortal were worthy of obtaining of Divine Providence one of those memorable decrees which constitute the grand epochs of history, I would ask Him to inspire some powerful nation, which had grievously offended Him, with the proud thought of constituting itself politically, beginning at the foundations. I would say, "Grant to this people every thing! Give to her genius, knowledge, riches, consideration, especially an unbounded confidence in herself, and that temper, at once pliant and enterprising, which nothing can embarrass, nothing intimidate. Extinguish her old government; take away from her memory; destroy her affections; spread terror around her; blind or paralyze her enemies; give victory charge to watch at once over all her frontiers, so that none of her neighbors could meddle in her affairs, or disturb her in her operations. Let this nation be illustrious in science, rich in philosophy, intoxicated with human power, free from all prejudice, from every tie, and from all superior influence; bestow upon her every thing she shall desire, lest at some time she might say, *this was wanting* or *that restrained me;* let her, in short, act freely with this immensity of means, that at length she may become, under Thy inexorable protection, an eternal lesson to the human race."

We cannot, it is true, expect a combination of circumstances which would constitute literally a miracle; but events of the same order, though less remarkable, have manifested themselves here and there in history, even in the history of our days; and, though they may not possess, for the purpose of example, that ideal force which I desired just now, they contain not less of memorable instruction.

We have been witnesses, within the last twenty-five years, of a solemn attempt made for the regeneration of a great nation mortally sick. It was the first experiment in the great work, and the *preface*, if I may be allowed to express myself thus, of the frightful book which we have been since called upon to read.

But, it will be said, *we know the causes which prevented the success of that enterprise.* How then? Do you wish that God should send angels under human guises commissioned to destroy a constitution? It will always be necessary to employ second causes; this or that, what does it signify? Every instrument is good in the hands of the great Artificer: but such is the blindness of men, that if, to-morrow, some constitution-monger should come to organize a people, and to give them a constitution made *with a little black liquid*, the multitude would again hasten to believe in the miracle announced. It would be said, again, *nothing is wanting; all is foreseen; all is written;* whilst, precisely because all could be foreseen, discussed, and written, it would be demonstrated, that the constitution is a nullity, and presents to the eye merely an ephemeral appearance.

I believe I have read, somewhere, *that there are few sovereignties in a condition to vindicate the legitimacy of their origin.* Admitting the reasonableness of the assertion, there will not result from it the least stain to the successors of a chief, whose acts might be liable to some objections. If it were otherwise, it would follow, that the sovereign could not reign legitimately, except by virtue of a deliberation of all the people, that is to say, *by the grace of the people;* which will never happen: for there is nothing so true, as that which was said by the author of the *Considerations on France,—that the people will always accept their masters, and will never choose them.* It is necessary that the origin of sovereignty should manifest itself from beyond the sphere of human power; so that men, who may appear to have a direct hand in it, may be, nevertheless, only the circumstances. As to legitimacy, if it should seem in its origin to be obscure, God explains Himself, by His prime-minister in the department of this world,—TIME.

But, since every constitution is divine in its principle, it follows, that man can do nothing in this way, unless he reposes himself upon God, whose instrument he then becomes. Now, this is a truth, to which the whole human race in a body have ever rendered the most signal testimony. Examine history, which is experimental politics, and we shall there invariably find the cradle of nations surrounded by priests, and the Divinity constantly invoked to the aid of human weakness. Fable, much more true than ancient history, for eyes prepared, comes in to strengthen the demonstration. It is always an oracle, which founds cities; it is always an oracle, which announces the Divine protection, and successes of the heroic founder.

The most famous nations of antiquity, especially the most serious and wise, such as the Egyptians, Etruscans, Lacedaemonians, and Romans, had precisely the most religious constitutions; and the duration of empires has always been proportioned to the degree of influence which the religious principle had acquired in the political constitution: *the cities and nations most addicted to Divine worship, have always been the most durable, and the most wise; as the most religious ages have also ever been most distinguished for genius.*

Not only does it not belong to man to create institutions, but it does not appear that his power, *unassisted,* extends even to change for the better institutions already established. The word *reform*, in itself, and previous to all examination, will be always suspected by wisdom, and the experience of every age justifies this sort of instinct. We know too well what has been the fruit of the most beautiful speculations of this kind.

To apply these general maxims to a particular case, it is from the single consideration of the extreme danger of innovations founded upon simple human theories, that, upon the great question of parliamentary reform, which has agitated minds in England so powerfully, and for so long a time, I find myself constrained to believe, that this idea is pernicious, and that if the English yield themselves too readily to it, they will have occasion to repent. *But,* say the partizans of reform, (for it is the grand argument,) *the abuses are striking and incontestable: now can a formal abuse, a defect, be constitutional?* Yes, undoubtedly, it can be; for every political constitution has its essential faults, which belong to its nature, and which it is impossible to separate from it; and, that which should make all reformers tremble, is that these faults may be changed by circumstances; so that in showing that they are new, we cannot prove that they are not necessary. What prudent man, then, will not shudder in putting his hand to the work? Social harmony, like musical concord, is subject to the law of *temperament in the general key.* Adjust the *fifths* accurately, and the *octaves* will jar, and conversely. The dissonance being then inevitable, instead of excluding it, which is impossible, it must be *qualified* by distribution. Thus, on both sides, *imperfection is an element of possible perfection.* In this proposition there is only the form of a paradox.

Voltaire, who spoke of every thing, during an age, without having so much as penetrated below the surface, has reasoned very humourously on the sale of the offices of the magistracy which occurred in France; and no instance, perhaps, could be more apposite to make us sensible of the truth of the theory which I am setting forth. *That this sale is an abuse,* says he, *is proved by the fact, that it originated in another abuse.* Voltaire does not mistake here as every man is liable to mistake. He shamefully mistakes. It is a total eclipse of common sense. *Everything which springs from an abuse, an abuse!* On the contrary; one of the most general and evident laws of this power, at once secret and striking, which acts and makes itself to be felt on every side, is, that the remedy of an abuse springs from an abuse, and that the evil, having reached a certain point, destroys itself.

The error of this great writer proceeds from the fact, that, *divided between twenty sciences,* as he himself somewhere confesses, and constantly occupied in communicating instruction to the world, he rarely gave himself time to think. "A dissipated and voluptuous court, reduced to the greatest want by its foolish expenses, devises the sale of the offices of the magistracy, and thus creates" (what it never could have done freely, and with a knowledge of the cause,) "it creates," I say, "a rich magistracy, irremovable and independent; so that the infinite power *playing in the world* makes use of corruption for creating incorruptible tribunals" (as far as human weakness permits). There is nothing, indeed, so plausible to the eye of a true philosopher; nothing more conformable to great analogies, and to that incontestable law, which wills that the most important institutions should be the results not of deliberation, but of circumstances. Here is the problem almost solved when it is stated, as is the case with all problems. *Could such a country as France be better judged than by hereditary magistrates?* If it is decided in the affirmative, which I suppose, it will be necessary for me at once to propose a second problem which is this: *the magistracy being necessarily hereditary, is there, in order to constitute it at first, and afterwards to recruit it, a mode more advantageous than that which fills the coffers of the sovereign with millions at the lowest price, and which assures, at the same time, the opulence, independence, and even the nobility* (of a certain sort) *of the supreme judges?* If we only consider venality as a means to the right of inheritance, every just mind is impressed with this, which is the true point of view. This is not the place to enter fully into this question; but enough has been said to prove that Voltaire has not so much as perceived it.

Let us now suppose a man like him at the head of affairs: he will not fail to act in accordance with his foolish theories of laws and of abuses. He will borrow at six and two thirds per cent. to reimburse his nominal incumbents, creditors at two per cent.: he will prepare minds by a multitude of paid writings, which will insult the magistracy and destroy public confidence in it. Soon Patronage, a thousand times more foolish than Chance, will open the long list of his blunders: the distinguished man, no longer perceiving in the right of inheritance a counterpoise to oppressive labours, will withdraw himself, never to return; and the great tribunals will be abandoned to adventurers without name, without fortune, and without consideration.

Such is the natural picture of most reforms. Man in relation with his Creator is sublime, and his action is creative: on the contrary, so soon as he separates himself from God, and acts alone, he does not cease to be powerful, for this is a privilege of his nature; but his action is negative, and tends only to destroy.

Withdrawn, by his vain sciences, from the single science which truly concerns him, man has believed himself endowed with power *to create.* . . . He has believed, that it was himself who invented languages; while, again, it belongs to him only to see that every human language is *learned* and never invented. He has believed that he could constitute nations; that is to say, in other terms, *that he could create that national unity, by virtue of which one nation is not another.* Finally, he has believed that, since he had the power of creating institutions, he had, with greater reason, that of borrowing them from other nations, and transferring them to his own country, all complete to his hand, with the name which they bore among the people from whom they were taken, in order, like those people, to enjoy them with the same advantages.

If the formation of all empires, the progress of civilization, and the unanimous agreement of all history and tradition do not suffice still to convince us, the death of empires will complete the demonstration commenced by their birth. As it is the religious principle which has created every thing, so it is the absence of this same principle which has destroyed every thing. The sect of Epicurus, which might be called *ancient incredulity,* corrupted at first, and soon after destroyed every government which was so unfortunate as to give it admission. Every where *Lucretius* announced *Cesar.*

But all past experience disappears before the frightful example afforded by the last century. Still intoxicated with its fumes, men are very far from being, at least in general, sufficiently composed, to contemplate this example in its true light, and especially to draw from it the necessary conclusions. It is then very important to direct our whole attention to this terrible scene.

It was only in the first part of the eighteenth century, that impiety became really a power. We see it at first extending itself on every side with inconceivable activity. From the palace to the cabin, it insinuates itself every where, and infests every thing. Soon a simple system becomes a formal association, which, by a rapid gradation, changes into a confederacy, and at length into a grand conspiracy which covers Europe.

Then that character of impiety which belongs only to the eighteenth century, manifests itself for the first time. It is no longer the cold tone of indifference, or at most the malignant irony of scepticism; it is a mortal hatred; it is the tone of anger, and often of rage. The writers of that period, at least the most distinguished of them, no longer treat Christianity as an immaterial human error; they pursue it as a capital enemy; they oppose it to the last extreme; it is a war to the death.

However entire Europe having been civilized by Christianity, the civil and religious institutions were blended, and, as it were, amalgamated in a surprising manner. It was then inevitable that the philosophy of the age should unhesitatingly hate the social institutions, from which it was impossible to separate the religious principle. This has taken place: every government, and all the establishments of Europe, were offensive to it, *because* they were Christian; and *in proportion* as they were Christian, an inquietude of opinion, an universal dissatisfaction, seized all minds. In France, especially, the philosophic rage knew no bounds; soon a single formidable voice, forming itself from many voices united, is heard to cry, in the midst of guilty Europe. "Depart from us! Shall we then forever tremble before the priests, and receive from them such instruction as it pleases them to give us? TRUTH, throughout Europe, is concealed by the fumes of the censer; it is high time that she come out of this noxious cloud. We shall speak no more of Thee to our children; it is for them to know, when they shall arrive at manhood, whether there is such a Being as Thyself, and what Thou art, and what Thou requirest of them. Every thing which now exists, displeases us, because Thy name is written upon every thing that exists. We wish to destroy all, and to reconstruct the whole without Thee. Leave our councils, leave our schools, leave our houses: we would act alone: REASON suffices for us. Depart from us!"

How has God punished this execrable madness? He has punished it, as He created the light, by a single word. He spake, LET IT BE DONE! —and the political world has crumbled.

Europe is guilty, for having closed her eyes against these great truths; and it is because she is guilty, that she suffers. Yet she still repels the light, and acknowledges not the arm which gives the blow. Few men, indeed, among this material generation, are in a condition to know the *date, nature, and enormity,* of certain crimes, committed by individuals, by nations, and by sovereignties; still less to comprehend the kind of expiation which these crimes demand, and the adorable prodigy which compels EVIL to purify, with its own hands, the place which the eternal architect has already measured by the eye for His marvelous constructions.

28 DONOSO-CORTÉS

The Fallacies of Liberalism

Don Juan Donoso-Cortés, Marqués de Valdegamas (1809–1853), has been described as "the subtlest intellect in the entire history of conservatism." A descendant of the conqueror of Mexico, Donoso-Cortés served in the Spanish Parliament and then as ambassador to Paris. He began his political career as a moderate liberal, in the fashion of his French contemporary, Alexis de Tocqueville. The more he saw of revolution and abstract liberalism, however, the more authoritarian he became. He became convinced of the necessity of limiting liberty. Because of man's imperfect nature, an extreme reliance on reason is unreasonable and is indeed a betrayal of all that men have learned from ages of struggle and hard thought. In his *Essay on Catholicism, Liberalism and Socialism,** he condemned what he called "self-worshipping man." The selection below is a part of that essay, first published in 1851. It was to have an influence on the thinking of Pope Pius IX, who incorporated some of its ideas in his famous *Syllabus of Errors*.

Mr. Proudhon, in his *Confessions of a Revolutionist*, has written these remarkable words: "It is surprising to observe how constantly we find all our political questions complicated with theological questions." There is nothing in this to cause surprise, except it be the surprise of Mr. Proudhon. Theology being the science of God, is the ocean which contains and embraces all the sciences, as God is the ocean in which all things are contained. . . .

He possesses political truth who understands the laws to which governments are amenable; and he possesses social truth who comprehends the laws to which human societies are answerable. He who

* Trans. by Madeleine V. Goddard (Philadelphia: J. B. Lippincott, 1862).

knows God, knows these laws; and he knows God who listens to what He affirms of Himself, and believes the same. Theology is the science which has for its object these affirmations. Whence it follows that every affirmation respecting society or government, supposes an affirmation relative to God; or, what is the same thing, that every political or social truth necessarily resolves itself into a theological truth. . . .

Through Catholicism man recognized the law of order, and through man this order entered into society. The redemption regained for the moral world the laws which it had lost through prevarication and sin. Catholic dogma became the criterion for the sciences, Catholic ethics the guide for human actions, and Catholic charity the standard for the affections. Human conscience, freed from the corrosive action of error and sin, was thus enlightened in its interior, as in its exterior darkness, and, guided by the light of these three criterions, was restored to the felicity of lost innocence.

Order was thus transmitted from the religious into the moral world, and passed from the moral into the political world. The Catholic God, the creator and preserver of the universe, subjects all things to the laws of his Providence, and governs them by his vicars. . . . The idea of authority is of Catholic origin. The rulers over the nations of antiquity placed their right of supremacy on human foundations; they governed for themselves, and they governed by force. The Catholic rulers did not claim to exercise authority through any inherent right, but only as the delegated agents of God, and as the servants of the people. When man became the child of God, then he ceased to be the slave of man. There is nothing more solemn, more impressive, and at the same time more respectable, than the words which the Church addressed to Christian princes at their consecration: "Receive this scepter as an emblem of the sacred power confided to you in order that you may protect the weak, sustain the wavering, correct the vicious, and conduct the good in the way of salvation. Receive this scepter as the rule of divine justice, which upholds the good and punishes the wicked; learn by it to love justice, and to abhor iniquity." . . .

People and rulers alike gained by this happy revolution. The latter, because their former power only extended over the bodies of men, and they had reigned by the right of force; while now they exercised a lawful authority over both bodies and minds. The former gained, because obedience to God is preferable to obedience to man, and because a willing compliance is better than an imposed consent; and this proves that the results of this revolution were more favorable for the people than for their rulers; for while princes, by the very act of governing in the name of God, represented humanity as impotent to constitute a legitimate authority of itself, and in its own name, the people, who only submitted to their princes in obedience to the divine command, became the representatives of the highest and the most glorious of human prerogatives, that of submitting to no yoke except the divine authority. This serves to explain, on the one hand, the singular modesty for which those happy princes are eminent in history, whom men call great, and the Church holy; and, on the other hand, the singular dignity and elevation for which truly Catholic nations are conspicuous. A voice of peace, consolation, and mercy had been heard throughout the world, and had penetrated deeply into the human conscience; and this voice taught the nations, that those of low and mean condition are so placed, in order to be cared for on account of their necessities, and that the rich and great are born to serve others, because they are great and rich. Catholicism, in deifying authority, sanctified obedience; and, in deifying the one and sanctifying the other, condemned pride in its most terrible manifestations, the spirit of domination and that of rebellion. Two things are entirely impossible in a truly Catholic society, despotism and revolutions. Rousseau, who was sometimes capable of sudden and great inspirations, has written these remarkable words: "The rulers of modern times are undoubtedly indebted to Christianity both for the stability of their authority and the less frequent recurrence of revolutions. Nor has its influence here ceased, for, acting upon the rulers themselves, it has made them more humane. In order to be convinced of this, one has only to compare them with the rulers of ancient times" (*Emile*, vol. i. ch. iv). And Montesquieu has said: "We are undoubtedly indebted to Christianity for the public law recognized in peace and respected by nations during time of war, and for whose benefit we can never be sufficiently grateful" (*Spirit of Laws*, b. iii. ch. iii). . . .

[The Church] has, in the defense of liberty, opposed those kings who have made a despotic use of power, and she has maintained the principle of authority in opposition to those nations who have attempted to effect an absolute emancipation. Everywhere she has upheld the rights of God and the inviolability of his holy commandments. There is no truth that she has failed to proclaim, nor error that she has not anathematized. Liberty in truth she has always held sacred, but liberty in error is as hateful to her as error itself. She looks upon error as born and existing without rights, and she has therefore pursued, resisted, and extirpated it in the most hidden recesses of the human mind. As the perpetual illegitimacy and ignoring of error has been a religious dogma, so has it also been a political dogma, proclaimed in all ages and by all rulers. All have considered as beyond the pale of discussion the principle on which their power rested; all have denounced as error, and have deprived of all legitimacy and right, any principle opposed to that principle. They have all considered themselves infallible in this judgment, without appeal, and if all political errors have not been condemned, it is not because the conscience of mankind recognizes the legitimacy of any error, but because it has never admitted, in any human potentates, the privilege of infallibility in the qualification of error. As a consequence of this radical incapacity of human potentates to discriminate error, has arisen the principle of freedom of discussion, the foundation of modern constitutions. This principle does not suppose in society, as might appear at first sight, an incomprehensible and culpable impartiality between truth and error; it is based upon two other hypotheses, one of which is true and the other false. The first supposition is, that those who govern are not infallible, which is an evident truth; the other is based on the infallibility of discussion, which is false in every point of view. Infallibility cannot result from discussion, if it does not previously exist in those who argue; and it cannot exist in those who argue, if it does not also exist in those who govern. If infallibility is an attribute of human nature, it is found in the first as well as in the second; but if it is not an attribute of human nature, neither the first nor the second possess it. Either all are infallible or all are fallible. The question then is to decide whether human nature is fallible or infallible; which question resolves itself into this other; whether human nature is in a sound condition or vitiated and fallen.

According to the first supposition, infallibility, an essential quality of a sound understanding, is the first and greatest of all its attributes, and from this principle the following consequences naturally follow: If the reason of man is infallible because it is sound, it cannot err because it is infallible; if it cannot err because it is infallible, then all men possess the truth, no matter whether we consider them collectively or separately. If all men possess the truth, either singly or collectively considered, then all their affirmations and negations are necessarily identical. If all their affirmations and negations are identical, discussion is inconceivable and absurd.

According to the second supposition, fallibility is a weakness of human reason, and is the first and greatest of human imperfections; and proceeding from this principle are the following consequences: If the reason of man is fallible because it is infirm, it can never be certain of discerning the truth, because it is fallible; if it can never be sure of the truth because it is fallible, then this uncertainty is an essential characteristic of all men, whether we consider them singly or in the aggregate. If this uncertainty exists in all men, collectively or individually, all their affirmations and negations must be a contradiction in terms, because they are necessarily uncertain; and if all their affirmations and negations are uncertain, discussion becomes absurd and inconceivable.

Catholicism alone, as on all other points, has given a satisfactory and legitimate solution of this fearful problem. Catholicism teaches the following doctrine: Man comes from God, and sin from man; ignorance and error, as well as sorrow and death, come from sin; fallibility comes from ignorance, and from fallibility results the absurdity of discussion. But it adds, man was redeemed; which does not mean that by the act of redemption, and without any effort on his part, he was delivered from the slavery of sin; but it signifies, that through the redemption he acquired the power to break these chains, and, ennobled and restored, to convert ignorance, error, sorrow, and death into means of sanctification by the proper use of his regained liberty. For this end, God instituted his Church, immortal, impeccable, and infallible. The Church represents human nature without sin, such as it came from the hands of God, full of original justice and of sanctifying grace; and this is the reason why she is infallible, and not subject to death. God has established his Church upon the earth, in order that man, aided by grace, which is granted to all, may make himself worthy of having the blood, which was shed for him on Calvary, applied to him, by a free submission to its divine inspirations. By faith he will be enabled to vanquish ignorance, by patience he will overcome sorrow, and resignation will conquer death; while death, sorrow, and ignorance only exist in order to be subdued by faith, resignation, and patience.

It follows, then, that the Church alone has the right of affirmation and negation, and that there can exist no right to deny what she asserts, or to assert what she denies. When society forgot the doctrinal decisions of the Church, and consulted either the press or the pulpit, the magazines or the public assemblies, as to what was truth or what was error, then all minds confounded truth and error, and society was plunged into a region of shadows and illusions. Finding it to be an imperative necessity to submit to truth and withdraw from error, yet finding it impossible to define what is error and what is truth, she forms a catalogue of conventional and arbitrary truths, and another of pretended errors; and then she attempts to dictate as to what is to be believed, and what condemned. But she does not know, so great is her blindness, that in asserting some things and denying others, she neither believes nor rejects anything; or, if she condemns and adores anything, she condemns and adores herself.

The doctrinal intolerance of the Church has saved the world from chaos. It has placed political, domestic, social, and religious truths beyond controversy. These primitive and sacred truths are not subject to discussion, because they are the basis of all discussion. The moment there arises a doubt about them, that moment the mind becomes unsettled, being lost between truth and error, and the clear mirror of human reason is obscured. . . .

If all beauty consists in the order originally established by God, and if beauty, justice, and goodness are the same thing, viewed under different aspects, it follows from this that, outside of this order established by God, there can be neither beauty, justice, nor goodness; and if these three things constitute the supreme good, order, which includes them all, must necessarily be the supreme good.

As there is no good except in order, everything not in conformity with order must be evil; nor can there be any evil which does not consist in a subversion of order; therefore, as order is the supreme good, disorder is the supreme evil, because outside of disorder there can be no evil, and outside of order no good. From what has been said, we deduce the inference that order, or, what is the same thing, supreme good, consists in the preservation of all things in that connection in which God placed them, when he created them out of nothing; and that disorder, or, what is its equivalent, supreme evil, consists in breaking this admirable connection and this sublime harmony. . . .

Discussion, the universal dissolvent, whose secret virtue you do not understand, has destroyed your adversaries, and will destroy yourself. As to me, I am resolved not to tolerate it, for if I do not suppress it, it will turn against me. Discussion is a spiritual sword, which turns the mind with bandaged eyes, and against its power neither dexterity nor an armour of steel avails. Death assumes the guise of discussion when it desires to remain concealed and unrecognized. Rome was too wise to be thus deceived, and when it entered her gates under the mask of a sophist, she saw the disguise, and hastened to dismiss it. According to Catholic doctrine, man fell only because he entered into an argument with the woman, and the woman fell because she listened to the devil; and later, in the midway of time, this same demon, it is said, appeared to Jesus in a desert, and attempted to provoke him to a spiritual contest, or, as we would express it, to a tribunal discussion. But here we find that the devil met a more prudent adversary. . . .

The fundamental error of liberalism is, that it considers questions of government as alone important, when they are in reality of no consequence whatever, compared to those of religious and social order. This helps to explain why liberalism is always and everywhere entirely eclipsed, from the moment that Catholics and socialists announce their tremendous problems and their contradictory solutions. When Catholicism affirms that evil comes from sin, that sin in the first man corrupted human nature, yet, nevertheless, good prevails over evil, and order over disorder, because the one is human and the other divine—there is no doubt that this doctrine, even before investigation, is satisfactory to reason, because it proportions the grandeur of the causes to that of the effects, and proposes an explanation equal to the question that is to be explained. When socialism affirms that man's nature is perfect, and that society is sick; when it places the former in open conflict with the latter, in order that the good which is in man may extirpate the evil that is in society; when it calls upon humanity to rise in rebellion against all social institutions, there is undoubtedly in this mode of presenting and explaining a question, false as it is, much that in dignity and grandeur is worthy of the terrible majesty of the subject. But when liberalism explains good and evil, order and disorder, by the diversity of governmental forms, which are all ephemeral and transitory; when, setting aside all social and religious problems, it discusses its political problems as alone worthy the serious consideration of a statesman, truly words fail to express our sentiments of the profound incapacity and radical incompetency of this school, we will not say to solve, but even to present these formidable questions. . . .

But if we consider the rationalist theory, from which all have their origin, it will be seen that rationalism is the sin that most resembles original sin, being, like it, an actual error, and the productive cause of all error. Consequently it embraces and comprehends in its vast unity all errors; and contradictions form no impediment to this union, for even these antagonisms are susceptible of a certain kind of harmony and union, where there exists a supreme contradiction which involves them all. In the case in question, rationalism is this contradiction, which comprises all the others in its supreme unity. In fact, rationalism is at once deism, pantheism, humanism, manicheism, fatalism, skepticism, and atheism; and, among the rationalists, he who is at the same time deist, pantheist, humanist, manicheist, fatalist, skeptic, and atheist, is regarded as the most consistent. . . .

The liberal school holds it as certain, that there is no evil except that which results from the political institutions which we have inherited from past ages, and that the supreme good consists in the overthrow of these institutions. The greater number of socialists consider it as established, that there is no other evil than that which exists in society, and that the great remedy is to be found in the complete subversion of social institutions. All agree that evil is transmitted to us from past ages. The liberals affirm that good may be realized even in the present day; and the socialists assert that this golden era cannot commence except in times yet to come.

Thus, both the one and the other, placing the realization of the supreme good in the entire destruction of the present order—the political order, according to the liberal school, and the social order, according to the socialist schools—they agree with regard to the real and intrinsic goodness of man, who, they contend, must necessarily be the intelligent and free agent in effecting this subversion. This conclusion has been explicitly announced by the socialist schools, and it is implicitly contained in the theory maintained by the liberals. The conclusion is so far maintained in this theory that, if you deny the conclusion, the theory itself must fall to the ground. In fact, the theory, according to which evil exists in man, and proceeds from man, contradicts that other theory, which supposes evil to exist in political and social institutions, and to proceed from them. If we adopt the first hypothesis, there would exist a logical necessity to commence by eradicating evil from the heart of man, in order to extirpate it from society and the state. If we adopt the second supposition, the logical consequence would be the necessity of commencing by eradicating evil directly from society or the state, where it has its center and origin. From which we see that the Catholic and rationalist theories are not only utterly incompatible, but likewise antagonistic. All subversion, whether it be in the political or social order, is condemned by the Catholic theory as foolish and useless. The rationalist theories condemn all moral reform in man as stupid and of no avail. And thus, the ones as well as the others are consistent in their condemnation; because, if evil neither exists in the state nor in society, why and wherefore require the overthrow of society and of the state? And, on the contrary, if evil neither exists in individuals nor proceeds from them, why and for what cause desire the interior reformation of man? . . .

If we adopt the theory of the innate and absolute goodness of man, then he is the universal reformer, and in no need of being himself reformed. This view transforms man into God, and he ceases to have a human nature and becomes divine. Being in himself absolute goodness, the effect produced by the revolutions he creates must be absolute good; and as the chief good, and cause of all good, man must therefore be most excellent, most wise, and most powerful. Adoration is so imperative a necessity for man, that we find the socialists, who are atheists, and as such refusing to adore God, making gods of men, and in this way inventing a new form of adoration. . . .

Mr. Proudhon affirms unity, solidarity, and social infallibility—precisely the three things that communism affirms or supposes to exist in the state—and he denies the capacity and right of individuals to govern nations, which is exactly what is denied by communism. From which it follows that Proudhonism and communism arrive at the same conclusions by different means. They both assert the right of government, and with it the unity and solidarity of human societies. The government is infallible for both, that is to say, it is omnipotent; and being so, it excludes all idea of liberty in individuals, who, placed under the jurisdiction of an omnipotent and infallible government, can only be regarded as slaves. Whether we hold that the right of government resides in the state, the symbol of political unity, or in society considered as a collective being, in either case, according to socialist doctrine, all social rights are condensed in the state, and consequently the individual considered as such is condemned to the most complete servitude. . . .

29 ACTON

Liberty: The Prime Political Value

John Emerich Edward Dalberg-Acton (1834–1902) was a Liberal Member of Parliament for several years before he was elevated to the House of Lords by his close friend William Gladstone. He has since been known as Lord Acton. In 1895 he was appointed (by another Liberal Prime Minister) Regius Professor of Modern History at Trinity College, Cambridge, where he edited the monumental *Cambridge Modern History*. Acton was both a rigorous Catholic and a devoted liberal who opposed the new dogma of papal infallibility. He firmly believed in the importance of legitimate authority and at the same time in the inviolability of the individual conscience. Like De Tocqueville, he was a conservative liberal, a Whig, who distrusted democracy and loved liberty. His great work, *A History of Freedom*, was never finished. The selection comprises parts of one of his essays for that book, "The History of Freedom in Antiquity," first published in 1877.*

Liberty, next to religion, has been the motive of good deeds and the common pretext of crime, from the sowing of the seed at Athens, two thousand four hundred and sixty years ago, until the ripened harvest was gathered by men of our race. It is the delicate fruit of a mature civilisation; and scarcely a century has passed since nations, that knew the meaning of the term, resolved to be free. In every age its progress has been beset by its natural enemies, by ignorance and superstition, by lust of conquest and by love of ease, by the strong man's craving for power, and the poor man's craving for food. During long intervals it has been utterly arrested, when nations were

* John Acton, *History of Freedom and Other Essays,* ed. by J. N. Figgis and R. V. Laurence (London: Macmillan, 1907).

being rescued from barbarism and from the grasp of strangers, and when the perpetual struggle for existence, depriving men of all interest and understanding in politics, has made them eager to sell their birthright for a mess of pottage, and ignorant of the treasure they resigned. At all times sincere friends of freedom have been rare, and its triumphs have been due to minorities, that have prevailed by associating themselves with auxiliaries whose objects often differed from their own; and this association, which is always dangerous, has been sometimes disastrous, by giving to opponents just grounds of opposition, and by kindling dispute over the spoils in the hour of success. No obstacle has been so constant, or so difficult to overcome, as uncertainty and confusion touching the nature of true liberty. If hostile interests have wrought much injury, false ideas have wrought still more; and its advance is recorded in the increase of knowledge, as much as in the improvement of laws. The history of institutions is often a history of deception and illusions; for their virtue depends on the ideas that produce and on the spirit that preserves them, and the form may remain unaltered when the substance has passed away.

A few familiar examples from modern politics will explain why it is that the burden of my argument will lie outside the domain of legislation. It is often said that our Constitution attained its formal perfection in 1679, when the Habeas Corpus Act was passed. Yet Charles II succeeded, only two years later, in making himself independent of Parliament. In 1789, while the States-General assembled at Versailles, the Spanish Cortes, older than Magna Charta and more venerable than our House of Commons, were summoned after an interval of generations, but they immediately prayed the King to abstain from consulting them, and to make his reforms of his wisdom and authority. According to the common opinion, indirect elections are a safeguard of conservatism. But all the Assemblies of the French Revolution issued from indirect elections. A restricted suffrage is another reputed security for monarchy. But the Parliament of Charles X, which was returned by 90,000 electors, resisted and overthrew the throne; while the Parliament of Louis Philippe, chosen by a Constitution of 250,000, obsequiously promoted the reactionary policy of his Ministers, and in the fatal division which, by rejecting reform, laid the monarchy in the dust, Guizot's majority was obtained by the votes of 129 public functionaries. An unpaid legislature is, for obvious reasons, more independent than most of the Continental legislatures which receive pay. But it would be unreasonable in America to send a member as far as from here to Constantinople to live for twelve months at his own expense in the dearest of capital cities. Legally and to outward seeming the American President is the successor of Washington, and still enjoys powers devised and limited by the Convention of Philadelphia. In reality the new President differs from the Magistrate imagined by the Fathers of the Republic as widely as Monarchy from Democracy, for he is expected to make 70,000 changes in the public service; fifty years ago John Quincy Adams dismissed only two men. The purchase of judicial appointments is manifestly indefensible; yet in the old French monarchy that monstrous practice created the only corporation able to resist the king. Official corruption, which would ruin a commonwealth, serves in Russia as a salutary relief from the pressure of absolutism. There are conditions in which it is scarcely a hyperbole to say that slavery itself is a stage on the road to freedom. Therefore we are not so much concerned this evening with the dead letter of edicts and of statutes as with the living thoughts of men. A century ago it was perfectly well known that whoever had one audience of a Master in Chancery was made to pay for three, but no man heeded the enormity until it suggested to a young lawyer that it might be well to question and examine with rigorous suspicion every part of a system in which such things were done. The day on which that gleam lighted up the clear, hard mind of Jeremy Bentham is memorable in the political calendar beyond the entire administration of many statesmen. It would be easy to point out a paragraph in St. Augustine, or a sentence of Grotius that outweighs in influence the Acts of fifty Parliaments, and our cause owes more to Cicero and Seneca, to Vinet and Tocqueville, than to the laws of Lycurgus or the Five Codes of France.

By liberty I mean the assurance that every man shall be protected in doing what he believes his duty against the influence of authority and majorities, custom and opinion. The State is competent to assign duties and draw the line between good and evil only in its immediate sphere. Beyond the limits of things necessary for its well-being, it can only give indirect help to fight the battle of life by promoting the influences which prevail against temptation,—religion, education, and the distribution of wealth. In ancient times the State absorbed authorities not its own, and intruded on the domain of personal freedom. In the Middle Ages it possessed too little authority, and suffered others to intrude. Modern States fall habitually into both excesses. The most certain test by which we judge whether a country is really free is the amount of security enjoyed by minorities. Liberty, by this definition, is the essential condition and guardian of religion; and it is in the history of the Chosen People, accordingly, that the first illustrations of my subject are obtained. The government of the Israelites was a federation, held together by no political authority, but by the unity of race and faith, and founded, not on physical force, but on a voluntary covenant. The principle of self-government was carried out not only in each tribe, but in every group of at least 120 families; and there was neither privilege of rank nor inequality before the law. Monarchy was so alien to the primitive spirit of the community that it was resisted by Samuel in that momentous protestation and warning which all the kingdoms of Asia and many of the kingdoms of Europe have unceasingly confirmed. The throne was erected on a compact; and the king was deprived of the right of legislation among a people that recognized no lawgiver but God, whose highest aim in politics was to restore the original purity of the constitution, and to make its government conform to the ideal type that was hallowed by the sanctions of heaven. The inspired men who rose in unfailing succession to prophesy against the usurper and the tyrant, constantly proclaimed that the laws, which were divine, were paramount over sinful rulers, and appealed from the established authorities, from the king, the priests, and the princes of the people, to the healing forces that slept in the uncorrupted consciences of the masses. Thus the example of the Hebrew nation laid down the parallel lines on which all freedom has been won—the doctrine of national tradition and the doctrine of the higher law; the principle that a constitution grows from a root, by process of development, and not of essential change; and the principle that all political authorities must be tested and reformed according to a code which was not made by man. The operation of these principles, in unison, or in antagonism, occupies the whole of the space we are going over together.

The conflict between liberty under divine authority and the absolutism of human authorities ended disastrously. In the year 622 a supreme effort was made at Jerusalem to reform and preserve the State. The High Priest produced from the temple of Jehovah the book of the deserted and forgotten law, and both king and people bound themselves by solemn oaths to observe it. But that early example of limited monarchy and of the supremacy of law neither lasted nor spread; and the forces by which freedom has conquered must be sought elsewhere. In the very year 586, in which the flood of Asiatic despotism closed over the city which had been, and was destined again to be, the sanctuary of freedom in the East, a new home was prepared for it in the West, where, guarded by the sea and the mountains, and by valiant hearts, that stately plant was reared under whose shade we dwell, and which is extending its invincible arms so slowly and yet so surely over the civilised world.

According to a famous saying of the most famous authoress of the Continent, liberty is ancient, and it is despotism that is new. It has been the pride of recent historians to vindicate the truth of that maxim. The heroic age of Greece confirms it, and it is still more conspicuously true of Teutonic Europe. Wherever we can trace the earlier life of the Aryan nations we discover germs which favouring circumstances and assiduous culture might have developed into free societies. They exhibit some sense of common interest in common concerns, little reverence for external authority, and an imperfect sense of the function and supremacy of the State. Where the division of property and labour is incomplete there is little division of classes and of power. Until societies are tried by the complex problems of civilisation they may escape despotism, as societies that are undisturbed by religious diversity avoid persecution. In general, the forms of the patriarchal age failed to resist the growth of absolute States when the difficulties and temptations of advancing life began to tell; and with one sovereign exception, which is not within my scope to-day, it is scarcely possible to trace their survival in the institutions of later times. Six hundred years before the birth of Christ absolutism held unbounded sway. Throughout the East it was propped by the unchanging influence of priests and armies. In the West, where there were no sacred books requiring trained interpreters, the priesthood acquired no preponderance, and when the kings were overthrown their powers passed to aristocracies of birth. What followed, during many generations, was the cruel domination of class over class, the oppression of the poor by the rich, and of the ignorant by the wise. The spirit of that domination found passionate utterance in the verses of the aristocrat poet Theognis, a man of genius and refinement, who avows that he longed to drink the blood of his political adversaries. From these oppressors the people of many cities sought deliverance in the less intolerable tyranny of revolutionary usurpers. The remedy gave new shape and energy to the evil. The tyrants were often men of surprising capacity and merit, like some of those who, in the fourteenth century, made themselves lords of Italian cities; but rights secured by equal laws and by sharing power existed nowhere.

From this universal degradation the world was rescued by the most gifted of the nations. Athens, which like other cities was distracted and oppressed by a privileged class, avoided violence and appointed Solon to revise its laws. It was the happiest choice that history records. Solon was not only the wisest man to be found in Athens, but the most profound political genius of antiquity; and the easy, bloodless, and pacific revolution by which he accomplished the deliverance of his country was the first step in a career which our age glories in pursuing, and instituted a power which has done more than anything, except revealed religion, for the regeneration of society. The upper class had possessed the right of making and administering the laws, and he left them in possession, only transferring to wealth what had been the privilege of birth. To the rich, who alone had the means of sustaining the burden of public service in taxation and war, Solon gave a share of power proportioned to the demands made on their resources. The poorest classes were exempt from direct taxes, but were excluded from office. Solon gave them a voice in electing magistrates from the classes above them, and the right of calling them to account. This concession, apparently so slender, was the beginning of a mighty change. It introduced the idea that a man ought to have a voice in selecting those to whose rectitude and wisdom he is compelled to trust his fortune, his family, and his life. And this idea completely inverted the notion of human authority, for it inaugurated the reign of moral influence where all political power had depended on moral force. Government by consent superseded government by compulsion, and the pyramid which had stood on a point was made to stand upon its base. By making every citizen the guardian of his own interest Solon admitted the element of democracy into the State. The greatest glory of a ruler, he said, is to create a popular government. Believing that no man can be entirely trusted, he subjected all who exercised power to the vigilant control of those for whom they acted.

The only resource against political disorders that had been known till then was the concentration of power. Solon undertook to effect the same object by the distribution of power. He gave to the common people as much influence as he thought them able to employ, that the State might be exempt from arbitrary government. It is the essence of democracy, he said, to obey no master but the law. Solon recognised the principle that political forms are not final or inviolable, and must adapt themselves to facts; and he provided so well for the revision of his constitution, without breach of continuity or loss of stability, that for centuries after his death the Attic orators attributed to him, and quoted by his name, the whole structure of Athenian law. The direction of its growth was determined by the fundamental doctrine of Solon, that political power ought to be commensurate with public service. In the Persian war the services of the democracy eclipsed those of the Patrician orders, for the fleet that swept the Asiatics from the Aegean Sea was manned by the poorer Athenians. That class, whose valour had saved the State and had preserved European civilisation, had gained a title to increase of influence and privilege. The offices of State, which had been a monopoly of the rich, were thrown open to the poor, and in order to make sure that they should obtain their share, all but the highest commands were distributed by lot.

Whilst the ancient authorities were decaying, there was no accepted standard of moral and political right to make the framework of society fast in the midst of change. The instability that had seized on the forms threatened the very principles of government. The national beliefs were yielding to doubt, and doubt was not yet making way for knowledge. There had been a time when the obligations of public as well as private life were identified with the will of the gods. But that time had passed. Pallas, the ethereal goddess of the Athenians, and the Sun God whose oracles, delivered from the temple between the twin summits of Parnassus, did so much for the Greek nationality, aided in keeping up a lofty ideal of religion; but when the enlightened men of Greece learnt to apply their keen faculty of reasoning to the system of their inherited belief, they became quickly conscious that the conceptions of the gods corrupted the life and degraded the minds of the public. Popular morality could not be sustained by the popular religion. The moral instruction which was no longer supplied by the gods could not yet be found in books. There was no venerable code expounded by experts, no doctrine proclaimed by men of reputed sanctity like those teachers of the far East whose words still rule the fate of nearly half mankind. The effort to account for things by close observation and exact reasoning began by destroying. There came a time when the philosophers of the Porch and the Academy wrought the dictates of wisdom and virtue into a system so consistent and profound that it has vastly shortened the task of the Christian divines. But that time had not yet come.

The epoch of doubt and transition during which the Greeks passed from the dim fancies of mythology to the fierce light of science was the age of Pericles, and the endeavour to substitute certain truth for the prescriptions of impaired authorities, which was then beginning to absorb the energies of the Greek intellect, is the grandest movement in the profane annals of mankind, for to it we owe, even after the immeasurable progress accomplished by Christianity, much of our philosophy and far the better part of the political knowledge we possess. Pericles, who was at the head of the Athenian government, was the first statesman who encountered the problem which the rapid weakening of traditions forced on the political world. No authority in morals or in politics remained unshaken by the motion that was in the air. No guide could be confidently trusted; there was no available criterion to appeal to, for the means of controlling or denying convictions that prevailed among the people. The popular sentiment as to what was right might be mistaken, but it was subject to no test. The people were, for practical purposes, the seat of the knowledge of good and evil. The people, therefore, were the seat of power.

The political philosophy of Pericles consisted of this conclusion. He resolutely struck away all the props that still sustained the artificial preponderance of wealth. For the ancient doctrine that power goes with land, he introduced the idea that power ought to be so equitably diffused as to afford equal security to all. That one part of the community should govern the whole, or that one class should make laws for another, he declared to be tyrannical. The abolition of privilege would have served only to transfer the supremacy from the rich to the poor, if Pericles had not redressed the balance by restricting the right of citizenship to Athenians of pure descent. By this measure the class which formed what we should call the third estate was brought down to 14,000 citizens, and became about equal in numbers with the higher ranks. Pericles held that every Athenian who neglected to take his part in the public business inflicted an injury on the commonwealth. That none might be excluded by poverty, he caused the poor to be paid for their attendance out of the funds of the State; for his administration of the federal tribute had brought together a treasure of more than two million sterling. The instrument of his sway was the art of speaking. He governed by persuasion. Everything was decided by argument in open deliberation, and every influence bowed before the ascendancy of mind. The idea that the object of constitutions is not to confirm the predominance of any interest, but to prevent it; to preserve with equal care the independence of labour and the security of property; to make the rich safe against envy, and the poor against oppression, marks the highest level attained by the statesmanship of Greece. It hardly survived the great patriot who conceived it; and all history has been occupied with the endeavour to upset the balance of power by giving the advantage to money, land, or numbers. A generation followed that has never been equalled in talent—a generation of men whose works, in poetry and eloquence, are still the envy of the world, and in history, philosophy, and politics remain unsurpassed. But it produced no successor to Pericles, and no man was able to wield the sceptre that fell from his hand.

It was a momentous step in the progress of nations when the principle that every interest should have the right and the means of asserting itself was adopted by the Athenian Constitution. But for those who were beaten in the vote there was no redress. The law did not check the triumph of majorities or rescue the minority from the dire penalty of having been outnumbered. When the overwhelming influence of Pericles was removed, the conflict between classes raged without restraint, and the slaughter that befell the higher ranks in the Peloponnesian war gave an irresistible preponderance to the lower. The restless and inquiring spirit of the Athenians was prompt to unfold the reason of every institution and the consequences of every principle, and their Constitution ran its course from infancy to decrepitude with unexampled speed.

Two men's lives span the interval from the first admission of popular influence, under Solon, to the downfall of the State. Their history furnishes the classic example of the peril of democracy under conditions singularly favourable. For the Athenians were not only brave and patriotic and capable of generous sacrifice, but they were the most religious of the Greeks. They venerated the Constitution which had given them prosperity, and equality, and freedom, and never questioned the fundamental laws which regulated the enormous power of the Assembly. They tolerated considerable variety of opinion and great licence of speech; and their humanity towards their slaves roused the indignation even of the most intelligent partisan of aristocracy. Thus they became the only people of antiquity that grew great by democratic institutions. But the possession of unlimited power, which corrodes the conscience, hardens the heart, and confounds the understanding of monarchs, exercised its demoralising influence on the illustrious democracy of Athens. It is bad to be oppressed by a minority, but it is worse to be oppressed by a majority. For there is a reserve of latent power in the masses which, if it is called into play, the minority can seldom resist. But from the absolute will of an entire people there is no appeal, no redemption, no refuge but treason. The humblest and most numerous class of the Athenians united the legislative, the judicial, and, in part, the executive power. The philosophy that was then in the ascendant taught them that there is no law superior to that of the State—the lawgiver is above the law.

It followed that the sovereign people had a right to do whatever was within its power, and was bound by no rule of right or wrong but its own judgment of expediency. On a memorable occasion the assembled Athenians declared it monstrous that they should be prevented from doing whatever they chose. No force that existed could restrain them; and they resolved that no duty should restrain them, and that they would be bound by no laws that were not of their own making. In this way the emancipated people of Athens became a tyrant; and their government, the pioneer of European freedom, stands condemned with a terrible unanimity by all the wisest of the ancients. They ruined their city by attempting to conduct war by debate in the marketplace. Like the French Republic, they put their unsuccessful commanders to death. They treated their dependencies with such injustice that they lost their maritime Empire. They plundered the rich until the rich conspired with the public enemy, and they crowned their guilt by the martyrdom of Socrates.

When the absolute sway of numbers had endured for near a quarter of a century, nothing but bare existence was left for the State to lose; and the Athenians, wearied and despondent, confessed the true cause of their ruin. They understood that for liberty, justice, and equal laws, it is as necessary that democracy should restrain itself as it had been that it should restrain the oligarchy. They resolved to take their stand once more upon the ancient ways, and to restore the order of things which had subsisted when the monopoly of power had been taken from the rich and had not been acquired by the poor. After a first restoration had failed, which is only memorable because Thucydides, whose judgment in politics is never at fault, pronounced it the best government Athens had enjoyed, the attempt was renewed with more experience and greater singleness of purpose. The hostile parties were reconciled, and proclaimed an amnesty, the first in history. They resolved to govern by concurrence. The laws, which had the sanction of tradition, were reduced to a code; and no act of the sovereign assembly was valid with which they might be found to disagree. Between the sacred lines of the Constitution which were to remain inviolate, and the decrees which met from time to time the needs and notions of the day, a broad distinction was drawn; and the fabric of a law which had been the work of generations was made independent of momentary variations in the popular will. The repentance of the Athenians came too late to save the Republic. But the lesson of their experience endures for all times, for it teaches that government by the whole people, being the government of the most numerous and most powerful class, is an evil of the same nature as unmixed monarchy, and requires, for nearly the same reasons, institutions that shall protect it against itself, and shall uphold the permanent reign of law against arbitrary revolutions of opinion. . . .

If the topic of my address was the history of political science, the highest and the largest place would belong to Plato and Aristotle. The *Laws* of the one, the *Politics* of the other, are, if I may trust my own experience, the books from which we may learn the most about the principles of politics. The penetration with which those great masters of thought analysed the institutions of Greece, and exposed their vices, is not surpassed by anything in later literature; by Burke or Hamilton, the best political writers of the last century; by Tocqueville or Roscher, the most eminent of our own. But Plato and Aristotle were philosophers, studious not of unguided freedom, but of intelligent government. They saw the disastrous effects of ill-directed striving for liberty; and they resolved that it was better not to strive for it, but to be content with a strong administration, prudently adapted to make men prosperous and happy.

Now liberty and good government do not exclude each other; and there are excellent reasons why they should go together. Liberty is not a means to a higher political end. It is itself the highest political end. It is not for the sake of a good public administration that it is required, but for security in the pursuit of the highest objects of civil society, and of private life. Increase of freedom in the State may sometimes promote mediocrity, and give vitality to prejudice; it may even retard useful legislation, diminish the capacity for war, and restrict the boundaries of Empire. It might be plausibly argued that, if many things would be worse in England or Ireland under an intelligent despotism, some things would be managed better; that the Roman government was more enlightened under Augustus and Antoninus than under the Senate, in the days of Marius or of Pompey. A generous spirit prefers that his country should be poor, and weak, and of no account, but free, rather than powerful, prosperous, and enslaved. It is better to be the citizen of a humble commonwealth in the Alps, without a prospect of influence beyond the narrow frontier, than a subject of the superb autocracy that overshadows half of Asia and of Europe. But it may be urged, on the other side, that liberty is not the sum or the substitute of all the things men ought to live for; that to be real it must be circumscribed, and that the limits of circumscription vary; that advancing civilisation invests the State with increased rights and duties, and imposes increased burdens and constraint on the subject; that a highly instructed and intelligent community may perceive the benefit of compulsory obligations which, at a lower stage, would be thought unbearable; that liberal progress is not vague or indefinite, but aims at a point where the public is subject to no restrictions but those of which it feels the advantage; that a free country may be less capable of doing much for the advancement of religion, the prevention of vice, or the relief of suffering, than one that does not shrink from confronting great emergencies by some sacrifice of individual rights, and some concentration of power; and that the supreme political object ought to be sometimes postponed to still higher moral objects. My argument involves no collision with these qualifying reflections. We are dealing, not with the effects of freedom, but with its causes. We are seeking out the influences which brought arbitrary government under control, either by the diffusion of power, or by the appeal to an authority which transcends all government, and among those influences the greatest philosophers of Greece have no claim to be reckoned.

It is the Stoics who emancipated mankind from its subjugation to despotic rule, and whose enlightened and elevated views of life bridged the chasm that separates the ancient from the Christian state, and led the way to freedom. Seeing how little security there is that the laws of any land shall be wise or just, and that the unanimous will of a people and the assent of nations are liable to err, the Stoics looked beyond those narrow barriers, and above those inferior sanctions, for the principles that ought to regulate the lives of men and the existence of society. They made it known that there is a will superior to the collective will of man, and a law that overrules those of Solon and Lycurgus. Their test of good government is its conformity to principles that can be traced to a higher legislator. That which we must obey, that to which we are bound to reduce all civil authorities, and to sacrifice every earthly interest, is that immutable law which is perfect and eternal as God Himself, which proceeds from His nature, and reigns over heaven and earth and over all the nations.

The great question is to discover, not what governments prescribe, but what they ought to prescribe; for no prescription is valid against the conscience of mankind. Before God, there is neither Greek nor barbarian, neither rich nor poor, and the slave is as good as his master, for by birth all men are free; they are citizens of that universal commonwealth which embraces all the world, brethren of one family, and children of God. The true guide of our conduct is no outward authority, but the voice of God, who comes down to dwell in our souls, who knows all our thoughts, to whom are owing all the truth we know, and all the good we do; for vice is voluntary, and virtue comes from the grace of the heavenly spirit within.

What the teaching of that divine voice is, the philosophers who had imbibed the sublime ethics of the Porch went on to expound: It is not enough to act up to the written law, or to give all men their due; we ought to give them more than their due, to be generous and beneficent, to devote ourselves for the good of others, seeking our reward in self-denial and sacrifice, acting from the motive of sympathy and not of personal advantage. Therefore we must treat others as we wish to be treated by them, and must persist until death in doing good to our enemies, regardless of unworthiness and ingratitude. For we must be at war with evil, but at peace with men, and it is better to suffer than to commit injustice. True freedom, says the most eloquent of the Stoics, consists in obeying God. A State governed by such principles as these would have been free far beyond the measure of Greek or Roman freedom; for they open a door to religious toleration, and close it against slavery. . . .

30 STEPHEN

Rejoinder to Liberal Dogma

Sir James Fitzjames Stephen (1829–1894) was a Victorian Englishman of wide talents and experience; he was a noted lawyer, a judge, an administrator in the Indian Civil Service, a professor and journalist. He recognized the gradual growth of democracy as an irreversible fact of history but was not very sanguine about it. "The waters are out and no human force can turn them back," he once wrote, "but I do not see as we go with the stream we need sing Hallelujah to the river god." It is not surprising that such a man should favor an empirical approach to conservatism. He strongly supported liberty under law and believed in a very wide area of personal freedom. But he strongly attacked John Stuart Mill's manifesto of liberalism, *On Liberty*. Stephen's rejoinder, *Liberty, Equality and Fraternity,* has been generally accepted as the classic conservative reply to Mill's liberalism. The selection is taken from the second chapter, "On the Liberty of Thought and Discussion." *

On the Liberty of Thought and Discussion

Though, as I pointed out in my last chapter, Mr. Mill rather asserts than proves his doctrines about liberty, the second chapter of his essay on the Liberty of Thought and Discussion, and the third chapter on Individuality as one of the Elements of Well-being—may be regarded as arguments to prove certain parts or applications of the general principle asserted in his introduction; and as such I will consider them. I object rather to Mr. Mill's theory than to his practical conclusions. I hope to show hereafter how far the practical difference

* James Fitzjames Stephen, *Liberty, Equality and Fraternity* (London, 1873).

between us extends. The objection which I make to most of his statements on the subject is, that in order to justify in practice what might be justified on narrow and special grounds, he lays down a theory incorrect in itself and tending to confirm views which might become practically mischievous.

The result of his letter on Liberty of Thought and Discussion is summed up, with characteristic point and brevity, by himself in the following words: —

We have now recognized the necessity to the mental well-being of mankind (on which all their other well-being depends) of freedom of opinion and freedom of the expression of opinion on four distinct grounds.

First, if any opinion is compelled to silence, that opinion may, for aught we can certainly know, be true. To deny this is to assume our own infallibility.

Secondly, though the silenced opinion be an error, it may, and very commonly does, contain a portion of truth; and since the general or prevailing opinion is rarely or never the whole truth, it is only by the collision of adverse opinions that the remainder of the truth has any chance of being supplied.

Thirdly, even if the received opinion be not only true, but the whole truth, unless it is suffered to be and actually is vigorously and earnestly contested, it will by most of those who receive it be held in the manner of a prejudice, with little comprehension or feeling of its rational grounds.

Fourthly, the meaning of the doctrine itself will be in danger of being lost or enfeebled and deprived of its vital effect on the character and conduct; the dogma becoming a mere formal profession inefficacious for good, but cumbering the ground, and preventing the growth of any real and heartfelt conviction from reason or personal experience.

The chapter in question is, I think, one of the most eloquent to be found in its author's writings, and it contains, as is not unfrequently the case with him, illustrations which are even more valuable for what they suggest than for what they say.

These illustrations are no doubt the part of this chapter which made the deepest impression when it was first published, and which have been most vividly remembered by its readers. I think that for the sake of them most readers forget the logical framework in which they were set, and read the chapter as a plea for greater freedom of discussion on theological subjects. If Mr. Mill had limited himself to the proposition that in our own time and country it is highly important that the great questions of theology should be discussed openly and with complete freedom from all legal restraints, I should agree with him. But the impression which the whole chapter leaves upon me is that for the sake of establishing this limited practical consequence, Mr. Mill has stated a theory which is very far indeed from the truth, and which, if generally accepted, might hereafter become a serious embarrassment to rational legislation.

His first reason in favour of unlimited freedom of opinion on all subjects is this: 'If any opinion is compelled to silence, that opinion may, for aught we can certainly tell, be true. To deny this is to assume our own infallibility.'

He states fairly and fully the obvious objection to this—that 'there is no greater presumption of infallibility in forbidding the propagation of error than in any other thing which is done by public authority on its own judgment and responsibility.' In other words, the assumption is not that the persecutor is infallible, but that in this particular case he is right. To this objection he replies as follows:—'There is the greatest difference between presuming an opinion to be true because, with every opportunity for contesting it, it has not been refuted, and assuming its truth for the purpose of not permitting its refutation. Complete liberty of contradicting our opinion is the very condition which justifies us in assuming its truth for purposes of action; and on no other terms can a being with human faculties have any rational assurance of being right.'

This reply does not appear to be satisfactory. It is not very easy to disentangle the argument on which it rests, and to put it into a perfectly distinct shape, but I think it will be found on examination to involve the following propositions:—

1. No one can have a rational assurance of the truth of any opinion whatever, unless he is infallible, or unless all persons are absolutely free to contradict it.

2. Whoever prevents the expression of any opinion asserts by that act that he has a rational assurance of the falsehood of that opinion.

3. At the same time he destroys one of the conditions of a rational assurance of the truth of the assertions which he makes, namely, the freedom of others to contradict him.

4. Therefore he claims infallibility, which is the only other ground on which such an assurance of the truth of those assertions can rest.

The first and second of these propositions appear to me to be incorrect.

As to the first, I think that there are innumerable propositions on which a man may have a rational assurance that he is right whether others are or are not at liberty to contradict him, and that although he does not claim infallibility. Every proposition of which we are assured by our own senses, or by evidence which for all practical purposes is as strong as that of our own senses, falls under this head. There are plenty of reasons for not forbidding people to deny the existence of London Bridge and the river Thames, but the fear that the proof of those propositions would be weakened or that the person making the law would claim infallibility is not among the number.

A asserts the opinion that B is a thief. B sues A for libel. A justifies. The jury give a verdict for the plaintiff, with £1,000 damages. This is nearly equivalent to a law forbidding every one, under the penalty of a heavy fine, to express the opinion that in respect of the matters discussed B is a thief. Does this weaken the belief of the world at large in the opinion that in respect of those matters B is not a thief? According to Mr. Mill, no one can have a rational assurance upon the subject unless every one is absolutely free to contradict the orthodox opinion. Surely this cannot be so.

The solution seems to be this. The fact that people are forbidden to deny a proposition weakens the force of the inference in its favour to be drawn from their acquiescence in it; but the value of their acquiescence considered as evidence may be very small, and the weight of other evidence, independent of public opinion, may not only be overwhelming, but the circumstances of the case may be such as to be inconsistent with the supposition that any further evidence will ever be forthcoming.

Again, an opinion may be silenced without any assertion on the part of the person who silences it that it is false. It may be suppressed because it is true, or because it is doubtful whether it is true or false, and because it is not considered desirable that it should be discussed. In these cases there is obviously no assumption of infallibility in suppressing it. The old maxim, 'the greater the truth the greater the libel,' has a true side to it, and when it applies it is obvious that an opinion is silenced without any assumption of infallibility. The opinion that a respectable man of mature years led an immoral life in his youth may be perfectly true, and yet the expression of that opinion may be a crime, if it is not for the public good that it should be expressed.

In cases in which it is obvious that no conclusion at all can be established beyond the reach of doubt, and that men must be contented with probabilities, it may be foolish to prevent discussion and prohibit the expression of any opinion but one, but no assumption of infallibility is involved in so doing. When Henry VIII. and Queen Elizabeth silenced to a certain extent both Catholics and Puritans, and sought to confine religious controversy within limits fixed by law, they did not assume themselves to be infallible. What they thought—and it is by no means clear that they were wrong—was that unless religious controversy was kept within bounds there would be a civil war, and they muzzled the disputants accordingly.

There are, in short, two classes of cases to which, as it appears to me, Mr. Mill's argument does not apply—cases in which moral certainty is attainable on the evidence, and cases in which it is not attainable on the evidence.

Where moral certainty is attainable on the evidence the suppression of opinion involves no claim to infallibility, but at most a claim to be right in the particular case.

Where moral certainty is not attainable on the evidence the suppression of opinion involves no claim to infallibility, because it does not assert the falsehood of the opinion suppressed.

The three remaining arguments in favour of unlimited liberty of thought and discussion are: 1. That the silenced opinion may be partially true and that this partial truth can be brought out by discussion only. 2. That a true opinion when established is not believed to be true unless it is vigorously and earnestly contested. 3. That it comes to be held in a dead conventional way unless it is discussed.

These arguments go to show, not that the suppression of opinion can never be right, but that it may sometimes be wrong, which no one denies. None of them show—as the first argument would if it were well founded—that persecution in all cases proceeds on a process involving distinct intellectual error. As to the first argument, it is obvious that if people are prepared to take the chance of persecuting a proposition which may be wholly true as if it were wholly false, they will be prepared to treat it in the same manner though it is only partially true. The second and third arguments, to which I shall have to return hereafter, apply exclusively to that small class of persons whose opinions depend principally upon the consciousness that they have reached them by intellectual processes correctly performed. The incalculable majority of mankind form their opinions in quite a different way, and are attached to them because they suit their temper and meet their wishes, and not because and in so far as they think themselves warranted by evidence in believing them to be true. The notorious result of unlimited freedom of thought and discussion is to produce general scepticism on many subjects in the vast majority of minds. If you want zealous belief, set people to fight. Few things give men such a keen perception of the importance of their own opinions and the vileness of the opinions of others as the fact that they have inflicted and suffered persecution for them. Unlimited freedom of opinion may be a very good thing, but it does not tend to zeal, or even to a distinct appreciation of the bearings of the opinions which are entertained. Nothing will give either but a deep interest in the subject to which those opinions relate, and this is so personal and deeply seated a matter that it is scarcely capable of being affected by external restraints, unless, indeed, it is irritated and so stimulated by them. . . .

To me the question whether liberty is a good or a bad thing appears as irrational as the question whether fire is a good or a bad thing? It is both good and bad according to time, place, and circumstance, and a complete answer to the question, In what cases is liberty good and in what cases is it bad? would involve not merely a universal history of mankind, but a complete solution of the problems which such a history would offer. I do not believe that the state of our knowledge is such as to enable us to enunciate any 'very simple principle as entitled to govern absolutely the dealings of society with the individual in the way of compulsion and control.' We must proceed in a far more cautious way, and confine ourselves to such remarks as experience suggests about the advantages and disadvantages of compulsion and liberty respectively in particular cases.

The following way of stating the matter is not and does not pretend to be a solution of the question, In what cases is liberty good? but it will serve to show how the question ought to be discussed when it arises. I do not see how Mr. Mill could deny its correctness consistently with the general principles of the ethical theory which is to a certain extent common to us both.

Compulsion is bad—

1. When the object aimed at is bad.

2. When the object aimed at is good, but the compulsion employed is not calculated to obtain it.

3. When the object aimed at is good, and the compulsion employed is calculated to obtain it, but at too great an expense.

Thus to compel a man to commit murder is bad, because the object is bad.

To inflict a punishment sufficient to irritate but not sufficient to deter or to destroy for holding particular religious opinions is bad, because such compulsion is not calculated to effect its purpose, assuming it to be good.

To compel people not to trespass by shooting them with spring-guns is bad, because the harm done is out of all proportion to the harm avoided.

If, however, the object aimed at is good, if the compulsion employed such as to attain it, and if the good obtained overbalances the inconvenience of the compulsion itself, I do not understand how, upon utilitarian principles, the compulsion can be bad. I may add that this way of stating the case shows that Mr. Mill's 'simple principle' is really a paradox. It can be justified only by showing as a fact that, self-protection apart, no good object can be attained by any compulsion which is not in itself a greater evil than the absence of the object which the compulsion obtains.

I will now proceed to apply the principles stated to the case of compulsion applied to thought and discussion. This Mr. Mill condemns in all cases. I should condemn it in those cases only in which the object itself is bad, or in which the means used are not suited to its attainment, or in which, though suited to its attainment, they involve too great an expense. Compare the results of these two ways of thinking. Few persons would be found, I suppose, in these days to deny the paramount expediency, the utility in the highest sense, of having true opinions; and by true I mean not merely honest, but correct, opinions. To believe true statements, to disbelieve false statements, to give to probable or improbable statements a degree of credit proportioned to their apparent probability or improbability, would be the greatest of intellectual blessings. Such a state of mind is the ideal state which a perfectly reasonable human being would regard as the one at which he ought to aim, as we aim at all ideals—that is to say, with a consciousness that we can never fully attain them. The most active-minded, the most sagacious, and those who are most favourably situated for the purpose, are in practice altogether unable to make more than an approximation to such a result, in regard to some few of the innumerable subjects which interest them. I am, of course, aware that this view is not universally admitted, but I need not argue at present with those who deny it.

Assuming it to be true, it will follow that all coercion which has the effect of falsifying the opinions of those who are coerced is coercion for an object bad in itself; and this at once condemns all cases of direct coercion in favour of opinions which are not, to say the least, so probable that a reasonable man would act upon the supposition of their truth. The second condition—namely, that coercion must be effective—and the third condition, that it must not inflict greater evils than it avoids, condemn, when taken together, many other cases of coercion, even when the object aimed at is good. For instance, they condemn all coercion applied directly to thought and unexpressed opinion, and all coercion which must be carried to the point of extermination or general paralysis of the thinking powers in order to be effective. In the first case the end is not attained. In the second it is attained at too great an expense. These two considerations are sufficient to condemn all the coarser forms of persecution. I have nothing to add to the well-known commonplaces which bear upon this part of the subject.

This being allowed, let us turn to the consideration of the other side of the question, and enquire whether there are no cases in which a degree of coercion, affecting, though not directly applied to, thought and the expression of opinion, and not in itself involving an evil greater than the evil avoided, may attain desirable ends. I think that such cases exist and are highly important. In general terms I think that the legal establishment and disestablishment of various forms of opinion, religious, political, and moral, their encouragement and recognition by law and public opinion as being true and useful, or their discouragement by law and public opinion as being false and mischievous, fall within this principle. I think, that is, that they are cases of coercion of which the object is or may be good, and in which the coercion is likely to be effective, and is not an evil great enough

to counterbalance the evil which is avoided or the good which is attained. I think, in short, that Governments ought to take the responsibility of acting upon such principles, religious, political, and moral,
as they may from time to time regard as most likely to be true, and
this they cannot do without exercising a very considerable degree of
coercion. The difference between, I do not say keeping up an Established Church at the public expense, but between paying a single
shilling of public money to a single school in which any opinion is
taught of which any single taxpayer disapproves, and the maintenance of the Spanish Inquisition, is a question of degree. As the first
cannot be justified without infringing the principle of liberty as stated
by Mr. Mill, so the last can be condemned on my principles only by
showing that the doctrines favoured by the Inquisition were not true,
that the means used to promote them were ineffective, or that their
employment was too high a price to pay for the object gained; issues
which I should be quite ready to accept. . . .

V
Contemporary Conservatism
in Europe

In Europe today, the tradition of both philosophic and practical conservatism, established by Burke, Hegel, De Tocqueville, Disraeli, and others, is being carried on by a new generation.

Particular social problems may vary from nation to nation, but the underlying principles remain the same. Burke's warning—that those who are not restrained from within must be restrained from without—remains as true as it was in 1789. Within this framework, however, every nation can cultivate its own kind of conservatism to suit its own character.

Bertrand de Jouvenel of France has contributed much, in his many writings, to our understanding of the modern world; one of his most insightful essays is on the subject of justice—the goal which has stimulated most political thought from the days of Plato to our own. The Western democracies, having solved the problems of production (for their necessities, at least), have since been preoccupied with "social justice," with the problem of distribution of wealth.

Arthur Seldon in Britain and Ludwig Erhard in Germany have changed, to a considerable degree, the accepted wisdom of their respective countries on such fiercely debated questions as: How much economic planning? and: What can the state do that private enterprise cannot? Erhard, of course, had the opportunity to put many of his economic theories into action, and as all the world knows, the German economic "miracle" was the result. Most of the socialist and "liberal" (in the American sense of the word) economists warned that chaos and depression would result if government controls were removed from the German economy in 1948. An almost perfect test of the two opposing economic philosophies of the West was thus arranged. It came as no surprise to Erhard that when restrictions were removed, a creative surge of new ideas and industry was the result and Germany soon outstripped her neighbors (most of whom started with many more material advantages) in the economic race. His book *The Economics of Success* is pertinent not only to his own country but to any nation, including those which are underdeveloped, that wants a higher standard of living for its people while preserving democratic values.

A prosperous nation will want to do everything it can to help those who lag behind the general affluence. There is little doubt that the collection of social services known as welfare states of the West are the result of piecemeal political pressures and could and should be drastically reformed along more equitable and efficient lines. Arthur Seldon, among many others, has pointed out that most of these social services are devoted to helping the middle class (who have the knowledge and the political influence to benefit most by them) and not the poor. In fact, there is considerable evidence that the really needy are actually worse off than they would be if the present welfare systems did not exist. Seldon's many provocative ideas are a most valuable contribution to a perennial political issue in all democratic countries.

No one in our time has been a more authentic spokesman for democratic conservatism than Winston Churchill, whose determination was largely responsible for bringing an end to Hitler and his National Socialist Party. Grandson of a duke, he refused a dukedom on the grounds that he knew of no higher title than that of Member of the House of Commons. He staunchly avoided a systematic exposition of his political philosophy (in itself a mark of his conservatism), but few, if any, were better able to evoke the spirit of all that is best in the conservative tradition. Conservatism is not without its faults. But if, once in a century, it can produce the leadership and vision of a Burke, a Disraeli, and a Churchill, it will have served its purpose.

31   DE JOUVENEL

The Meaning of Social Justice

Bertrand de Jouvenel (1903–   ) is one of the most distinguished students of politics in France, or indeed the world, today. A professor at the University of Paris, he is the author of *On Power* and
Sovereignty; he is also the editor of *Futuribles,* a scholarly journal concerned with coming trends. His book *Sovereignty* is subtitled *An Inquiry
into the Political Good,* and it includes an examination of such ideas as
justice, the common good, and liberty. The problem of social justice is
one of the most pressing of our time; De Jouvenel provides some insights into how a sensible and intelligent definition of social justice may
be worked out. The selection is the chapter from *Sovereignty* entitled
"Justice." *

In every age justice has been called the keystone of the social edifice. By acting towards each other justly, the citizens maintain the
condition of trustfulness and friendship which is the basis of an un-
forced and fruitful co-operation; by acting with justice towards each
and all, the public authority wins the confidence and respect which
render it effective. Authority finds in its justice, taken as a whole, the
end and the means of its activity.   The sceptre and the sword of
justice are the traditional attributes, closely associated, of the monarch; to be just—to resist the pressures which would cause him to
give unjust decisions—he must be strong, and his justice increases his
credit, whence he draws his strength.

Preoccupation with justice is, therefore, the political preoccupation
par excellence and it is no bad thing that 'social justice' should be

* Trans. by J. F. Huntington (Cambridge, U.K.: Cambridge University
Press, 1957). By permission.

the obsession of our time. To all appearances, however, it acts as a principle not of concord but of discord. Intellectuals speak of 'realising' or 'winning' it and political groups fight each other for the honour of leading this crusade; for the enterprise is conceived as a struggle against forces hostile to a species of justice the precise nature of which its champions do not doubt. Unfortunately, not all see it alike. Hence comes the spectacle of society splitting and crumbling in the name of the justice which should harmonise it and cause peace to reign.

Of What or of Whom Is Justice the Attribute?

The classical definitions all attest that the place where justice dwells —or should dwell—is the hearts of men. So say the Institutes of Justinian: 'Justice is a firm and unceasing determination to render to every man his due.' Here, then, justice appears as a matter of will. Saint Thomas Aquinas goes a step further: 'Justice is a habit of mind which maintains in us a firm and unceasing determination to render to every man his due.' So he links up with Aristotle, for whom 'justice is that quality in virtue of which a man is said to be disposed to do by deliberate choice that which is just, when distributing things between himself and another, or between two others.'

Thus justice is conceived as a human attitude of mind which habit strengthens—a virtue. But when people talk of justice today they no longer mean this virtue of the soul, but a state of things. The word no longer conveys to the mind a certain human attribute but a certain configuration of society; it is no longer applied to certain personal attitudes of mind but envisages certain collective arrangements. Whereas it used to be thought that social relationships are improved by justice in men, it is now thought, contrariwise, that the installation in institutions of a state of things called just promotes the improvement of men. This reversal is in the fashion of thought today, which makes morality the creature of circumstance.

We see then that justice today is not a habit of mind which each of us can acquire in proportion to his virtue and should acquire in proportion to his power; rather it is an organisation or arrangement of things. For this reason the first part of the classical definitions, which links justice with the human being, no longer finds a place in modern preoccupations which link justice with society. People no longer say with Aristotle that justice is the moral attitude of the just man, or with the jurists that it is a certain exercise of the will, for these talk of an intimate quality of the soul. The justice now recommended is a quality not of a man and a man's actions, but of a certain configuration of things in social geometry, no matter by what means it is brought about. Justice is now something which exists independently of just men.

Men now seek to establish 'the thing which is just', and it is supposed that the difficulty of doing so is entirely in the execution; no doubts are felt that this conception of the just thing is the true one. Yet very different conceptions of it are possible, and that is why the sages of old treated it as a mental state of moral agents, rather than as an arrangement of things of which the secret was available. In speaking of this arrangement, we must be quite clear what we mean by it: what is the arrangement that can be called just? Let us see if the classical definition can help us here, if we drop its relation to man and concentrate on what it tells us about the thing which is just— on, that is to say, 'tribuere jus suum cuique' or 'reddere jus suum cuique'. Anyone determined to see in justice only a state of things may make it consist in the 'suum cuique'; but then the question has to be faced. 'What is this *suum?*' Different answers to this question are possible.

First Conception of Justice: Respect for Rights

The simplest conception of the *suum* is that suggested by the verb *reddere* with which we find it habitually associated; the verb carries the idea of restitution, or restoration: 'If thou meet thine enemy's ox or his ass going astray, thou shalt surely bring it back to him again.' The 'his' which must be rendered to each is, essentially, something which he already had and of which he found himself deprived wthout just cause.

Justice here appears in the character of preserver or restorer. The dative is determined by the genitive and the ablative: 'this is Peter's, it has been taken from Peter, give it to Peter.' It is a currency which bears the image and superscription of Caesar and comes from his mints: *Redde Caesari*. Justice of this kind may be divided into three parts. It is unjust to assault Peter with a view to taking from him what is his, and it unjust to covet what is his: 'Thou shalt not covet thy neighbour's house, thou shalt not covet thy neighbour's wife, nor his manservant, nor his maidservant, nor his ox, nor his ass, nor any thing that is thy neighbour's.' It is just to defend what is Peter's against another's aggression, and it is just to restore to him what he has lost. Under this aspect justice appears as an active respect for what belongs to another. We may note in this connection that 'the defence of the widow and fatherless' was understood in former times not as the attribution to them, as widows and orphans, of any new rights, but as an intervention to uphold whatever rights they had already—rights which their weakness made them incompetent to defend by themselves.

This preservative conception of justice was that which was incorporated first in the Covenant of the League of Nations and afterwards in the Charter of the United Nations. These sought to guarantee to each nation, the weak as well as the strong, the tranquil enjoyment of what each had; this was to be achieved by moral condemnation of aggression and by laying on the associated nations the duty of intervening to maintain the nation attacked in possession of what was in dispute, or, if it was taken by force, to restore it.

Justice, then, makes its first appearance as preserver and restorer. Its preservative function is accomplished out of sight by means of its restorative activity. Every time that it puts back landmarks and punishes the act which removed or displaced them, all existing landmarks are made more secure thereby. Thereby it upholds the fundamental condition of social co-operation. The increasing benefits which men derive from the ever more intricate intersection of their activities are completely dependent on mutual confidence and the reliance of each upon the respect of all others for his stated rights. Whoever boldly invades such rights not only offends against his victim but against the general value of mutual confidence. While the preservation of this mutual confidence must rest primarily on moral education, its ultimate warden is the public authority, which never fails more fundamentally in its duty to society than when it is lax to repair the torts which injure mutual confidence. It is, therefore, obvious that any indulgence shown to aggression against rights is a breach of mutual confidence, is an act or feeling directed against society as a whole.

Prestige of the Preservative Notion

The notion that justice consists in the upholding of existing rights finds little favour with our time, which considers that it is to be found in the creation of new rights. But what new rights will be just? If each man's existing rights are recognised as a criterion of justice, what is the criterion to be when it comes to creating rights? Awareness of this difficulty shows itself in the form habitually taken by demands for rights.

Throughout the *ancien régime,* the new demands which were proposed for acceptance were presented in the guise of 'restorations of ancient rights, franchises and privileges'. When men desired to change the French constitution, they made reference to the mythical constitutions of Pharamond, mythical himself. And even today demands for new rights are styled 'claims', a word which, in the phrase 'statements of claim', denotes actions in law for the recovery of something which was yours and has been taken from you.

The most daring innovators instinctively use the past as a criterion and present their demands as the re-establishment of what has already been. This instinct sometimes leads to odd results, as in the case of the prophets of communism—evolutionists, all of them, who hold that man has emerged from the animal state to that of conscious co-operation, and have yet thought to make their advocacy of communism more effective by attempts to prove that it had been the primitive way of life. Mental approaches of this kind are evidence for the fact that unconscious search is always made for the reinforcement which comes from presenting a demand as a 'claim' in the true sense. It springs from the deep conviction that the way to get something accepted now is to be able to represent it as having existed in the past, and that acceptance of an inauguration of new rights will be that much the readier the more successfully it can be represented as a restoration of a past state of things.

If there is no known precedent for what is sought, recourse can be had to pre-history. The invention of a 'state of nature' on which to base claims was the great resource of the eighteenth-century writers; the notion of a primitive order to which return must be made—the secular exploitation of the religious conception of the Fall—lacks all positive authority in the spheres to which it is applied.

We have just been observing a very general tendency to present demands for rights in the form of 'claims'. The reason for it is the great difficulty found in defining the just as soon as the customary is no longer available as a criterion. The notion of maintaining as it is what is established or earmarked is a clear one. It is just to respect rights and just to safeguard them. These rights are those which are in force. To do justice in this sense is to maintain in being. So ran the royal oath: 'As for me, I will, so far as I know and can, God helping me, honour and safeguard each one of you, according to his rank and dignity; and I will preserve him safeguarded from all mischief, whether hurt or deception; and I will maintain for each the law and justice which pertain to him.'

Nothing is more necessary to intercourse between men than the justice which preserves—which asks no other title for what is than that it has been. But, it is certain, this is not the justice at which innovators aim. The justice of their seeking is a more perfect kind, in which rights are founded, not on long possession, but on reason. The difficulties involved lead to a search for support in the 'conservative' fiction: let us see what these difficulties are.

Second Conception of Justice: The Perfect Order

Today, reasoning on justice is focused on the distribution of rights, the existing distribution being thought unjust. But how, on our argument so far, can any given distribution of rights be assessed in terms of its justice? If justice exclusively consists in preserving established rights or restoring them as against the aggressor, such an assessment is impossible. Today, however, this is not the model on which justice is conceived; injustice consists not only in the neglect or invasion of existing rights but also in their existing distribution. What is now sought is, in short, an order which is just absolutely. But now comes the problem: how can we tell what order is just absolutely? In this second conception of justice, as in the first, what is involved is a conformity. In the first, justice was what conformed with the existing order, which was the touchstone; in the second, the existing order is just or unjust according as it conforms or fails to conform with a model entertained in the mind. In other words, the existing order will be called unjust in so far as it falls short of the vision of a just order which haunts our spirit and has become our touchstone.

There is no obscurity about our second meaning of the word 'just'. It is a question of adjusting what is to what it is considered ought to be. Thus, for everyone to know what the just is, two conditions only must be fulfilled: that the same scheme of what should be is present in the minds of all, and that what is should be seen by all in the same colours. In that event the changes which must be effected in the existing order to realise the ideal order will have received perfect definition.

Unfortunately, opinions differ both as to how what is should be viewed and as to the merits of the scheme of what should be. If rights are regarded not as already assigned but as still available for perfect distribution, it is impossible to expect unanimity on their next assignment, for different minds entertain different models of the ideal order. The sense of justice bids each one of us change the existing order that it may conform with the just order. But the just order is not identical for all minds, and any presumed identity, so long as we confine ourselves to generalities, dissolves when it comes to application. For this reason, agreement to discard the existing order for a just order is an agreement in words only, for our agreement on movement towards the just order implies no agreement as to wherein this just order consists. All we are agreed on is the need to change—not the goal. The past is repudiated as a criterion and there is no agreement as to what to put in its place. It is something which Montaigne notes time and again: 'It is easy to bring the charge of imperfection against a polity, for all mortal things are full of imperfection; it is easy to engender in a people contempt for its ancient usages—no one ever attempted it who did not succeed; but to establish there a better order in place of the one destroyed is a task in which many of those undertaking it have failed dismally.'

Pascal, too, is sceptical and couches his scepticism in much more positive form: 'Justice is what is established; and so all our established laws must necessarily be accepted as just without examination, because they are established.' Beyond that, agreement is impossible: 'Justice is subject to disputes.' 'The art of factious opposition and revolution is the disturbance of established customs, exploring them to their source in order to bring to light their defect of justice. We must, they say, return to the fundamental and primitive laws of the state, abolished by an unjust custom. That is a game leading straight to ruin; the scales are quite untrustworthy.' Pascal leaves no doubt as to his meaning: 'If we follow reason alone, nothing is just in itself; everything changes with time.'

Even though nothing is just in itself, it does not follow—and let us note this—that an individual or a ruler cannot act justly. The virtue of justice is not hit by this scepticism; but the idea of a particular order incarnating justice is hit hard. The authority of Pascal avails to dissipate the illusion that the just order comes naturally to the mind. But we are not bound to concede to him that justice is undiscoverable, though we will admit that it must be sought. For many of our contemporaries it will be a discovery indeed.

Should Justice Be Identified with Other Qualities of Social Arrangements?

If justice is a quality which we look for in social arrangements, and if we find it difficult to form a clear idea of it, it is very tempting to identify it with other good features of social arrangements—features of which it is easy to form a clear picture.

For instance, are there not among the various social configurations some which present a natural stability, so that a configuration of this kind tends to reassemble of its own accord on any attempt to pull it apart? We see in it a condition of stable equilibrium. Having this property, it is, other things being equal, certainly preferable to a configuration which is without it. If we forbid ourselves to choose among arrangements based, each of them, on subjective preferences, we may ascribe an objective superiority to an arrangement having the property of stability, and we may be tempted to say that such a configuration is 'just'. But its quality is in fact sufficiently denoted by the word 'stability', and there is neither rhyme nor reason in making the word 'justice' play the part of a useless synonym.

Yet another conception of justice can be put forward; it too is objective in character, though its objectivity is merely instrumental and conditional. Provided that we have an idea as to what the good of a whole is, that internal configuration will be the best which will carry the whole to the fullest achievement of its particular good. Take, for example, the case of an army as to whose end, victory, there is no dispute; the configuration which fits it best for realising its end is the best for it. The realisation and the maintenance (or the restoration) of this configuration or shape should be the desire of anyone aiming to promote the good peculiar to this particular whole, and this desire is a manifestation of the virtue of justice in relation to the given whole and its pre-determined end. But, all the same, what the man serving this whole and this end will desire—and rightly desire in his capacity as their servant—may be deemed unjust by one who is not their servant, or by one who, in his capacity as servant of this whole, does not see clearly what is necessary to its end.

It may happen, for instance, that a general employs severity against insubordinate elements, thereby serving the cause of victory, and that his conduct may then be deemed unjust either through ignorance of its necessity in relation to the end pursued or through indifference to this end—these being, of course, two very different cases, of which the second is much the most interesting. If the justification of an act lies in its power to steer a given whole to a given end, the acceptance of these data creates, it is clear, the frame of reference within which those who would appraise the justice of the act must place themselves. Judge the act from within another frame of reference and its justice may be denied, because, for instance, the critic is thinking of the soldiers not as members of an army whose business it is to win or be in good shape to win, but as mainstays of a family. The conclusion is that appraisals of justice are most unlikely to coincide, unless they are founded on a feeling of belonging together for a common purpose.

Justice as Mere Conformity to the Rule Laid Down

Many authors have considered that all pursuit of the just outside the sphere of positive law is a vain thing. Just, in their view, is what conforms to the published rule, unjust is what does not. The rule is the criterion of the just and the unjust, and the criterion itself defies measurement. A rule cannot be called just or unjust, for to decide the point there must be something to measure it against.

This intellectual standpoint may have quite different consequences, according as it is adopted by theologians and accepted by believers, or as it is applied by philosophers and jurists who are not believers. Let us examine the two cases in turn. All theologians agree in saying: 'Just is what accords with the commandments of God, unjust is what is contrary to them.' But whereas some think that what is commanded by God is just because God's will has made it just, others consider that God commands it because it is just. For the latter, the just is older than any command, even God's; for the former, only the will of God gives it meaning. On the second view God's commandments are not confined to giving us knowledge of good and evil, but determine, what was till then indefinite, what good and evil are to be. These decrees of his He can issue as He pleases, and their purport might as easily have been to bid us do what is forbidden and to forbid us do what is bidden; in the precepts of the Omnipotent there is no element of necessity, for there is nothing to bind Him who binds everything. We see, then, that theology makes room for two points of view, the contrast between which has been clearly expressed by Leibniz; on either view God commands what is just, but on the first view something has been commanded because it is just, and on the second it is just because it has been commanded. Both points of view have been maintained in their time by Doctors of the Church, but the Christian point of view *par excellence* is certainly the first one, whereas in Islam the second prevails.

In a society of believers which is religious through and through, the general idea that justice is conformity with the rule laid down will shape, necessarily and unequivocally, the positive laws stemming from the divine commandments—the laws will receive an induced respect from the commandments. But the same idea will have very different results in an unbelieving society, or one in which social life has been secularised to its roots. If justice is no more than conformity with the rules, there will be no place in the social order for discussing the justice of the rules. Just as a religious society conceives morality as obedience to the rules laid down by the Omnipotent in the plenitude of His power, so in a secularised society morality must be conceived as obedience to the rules laid down by the prince of this world in the plenitude of his sovereignty. But in the latter case, instead of the just being unchanging and surely ascertainable by the exercise of casuistry on the divine decrees, it will be infinitely variable at the good pleasure of the sovereign introducing changes into it. This was the thesis maintained by Hobbes and criticised by Leibniz. This is not the place to expatiate on so large a subject, which is not the one under consideration here; our purpose is only to emphasise the fact that there are high authorities for the proposition that anyone saying that 'some rule or other is unjust' is talking nonsense, the reason being that the rule itself is the only criterion of justice.

Yet it is an observable fact that every day of the year men direct criticism at the existing rules, which they tax with injustice.   The answer made by contemporaries is that men call unjust the rules which they dislike, that what they represent as just is what suits them, that 'just' is the high-sounding title which they give to their preferences, and that their notions of the just are as various as their preferences. From this it is concluded that the search for justice is the pursuit of a will-of-the-wisp, with each man calling just whatever happens to attract him.

The Feeling for the Just

But before we conclude, as modern positivists invite us to do, that the word 'just' is merely a term of approval applied by each man as suits his taste, we must examine whether there is nothing in common to be found between the various opinions held of the just. To bring home to us the ambiguity surrounding the just, an ingenious author points out that a fiscal measure may be called just in so far as it places the burden of tax on those who are at the moment best able to support it, but unjust in that it penalises those who have in the past been energetic and thrifty. Now is it not evident that we have here two evaluations of the same measure by a single operation of the mind, applying itself to different aspects? On the one hand, unequal incomes in the present should, it is considered, support unequal burdens; on the other, unequal efforts in the past should ensure unequal results in the present. Always it is a case of ensuring the equality of proportion of one thing to another.

If there is no agreement among men as to what is just, at any rate the ways in which different minds work when it comes to appraising justice in a particular aspect are identical.   What they find just is to preserve between men as regards whatever is in question the same relative positions as exist between the same men as regards something else. One man says that the wage of Primus should be half as much again as that of Secundus, because Primus does that much more work; another man says that the wage of Secundus should be half as much again as that of Primus, because Secundus has to feed a family larger by half than that of Primus. So far as the solution is concerned, the opinions of our two advisers, call them Black and White, are diametrically opposite. Out of a total wage of 250, Black would give 150 to Primus and 100 to Secundus, White would give 100 to Primus and

150 to Secundus. Black and White certainly do not see eye to eye; but can we fail to note that Black and White have used exactly the same mode of reasoning, though their starting points are different properties in the persons compared? Let us call in a third adviser—call him Red; he may argue that Primus and Secundus should receive precisely the same wage, because he has considered them under some aspect in which⁻ they are demonstrably equal, as, for instance, their having worked the same number of hours. This disagreement between Black, White and Red is a disagreement as to what solution is just, but it is important to stress that their common manner of reasoning implies that the sense of justice is in fact the same in all three advisers.

Let us represent Primus and Secundus as two points in space, situated by reference to three axes; on one of these axes is set the work accomplished, on the second, family requirements, on the third, hours worked. The relative positions of Primus and Secundus will be differently ranged on each of these axes, and anyone who measures the rewards due to them by reference to their positions on one axis only, just though he may aim at being, will seem unjust to anyone measuring on another axis.

It will be noted that the concept of equality, which plays a basic but far from simple role in the appreciation of justice, enters into all three judgments. It seems worth our while to labour the point. A total payment of 250 is to be divided between Primus (40 hours of work, two mouths in the family, 150 units produced) and Secundus (40 hours of work, three mouths in the family, 100 units produced). Of the total payment of 250, 150 should go to Primus, says Black, only 100, says White, 125, says Red. It is immediately clear that if the Red solution is chosen (i.e. 125 paid to each), it must offend equality in the eyes of Black because Primus is paid only 0·83 per unit produced while Secundus is paid 1·25 per unit produced. But also it must offend equality in the eyes of White because the Primus family obtains a payment of 62·5 per mouth and the Secundus family a payment of only 41·7 per mouth. In the same manner, the Black and the White solutions must each seem inequitable to the two other judges. Black's solution will displease Red because Primus is to be paid 1·5 times as much per hour of work as Secundus, and will scandalise White because the Primus family will obtain 0·75 per mouth as against 0·33 per mouth in the case of the Secundus family. White's solution (100 to Primus, 150 to Secundus) will result in rewarding Primus one-third less

than Secundus per hour worked, and per unit produced less than one-
half as much.

The identical aim of all our three disputants is to treat equal things
equally and proportional things proportionally; only the proportions
which serve as starting-points are different for each of them. Light
has been thus thrown on the relations between equality and justice;
justice, as Aristotle said, is an equality of proportions. Every allocation of reward which is, as it must be to be just, founded on equality
under a certain aspect, will be hierarchical and contrary to equality
under another aspect. Take a very simple example; the case of a man
with orders to spread among different factories with very different
capacities. If he shares them out equally, the time of the factories will
be the less taken up by the orders the more important that the factories are, and the factories will from this angle have been treated un-
equally; if on the other hand he shares out the orders in proportion to
each factory's capacity, this division of them, though aiming at equality, will be unequal. Complications may be introduced into the problem. Unequal in capacity, the factories were, before the orders were
given, in a state of unequal activity by reason of other orders; does
justice demand that the new orders should bring them all to a state
of equal activity, or will doing so penalise unjustly those which had
by their own efforts made themselves busier?

Justice is thus seen to be as simple in principle as it is varied in application. A simple algebraic analogy will perhaps make the point
clearer. Let us postulate points in a multi-dimensional space. Each of
these points is distinguished by its own set of co-ordinates, and
there are as many co-ordinates as there are dimensions. The problem
now set us is to project these points on to a single vector in such a
way as to preserve the relations existing between them in the multi-
dimensional space. To this problem there are an infinite number of
possible solutions. We may, to start with, arrange the points on the
vector according to the values of one of the co-ordinates affecting
them—an arrangement which produces as many solutions as there
are dimensions in the space in question. These are the simpler solutions, each of which neglects all but one of the co-ordinates with
which our points are endowed. But all the co-ordinates may more
plausibly be taken into account. In order, however, to combine the
several or many co-ordinates which together fully characterise one
point into a single value for this point, we must use a set of 'weights',

or parameters. The single value will be the sum of the co-ordinates each multiplied by the specific parameter we shall have seen fit to assign to it; provided we apply to each set of co-ordinates of each point the same set of weights or parameters, our single values will be comparable. But, quite obviously, the adoption of the same set of weights is arbitrary, and, as different minds use different sets of weights, the single values arrived at will be different.

Each solution offered will be an answer to the problem set, but each will be different from the rest and none will be more valid than another in terms of the problem. For there to be one, and only one valid solution, we must be told at the start one of two things: either that classification is to be based throughout on a single specified co-ordinate or on a combination of specified co-ordinates by means of a specified set of parameters or weights.

As the single values of these points in space can stand in innumerable different orders, according to the co-ordinate or the weighted combination of co-ordinates retained for their ordering, so also it is with men, who can be regarded under a great many different aspects and present under each aspect different relations of inequality. It is, therefore, impossible to classify these different relations unless it is stipulated either that only one aspect or a specified combination of specified aspects is considered. Only if such a condition is made can a definite classification be achieved; but this classification is not valid absolutely, it is valid only in relation to the particular criterion applied. Change the criterion, the classification changes. Take the example of a competitive examination: it cannot be said that it selects the best men absolutely, but only those who do best at a given set of tasks; these tasks, which have different values assigned to them, furnish each single man with a general co-ordinate which makes classification possible. But the classification produced by the competition is not the only one possible; there is an infinity of possible ones to be had by varying the tasks themselves and the value to be assigned to each. All that the defenders of the competitive test say for it is that the classification obtained thereby is the most relevant to their particular purposes.

The Notion of Relevance

Suppose that I am a millionaire and that I have the benevolent idea of establishing a fund to enable young people to visit the picture-galleries of Italy. Suppose further that I lay down the following criterion for choosing fifty annual beneficiaries: the committee of selection must choose the applicants with the fairest heads of hair. This being the rule laid down by me, the donor, the members of the committee will have to arrange the applicants by degrees of blondness; they will be just if they follow this rule exactly, they will be unjust if they depart from it (so that a less blond man is admitted into the annual contingent to the exclusion of a more blond man). Yet everyone will concur in saying that the rule which they are applying is an absurd one; the journey to Italy can be looked on as a reward for merit, but what merit is there in being blond? Or, more plausibly perhaps, the journey to Italy can be looked on as a means of cultural advancement which should be awarded to those who will derive most profit from it; but blondness indicates nothing as to artistic or cultural propensities. Thus the criterion which I have laid down is not a relevant one.

This notion of relevance is fundamental to all problems of justice. If I have to effect a distribution of something among a series of individuals, I must, if I am to be just, found my classification and proportions on the serial order of these individuals in another plane; this serial order is my standard of reference. And if my final share-out does not conform to the serial order of reference, I show myself unjust. But, in addition, the serial order which I make my standard of reference must be relevant to the final share-out. If, for instance, it is a case of leaving my goods at death and I take as my standard for their share-out the serial order of degrees of relationship with myself, this standard of reference will be thought relevant; but if, as head of a government, I take the serial order of degrees of relationship as my standard for nominating to high office, my choice will be thought scandalous, because the standard of reference is irrelevant for the purpose.

There is injustice whenever the mind is scandalised by false proportions—a thing which happens either when the serial order laid down is not respected or when that serial order is clearly irrelevant. Let us take a concrete case. An industrialist, compelled by a falling off in orders to discharge several members of his staff, dismisses not the most recently engaged but those who are the least useful to him in his business; this choice may seem just to him and unjust to his employees, who consider that he ought to apply the seniority rule, under which he would discharge those who had least service with him— the latest arrivals. There is in this case a clash between two conceptions of the just. Now let us suppose that the employer acts in the same way but that there is a general contract laying down the rule of seniority; in this case the conduct of the employer is unjust because it does not conform to the rule laid down. Lastly, let us suppose that the employer himself enunciated the rule of seniority, which he claims to apply but in fact violates; in this case there is injustice of a radical and absolute kind.

Analogous instances to the last two cases frequently occur in social life, and cause reactions which are as violent as they are legitimate; they involve, however, no intellectual problem. The intellectual problem is directly posed by whatever has affinity with the first case; for here there is a clash between two conceptions of the just, each of which is solidly founded.

The Problems of Justice

There is no problem of justice when those who have to make a share-out know by reference to what serial order, whether agreed or by common consent relevant, this share-out must be made. The just share-out is that which conforms to the relevant serial order, and the man who aims at applying it conscientiously displays the virtue of justice, since his purpose is to assure to each his due. On the other hand, there is a problem of justice when there is doubt or dispute as to the serial order relevant to the occasion. More than that, and this is what makes for trouble, two or more men may be in conflict as to what is just in a case in which each of them displays the virtue of justice, each being determined to apply conscientiously the serial order which he thinks relevant. So we see that the thorny problems are those concerned with the choice of a criterion relevant to the occasion.

The choice of the relevant criterion is particularly easy in the case in which the thing to be shared out is seen by everyone as means in the service of an end on which everyone is agreed. Suppose, for instance, that on a given day I have ten pairs of skis at my disposal and that there are fifty young men all anxious to put them on; the allocation will be quickly made and accepted by all if one of their friends is lost on the mountains and it is essential to bring him back before nightfall—the skis then go to the best skiers. When action has an obvious end, the just share-out is that which maximises the particular action's chances of success. If we take up again the example of the fund for visiting the Italian picture galleries, there will be a simple criterion of allocation if its aim is to draw up a systematic catalogue of these galleries. Mistakes of fact are, of course, always possible; for instance, if I am the selector of the French team for the Davis Cup and I have chosen and sent off four tennis players, one of whom plays much below the level of someone else who could have been chosen, I can be charged with an error of judgment but not with injustice, if I had in fact taken the four players who were generally considered to be the best and classed as such.

The imperative of the end governs the share-out of what are seen as resources directed to that end. And it leaps to the eye at once that all sorts of contradictory judgments are possible. For instance, the French Prime Minister needs to designate three delegates for an international conference of the highest importance; the end which he has in mind is a successful issue to the conference for his country, the places which he has to fill are regarded by him as resources to this end, and he is careful to choose the three men who will, he thinks, be the most effective for the purpose. His principal adviser criticises this choice, pointing out to the Prime Minister that his primary consideration should be to stay in power (an alternative end) and that the nomination of three delegates who will be away for some time gives him the chance of getting out of the way three individuals whose intrigues are harassing him. The secretary of the party now appears on the scene with yet another opinion; the three places are eminently desirable and should be given as rewards to the three people who have done most for the victory of the party. (Here the notion of end takes flight and what is to be shared out is looked on as means of satisfaction.) This example comes from the daily realities of politics; it will be generally agreed that the first point of view impresses itself irresistibly as the only just one for the occasion.

When there is agreement on an end to be achieved and all are united in thinking that certain resources should be put to the service of that end, the right and necessary share-out of those resources is by reference to the serial order of competence for the purpose among those dedicated to the end. The only point on which disagreement could then be possible would be as to the internal structure of the serial order adopted, for the classification of those dedicated to the end is not necessarily the same in the eyes of different judges; but these judgments are various rather than conflicting, for all are concerned to measure one and the same objective competence and it will be possible to reach agreement on some particular classification as the most likely to be right. Very different is the case when two rival groups of opinion regard the resources to be shared out as having to serve two different ends, in relation to which the recipients are drawn up in two different serial orders; or, again, when the two groups admit the legitimacy of both ends but are divided as to their relative importance. And the problem gets more complicated with every addition to the ends to which the resources are applicable and the more the degrees of importance attached by different minds to different ends become differentiated.

In considering the resources to be shared out as means of action which must serve the realisation of some given end of action, we have equated the problems of justice with the problems of action. But men admit justice of this kind only so far as a particular end of action obsesses them, and not otherwise. A newspaper publisher, for instance, has profits to allocate, and ascribes this success to large-scale reporting; his obsession is to make his paper more successful, and to that end he decides, having now more to spend, to spend it on more reporting. But his editorial staff, on the other hand, not sharing the preoccupation which governs his conduct, want him to disburse his surplus in salary increases to them. In their eyes, the resources arising from a common undertaking are not means for advancing the fortunes of the common undertaking, but should rather, being the consequences of the undertaking, serve as means for enriching individual lives. Anything to be shared out, whatever it is, is always liable to be looked at under two different aspects: as means of action to be shared out by reference to the criterion relevant to an end of action, and as means of existence to be shared out by reference to a different criterion. Each of the two points of view has its validity, varying according to circumstances. If, for instance, I am commanding a company of infantry on an important march when the nation is at war, and on coming to a township I requisition all the bread available, the mayor will back up my action;

nor will it seem unjust to the inhabitants whose minds are attuned to the end of what I have done. Yet the same requisition, if made on peacetime manoeuvres, will seem unjust to them, because the end to which it is directed is not looked on as of sufficient importance.

Thus, the amount of resources which it will be thought just to devote to an end will turn on the importance attached to that end. But men are very unevenly taken up with distant ends necessitating collective action; thus a minority of promoters with a lively sense of ends requiring action, who therefore regard resources as first and foremost means of action, is naturally bound to come into conflict with a majority whose nature it is to regard resources as means of existence. The result is that tension underlies every process of share-out; it is the more serious with every rise in importance of the blocks of resources to be divided. That is the reason why it is wise to break up the general process of share-out into as many small, disconnected share-outs as possible. The more comprehensive the process the more serious the tension.

The simplest method of effecting this fragmentation of share-out is to attribute every new element of resources to its owner as it appears. As, with exceptions, new elements do not appear of themselves but as the result of determined efforts, it is generally allowed that they should go to those whose efforts have produced them. This leads us to an examination of the problem of the just in regard to the share-out of the fruits.

That Resources Are Fruits and What Follows From It

It is of the greatest importance to recognise that resources are fruits: we are about to see why this is so. Let us imagine any gathering of men whatsoever among whom I am empowered to share out all resources as I see fit. As I am free to do what I like, I shall draw up my decree of allocation by reference to my own serial order of choice, whatever it is. The share-out which I enjoin may be made either equally or by reference to the amount of affection which I feel for particular people or in some other way. Anyhow, here is my allocation made and the shares fixed proportionally. This share-out of mine represents a settled policy, and applies as much to the resources that will be available in the future as to resources which are available in the present. But the resources of the future are themselves contingencies of the future. At some future moment, which we will call the 'second day', these shares of mine, though they accord with the proportions laid down, are found to be each of them smaller than on the 'first day', because the total resources are smaller, and everyone is then heard complaining of his diminished share. Alarmed by this discontent, I go for advice to Mentor, who adresses me as follows:

'From the earliest times, all peoples have regarded increasing plenty and the proliferation of resources as the mark of a good government; naturally, therefore, yours stands condemned. You should have taken thought for what economists in every age have called the maximisation of the future product. You ought to have foreseen that Primus, a generic name for any single one of your citizens, would read your edict as meaning that his livelihood in future would depend not on his own activity but on the collective activity, in which what he does himself cuts a most diminutive figure and which he regards as being in essence the activity of other men; and that Primus would for the future do no more than is enough to satisfy custom and opinion. It is that spirit which has diminished the collective livelihood.'

Much upset by what I hear, I deplore to Mentor that justice and collective utility should be at variance. But he will have none of it:

'You say they are at variance because I have made you see that what you considered your just edict is contrary to collective utility. But are you sure that you were just? Ask Primus what he thinks. Justice for him meant that the fruits available to him should be proportional to his activity; he finds it unjust that this relationship should be disturbed. I have still another answer in my locker to give you: in an ensemble of men nothing should be considered just which sets it in the path of its own decline, for justice is essentially constructive.'

From this I draw the conclusion that, on the one hand, I have no discretion at all as regards the share-out of future benefits—it must follow the serial order of the contribution made—and that, on the other hand, it will be a task of immense difficulty to apply this serial order. But what Mentor says next to a large extent relieves me of this task:

'The great pile of fruits which haunts your mind exists only in your imagination; it is in fact a thing of modest fractions, each of them the product of a specific team which carries out its own process of share-out within itself. Your part is merely to be called in to arbitrate the disputes which constantly arise on these occasions.'

It now seems to me that what Mentor is recommending is that I should concern myself with share-out as little as possible. But on my exposing to him the way my mind is moving he contradicts me: 'Certainly not. You can effect all sorts of improvements. All that I have sought to bring home to you is that the idea of regulating from on high the entire share-out was a presumptuous chimera.'

The Share-out of the Fruits Within the Team

Now that we are clear that what is to be shared out should be looked on as fruits and that the primary process of share-out should take place within the team which produces them, let us address ourselves to the problem as so defined.

Let us suppose that it is of capital importance to me to have the manuscript of this book copied in a single day, that for this purpose I get together ten typists who are unacquainted and belong to different milieus, and that I offer a very high total reward for the achievement of the task in a single day. When it comes to sharing out this total reward, the just allocation will seem to be that which is proportional to the number of pages typed and initialled by each typist. Objection to this share-out can be made only on the ground that it has been possible to finish the work within the time laid down—thus earning the total reward—only by reason of the individual contributions which were of more than average merit, whereas the collective success was endangered by the individual contributions which were of less than average merit; for that reason the typists should be paid, not simply by reference to the number of pages completed by each, but on a progressive tariff graduated by reference to that number of pages. Probably, however, this solution will enter nobody's head, and, if it is suggested, will certainly be rejected as being hard of comprehension for the less intelligent; a rule of justice must always be intelligible to all. Therefore the share-out of the product will be proportional.

If, however, my intention in committing to them this work of copying was merely to employ workless people with a view to giving them a helping hand, the principle of share-out will be a quite different one: equal rewards or rewards proportional to the number of mouths to be fed. This example brings out clearly the contrast between share-outs made with a view to a practical object and those made with a view to the subjects.

In social life this contrast tends to fade out. In my example I made it clear that the typists did not know each other and did not belong to the same milieu. Now let us make the hypothesis that they are used to working together and that each is aware of each other's personal needs, which are like her own. In that case repugnance will be felt to the inequality, clear cut and sharply angled, in wages, which is based on the contribution of each to the common task. This psychological tendency will make for the flattening out of the angles, and will be the more pronounced the more that the workers are used to coming together on the same sort of task.

The newer an action-group, the less linked by habitual co-operation its members and the more exceptional its fruits, so much the readier are those engaged in it to agree on the justice of a share-out of these fruits by reference to the individual contributions. Contrariwise, the more that members of the team see each other as 'neighbours' and the more that the team gains in social coherence, the more the idea of 'all alike' gains at the expense of that of superior and inferior performance. But this is a tendency which, though it may be accounted common to all those taking part, has naturally more force with those with whose personal interest it runs than with those to whose personal interest it runs counter. It is, in consequence, a safe prediction that, in a first stage, all the participants will agree in favouring unequal share-out of fruits by reference to proportional equality, that, in a second stage, they will agree in favouring a moderate rounding off of the angles, but that, in the end, they will no longer be in agreement, with some wanting to carry the process of levelling down further and others not. If a conflict of this kind is settled by counting heads, levelling down will always win, for it is certain that the number of performances which are below the average will be greater than the number of those which are above the average. A settlement on these lines will be the more readily borne by those whom it damages the stronger their emotional attachment to the group. It will, in other words, be borne with unequal complaisance, and there will be those who leave the group from a desire to seek elsewhere fruits which are proportional to what they do.

This scheme of thought suggests a way of classifying a society's teams of action. If we arrange them in order of age, we shall find, on the assumption that the scheme is valid, a rounding off of angles of share-out as we proceed from newest to oldest; this gradual process of levelling down itself starts off a process of escape from old groups and formation of new ones—tends, in other words, to create centres of unequal share-out in proportion as it tends to equalise share-out. This would explain why, in sum, the margins of inequality introduced into society by the process of share-out always present a fairly constant general profile.

Thus, at the same time that society is continually maintained in resources by the functioning of work teams (or action groups), it is continually maintained in inequalities by those resulting from the processes of share-out of fruits which go on within the teams of work. But, society being itself a large milieu of existence, the same tendency to the erosion of inequalities shows itself there as in small milieus; in the result the inequalities produced by action groups undergo a certain flattening out *a posteriori*. Thus we see that contrary influences are forever at work in combination. The work teams, which provide society with resources, affect it, so far as equality is concerned, like some hot spring which breeds inequalities, whereas society, which uses the resources, functions like a cold spring which attenuates these inequalities. The state of inequality, photographed at any given moment, is the product of a crowd of phenomena, on each of which certain actions can no doubt be brought to bear; it is, however, utopian folly to seek to annul *en masse* all their consequences with a view to creating a condition of share-out which is the result of mental choice and transcends the phenomena of social life.

However high may be my place in society and however great my authority, it is never my affair to share out everything among all, but only, at a given moment, certain things among certain people. If, when the moment comes, I use reflection and counsel to seek out the serial order relevant to the occasion, and if I apply that order, then I have acted with justice and have displayed the virtue of justice; and that is all that can be asked of me. If I hold a military command and consideration of the part played by a particular officer in a battle leads me to recommend him for an important decoration, no-one will reproach me for not having taken into account the fact that there were already many decorations in his family. If I am president of a selection board and the insufficiency of marks to a candidate's credit leads me not to choose him, no-one will reproach me for not having taken into account the fact that the situation of the candidate's family made it particularly important for him to get the post for which he has been turned down. It has often been said that justice is blind; let us go so far as to agree that to be just she must be myopic. Just as the situation of the family of the unsuccessful candidate is not a circumstance which could lead me to pass him notwithstanding his inadequacy, so, if I am an official administering public assistance, I am not to rebuff him when the needs of his family cause him to seek help on the ground that he would not have needed help if he had worked harder for his examination. In every share-out what has to be considered is its particular end, which is sometimes to select the most promising candidates and sometimes to assist the most necessitous families: categories must not be confused.

Sadly and too frequently found together are the presumption which claims to have found a formula of overall distributive justice and indifference to the immediate obligations of commutative justice. The scrupulous practice of commutative justice by the citizens, the backing of public opinion for its observance and its forcible endorsement by the government—these do between them more for the common good than is done by proposals for overall distributive panaceas. It is, moreover, a product of barren and lazy thinking to picture distributive justice as the work of a supreme legislator. Rather it is the duty of each single person, for there are none so free of ties that they do not have to take decisions on share-out to others, even if, as in the case of the mother of a family, what is to be shared among others —her children—is only work, patience and love. Each of us in his efforts to render the equivalent of what he has received practises commutative justice, and each of us, in making conscientious share-out and in lining-up our fellow-recipients in the order relevant to the occasion, practises distributive justice.

To suppose that the just authority is one which inaugurates an impeccably just order at all points is the broad way to follies of the most dangerous kind. An authority is just when it gives an example of justice in all the activities proper to itself—and that it finds hard enough. The logical end of the illusions now in vogue is the quite absurd one of a society in which everything would be arranged justly and no-one would have to be just.

That It Is Impossible to Establish a Just Social Order

No proposition is likelier to scandalise our contemporaries than this one: it is impossible to establish a just social order. Yet it flows logically from the very idea of justice, on which we have, not without difficulty, thrown light. To do justice is to apply, when making a share-out, the relevant serial order. But it is impossible for the human intelligence to establish a relevant serial order for all resources and in all respects. Men have needs to satisfy, merits to reward, possibilities to actualise; even if we consider these three aspects only and assume that—what is not the case—there are precise *indicia* which we can apply to these aspects, we still could not weight correctly among themselves the three sets of *indicia* adopted. The attempt comes up against a basic impossibility.

Is it, on the other hand, necessary to call attention to the fact that nothing is more absurd than the defence of an exising social order as just? What is this serial order of yours that you should make me see the reflection of it in the existing order? There is no such thing. Your proposition merely is that whatever is, is just.

Must our conclusion be, then, that justice cannot rule in society? It must be so if justice is found only in an arrangement of things which coincides with some intellectual prepossession, whatever it is. But our conclusion is that justice is not there.

In What Does the Rule of Justice Consist?

Justice is a quality, not of social arrangements, but of the human will. The cardinal phenomenon in the positive history of human societies is the successive mastering of new processes, which call for operational reorganisation. Thus, new goals become attainable by new modes of co-operation and new relationships come about. There is no once-for-all scheme of things to be established and preserved; our own conceits in this respect should be abated by our poor opinion of the different conceits held by our forefathers. Therefore what we should be concerned with is that the whole ceaseless process of change should be increasingly permeated by the quality of justice in our individual wills. Every immediate field of choice open to us, in either our private or public capacity, offers us opportunity for the exercise of justice. Whenever we miss this opportunity we feed the sum of social injustice—a sum which it is comfortable but untrue to regard as the product of some single institution or mode of arrangement.

32 SELDON

The Future of Social Services

Arthur Seldon (1917–   ) is well known in Britain as one of the most original and constructive critics of the welfare state. An honors graduate of the London School of Economics, he is an examiner in economics at the University of London and research director of the Institute of Economic Affairs in London, which regularly publishes new proposals for reforming one or another of the social services. Seldon's main point (shared by many decentralist liberals or conservatives) is that government-run welfare services are usually more costly and less efficient than services regulated by the discipline of the market. The way to better services, in keeping with what people actually want, he argues, lies through a freer, more voluntaristic system. In the December, 1967, issue of *Encounter* he put forth some radical ideas for reform in an essay entitled "Crisis in the Welfare State."*

The theory and philosophy of the state services we collectively describe as "Welfare," mainly education, health, housing, and pensions, are based on the myth that they are or can be free. The myth has been absorbed in the social sciences (except economics), in most journals of opinion, in all political parties. It is the essential reason why state welfare faces debilitation, disintegration, and decay. It persists because policy has for twenty years until the last few months been made with sparse hearing for the inconvenient sceptics who introduce doubts, provoke agonising reappraisals, and endanger intellectual conservatism.

State welfare services take a fifth, some £7,000 million, out of the national income of £34,000 million or about a half of the public sector of £13,000 million. They invade every main facet of personal and

* Reprinted with the permission of the author and of *Encounter*.

343

public life. They evoke our humanity and compassion; and they reflect our ethics in the scale and aptness of the aid they give neglected children, the disabled, the long-term sick, penurious widows, bewildered families, the impecunious aged. They help to decide the cultural and physical conditions of life in the effectiveness with which they apply limited resources to education, to medical care, to housing, to pensions. They furnish the stuff of local and national politics. They closely affect and are affected by living standards, national finances, balance of payments crises, international wars and rumours of wars.

The education of politicians in office and stubborn economic realities are forcing the diagnosis of the critics of "free" welfare to the forefront of public debate. The sanguine hopes of the 1940s, aroused by Lord Beveridge's visions inflated by sociological wishful thinking and political ambition, have been fermenting into the bitter fruit of stringency for the "submerged," the "deprived," the "disadvantaged," frustration for parents and teachers, patients and doctors, tenants and owner-occupiers, impoverishment for pensioners. In spite of unprecedentedly massive sums spent on state welfare there is *still* not enough; and there never will be. What there is *does not go to people who need it most.* "The language of priorities" bears the dreary accent of political calculation; and the dialogue on poverty between academics and the Labour politicians they once advised has become almost acrimonious.

There are "solutions" in plenty: *more money;* better administration; more centralised control; increased taxes; more doctors, nurses, teachers; higher pay for ditto; "education" of patients in the "proper" use of doctors and hospitals; "education" of administrators and consultants in the courteous treatment of family doctors and patients; discouragement of emigration; obligatory employment of state-financed students in the National Health Service or state education; funds from armaments; prohibition or inhibition of independent education, higher charges for private beds in state hospitals; more rent restriction; state control of pension funds; *more money.*

These solutions are mostly pretexts or placebos. Even if they were all practicable they would not remove the central weakness: the pretence that education is "free" for all, that medical care is "free" for all, that housing is partly "free" for millions. Free services are advocated with fervour or resignation for reasons of compassion, administrative convenience, social philosophy, or political practicability. . . .

Yet the evil effects of the myth are the common currency of first-year economics: that if you depress a price you inflate the demand and choke off supply. This is the essential reason for shortages and waiting lists, for arrogance and arbitrariness from officials (who ration in the absence of price); for frustration and emigration; for concentration on electorally-sensitive medical services and postponement of hospital-building; not least, for the diversion of purchasing power to pleasurable consumption that moralising politicians can conveniently denounce as candy-floss.

The social policy emerging from the myth is deceptively simple. People must have education, medical care, housing, pensions; many people cannot, or will not, pay the price; *ergo,* supply them wholly or partly free; and, for administrative convenience, supply them to *everyone.* This is the solution of the Universalists and the Egalitarians in all three British political parties.

The pretence that the social services are "free" is one of the most deceptive that disfigure British public life. Sir Norman Angell condemned the claim that war really pays as the Great Illusion of the pre-war years. The pretence that people do not pay for welfare is the great illusion of the post-war years. The offer of "free" plastic flowers or dish-cloths by business men advertising soap is derided by British sociologists and *literati* for misleading the housewife. The politician who offers "free" welfare magnifies the offence immeasurably. Even Professor J. K. Galbraith's risible caricature of the industrial corporation that can make the consumer buy what it chooses to produce did not attribute to its directors the altruistic motives professed by sanctimonious politicians.

The alternative solution to abolishing market prices for welfare is to restore them and enable everyone to pay them. The function of the state in a society that respects the individual is not to organise and provide welfare but to give the purchasing power to people without it, and perhaps to lay down minimum requirements for buyers and minimum standards for sellers. This is the solution of the Selectivists and the Liberals; and again they are to be found in all three parties.

The role of pricing is generally misunderstood by Universalists. The *New Statesman* recently admonished the Minister of Health to maintain the National Health Service "free to all comers," but also to ensure that it continued in being. Astonishingly, there was no hint of recognition that pricing and supply might perhaps be linked. Was [the Minister of Health] being asked to run a press-gang in reverse and shanghai intending emigrants? Was he to require hospital house surgeons, nurses, and family doctors to work even longer hours? Was he to organise indentured medical labour gangs from Asia?

Oddly enough [the editor of the *New Statesman*] has shown that he can see the purpose of pricing. He has welcomed the announcement by the Minister of Transport that she was considering road pricing because "it will embody a principle of justice—that people should pay for the trouble they cause and the benefits they receive." He also saw that the main alternative to rationing by price was "a permit system [which] would entail a vast bureaucracy, a probable black market and discrimination. By what criteria," he properly asked, "would you decide which drivers were 'essential' and which not?" Mr. Mervyn Jones saw it even more clearly when he said in the *New Statesman*: "The alternative . . . to compulsion . . . is to exercise persuasion by price . . . to let the motorist decide for himself whether his use of the car is worthwhile *and to make sure that he thinks twice about it.*" (My italics.) Precisely: the "social purpose" of pricing is to make you think twice before using scarce resources and denying them to other uses that may be more urgent or productive. In principle this is as true of education, medical care, housing, pensions, as of roads, land for car-parking, water, or any other commodity or service hitherto supplied "free."

These are the two basic principles, Universal and Selective, on which British social services will be debated in the coming decade. Mr. Anthony Crosland [the author of *The Future of Socialism*] has said, "The relief . . . of distress and the elimination . . . of squalor is the main object of social expenditure." This principle puts humanity before equality, selectivity before universalism. It is approved by "individualists," rejected by "socialisers." In practice the selective principle is the only one that will work in a period of rising incomes and growing aspirations. The main objections to it, that it requires identification of people whose incomes require topping up and that some will not ask for aid unless it is shared by all, is a smoke-screen in an intellectual rearguard withdrawal by the Universalists. They are also magnified for party political purposes. But the selective principle does not require the "Household Means Test" that broke up families in the 1930s: means can be identified by an impersonal periodic record of income. The objections lack cogency since a Means Test *is* applied in rate rebates, Council house rent rebates, students' grants, legal aid, the Option Mortgage scheme, and the "income guarantee" by Supplementary Pensions. It has been urged for nursery school fees by Professor A. J. Ayer, Professor D. V. Donnison, and Dr. Michael Young. It is to be applied to an increase in the price of school meals, and it will have to be used by the Government even more if increased help is to be given to families with low incomes because there will simply not be enough public money to give every social benefit to everyone. And by now it must be clear to even the most committed egalitarian that it is foolishly wasteful and inhumane to hand state funds to 100% of the populace in order to make sure that the 10%, or 15%, or 20%, who need it get it.

The argument on "social divisiveness" may, if it is not rebutted, become as stubborn an obstacle to clear thinking and humane reform as the means test. It was put recently by a journalist with Universalist sympathies but an open mind, Mr. Rudolf Klein, in the *Observer*: The fundamental objection, he said, to allowing people to pay for welfare services privately was that it would introduce a double standard, one for the rich, one for the poor, because the middle classes who would leave the welfare state are those most anxious to raise standards.* On the contrary, it is state welfare services that would be "socially divisive" because they cannot, outside rigidly totalitarian societies, be made completely universal. No degree of comprehensivation of secondary schooling in Britain, or "integration" of private with state schools, would prevent some families from giving their children a better formal education than the state provides, either because their income is higher or because they prefer to spend more on education and less on eating, clothing, smoking, drinking, motoring, or holidaying. No discouragement to private medical care will prevent some families from seeking more choice, convenience, privacy, or comfort in sickness than is provided by the National Health Service. No encouragement to Council building or discouragement of Council house purchase by tenants, or inhibition of the building societies, will prevent some families from finding better homes than others think worth paying for. No degree of expansion in state pensions will prevent

---

* The middle classes who use state services get what they can for themselves, often at the expense of the working classes. It is an illustion to suppose that there is one standard in state education or the N.H.S.

many people from accumulating more for their retirement than they are compelled to accumulate by (and through) the state.

If the Universalists believe otherwise, let them say that no man shall be able to buy better education, medical care, housing or a standard of life in retirement than the state can provide for all out of taxation. And then let them show that the Universalist welfare state is more than an egalitarian mirage by drafting the apparatus of controls required to create and enforce it at rising standards financed by increasing taxation: rules governing personal expenditure, inspected and policed; direction (and dilution) of labour for teachers, doctors, and nurses; the penalties of political displeasure and social disapproval of tax avoidance, even by restricting work in favour of leisure; increasingly savage penalties for tax evasion; control or prohibition of emigration.

It is difficult to believe that the Universalists accept or can practise the logic of their philosophy. They must find it especially difficult when rising incomes facilitate and encourage growing social aspirations; and even more difficult when they see communist countries resort to pricing in welfare: Russia charges for nursery schools, Czechoslovakia imposes health prescriptions charges, Poland changes from housing subsidies to housing allowances to families to enable them to pay market rents, Russian doctors advocate charges for hospitals. Do the Universalists really suppose that the notion of equality in state welfare, as a lowest common denominator, will be freely accepted by wage-earners accustomed to rising standards in everyday consumption?

Many Universalists earn middling or above-middling incomes of £2,000 to £5,000 or more as academics, writers, journalists, civil servants, lawyers, doctors, politicians. If they send their children to state schools, occupy state hospital beds when ill, live in subsidised Council or rent-restricted houses, and refrain from private saving for retirement in order to avoid privilege and share in parity of esteem, what do they do with their money? And if they buy books, records, go to concerts, the opera, live in spacious houses, entertain interesting people, holiday abroad, how do they prevent their children from deriving educational, social or cultural advantages denied the child of the plumber, the boilermaker, the railwayman? Do they really prevent their wives from seeing Harley Street doctors? Do they really buy the furniture and furnishings common in Council houses? Do they really avoid saving to supplement the state pension? Do they really reject scholarships or free places at public schools? How do they spend their money on goods and services that yield no social privilege? And if they perform this feat in their lifetime, how do they avoid advantaging their children when they are dead?

The notion that state welfare can ever be completely universal is a chimera. At the best it will fight a gradually losing rearguard action against rising incomes, a man's natural wish to do better for his family than he had in his lifetime, the family's concern to subsidise its weaker members and shelter them from the competition of the meritocracy, and the foreign example of countries in Europe, Australasia and America that permit growing incomes to yield widening choice.

A system that sets out to provide state welfare universally will, in any society, capitalist or communist, have to permit growing "social divisiveness." But there is a method of creating social parity of esteem. It is to give purchasing power selectively to people who are in need in order to enable them to exert the authority of those who are not. State benefits in cash or coupon would enable everyone—wage-earner as well as salary-earner—to act as a buyer with enough purchasing power in the market to pay for education, medical care, housing or pensions from competing state, local authority, benevolent, charitable, "mutual" or commercial suppliers. Every man and woman would in time appear as a buyer, not a "beneficiary." Social origin and accent would become irrelevant. The market is tone-deaf. Such a system would remove the social divisiveness in the pseudo-Universalist system between the few who pay for a choice and the many who receive free state services with no option. The physically or mentally incapable who could not use cash or coupons would need services in kind or personal care; they are the helpless unavoidable in any society. Everyone else would be buying and paying for welfare with choice. Everyone would be a school fee-paying parent, a private patient, a tenant paying market rents, or an owner-occupier buying a home. In a market the discriminating, articulate, "middle-class" consumers (who subscribe to *Which?* and *Where?*) would keep up standards for the "working-class" consumers (who do not) in welfare as they now do in food, footwear, and furniture.

And they would do so much more effectively than in Parent-Teacher or Patients' Associations because withdrawal of custom and loss of profits is a more powerful sanction for the supplier in competition than political agitation by captive customers is for politicians, civil servants, Councillors, local education officers, regional hospital boards, headmasters, Council housing managers, or directors of hospitals.

The academic and the political Universalists have been rethinking welfare policy. The academics have come up with little new except more detailed evidence of poverty, a new emphasis on deprivation as relative rather than absolute, and no new solutions to two dilemmas: the conflict between *equal* benefits and *humane* benefits, and the scope for choice in state welfare. At the 1966 Fabian lectures, by what the *Guardian* has called "the poverty lobby," Professor Townsend combined a complaint that Labour had not done enough for people in need with a demand that it should give more aid to all and sundry. He has never explained how he reconciles humanity with equality, and his claim that there is general public rejection of Means Tests is wishful thinking. . . .

Professor Abel-Smith did much better in the third part of his lecture, as his 1965 Fabian Tract *Freedom in the Welfare State* suggested he might do. The first part was a complaint that Labour had slowed down the rate of increase in expenditure on the social services below its rate under the Conservatives. Even the increase of 28% for 1964 to 1970 in the National Plan, disembalmed for the evening, was lower than the Conservatives' 34·5% for 1958 to 1964. How to find the money for more state welfare? Easy: raise taxes. He does not see that choice in welfare might itself encourage effort and yield tax revenue. The second part was another complaint that Britain was spending proportionately less on social welfare than countries with smaller national incomes. He did not consider the reasons for these shortcomings: do they really lie in the mendacity of Conservative and Labour politicians? The third part contained, it seemed, a new note: the admission, at long last, that universal "free" benefits could not continue: perhaps the state might charge fees for some of its services and replace students' grants by loans.

But there was no effort to show how choice, the case for which he had recognised in *Freedom in the Welfare State*, could be ensured in state welfare. Recently he has conceded that in the end the solution is "to concentrate help where it is needed and to stop giving it where it is not." But this system requires Means Tests; there are "administrative snags" in Means Tests, so for a decade until they are solved higher benefits should be given to all. The case for Universalism has thus toppled from the philosophic principle to a technical convenience. Now perhaps the debate can concentrate on how to devise the simplest, least inquisitive technique for identifying income and needs.

The political Universalists have shown more wisdom. First, Mr. Douglas Houghton, then Mr. Brian Walden and Mr. Desmond Donnelly (and now Mr. Ray Gunter) [all leaders of the Labour Party] have virtually abandoned Universalism and embraced Selectivity though not without ambiguity and reluctant compromise that may prove impracticable. The academics are now in a quandary. Professor Titmuss' formula, "an infrastructure of Universalist services . . . within and around which can be developed socially acceptable selective services" is an attempt to save the academic argument but concedes its invalidity and impracticability. It is hardly tenable to argue that social benefits should be both equal and unequal. If selectivity is noxious or offensive, it should be avoided; if it is acceptable there is no argument for retaining universalism to avoid the social stigma.

His most recent formulation, in a forthcoming book, *Commitment to Welfare*, is ingenious but abortive. It is to combine universalist services with selective services based on "the *needs* of specific categories, groups and territorial areas and not dependent on *individual tests of means*" (his italics). But the composition of categories and groups changes: "Council house tenants" now includes people who are not in need of subsidy, and many who should have the subsidy are not Council house tenants. "Territorial areas" designated for state aid would contain people who do not need it, and others who do would live elsewhere. There is no escape: universal benefits must be replaced by benefits matched to the circumstances not of "groups" or "areas" but of *individual people*.

Professor John Vaizey has demonstrated the dilemma of the Universalists in pointing (in a recent *Spectator*) to the "grave internal contradiction" in "the ideology of equality, an ideology to which I subscribe," of concentrating education on the able and on the deprived. The progressives and the egalitarians do not seem to be able to make up their minds whether they wish to open the world to the gifted child or to rescue the ungifted from his environment. Their dilemma is even worse than that: by wanting to make the comprehensive school a monopoly rather than an experiment, and by limiting the expenditure on education to the revenue that can be raised in taxes, they are putting equality before quality. The tragedy in their position is that there is no need for this unpalatable choice. It is possible to raise the minimum education that could be made available for *all* children by allowing parents who value it more to pay for more in the market. The egalitarians are not only inhibiting the gifted; they are also repressing the ungifted.

But the notion that people who value welfare and who can pay for it *should* pay is spreading. Mr. David Marquand, Dr. David Owen, and Professor John Mackintosh tentatively acknowledge ("Change Gear," *Socialist Commentary*) the relevance of selectivity for concentrating resources on people in most need and the case, in principle, for welfare charges. In their anxiety to recognise economic reality but not to abandon their philosophic moorings they strain after both but risk emerging with neither. They see that taxation is not always a better method of financing welfare than charges, and that users may be more willing to pay if they see a connection between payment and service, but they confuse the *purpose* and the *effect* of charging. They want charges but not if they "deter." But charges necessarily deter, and they should deter—that is how they husband resources and minimise waste. The solution is not to avoid charges but to enable people in need to pay them by supplements to income.

A decisive defect of the Universalist principle is that it is *inhumane*. It gives cake to people with cake and denies a second loaf to those with one. Some universal benefits, pensions, for example, are taxed: even so, much remains with the well-off and wealthy (pensions are taxed as earned income). But some benefits are not taxed at all. A state education is worth £280 a year to a family with two children at a secondary school, £560 if in a sixth form; medical care is worth perhaps £80–£100 a year to a family of four; Council housing £60 a year or more. Hundreds of millions of pounds remain in such pockets that could be distributed in larger family allowances, widows' grants, disablement benefit, retirement pensions to people in need.

Some Universalists support the inhumane system because of a political fallacy: that social benefits must be equal and shared by all. For Professor Titmuss "the real argument is about equality." *But equal treatment of people in unequal circumstances is not equality.* It satisfies the yearning for equality less than a selective system which would relate aid to need.

Nor can the Universalist principle be maintained by higher tax yields out of rising incomes and faster economic growth. This was the doctrine propounded at the 1964 and 1966 elections; and it is implied by foreign example in writings from the National Institute of Economic and Social Research and from the Economics Correspondent of *The Times Business News*. There is no evidence that as incomes rise people will readily yield the increases to the state for enlarged collective welfare (or any other) services. Governments in political democracies may devise new taxes on employment, corporations or wealth; but they have yet to show that they can extract more than 40 to 45% of total incomes—even in wartime. And the contrast with European countries that spend more on state welfare despite lower national incomes demonstrates no more than that state welfare is desirable precisely where incomes are low—and provided they are unequal enough to furnish some large enough for redistributive taxation. State welfare should recede as living standards rise. It becomes increasingly superfluous.

British social policy since 1964 amply demonstrates the fiscal limits to state welfare when taxation is high. It is easy to ask for more state benefits but not to show how to raise the additional taxes. To his credit Professor Abel-Smith did not resort in his Fabian lecture to the too easy option of reduced armaments. The amount that could be saved by reduction in the £2,250 million defence bill would not provide the vast sums required to raise the amount and quality of the social services to the level required for the most needy, still less to satisfy rising expectations, so long as they must be provided for everyone. It is the universality and "free"-dom of state welfare that remains the fundamental weakness of the British welfare state.

The latest effort to find tax revenue has passed from unchanged tax rates on rising incomes to higher taxation of static incomes. The Universalists would like higher family allowances (for all) to be financed by lower income tax allowances for children. This clumsy proposal confuses aid for the needy with the equity of the taxation system as a whole. But its significance is that it illustrates the dire straits of the Universalists. The politicians will have to recognise what the social administrators cannot see: that economic causes have political and fiscal consequences: Ossa cannot be piled on Pelion for all time. There is not much more room for adding taxes on personal incomes. Ingenuity in avoiding and evading taxes is not yet exhausted. . . .

Until recently, the common conclusions favoured universal state benefits. The appearance of a change in all three parties is therefore significant.

In Labour it seems to have begun in 1962 with the admonition by Young Fabians of their elders to reject the "utterly naïve" notion that the basic state pension could ever be raised sufficiently to take all pensioners off National Assistance and to see that some form of Means Test was unavoidable. . . .

The Liberal Party's spokesman on social security in the House of Commons, Mr. John Pardoe, has quickly seen the incongruity of universal social benefits and rising incomes. And at the 1966 Liberal Assembly he made no bones about the common sense of abandoning opposition to a Means Test.

In spite of one of the least unsordid acts in recent social policy, the 1961 graduated state pension (introduced to raise revenue without the unpopularity of a tax and to dish Labour), the Conservatives are also increasingly accepting the second half of the 20th century and are promising to reconstruct the welfare state to give more aid to the needy. Younger Tories like Geoffrey Howe and John Biffen are streets ahead of their elders, and Sir Keith Joseph is revealing a subtle and sensitive mind.

The change from universal to selective benefits is impeded by a variant of the equality principle that ranges from a wholesome rebellion against privilege to a little-minded indulgence in envy. It ordains that no one shall have anything—better schooling, nursing, housing—unless and until everyone can have it. It is as potent a precept as any for postponing the day when all can have it. What is at stake is more than the blunting of incentives to individuals to earn more for their families, or indeed the role of the family in social life. It is even more than the logical dilemma of the egalitarian who is prepared to allow some inequality in income after taxation but no inequality in expenditure on education, medical care, even housing, and is content to see vast sums go to everyday consumption. The dilemma of the Egalitarian is that insistence on equality is insistence on *less than that possible for all*. Luton Council has told parents that a shortage of teachers prevents its schools from taking children at five; they must wait until they are six. Rebellious parents sought out local former teachers prepared to take their children for a year. The Council's Education Officer objected that no five-year-olds could have the teaching because all could not have it. If welfare services are to be organised by public authority on the principle "nobody until everybody," then everybody will have less than they could have and wait longer for more.

There is a further difficulty for the Egalitarians. If no one may move up in earning or spending income until all move up, there may be no movement at all. Example and demonstration are the *conditio sine qua non* of improvement. If no one may have something *different* which can be considered *better*, movement will be stultified. Equality is an idea reserved for a world without scarcity. Lenin saw it in *State and Revolution;* and John Strachey saw it in his Left Book Club era of the 1930s, although he was naïvely sanguine about the imminence of superabundance. But even if Utopia is still far off and differences in earnings are unavoidable and (in the Marxist phrase) socially necessary, we can top up the lower ones and make them *less unequal* bundles of purchasing power. To add to all of them in the name of equality, social cohesion, or parity of esteem, is to add champagne to the rich man's table and shin-bone to the pensioner's.

Sooner or later enough people in the Labour, Liberal, and Conservative parties will see that three basic aims in welfare are within our grasp: humanity, liberty, and relative plenty. We could within a few years give much more help to the needy, create choice for all capable of using it, and secure much more expenditure on welfare out of the national income. But all three parties will have to abandon their conservatism and think more radically and adventurously. Labour will have to abandon its false egalitarianism, the Liberals their out-dated Beveridgism (which Beveridge himself might have abandoned), the Conservatives their propensity to ape anything that seems momentarily fashionable or expedient.

The notion that change in the welfare state is "politically impossible" has been blown sky-high by the field surveys of public attitudes and preferences in the last four years conducted by Mass Observation for the Institute of Economic Affairs, largely confirming or confirmed by surveys by Dr. Mark Abrams for *Socialist Commentary* in 1960, by Mr. W. G. Runciman in 1962 (discussed in *Relative Deprivation and Social Justice* in 1966), by *New Society* in 1963, by the National Opinion Polls in 1966, and by newspaper polls in the last few months. The findings of the I.E.A. research are that there is no majority political preference for universal social benefits irrespective of needs. On the contrary, it has found that half or more of the varying samples of the population would favour social benefits related to need. The survey by Mass Observation (for the I.E.A.) in June 1966 found that 53% of the sample of men and women thought that free health prescriptions should be confined to people in need, 57% family allowances, 73% subsidised Council houses, and 38% increases in state pensions.* A survey in April 1967 found that 65% of a national sample said they would be more ready to pay taxes if their money went to people in need than if it went to all and sundry.

There is no insurmountable political obstacle to a change in welfare policy that could give more to people in need, choice to everyone as soon as they could use it, and more welfare all round.   It could, I believe, be achieved by reform in four stages.

Stage I, in which all social benefits, in kind as well as in cash, would be taxed. This gradual closing of the gap between "free" state services and full market fees for private services would ease:

Stage II, in which fees from people who could pay them would be charged for state services, the scope for charges widening in:

Stage III, in which cash (for coupons) would be distributed to enable everyone to pay for welfare, state or private:

Stage IV, in which taxation would be reduced and cash allowances or coupons gradually withdrawn. The stages would be reached at varying rates in different services, and some by-passed or telescoped.

The philosophy of "free" state welfare is based on jejune sentimentality about human affairs that does no credit to the common sense or practical judgment of the academics, the *literati*, the doctors, teachers, lawyers, or the politicians who profess it. In the conduct of their private affairs they reject the assumption that human beings will not try to get as much as they can for nothing, or are not concerned about personal, private, family interests, or that to appoint a man a public official is to transform him into a selfless public benefactor. Yet they persist in espousing a system of universal benefits because it satisfies their yearning for a pseudo-egalitarianism, because it assuages their guilty conscience about inherited or acquired wealth and social advantages, or because, contrariwise, it offers the prospect of political power in aggrandisement of the state. And all this in spite of its denial of help for the neglected, the sick, the suffering, the be-

---

* The findings are detailed and alternative policies discussed in Seldon and Gray, *Social Benefits: Universal or Selective?* Research Monograph 8, Institute of Economic Affairs, 1967.

wildered, and the aged, its denial of the liberty to choose, its incite-
ment to spend on everyday consumption.

The U.S.A. is installing state welfare just when we are learning its
defects, but Socialist and Communist countries are having second
thoughts despite a political philosophy that requires universal benefits. Young men—and unclosed minds—avid for change should look
East. The welfare state in Britain reached its present shape in the
last twenty years. The longer it is left unchanged the more convulsive
the upheavals when change is enforced by rising incomes, growing
social aspirations, and overseas example.

33   ERHARD

Prosperity for All

Ludwig Erhard (1897–   ), former Minister of Economics and Chancellor of the Federal Republic of Germany, presided over the "economic miracle" which transformed that country after price and wage controls were finally removed and a "social market economy" instituted.   A scholar who taught economics at the University of Munich, Erhard insisted that the way to prosperity is to release the creative energies of the people rather than attempt to stifle them under mountains of paperwork and controls. In no uncertain terms his views have been confirmed by Germany's remarkable recovery from the devastation of war. In his book *The Economics of Success** he describes the basic policies which he had put into practice ; the selection is taken from two speeches reprinted in that book: "Free Economy Versus Planned Economy" and "Prosperity for All!"

Free Economy Versus Planned Economy†

In the work of threshing out the *Länder* [province] constitutions, discussion of what shape the future economic order should take naturally occupied an important place. I shall attempt in this article to disentangle the specific problems of the moment from the web of polemics and to make a sober assessment of our position by formulating what is common to all the proposals that have so far emerged. It is typical of our present situation that these conflicting views should invariably be pushed to extremes terminating on opposite sides of a supposedly unbridgeable gulf—on one side free economy, on the

---

* Trans. by J. A. Arengo-Jones and D. S. S. Thomson (London: Thames & Hudson, 1963). By permission.

† Article in *Die Neue Zeitung* of October 14, 1946.

other planned economy, here socialism, there capitalism—although the economic developments actually taking place should rather make us ask ourselves whether influences are not in fact emanating from both fronts and tending to bridge the gap between conflicting viewpoints. To imagine, for instance, that any free economy must exhibit symptoms of the uninhibited exploitation associated with the early days of capitalism is to misunderstand the dynamism of the advanced economies of today as completely as does the detached individualist for whom any kind of economic planning is tantamount to the life-destroying levelling of a soulless bureaucracy. And the same applies in regard to the concepts of capitalism and socialism. Today it is just as hopelessly biased to think that capitalism means exploitation of the workers as it is to think that socialism means the ruthless denial of the last trace of freedom. If, for example, the main characteristic of a capitalist economy is taken to be merely the capitalist mode of production involving the large-scale investment of capital formed within the national economy, then there is no difference between it and a socialist economy. Conversely, a free economy, which simply because it is free is commonly dubbed 'capitalist', need not preclude full regard for the social needs of the day. And whereas in capitalist countries with a free market economy the accumulation of capital is often violently criticized, the formation and use of capital in socialist countries is often not subjected to such effective public scrutiny and criticism. In other words, catch-phrase criteria are no longer applicable in appraising an economic system, least of all its social aspects. When it is remembered that a capitalist and a socialist economy are equally compelled to make provision for the building up of capital resources, and at the same time it is agreed that this can only be done, whatever the shape of the economic structure may be, by saving and consumer restraint, then it looks very much as if the systems are not so irreconcilable after all.

It is indeed true that a socialist economy cannot do without planning on an extensive scale, but this does not mean that a free economy —or, to be more precise, a market economy—can be written off as aimless or anarchical. The fact is that it uses the highly developed methods of market research so extensively for the systematic recording of economic data and the evaluation of trends, that with this type of economic order there is a very strong and growing tendency to put plans first. In an earlier article I pointed out that between an economy which embraces many plans and a fully planned economy there are any number of possible systems, varying according to the particular kind or degree of influence or guidance brought to bear on the functions of the economy, and that it is therefore wrong and dishonest in this connection to play around with absolutes.

The real contradistinction is not between free and planned economic systems, nor between capitalist and socialist economic systems, but between a market economy with free price-level adjustment on the one hand and an authoritarian economy with state controls extending into the sphere of distribution on the other. In the last analysis it is simply a question of whether the market as the voice of the economic society as a whole or, alternatively, the state or some other collective entity is better able to decide what is conducive to the common good or the well-being of all. It is still a widely held fallacy that the outcome of free competition is to arrest movement and change within the social structure or at least to set up economic strains and stresses. In actual fact, all liberal-minded experts with a sound knowledge of the social organisms are agreed that it is precisely the other way round, that it is the limiting of freedom of movement that throws the economy out of balance and produces crisis after crisis, each more unmanageable than the last. Provided in future the state sees to it that neither social privileges nor artificial monopolies impede the natural process by which economic forces reach and maintain a state of equilibrium, and that the operation of supply and demand is allowed free play, the market will adjust the total input of economic forces so as to create optimum running conditions and to compensate any mistakes made at the controls. Anyone who wishes is welcome to believe that a planning and regulating economic authority might be a better judge of the economic intentions and wishes of society; but just let him try to prove it. What can be said is that in a free market economy mistakes of judgment in the management of affairs automatically produce price changes with all their attendant repercussions, whereas in a state-directed economy there is always the danger that equally serious mistakes can be covered up and left to fester until they ultimately erupt with elemental force. We have had experience in recent years of how easily a state-directed economy can deteriorate, by imperceptible stages, into a travesty of what an economy should be.

Our criticism is thus not directed against the planned economy *per se,* whose manifold forms can be variously interpreted, but most definitely against the state-controlled authoritarian economy, which if carried to its logical conclusion wipes out the market and robs the consumer of all freedom of choice. On the other hand, a collectively managed economy responsive to market reactions is a contradiction in terms and therefore unthinkable; disregard for the wishes of the consumer as reflected in market reactions is bound to destroy freedom of action and stems from the fallacy that human happiness can be secured by maximum satisfaction of statistically measurable needs. So, even assuming that the authority wielding economic control had no other motive than to serve the good of the community—and this not even the socialist state guarantees—it is still open to doubt whether the people as a whole would prefer any form of collective economy to the free market economy.

As things are today, the state must provide the economy with the principles and broad lines of a policy and with objectives designed to guide and regulate its functioning. In this respect the state indisputably has and should have the initiative. But to go further and reduce the independent businessman to the status of a mere puppet or servant of the authority's will would be to destroy all the values derived from personality and to rob the economy of its most precious source of inspiration and strength. Now, if ever, is the time to realize that the economy is not opposed to social progress but, on the contrary, treats it as a yardstick. All steps capable of contributing to a fair distribution of the national product, and with it of the national income, deserve our most careful consideration. But then we have the chance to do this through the very act of honouring the obligations arising from our country's distress, if only we put actuality before dogma.

I am convinced that the tasks of today call for the full participation of the individual. We shall be doing our country a real and lasting service if we establish an economic order which is purged of the theorizing and bureaucratic spirit that everyone hates and which enables people to act freely in response to a sense of their social responsibilities.

Prosperity for All! *

'Prosperity for all', merely as a policy directed to improve the

* Speech at the 7th Parliamentary Party Congress of the Christian Democratic Union in Hamburg on May 14, 1957.

material living standards of our people, would be important enough to become an article of faith for a party which embraces all classes of the population. But we cannot be accused of being materialists, if in our policy of 'Social Market Economy'—inspired by the will to create a new society on and out of the ruins of the war and the post-war period—we had to give top priority to providing our German people once more with the basic necessities of life. How else could we have effectively overcome the want which threatened us in every walk of life?

Our people would have had no political, no economic, no social future, if we had not succeeded in removing the quite intolerable burden of material hardship, in once again giving labour a purpose by increasing the rewards, in restoring productive and competitive capacity and so steering the Federal Republic back into the world economy, and in regaining the confidence and friendship of the world by honest work and equally honest intentions. The alternative would have been to condemn ourselves to a primitive way of life, which would have marked the end of our nation's history. But without this new Germany, for whose political regeneration in those historic years the CDU was largely responsible, the political situation in Europe would also have taken a very different turn. We are not making ourselves out to be strong and we are certainly not forgetting the help we received, particularly from America, in our greatest need, when we say that the success of Germany's reconstruction has contributed to the security of Europe and to closer and freer international co-operation. On such international links depend the peace and freedom of those nations in our continent, to whom these ideals are sacred. While we should, and must, always bear in mind that material values are relative, we cannot afford on the other hand to underestimate the political and social implications of a new and broadly based prosperity. It seems to me that it was a simple Christian act on our part to free our fellow-Germans from need and misery and give them back a sense of security and dignity.

Let me illustrate what we have achieved in this field by quoting a few figures. Our gross national product, which is a measure of our economic position, is double what it was in 1936. Compared with the same year, our industrial production is 220%. Over the past eight years the Federal Republic's foreign trade has shown a rise in exports at an average rate of 245 million marks a month to the

present level of 3·2 milliard marks. This improvement has been reflected particularly in our gold and foreign currency reserves, which
stand at nearly 19 milliard marks. The total of net wages and salaries
has risen in the past five years alone from 34 to 68 milliards and
the gross income figure rose in exactly the same proportion from 45
to 90 milliards; in other words, it has doubled. Another effect of our
economic policy during the past eight years has been to increase the
employment figure from 13·5 to 18·6 million. . . .

This is not mere theory but proven fact, which we have all experi-
enced. Over the past nine years, for example, since 1948 the prevailing economic trend has been one not of cycles with regular ups and
downs but rather of steady and even very rapid growth. This is certainly no mere accident or gift of providence but the result of a deliberate policy. I suggest, therefore, that this same steady and assured
process of economic development has done much to strengthen the
feeling of security of all engaged in the economy, employers as well
as labour. It has made it possible to plan ahead and has freed everyone from the fear of an uncertain future, to which they had previously
seemed hopelessly exposed. Anyone who regards shifts of political
emphasis or periodic changes in investment policy and the production of consumer goods as contradictory or inconsistent knows very
little about modern economic machinery. Our motto here is: 'Judge
them by their deeds, not (and this is intended for our critics) by their
words.' . . .

We, meanwhile, will continue honestly and doggedly to increase the
social welfare and the prosperity of the nation. The communal and
individual incomes can only be raised by increasing the national product, in other words, by stepping up production, and only by increasing prosperity for all can we acquire the means, that is, the capital,
which enables us, as a modern industrial country, to keep pace with
technical progress and to compete in world markets. Capital does not
drop from heaven but must first be earned by the sweat of our brows
and then consolidated by cutting back on immediate consumer demands. This applies, moreover, to all economic or social systems.
The crucial question is always how much capital is amassed and how
it is spent. And the main problem which concerns us from a social
and political view-point is into whose hands the capital goes and who
should dispose of it.

This brings me very close to the position taken by my friend Karl

Arnold in his speech, for, if the concepts of capital-ownership and the disposal of capital are not identical with that of 'Ownership for all', both reveal the direction and the aim that our party is pursuing in its efforts to mould Germany's social system. We do not accept the Socialist idea of 'redistribution' of productive capital or of the titles of ownership which represent this capital, because such terminology could encourage the dangerous illusion that some institution like the state should have the power to take over ownership of capital at will and to distribute it or even give it away, as it thinks fit. So long as capital ownership is synonymous with free and private property, it can only—and must only—be acquired by work and restricted consumption. Romantic ideas will not help us here; they will only lead to confusion and error.

Even a superficial study of Germany's post-war capital resources and capital investment policy is enough to show that our efforts to revive the productive capacity of our economy were successful and indeed had to be successful, if they were to create opportunities of permanent employment for all workers, and particularly for the refugees and expatriates. At the same time the raising of capital was, to a considerable extent, in the hands of the state and private employers, while the savings of the mass of the people—although they increased over the past seven years from 3 to 24 milliard marks—lagged somewhat behind. One might regard this as a regrettable defect—possibly even as something more serious—but one must also realize in all fairness that, during the period in question, this was the only possible method of reconstruction. For example, how could the state have solved all the pressing problems before it without acquiring the necessary means through taxation? And, having lost our former capital reserves, how could our economy, with no capital market to draw on, have embarked upon such a rapid programme of reconstruction without financing itself? All the normal standards for a 'just' accumulation of capital simply did not apply, nor were there any historical analogies to help us; our course of action was dictated by the pressure and urgency of external circumstances. Moreover, it seemed only natural that those in employment and those seeking it, after the hardships they had suffered, should feel like consuming and not saving, at least to begin with.

In such a situation an ostensibly just but necessarily free distribution of fresh capital, both money and equipment, would have led inevitably to a very substantial slowing-down of development in the public and private sectors of the economy. Taking all the circumstances into account, the price we would have had to pay for a prolonged period of hardship would have been too high. In the final analysis, all classes of the population have profited by the rapid and expansive advance of Germany's reconstruction programme. Let me remind you, for example, that in two periods of legislation the Federal Republic built 3½ million new dwellings, that in the past six years nominal wages have risen by more than 55%, real wages by more than 40%, that social expenditure from the Federal Budget alone was doubled during the same period and the great insurance reform brought annual insurance payments up from 7.4 to 13 milliards. . . .

We regard it as our duty and responsibility, however, not merely to improve over-all living standards but also to awaken a social consciousness which will produce a more mature and more intelligent awareness in the individual and at the same time lead us as a nation to a new way of life. This presupposes that we should cease to think in terms of classes or even groups, that we can look beyond our immediate group-interests, acquire a real sense of community life and feel responsible, as a community, for the future destiny of our country and our people. For this reason I am not addressing myself today to any professional or commercial groups, for, as a true People's Party and especially on the eve of such an important election, we cannot take the easy way of promising everyone everything. Either we prosper as a people, or we all suffer.

The consciousness of a common responsibility should make it impossible for us, for any one of us, to live thoughtlessly only for the day. But each citizen will be the better able to see things in this way as he gains confidence that he, his children and his children's children will share in the happy future of our people. The more pronounced this sense of individual responsibility becomes, the sooner will we be in a position to put the state and all other collectivist organs of power in their place; the greater the longing of every single person to gain independence and inner freedom by his own efforts and without any collectivist security, then the more confident we can be that increasing wealth will not enslave but liberate us.

The Socialists believe, and have, in fact, expressly said so, that the capital requirements resulting from the application of modern technical methods cannot be satisfied through the traditional channels of the so-called capitalist system and that the spectre of automation, which they invoke for reasons that are all too transparent, could become such a menace that once more the state, and only the state, should be empowered to shape the present and future of our national economy, or at least to control and direct it. For reasons that are not difficult to understand, the SPD no longer have the courage to preach a planned economy, but they lose no opportunity of smuggling their dogma into the German economic and social structure by the back door. So we shall have to be constantly on our guard never to lose sight of this threat to the prosperity and freedom of the German people.

As no power on earth can produce capital by waving a magic wand, the state can only raise capital if it is prepared and in a position to tax the people. That sounds relatively harmless but in practice it means that the citizen is expropriated, without compensation, in order to provide the state with an accumulation of capital and wealth. It means that, as a result of this specific form of national compulsory saving, the fruits of restricted consumption fall not to the saver or taxpayer but to an increasingly powerful state.

There is no more false ideology than that it would be in the interest of the people, that is of workers and traders, to hand over the nation's productive capital to state ownership and public control, because—it is cunningly argued—what belongs to the state also belongs to the people. There was a time when it was thought that the demand for socialization or nationalization might arouse the enthusiasm of the masses; today only the most diehard ideologists and cynical bureaucrats can derive any warmth from their lukewarm memories of that false social ideal. In the long run the concepts of prosperity and of property are inseparable; in fact, I will put it even more plainly: the CDU have made it their political aim that, with each stage of economic expansion, ownership of the means of production should spread more and more widely, in other words, regardless of whether and in what sectors technical progress leads to a concentration of the means of production, that there should be a steady process of deconcentration in the ownership of this national economic capital. This applies in the first instance to productive resources at present under public ownership, for the citizen's imaginery, anonymous claim to these capital goods is, to put it bluntly, not worth a straw, because pseudo-property of this kind is not freely negotiable by the individual. It only serves to reinforce the power, or indeed the omnipotence, of the state or any other collectivist authority to the point where the central power is deified, and at the same time it increases the dependence of the citizen to the point of slavery. And if the individual's scope for creative work and expansion is more and more restricted by the growing intervention of the state in the economy, the possibility of personal advancement is not strengthened but reduced.

A glance at the economic system and methods of totalitarian states —of the Soviet bloc, for example—is enough to show that state-ownership of the means of production does not lead to an increase of wealth for the people but, on the contrary, to their exploitation, whereas the reverse is true of the free countries and peoples, which are denounced for their so-called capitalism but which clearly illustrate how private ownership of the means of production is contributing more and more to the general welfare. So we decline with thanks to adopt as a model for the whole German people, when the long-awaited day of reunification finally comes, the kind of social system represented by the so-called 'social achievements' of the ostensible German Democratic Republic. I simply cannot imagine, and I would be sadly out of touch with the spirit of the German people and especially of the German worker if I believed, that he could derive happiness and satisfaction from knowing that so-called 'People's property' was being run by party officials. After all, what could he buy for it!

But, as I have already said, a wider distribution of ownership in the nation's productive capital should also extend to private enterprises. This certainly does not mean that the returns and profits which help firms to finance themselves would fall into disrepute; on the contrary, it must be the aim and object of every management to work along those lines. Even socialized concerns must make a profit, otherwise there is a deterioration in the living standards and way of life. . . .

34 CHURCHILL

Conservatism and Liberty *

Few would deny that Winston Churchill (1874–1965) was the great statesman of his century. "Men now alive," the *Economist* stated shortly after his death, "will boast the rest of their days that they once lived in the age of Winston Churchill." It may seem strange that a man who did so much and wrote so much said very little about his political philosophy. Herein is expressed his essential conservatism. He was so involved in the defense of the rights of men and the functioning of the state that he had no time for speculation about them and in any event was generally skeptical about visionary plans for utopian reform. The selection is taken from several speeches in which he did try to express his basic political philosophy.

The wisdom of our ancestors for more than 300 years has sought the division of power in the Constitution. Crown, Lords and Commons have been checks and restraints upon one another. The limitation of the power of the Monarchy was the cause for which, as Liberals used to say, 'Hampden died in the field and Sidney on the scaffold.' The concentration of all power over the daily lives of ordinary men and women in what is called 'the State', exercised by what is virtually single-chamber government, is a reactionary step contrary to the whole trend of British history and to the message we have given to the world. The British race have always abhorred arbitrary and absolute government in every form. The great men who founded the

* From Winston S. Churchill's "Election Address, October 15, 1951," in *Stemming the Tide,* ed. by R. S. Churchill. Reprinted with the permission of Houghton Mifflin Company, Boston, and McClelland & Stewart Ltd., Toronto, Canada.

American Constitution embodied this separation of authority in the strongest and most durable form. Not only did they divide executive, legislative and judicial functions, but also by instituting a federal system they preserved immense and sovereign rights to local communities, and by all these means they have preserved—often at some inconvenience—a system of law and liberty under which they have thrived and reached the leadership of the world. The Socialist conception of the all-powerful State entering into the smallest detail of the life and conduct of the individual and claiming to plan and shape his work and its rewards is odious and repellent to every friend of freedom. These absolute powers would make the group of politicians who obtained a majority of seats in Parliament the masters and not the servants of the people and would centralize all government in Whitehall. So far we are only at the first stage of this evil journey. But already enterprise, daring and initiative are crippled. Thrift is penalized by the heaviest taxation in the world. Regulations increasingly take the place of statutes passed by Parliament. There are many hundreds of new crimes unknown before the war, punishable by fines or imprisonment. And all this is avowedly only a step to complete Socialization.

'All men are created equal,' says the American Declaration of Independence. 'All men shall be kept equal,' say the British Socialist Party. The only exceptions are no doubt to be the Ministers and the members of the Government and their associates. If this is already taking place before our eyes, when only one-fifth of our industries have been nationalized, and while we still retain our political rights and freedom, we can judge what will happen when the whole process is complete. The worship of an all-powerful State, beneath which the ordinary mass of citizens lie prostrate, is one of the most deadly and insidious delusions by which a free people as we still are can cast away rights and liberties, which for their own sake and the sake of their children, they ought to hold dearer than life itself.

The British nation now has to make one of the most momentous choices in its history. That choice is between two ways of life; between individual liberty and State domination; between the concentration of ownership in the hands of the State and the extension of a property-owning democracy; between a policy of increasing control and restriction, and a policy of liberating energy and ingenuity; between a policy of levelling down and a policy of finding opportunity for all to rise upwards from a basic standard. . . .

35 CHURCHILL

Socialism and Centralization of Power *

Every tendency of Socialist government is towards the centralization of power. It is inherent in their conception of State control. But,
as history shows, the division of ruling power has always been for
more than 500 years the aim of the British people. The division of
power is the keynote of our Parliamentary system and of the constitutions we have spread all over the world. The idea of checks and
counter-checks; the resistance to the theory that one man, or group
of men, can by sweeping gestures and decisions reduce all the rest of
us to subservience; these have always been the war cries of the British
nation and the division of power has always been one of the war cries
of the British people. And from here the principle was carried to
America. The scheme of the American Constitution was framed to
prevent *any one man or any one lot,* getting arbitrary control of the
whole nation. Of course in America there are forty-eight States in the
Union, all of which by their power to lead their own life in their own
way within their wide limits, and to argue it out among themselves,
are defended and protected against anything in the nature of a one
man or one caucus autocracy. . . .

We Conservatives want the future planning to take place primarily
in the individual home and family. If they do not plan for the future,

* From Winston S. Churchill's "Speech to Conservative Annual Conference,
October 14, 1950," in *In the Balance,* ed. by R. S. Churchill. Reprinted with
the permission of Houghton Mifflin Company, Boston, and McClelland &
Stewart Ltd., Toronto, Canada. See introductory remarks to Selection 34.

no State organization can. It is only on their motive power that the larger progress can be made. There are the long-established laws and customs of our island. The State organization must go ahead and fore-see developments in science and industry. Why do we elect these eminent men to power unless they are able to show us the way? But after all, it is the people who have to move forward from generation to generation, and it is their impulse and self-restraint which consti-tutes the life of our country. If the impulse of the people fails, no kind of planning of the road ahead will be any substitute. Socialism operating through bureaucracy destroys the individual impulse of millions of homes. The orthodox conclusion which many members of the Socialist Party draw from whatever happens is that they have only to vote Socialist and the State will look after the rest. But how little this has to do with the facts of the situation, when we have to struggle to earn our living at home and in the world, and when we have to defend our life against the challenge of armed and aggressive Communism as it presents itself in Soviet Russia. Believe me, the mainspring of British life and power is the home and the family. But in these you have had a free chance. Let the people use their good common sense, multiply the choices which are open to them at every difficult phase in their lives. Make freedom spring from its source in their hearts and then indeed you will have a country which with wise government may be made to play a great part in the world; but stifle the spring, hamper and restrict and fetter the necessary operations of thought and consultations that go on inside the home and all your fine Utopias will come crashing to the ground. . . .

36 CHURCHILL

Conservative or Socialist Planning? *

Now I turn to another aspect of the same problem and must ask your indulgence if I unfold these matters to you as this is an occasion of great importance. The question is asked: 'Are Conservatives opposed to planning?' There is nothing new in planning. Every Government, ancient or modern, must look ahead and plan. Did not Joseph advise Pharaoh to build granaries and fill them for the lean years when the Nile waters failed? He followed the opposite course to the present Government, which is to waste the favourable period of getting the country on to its feet and meanwhile squander all the accumulated resources. But of course we are in favour of planning. But planning what for?

We hold that in these modern times planning, with all the resources of science at its disposal, should aim at giving the individual citizen as many choices as possible of what to do in all the ups and downs of daily life. The more a man's choice is free, the more likely it is to be wise and fruitful, not only to the chooser but to the community in which he dwells. Now there is an important distinction between the quality and kind of planning. This kind of planning differs fundamentally from the collectivist theme of grinding them all up in a vast State mill which must certainly destroy in the process the freedom and independence which are the foundation of our way of life and the famous characteristic of our race.

* From Winston S. Churchill's "Speech to Conservative Annual Conference, October 14, 1949," in *In the Balance*, ed. by R. S. Churchill. Reprinted with the permission of Houghton Mifflin Company, Boston, and McClelland & Stewart Ltd., Toronto, Canada. See introductory remarks to Selection 34.

The Socialist policy and aim is to flatten out all those differentials—to use an important trade union expression—which result from the efforts and qualities of individuals and at all costs to establish a dead level above which no one but Socialist lackeys and politicians shall be allowed to rise. Of course they can only bring this about gradually, but that is the goal they seek, and that is the only goal that their political philosophy can reach.

I am glad to see that responsible trade union leaders, Socialists though they may call themselves, who are in daily contact with the realities of industry and of labour, do not hesitate to resist this ironing-out process. That process would be fatal to all those forces which make more abundant and progressive production, and would deny to every man that right to make the best of himself and his abilities for the benefit not only of his family but of his fellow countrymen, within the limits set by the old broad and well-known laws upon which our way of life in this island has been built. . . .

37 CHURCHILL

Socialist Jargon *

I hope you have all mastered the official Socialist jargon which our masters, as they call themselves, wish us to learn. You must not use the word 'poor'; they are described as the 'lower income group'. When it comes to a question of freezing a workman's wages the Chancellor of the Exchequer speaks of 'arresting increases in personal income'. The idea is that formerly income taxpayers used to be the well-to-do, and that therefore it will be popular and safe to hit at them. Sir Stafford Cripps does not like to mention the word 'wages,' but that is what he means. There is a lovely one about houses and homes. They are in future to be called 'accommodation units'. I don't know how we are to sing our old song 'Home Sweet Home'. 'Accommodation Unit, Sweet Accommodation Unit, there's no place like our Accommodation Unit.' I hope to live to see the British democracy spit all this rubbish from their lips. Mr. Herbert Morrison made a complaint the other day. 'Socialized industries,' he said, 'are the subject of the most persistent misrepresentation, whereas the difficulties and deficiencies of private industries are glossed over.' How does he mean, *'glossed over'?* If private enterprise fails the owners may find themselves in the bankruptcy court. Is that being glossed over? . . .

---

* From Winston S. Churchill's "Election Address, February 8, 1950," in *In the Balance,* ed. by R. S. Churchill. Reprinted with the permission of Houghton Mifflin Company, Boston, and McClelland & Stewart Ltd., Toronto, Canada. See introductory remarks to Selection 34.

38 CHURCHILL

Conservative Principles *

The principles of our Party are not up for auction. We propose no bargain to any section of public opinion. If however there are others who, in growing numbers, are marching along the path which Duty marks out for us, no memories of past differences or outworn quarrels should be allowed to stand in the way of these natural unities which spring from a common policy and a single aim.

I do not believe in looking about for some panacea or cure-all on which we should stake our credit and fortunes trying to sell it like a patent medicine to all and sundry. It is easy to win applause by talking in an airy way about great new departures in policy, especially if all detailed proposals are avoided. We ought not to seek after some rigid, symmetrical form of doctrine, such as delights the minds of Socialists and Communists. Our own feelings and the British temperament are quite different. So are our aims. We seek a free and varied society, where there is room for many kinds of men and women to lead happy, honourable and useful lives. We are fundamentally opposed to all systems of rigid uniformity in our national life and we have grown great as a nation by indulging tolerance, rather than logic.

It certainly would be an error of the first order for us to plunge out into a programme of promises and bribes in the hopes of winning the public favour. But if you say to me: "What account are we to give of the policy of the Conservative Party? What are we to say of our

* From Winston S. Churchill's "Speech to Conservative Party Conference, October 5, 1946," in *The Sinews of Peace*, ed. by R. S. Churchill. Reprinted with the permission of Houghton Mifflin Company, Boston, and McClelland & Stewart Ltd., Toronto, Canada. See introductory remarks to Selection 34.

theme and our cause and of the faith that is in us?" That is a question to which immediate answer can always be given.

Our main objectives are: To uphold the Christian religion and resist all attacks upon it. To defend our Monarchical and Parliamentary Constitution. To provide adequate security against external aggression and safety for our seaborne trade. To uphold law and order, and impartial justice administered by Courts free from interference or pressure on the part of the executive. To regain a sound finance and strict supervision of national income and expenditure. To defend and develop our Empire trade, without which Great Britain would perish. To promote all measures to improve the health and social conditions of the people. To support as a general rule free enterprise and initiative against State trading and nationalisation of industries.

To this I will add some further conceptions. We oppose the establishment of a Socialist State, controlling the means of production, distribution and exchange. We are asked, "What is your alternative?" Our Conservative aim is to build a property-owning democracy, both independent and interdependent. In this I include profit-sharing schemes in suitable industries and intimate consultation between employers and wage-earners. In fact we seek so far as possible to make the status of the wage-earner that of a partner rather than of an irresponsible employee. It is in the interest of the wage-earner to have many other alternatives open to him than service under one all-powerful employer called the State. He will be in a better position to bargain collectively and production will be more abundant; there will be more for all and more freedom for all when the wage-earner is able, in the large majority of cases, to choose and change his work, and to deal with a private employer who, like himself, is subject to the ordinary pressures of life and, like himself, is dependent upon his personal thrift, ingenuity and good-housekeeping. In this way alone can the traditional virtues of the British character be preserved. We do not wish the people of this ancient island reduced to a mass of State-directed proletarians, thrown hither and thither, housed here and there, by an aristocracy of privileged officials or privileged Party, sectarian or Trade Union bosses. We are opposed to the tyranny and victimisation of the closed shop. Our ideal is the consenting union of millions of free, independent families and homes to gain their livelihood and to serve true British glory and world peace.

Freedom of enterprise and freedom of service are not possible without elaborate systems of safeguards against failure, accident or misfortune. We do not seek to pull down improvidently the structures of society, but to erect balustrades upon the stairway of life, which will prevent helpless or foolish people from falling into the abyss. Both the Conservative and Liberal Parties have made notable contributions to secure minimum standards of life and labour. I too have borne my part in this. It is 38 years ago since I introduced the first Unemployment Insurance Scheme, and 22 years ago since, as Conservative Chancellor of the Exchequer, I shaped and carried the Widows' Pensions and reduction of the Old Age Pensions from 70 to 65. We are now moving forward into another vast scheme of national insurance, which arose, even in the stress of war, from a Parliament with a great Conservative majority. It is an essential principle of Conservative, Unionist, and Tory policy—call it what you will—to defend the general public against abuses by monopolies and against restraints on trade and enterprise, whether these evils come from private corporations, from the mischievous plans of doctrinaire Governments, or from the incompetence and arbitrariness of departments of State. Finally, we declare ourselves the unsleeping opponents of all class, all official or all Party privilege, which denies the genius of our island race, whose sparks fly upwards unceasingly from the whole people, its rightful career, reward and pre-eminence alike in peace and war.

How then do we draw the lines of political battle? The British race is not actuated mainly by the hope of material gain. Otherwise we should long ago have sunk in the ocean of the past. It is stirred on almost all occasions by sentiment and instinct, rather than by programmes or worldly calculation. When this new Parliament first met, all the Socialist Members stood up and sang "The Red Flag" in their triumph. Peering ahead through the mists and mysteries of the future so far as I can; I see the division at the next election will be between those who wholeheartedly sing "The Red Flag" and those who rejoice to sing "Land of Hope and Glory". There is the noble hymn which will rally the wise, the soberminded and the good to the salvation of our native land.

Suggestions for Further Reading

I. BASIC BOOKS

There is, unfortunately, no good history of European conservatism. Peter Viereck's *Conservatism from John Adams to Churchill* (Princeton, 1956) comes closest to such a survey; it is written in handbook style, however, and the selections from conservative writers which are offered rarely run to more than a few paragraphs. It must still be regarded as a useful and stimulating introduction, written by an original thinker. Russell Kirk's *The Conservative Mind from Burke to Eliot* (Chicago, 1954) is undoubtedly the best historical study of conservatism published; it includes both British and American writers but unfortunately was not intended to deal with Continental thought.

What Is Conservatism? (New York, 1964) is a collection of essays written by both American and European scholars in a joint attempt to arrive at some definition of conservatism in the modern world. The editor, Frank S. Meyer, attempts to reconcile the differences between the classical liberals and the traditional conservatives. A valuable anthology of British conservative ideas, *The Conservative Tradition* (London, 1950), has been edited by R. J. White.

A third anthology which ought not to be neglected by the student of conservative thought is *The Development of the Democratic Idea: Readings from Pericles to the Present* (New York, 1968). The editor, Charles M. Sherover, skillfully presents and criticizes (from a standpoint more often than not traditional and conservative) the leading contributors to the history of democratic theory, including several writers included in this volume.

Quintin Hogg (formerly Lord Hailsham), one of the most brilliant leaders of the British Conservative Party, stated the general principles motivating contemporary conservative politicians in Britain in *The Case for Conservatism* (London, 1947). A more recent sampling of the ideas of influential younger Tories is provided in *The Conservative Opportunity*

(London, 1965), published by *Crossbow* and the Conservative Political Centre and including such contributors as Michael Wolfe, Geoffrey Howe, John McGregor, John Biffen, Philip Goodhart, and Julian Critchley.

An introductory analysis of political thought which ought not to be uncongenial to conservatives is J. R. Lucas' *Principles of Politics* (Oxford, 1966). The best book of conservative thought written by a European in recent years is probably Michael Oakeshott's *Rationalism in Politics* (London, 1962). For a splendid restatement of the classical liberal tradition, consult F. A. Hayek's *The Constitution of Liberty* (Chicago, 1960). Sir Karl Popper (also a defender of Whiggism) has written a brilliant critique of social engineering, *The Open Society and Its Enemies* (Princeton, 1950).

Elie Kedourie has just completed a new introduction to conservative philosophy entitled *Conservatism,* to be published by Watts (New Thinkers' Library) in London in 1970. Angus Maude, M.P., and Norman St. John-Stevas, M.P., are both working on their own versions of the philosophy of conservatism to be published in the near future.

A very useful bibliography of articles and books on conservatism (mostly, but not exclusively British) has been compiled by Geoffrey D. M. Block. Entitled *A Source Book of Conservatism,* it is published by the Conservative Political Centre (London, 1964).

II. BOOKS BY AND ABOUT CONSERVATIVES

A. Classical and medieval conservatives

It would be a terrible oversimplification, of course, to label Plato, Aristotle, and Cicero as "conservatives"; what is true, however, is that many varieties of conservative thought have drawn sustenance from many of the ideas in Plato's *Republic, Laws, Statesman,* from Aristotle's *Politics,* from Cicero's *On the Commonwealth* and *Laws.* A penetrating attack on Plato's ideal of the philosopher-king is found in Sir Karl Popper's *The Open Society and Its Enemies* (Princeton, 1950). The case for Plato's politics has been marshaled by Ronald B. Levison in his *In Defense of Plato* (Cambridge, Mass., 1953). A more dispassionate study is Ernest Barker's *The Political Thought of Plato and Aristotle* (London, 1906).

A good general introduction is provided by C. H. McIlwain's *The Growth of Political Thought in the West, from the Greeks to the End of the Middle Ages* (New York, 1932). *Selected Political Writings of Thomas Aquinas* has been edited by A. P. d'Entrèves (Oxford, 1948). A classic defense of the ideals of feudalism is *The Statesman's Book of John of Salisbury* (New York, 1927).

B.   Continental conservatives prior to the twentieth century

Although he is not usually regarded as a conservative, a close examination of Jean-Jacques Rousseau's thought will reveal the common concern for social harmony and the stability of the community which he shared with Edmund Burke. See, for instance, *The Political Writings of Jean-Jacques Rousseau,* edited by C. E. Vaughan (Cambridge, 1915), and Annie M. Osborn's study *Rousseau and Burke* (New York, 1940). G. W. F. Hegel was to carry forward the work begun by Burke and Rousseau in analyzing man's place in society in his monumental *Philosophy of Right* (Oxford, 1942). Hugh A. Reyburn's commentary on this work, *The Ethical Theory of Hegel: A Study of the Philosophy of Right* (Oxford, 1921), will be useful. The fear of revolution, as might be expected, motivated most of the conservative writers of the nineteenth century.

Jack Lively has recently given us a welcome edition of Joseph de Maistre's *Works* (London, 1965) in English translation. *Les Soirées de Saint Petersbourg* (Lyon, 1845) and *The Pope,* translated by Aeneas Dawson (London, 1850), repay careful reading for De Maistre's insights into the workings of society. It is unfortunate that very little has been published on the thought of Don Juan Donoso-Cortés, in some ways a more penetrating critic of his time than De Maistre; H. A. Rommen's *The State in Catholic Thought* (London, 1945) is a good introduction, however, to the influential tradition of which both men were a part.

Alexis de Tocqueville, of course, was a communicant of the same church as Donoso-Cortés and De Maistre but held rather different political ideas. His greatest work, *Democracy in America* (New York, 1954), must rank as one of the half dozen most important studies of that system of government now prevalent in the West. He has demonstrated his skill not only as a political theorist and sociologist but also as a historian in his other works, *The Old Regime and the French Revolution* (New York, 1955) and his *Recollections* (London, 1948). At least two valuable commentaries on De Tocqueville will be of interest to readers: Jack Lively's *The Social and Political Thought of Alexis de Tocqueville* (Oxford, 1962) and Marvin Zetterbaum's *Tocqueville and the Problem of Democracy* (Palo Alto, 1967).

The thoughts of three very practical statesmen who were pillars of the Austrian, German, and Russian empires are an essential part of the Continental conservative tradition. The Habsburg chancellor, Clemens von Metternich, has left us his *Memoirs* (London, 1880), and Henry A. Kissinger has drawn some conclusions for our time in his study of the statecraft of Metternich and Bismarck, *A World Restored* (New York, 1954). Otto von Bismarck's own memoirs were published under the title *The*

Man and the Statesman (London, 1898), and his distinguished contemporary and sometime rival Konstantin Pobiedonostsev found time to write Reflections of a Russian Statesman (London, 1898).

Those interested in what has been called "cultural conservatism" ought not to neglect Jakob Burckhardt's Civilization of the Rennaissance in Italy (New York, 1954) and the works of Friedrich Nietzsche, readily available with a good introduction in The Portable Nietzsche (New York, 1954).

C. British conservatives prior to the twentieth century

In the eighteenth century, across the Channel, David Hume, Viscount Bolingbroke, and Edmund Burke were, in their diverse ways, laying the foundation of Anglo-Saxon conservatism. Empirical conservatives have learned much from David Hume's Political Essays (New York, 1953), while the more idealistic have drawn sustenance from Bolingbroke's Idea of a Patriot King (London, 1738). An engaging study of the latter, Bolingbroke: Tory Humanist (New York, 1965), has recently been published by Jeffrey Hart. The best edited short selection of the works of Burke is probably The Philosophy of Edmund Burke, introduced by Louis I. Bredvold and Ralph G. Ross (Ann Arbor, 1960). For a one-volume biography with a good bibliography, consult Russell Kirk's Edmund Burke: A Genius Reconsidered (New Rochelle, N.Y., 1967). Another eminent scholar of conservatism, R. J. White of Cambridge University, has made available the best of Samuel Coleridge's political writings in The Political Thought of S. T. Coleridge (London, 1938).

A link with the Continent is provided by two of England's most distinguished Catholics, John Dahlberg-Acton (Lord Acton) and John Henry Cardinal Newman. Gertrude Himmelfarb has edited a most useful collection of Acton's work under the title Essays on Freedom and Power (Boston, 1948) and has published a brilliant intellectual biography: Lord Acton: A Study in Conscience and Politics (Chicago, 1952). Two of Acton's friends, J. N. Figgis and R. V. Laurence, edited his History of Freedom (London, 1907) and Lectures on Modern History (London, 1906). My own political biography, Lord Acton: Historian of Liberty, will be published by Arlington House, New Rochelle, N.Y., in 1970. John Henry Cardinal Newman's classic essay, of course, is his Apologia Pro Vita Sua (London, 1864). T. Kenny has written an admirable study of The Political Thought of J. H. Newman (London, 1957).

For two of the most provocative of the Victorian critiques of democracy and liberalism, students should consult Henry Maine's Popular Government (New York, 1888) and R. J. White's edition of Liberty, Equality and Fraternity by J. F. Stephen (Cambridge, U.K., 1968). Maurice Cowling has written one of the best critiques of Mill and Liberalism under that time (Cambridge, U.K., 1963).

Several biographies of Tory political leaders are valuable for illuminating some of the various ways in which conservative ideas may be put into practice. Lord David Cecil's biography of that most Tory of Whig Prime Ministers, *Melbourne* (London, 1965), is a genuine masterpiece of its genre and is my own favorite book. Another Cecil, Lady Gwendolin, has given us the best biography of her father in her *Life of Robert, Third Marquis of Salisbury* (London, 1921), and Michael Pinto-Duschinsky recently published *The Political Thought of Lord Salisbury, 1854–68* (London, 1967), an instructive analysis of the mind of an empirical conservative.

Paul Smith has edited *A Selection from Lord Salisbury's Articles in the 'Quarterly Review,'* to be published by Cambridge University Press in early 1970, and Robert Rhodes James is presently writing a new biography of Lord Salisbury for Weidenfeld and Nicolson in London.

Mr. Secretary Peel (London, 1961), by Norman Gash, and *Disraeli* (London, 1966), by Robert Blake, are distinguished examples of political biography and S. A. Granbard's *Burke, Disraeli and Churchill* (Cambridge, Mass., 1961) ties together the strands which unite conservatives over three centuries.

D. Continental conservatives of the twentieth century

José Ortega y Gasset's *Revolt of the Masses* (New York, 1932) is a classic of conservative thought, more relevant today than ever. Another Spanish scholar (although he resided in the United States for many years), George Santayana, is best known for his philosophic work, *Dominions and Power* (New York, 1951).

A. P. d'Entrèves, of the University of Turin, has written two influential defenses of the classic tradition in political theory, *The Law of Nature* (London, 1951) and *The Notion of the State* (London, 1967). The late Bruno Leoni of the University of Pavia was the author of a notable exposition of classical liberalism, *Freedom and the Law* (Princeton, N.J., 1959). Perhaps the best recent analysis of the problem of democracy, written from a point of view not uncongenial to classical liberals and empirical conservatives, has been published by Giovanni Sartori of the University of Florence: *Democratic Theory* (New York, 1965).

The venerable Catholic philosopher Jacques Maritain is perhaps best represented by his *Two Humanisms* (London, 1938). For further reading, consult *The Social and Political Philosophy of Jacques Maritain,* by J. W. Evans and L. Ward (London, 1956). The most eminent political theorist in the classical liberal tradition writing today in France is undoubtedly Bertrand de Jouvenel of the University of Paris. Interested students will derive much benefit from all his works, especially *Power* (Geneva, 1945), *Sovereignty* (Cambridge, U.K., 1957), *The Ethics of Redistribution* (Cambridge, U.K., 1951), and *The Pure Theory of Politics* (Cambridge, U.K., 1963).

Some idea of the clarity of thought of the respected French economist Jacques Rueff may be derived from his "A Letter to the Advocates of a Controlled Economy," in *Essays in European Thought,* edited by Louis Sommer (Princeton, N.J., 1960). Most of the other essays in this anthology ably put forward points of view by leading European free market economists. Another French scholar, Jacques Ellul, has written a provocative book on the limits of government power in an advanced technological civilization: *The Political Illusion* (New York, 1967).

In the German-speaking world, Ludwig von Mises, long at the University of Vienna, stands out as a fountainhead of ideas in the classical liberal tradition. See especially *Socialism* (London, 1951), *Bureaucracy* (London, 1945), and his chief work, *Human Action* (London, 1949). Writing principally in Switzerland, Wilhelm Röpke's many works combined much of what was best in the old liberalism and the new conservatism. Of particular interest are *Economics of the Free Society* (Chicago, 1963) and *A Humane Economy* (Chicago, 1960). For a profoundly Christian interpretation of history, the student should turn to the monumental *Order and History series* (London, 3 vols., 1952–55) by Eric Voegelin, formerly of the University of Munich. A new collection of Voegelin's essays, translated by William K. Fitzpatrick, has just appeared: *Science, Politics and Gnosticism* (Chicago, 1968).

E. British conservatives in the twentieth century

Few men have made so many contributions to philosophy, economics, law, and political thought as has F. A. von Hayek, long a British subject, now teaching at the University of Freiburg in Germany. See especially his *Constitution of Liberty* (Chicago, 1960), *Road to Serfdom* (London, 1944), *The Counter-Revolution of Science* (Glencoe, Ill., 1952), and his latest work, *Essays in Philosophy, Politics and Economics* (London, 1967). Two of Britain's most eminent economists have published searching critiques of the effects of the planned economy. See *The New Ordeal by Planning* (London, 1968) and *Public and Private Enterprise* (London, 1965), by John Jewkes of Oxford University, and *A Case for Laissez-faire* (London, 1929), by James W. Nisbet of St. Andrews University. Arthur Seldon and Ralph Harris, directors of the Institute of Economic Affairs in London, have presided over the publication of almost 200 essays and books on current economic policy. To cite but two examples, the student may be interested in *Economics, Education and the Politician* (London, 1967), by Edward G. West of the University of Kent, and *Universal or Selective Social Benefits?* (London, 1968), by Arthur Seldon and Hamish Gray. For an insightful critique of current politics in Britain from the viewpoint of a libertarian in economic policy see Anthony Lejeune's *Freedom and the Politicians* (London, 1964).

The most rigorously intelligent and most consistently provocative politician writing in Britain today is doubtless J. Enoch Powell, M.P., former Conservative shadow Minister of Defense. A collection of his speeches under the title *Freedom and Reality* has just been edited by John Wood (London, 1969). British philosophers and historians of a conservative persuasion have not been idle in the past few decades. Sir Herbert Butterfield of Cambridge University has done his best to undermine the simplistic belief in "progress" so common among academics in his *The Whig Interpretation of History* (London, 1931) and *Christianity and History* (London, 1949). Maurice Cranston of the London School of Economics has cleared away many of the confusions about the meaning of liberty as it is understood by many liberals in his valuable *Freedom: A New Analysis* (London, 1954). Students should not fail to read Michael Oakeshott's *Rationalism in Politics and Other Essays* (London, 1962), probably the most important restatement of Anglo-Saxon conservatism in our generation. Although he always denies that he is a conservative, students of the subject will find much of interest in the writings of Sir Isaiah Berlin of Oxford University, especially his *Two Concepts of Liberty* (Oxford, 1958) and *The Hedgehog and the Fox* (New York, 1953), in which he relates De Maistre to Stendhal and Tolstoy. No survey of English conservatism would be complete without a familiarity with two of that nation's principal men of letters, C. S. Lewis and T. S. Eliot. Eliot's *The Idea of a Christian Society* (London, 1939) in particular is a lasting contribution to the conservative search for the good society.

III. CURRENT EUROPEAN PERIODICALS OF CONSERVATIVE THOUGHT

Students interested in European journals which regularly publish scholarly articles by contemporary conservative thinkers should consult *Il Politico* (University of Pavia, Italy), *The Swinton Journal* (Swinton Conservative College, near Ripon, Yorks, England), and for emphasis on economic matters, *Economic Age* (10 Upper Berkeley Street, London). The Institute of Economic Affairs (2 Lord North Street, London), directed by Ralph Harris and Arthur Seldon, publishes a steady stream of books and pamphlets criticizing various aspects of government intervention in the economy, as does the Reform Group ("Granville," Largo Rd., St. Andrews, Scotland). The Conservative Political Centre (32 Smith Sq., London) has also produced a long series of essays on contemporary conservative thought and policy; its director, Russell Lewis, has just written a general statement of Tory views entitled *Principles to Conserve* (London, 1968). The Bow Group, an organization of scholarly young conservatives, publishes a quarterly, *Crossbow* (240 High Holborn, London, England). There are at least four American journals which publish essays by European conservatives in most issues: *National Review* (New York), *New Individualist Review: A Journal of Classical Liberal Thought* (University of Chicago), *Modern Age* (Chicago), and *The Intercollegiate Review* (Intercollegiate Studies Institute, Bryn Mawr, Pa.).